IN THE FOOTSTEPS OF CHURCHILL

In the Footsteps of Churchill is both a study in character and the story of an extraordinary career. Historian Richard Holmes uses new material to investigate the influences that shaped the man: his schooldays, his flamboyant father, Randolph, and his attractive American mother, Jennie. Holmes argues that the qualities that made Churchill great also led him to commit catastrophic blunders. The recklessness that made him a hero when he was a young correspondent during the Boer War, for example, cost thousands of Allied lives during his planning of the Gallipoli campaign in 1915, and may also have contributed to the fall of Singapore in 1942.

In the Footsteps of Churchill takes us on an exhilarating journey through Harrow School, The North-West Frontier, the Sudan, South Africa, 10 Downing Street and his beloved Chartwell; a journey that begins in the aristocratic splendour of Blenheim Palace and ends in the quiet of a country churchyard not far away—the compass of an extraordinary life in a few Oxfordshire acres . . .

IN THE FOOTSTEPS OF CHURCHILL

Richard Holmes

BBC
LARGE
PRINT

First published 2005
by
BBC Books to accompany the television series
In the Footsteps of Churchill produced for BBC
television by Quickfire Media
This Large Print edition published 2005
by
BBC Audiobooks Ltd
by arrangement with
BBC Worldwide

ISBN 0 7540 9453 7

British Library Cataloguing in Publication Data available

Printed and bound in Great Britain by
Antony Rowe Ltd., Chippenham, Wiltshire

CONTENTS

INTRODUCTION

In one sense, only the exercise of the most sensitive historical imagination will let us follow in the footsteps of Churchill, for the social and political paths he walked have vanished almost as if they had never been. To a very great extent this had already happened during his lifetime: in 1930 he wrote that 'the character of society, the foundations of politics, the methods of war, the outlook of youth, the scale of values, are all changed, and changed to an extent I should not have believed possible in so short a space without any violent domestic revolution'.[1] The process he described continued for the rest of his life, the only constant being that the domestic power of the state relentlessly increased, almost as if to compensate for the rapid shrinking of the international space occupied by Great Britain. Winston was born to a class and a nation alike confident in their right to rule. But before he died the great aristocratic dynasties had become the museum curators of their heritage, while in the House of Commons rhetoric echoed, almost nostalgically, in the void of diminishing ability to influence world events. As he once observed, 'when nations are strong they are not always just, and when they wish to be just they are no longer strong'.[2]

And yet it is remarkable that if the cultural landscape has been so profoundly transformed, the physical surroundings Churchill would have remembered have changed far less. His birthplace,

Blenheim Palace, still sends its glare of cold command across the landscape; his London apartment in Morpeth Mansions sits comfortably in the shadow of Westminster Cathedral; one can almost catch the whiff of his cigar in the Pinafore Room at the Savoy, and his presence at his beloved Chartwell is somehow palpable. The young man who charged the Dervishes at Omdurman in 1898 or the youthful Home Secretary who characteristically turned up to watch Scots Guardsmen supporting the civil power at the 'Siege of Sidney Street' in 1911 may seem impossibly remote. But the senior statesman, painfully past his best but still a symbol of hard-won glory, was Prime Minister when I was at primary school. He died in 1965, when I was about to go up to Cambridge. Although I was anxious to grab my share of what were very evidently the swinging sixties (and could scarcely have conceived of ever becoming a professional historian), I knew then that his death marked the end of an era. I saw it in my parents' faces. Although my mother had a good deal to put up with, like many of her generation she was not much given to tears: but I remember how Churchill's death broke in even upon my family's recognition that my father's illness was his last. Churchill is buried behind the little church at Bladon, in the same plot as his parents and just outside the park walls of Blenheim. It struck me all those years ago, as I watched his funeral on television, that there was a fitting symmetry to birth and death: the soaring trajectory of a long life somehow confined within the narrow compass of a few Oxfordshire acres.

There was none of this sense of personal contact

in my other two biographies, of Field Marshal Sir John French, commander of the British Expeditionary Force in 1914–15, and the great Duke of Wellington. And they were a good deal easier to write about. Although neither subject shirked controversy, it was always relatively easy to steer a consistent path and not to let my own view of the world influence what I wrote. It has been far harder with Winston. Indeed, the fact that I generally refer to him in these pages as Winston is indicative, for I would no more have routinely styled Wellington Arthur than I would have called French Johnny. And yet, despite the fact that there are already rafts of books about Winston, I felt irresistibly impelled to take him on. Over a busy career as a military historian I have written at length about both world wars, and most recently, in *Tommy: The British Soldier on the Western Front*, I examined the generation (of which Winston himself was part) that fought in the trenches. No study of British military policy in either war can be complete without Winston: neither can he be spared his share of responsibility for the fact that the warriors who returned home in 1918 did not find a land fit for heroes to live in. Indeed, his electoral defeat in 1945 was, at least in part, a demonstration that returning servicemen that year felt entitled to better treatment than that accorded to their fathers. So he stands like a rock, immovable and distinctive, in twentieth-century British military history: there is simply no way round him.

I cannot deny Winston's extraordinary resonance for me personally. But in writing about him I am in the No Man's Land of historiography, and am conscious that some of what follows will inevitably succeed in offending both supporters and critics. Yet this is a measure of the man. He was neither wholly good nor wholly bad, as completely right about as often as he was hopelessly wrong, and the occasional frail raft of quiet humility was swamped by his raging ego. And even when my head urges me in one direction, my heart pulls me in the other.

Visiting so many of the places that had played such a part in his own long life certainly coloured my view of the man. Churchill the politician was not simply the product of a frustrating childhood, but was powerfully influenced by Churchill the soldier. By the time he entered politics he had risked his life a dozen times, and had twice come close to winning the Victoria Cross, his country's highest award for gallantry. Things like charging at Omdurman, escaping from a prisoner-of-war camp and having the plume snipped from his hat by a Boer bullet at Spion Kop left him with an abiding sense of destiny, and his experiences as a soldier and then as government minister responsible for the largest navy the world had ever seen were all part of the heady cocktail that he took to Downing Street in 1940.

This is not a full-dress biography that catalogues each twist and turn of a long life. It is instead an effort to illuminate the character of the man whom a BBC poll in 2002 established as the greatest Briton, and to show how that character (never bland, comfortable, evenly balanced or free from controversy) spun him from one crisis to another like a frenetic pin-ball, building up painful experiences and gaining hard-won wisdom until he was at last granted the opportunity to throw it all into battle against a monstrous evil. In a broadcast on 14 July 1940, after the fall of France, Winston declared 'we are fighting by ourselves alone; but we are not fighting for ourselves alone'. So it proved. That year Britain could indeed have lost World War II, for had it capitulated (as logic might have urged) the issue would have been settled in favour of either Nazi or Soviet tyranny, without the USA being able to intervene. Unfortunately, being on the winning side, although manifestly better than the alternative, permitted the survival of a constellation of institutional weaknesses, restrictive practices and comforting illusions that bedevilled post-war recovery. None the less, Winston's eloquence, courage and honour left a legacy of quiet pride to his people, and set an example to which so many of his successors have aspired ever since. Winston would earn greatness from this alone, and his courage in that blazing summer goes far to counteract his many faults.

My task is made all the harder by the fact that following in Winston's footsteps involves being wary of the false trails he laid, as well as of the places where his tracks have been deliberately obscured by the enraged trampling of those upon whose toes he trod. Also, although he was central to his own time, that age may not have been particularly representative of the broader history of his nation. As far back as the fourteenth century, the French chronicler Jean Froissart commented that the English were hard to govern, being 'of a haughty disposition, hot-tempered and quickly moved to anger . . . incapable by nature of joining in friendship or alliance with a foreign nation'. So might an embittered European civil servant write no less feelingly today. Four hundred years after Froissart, the pamphleteers who promulgated the American Revolution justified their action by denouncing the corruption, bawdiness and drunken violence of the British. It could be that the relatively well-mannered, self-regulating and deferential Britain of Winston's lifetime was an historical aberration. Just as the separate identities of the Irish, Scots and Welsh have now surged up through the cracks in the imperial construct known as Great Britain, so also the English may have shrugged off the constraints of ambition and reverted to type, almost with a Falstaffian belch of relief.

We should not necessarily suppose that all Winston's patrician sensibilities would have been offended by the rawness of contemporary British society, for the historian in him might well have noted some similarities with the reign of the first Elizabeth. This may seem strange to those who think of Winston's era as one of cringing deference, unthinking patriotism and world-girdling arrogance, but there has always been an earthy, buccaneering streak in the British character, and it was strongly represented in him. There can be no doubt that his love of the British people and his own unbounded self-belief were virtually one and the same. They were the binoculars of his existence, and every word he wrote, every action he initiated can be seen clearly only when the two are focused together. Thus in 1963, in a message accepting the unprecedented honour of Honorary Citizenship of the USA, he rebuked those who believed the sacrifices of two world wars had permanently crippled Britain, affirming that: 'Our past is the key to our future, which I firmly trust and believe will be no less fertile and glorious. Let no man underrate our energies, our potentialities and our abiding power for good.'

That robust, limitless view of the future has always sat ill with some of his countrymen, whose principal characteristics were identified in 1842 by Charles Dickens: 'There is a horrid respectability about the most of the best of them—a little, finite, systematic routine in them, strangely expressive to me of the state of England herself.' Winston would have recognized some of those who snipe at his memory today as the spiritual descendants of those who helped create the moral climate for the appeasement of Hitler in the 1930s:

> The worst difficulties from which we suffer do not come from without. They come from . . . a peculiar type of brainy people always found in our country, who, if they add something to its culture, take much from its strength. Our difficulties come from the mood of unwarrantable self-abasement into which we have been cast by a powerful section of our own intellectuals.[3]

The mind-set thus described has cast a long shadow. Martin Gilbert, Winston's official biographer, comments that the prejudice of his Oxford tutors was such that, when he graduated in 1960, his awareness of Churchill's enormous contribution to the public life of Britain in the early twentieth century was 'not very far from nil'.[4] The reasons for this deliberate neglect are not difficult to identify. Winston's passionate belief that myths and legends are scarcely less important in a nation's history than the provable facts was ludicrously 'old-fashioned' to academics who considered themselves progressive, and a towering statesman-scholar with no educational credentials was anathema to them. There was, however, something else at work. J. H. Plumb, a leading historian during my time at Cambridge, believed that 'what gave Churchill his confidence, his courage, his burning faith in the rightness of his cause—his deep sense of the miraculous English past—has been lost. It no longer explains our role or our purpose.'5 But if history is perceived as an expression of national identity, as it was by Winston, then it will generally be written on a grand scale, and between one who treated it as a glorious epic and another seeking to redefine it in wholly objective terms there will be a difference more of animating intent than of mere methodology.

Plumb went on to declare: 'In those fields where his work challenges comparison with professional history, Churchill remains, by the most generous assessment, a gifted amateur.'6 Winston was awarded the 1953 Nobel Prize for Literature, preceded by François Mauriac in 1952 and followed by Ernest Hemingway in 1954, and it really is as literature rather than as history that we should interpret his work. If his ranking as a serious historian is indeed in doubt, his immense stature as a story-teller on a par with Edward Gibbon and Thomas Macaulay is secure. Another critic acknowledged his link to Macaulay, with whom he shared 'towering gifts of language' as well as 'obliquity and partiality':

> Both grind their axes with formidable
> certainty, both carry their points with breath-
> taking use of language, both speak vividly to
> the common reader. To neither does one look
> for balanced portrayal, to neither does one
> look for objectivity. One seeks instead, and
> finds, majestic English, wide-ranging vision,
> and a continuing and passionate belief in the
> greatness of their country.[7]

Although I opened by affirming that the paths
walked by the historical Winston have vanished, the
same cannot be said for his legacy, which remains
very much in play. While much of the world seems
content to accept that he was indeed a great man,
albeit of and for his time, in Britain his reputation
remains one of those issues that never quite seem
to achieve closure. Part of the reason is that for all
our apparent interest in history we appear to be
remarkably unwilling to learn from it. The authors
of the 1940 book *Guilty Men*, which denounced
those responsible for British lack of military
preparedness prior to the outbreak of war in 1939,
had demanded unilateral disarmament in the 1930s
and did so again 30 years later. One of them,
Michael Foot, went on to become the leader of the
Labour Party and then to support military action by
a Conservative government in response to the
invasion of the Falkland Islands, a British
dependency, by a dictatorship. The British
counterstroke succeeded only because recently
announced cuts in defence spending had not yet
been implemented. Rescued by the very armed

9

forces it had been about to emasculate, the same government went on to wrap itself in the Churchillian mantle. It is not yet the task of a historian to judge the wisdom of Britain's stance in the Iraq War of 2003, but it is significant that one of the Prime Minister, Tony Blair's, leading political supporters explicitly compared him to Churchill, and that the same government is bent upon defence 'restructuring' as I write.

If the same short-term policies, and even in some cases the same people, still swilled around in British politics 50 years after he first warned against their evident folly, it is no wonder that Winston's shade still tramps round the revolving treadmill of British national discourse. In addition, of course, his legacy is a standing rebuke to the envious levelling that has been such a feature of British society over the past 60 years. Ralph Waldo Emerson declared a foolish consistency to be the hobgoblin of small minds, but sadly it seems that greatness may be the real bugbear of those unable to aspire to it. The wish to lop the head off the tallest poppy is very pronounced in Britain, and is by no means limited to those who believe themselves to be progressive. The late Conservative MP and military historian Alan Clark was of the opinion that Britain should have avoided involvement, or negotiated a truce, in World War II. Therefore, he argued, the refusal to capitulate in 1940 was not Britain's finest hour but the time when, misled by Winston, the nation ruined itself, a consummation devoutly wished for and partly engineered by the Americans.[8] The words Shakespeare put in the mouth of thoroughly modern Cassius spring to mind:

10

> Why, man, he doth bestride the narrow
>   world,
> Like a Colossus; and we petty men
> Walk under his huge legs, and peep about
> To find ourselves dishonourable graves.
> Men at some time are masters of their fate:
> The fault, dear Brutus, is not in our stars,
> But in ourselves that we are underlings.[9]

Cassius was inciting Brutus to the murder of Julius Caesar, another eloquent egoist who, like Winston, not only played a leading role in the events of his time but also sought to assure his place in history by writing it. This is not unusual. I hope I may be forgiven for quoting, from my own *Battlefields of the Second World War*, a passage that could have been written about Winston or, for that matter, Caesar:

> History is not really the tricks we play on the dead, but rather the uncovering of the tricks they played while alive. One has to steer between the Scylla of accepting an often carefully constructed mask and the Charybdis of tearing it down as though what lay behind it was the 'real' person. In life the two are inseparable and there are very few areas of human endeavour in which the talents of the actor or even the showman are not rewarded.[10]

As a stylist Winston drew deeply on Gibbon and Macaulay, but there is a strong case for seeing him as a Shakespearian character, in which a talented actor and a magnificently scripted role became one. A follower of Carl Jung might argue that Winston, as a man of intuition rather than rational calculation, was in closer contact than most with the collective unconscious. Both hypotheses have merit. Winston was not only his own scriptwriter but also played most of the supporting roles before assuming the lead. In Chapter Six I explore the moment when he subconsciously cast himself in the role of Moses for the period he himself revealingly described as the 'Wilderness Years'. Although his most resonant words were tailored to the requirements of a particular audience at a very unusual time, the hold he still exerts over the imaginations and sentiments of people all over the world suggests he may have acquired the attributes of Jung's Child archetype, with Adolf Hitler as the Shadow.

Whatever Winston's iconic stature, many of his sayings retain practical topicality because they are crisp expressions of common sense. To go no further than the interminable debate about Britain's place in Europe, the case for first putting one's own house in order has never been better stated than by Winston, 60 years ago:

> There is also a European duty and talk about our being good Europeans. The best way in which a British Member of Parliament or statesman can be a good European is to make sure that our country is safe and strong in the first instance. The rest may be added to you afterwards, but without that you are no kind of European. All you are is a source of embarrassment and weakness to the whole of

the rest of the world.[11]

The sort of person capable of defacing his statue in Parliament Square because he was 'an imperialist' may never be able to navigate the contradiction in Winston's belief that the Empire was the necessary support, against a hostile world, for the individual liberties enshrined in English Common Law. In *The Story of the Malakand Field Force*, his first book, he wrote of 'Imperial Democracy' and it would be as well to chew that concept carefully before spitting it out. In common with most of his contemporaries he used the word 'race', rather than today's preferred and more accurate 'culture', until the rise of stridently racist Nazism forced a change in vocabulary. He then wrote of the English-speaking peoples, but failed to include the millions in Africa and Asia who spoke the language—because they did not, in his view, share the cultural values he espoused. He was wrong, and his views on race were broadly typical of someone of his class and education, but he did more than any other man to combat Social Darwinism, the belief widespread in the first half of the twentieth century that nations are the expression of genetic values, and great nations the product of a specific set of (mainly military) virtues associated with genetic purity.

The accusation of racism is often accompanied by selective misquotation from a speech Winston made in 1931, in which he declared it 'alarming and also nauseating to see Mr Gandhi, a seditious Middle Temple lawyer, now posing as a fakir of a type well known in the east, striding half-naked up the steps of the viceregal palace, while he is still

13

organizing and conducting a defiant campaign of civil disobedience, to parley on equal terms with the representative of the king-emperor'.[12] Gandhi attended the Inner, not the Middle, Temple and he successfully skewered British imperialists on their own Common Law. Think for a moment what his fate would have been at the hands of the French, Germans or Japanese, and the power for decency in the tradition he invoked at once becomes apparent. Winston was not alone in believing Gandhi a clever barrister first and a Hindu mystic some way second, and dislike of politically ambitious lawyers, even if dark-skinned, cannot be branded necessarily racist without, to use a phrase Winston employed in another context, some risk of terminological inexactitude.[13]

The population of a few small offshore islands could only exercise authority over many millions as long as their own confidence in their right to rule remained firm, and was not seriously challenged by those they governed. Winston believed the maintenance of that confidence was paramount, whereas wiser men realized the crucial factor was its acceptance by the subject peoples. Once that acceptance was gone, then the Empire was moribund and an orderly retreat was imperative. When Winston spoke against relaxing imperial supremacy over India (which then included the separate modern nations of Pakistan and Bangladesh) he declared it was only kept united by British rule, which proved to be true. He was dismissive of Hindu polytheism, less so of the brand of warrior Islam he had encountered on the North-West Frontier and in the Sudan, and believed neither provided the basis for benevolent governance. There is no denying that he mouthed the clichés of progressive eugenics when he was young, that he regarded native peoples as inferior, or that he appealed to racial prejudice in his speeches against Indian self-government. But there is equally no doubt that his opposition was based on a correct estimation that an independent Gandhian India would not support Britain in any future war. Some argue that his views on India detract from his later incarnation as the standard-bearer of freedom; but it is illogical to praise him for seeking to put some backbone into British foreign policy in the 1930s while condemning his efforts to retain India, a vital source of economic and military strength, which indeed proved so valuable in 1939–45 when it raised—let it never be forgotten—the largest all-volunteer army in history.

Oddly, Hitler's pot-calling-the-kettle-black accusation that Winston was a warmonger has recently been revived, mainly by those who wish first to define Britain in Europe, and then to define Europe in opposition to the USA. Those who tried this while he was alive expensively discovered it was libellous. And although he was fascinated by the drama of war and felt energized by being involved in it, he was repelled by its realities. 'Much as war attracts me & fascinates my mind with its tremendous situation', he wrote from Germany in 1909, 'I feel more deeply every year . . . what vile and wicked folly and barbarism it all is.'[14] Half a century later he coined the phrase 'to jaw-jaw is better than to war-war'.[15] Winston loved wearing uniforms, but apart from that foible he was the antithesis of a militarist.

Winston was elitist but, despite outraged grumbling when the vote went against him, he believed he should either win over the electorate or adapt to its will: this is not something that those who count themselves among the intellectually chosen are always so willing to respect. He was sexist, in that he believed men and women were different in outlook and abilities and that leadership was properly the preserve of men. But I suspect his reaction to Golda Meir, Indira Gandhi and Margaret Thatcher would have been a wry chuckle followed, perhaps, by a reference to Joan of Arc and Elizabeth Tudor. He had many prejudices, but was no bigot. Despite Winston's admiration for the political principles of the English Revolution (he strove as unsuccessfully as unwisely to have a warship named for Oliver Cromwell), he disliked the Puritans, and his romantic monarchism made him an object of ridicule when he cast himself in the role of 'King's man' in the abdication crisis of 1936. Like most of his class he could not have cared less about people's sexual proclivities so long as they did not intrude into the public arena. His stance to the contrary in the case of Edward VIII was not solely an expression of personal loyalty: he was seeking an issue, any issue, with which to unsettle the Prime Minister, Stanley Baldwin. In 1947, when asked to join a tribute to mark Baldwin's eightieth birthday, Winston said he *could* not. With a vindictiveness not usually associated with him, he told the organizers of the tribute that 'it would have been better for our country if he [Baldwin] had never lived'.[16]

As to the oft-repeated charge of drunkenness,

16

Winston may indeed have had a genetic predisposition to alcoholism, but he was 'brought up and trained to have the utmost contempt for people who got drunk—except on a very few occasions and a few anniversaries'.[17] As a result, and sadly unlike his son Randolph and daughters Diana and Sarah, he never surrendered to it. He required a steady but seldom excessive intake (which today we might term 'maintenance drinking') to feel fully functional, although it probably also contributed to those recurrent episodes of depression he called the 'black dog'. In hospital in New York after being hit by a car in 1931, when America was still Prohibition-bound, he convinced a physician to write a prescription affirming that his health 'necessitates the use of alcoholic spirits especially at mealtimes', specifying a minimum of 250cc per day.[18] He told the Liberal politician Lady Violet Bonham Carter that he could remember no time when he 'could not order a bottle of champagne for myself and offer another to a friend'.[19] But his wartime Cabinet colleague, the newspaper magnate Lord Beaverbrook, was right to observe that: 'He exaggerated his drinking habits by his own remarks in praise of wine and brandy.'[20] In old age Winston declared that he had taken more out of alcohol than it had taken from him and, given what is now known about the interplay of willpower, social standards and biochemistry in alcoholism, this seems a fair assessment.

Above all else Winston was a patriot, not a nationalist, a crucial distinction best illustrated by contrasting his view of Britain as the ever-changing expression of its inhabitants with Charles de

Gaulle's vision of a sacred, eternal France that could not be itself without greatness, so that if 'mediocrity shows in her acts and deeds, it strikes me as an absurd anomaly, to be imputed to the faults of the French, not to the genius of the land'.21 Winston's words were never appeals to live up to an ideal of a nation superior to the interests and concerns of its people. He never believed his countrymen were not worthy of him, and his speeches during the war years were addressed to what he believed were the eternal strengths and personal values of the British people.

Finally, if he can rightly be faulted for returning to office in 1951–5 when he was no longer physically or mentally fit for the job, it was also an expression of a general mood of national sentimentality and, perhaps, of atonement for having voted him out in 1945. The blame must attach more firmly to the Conservative Party, which for much of his career regarded him as an interloper, for exploiting that mood and for failing to force an earlier retirement. Like most great leaders Winston was a monumental egoist, and if people continued to indulge him he saw no reason to make them stop. He knew that he was declining, and admitted: 'In the midst of the war I could always see how to do it. Today's problems are elusive and intangible.'22 But he did not believe in an afterlife, and thought that only involvement in the affairs of state could sustain his waning vitality. He was at one with Dylan Thomas about growing old ungracefully:

> Do not go gentle into that good night,
> Old age should burn and rave at close of day;

Rage, rage against the dying of the light.

Yet beyond the accusations made by those who attack Winston more as a symbol of some current preoccupation than as an historical figure, there is a case for the prosecution that cannot be easily dismissed. By far the most serious charge relates to his share of the collective responsibility that weighs on the Liberal government of 1914 for committing the small British army to a land war among continental giants. Aggravating circumstances include persisting in voluntary recruitment until early 1916, long after it had become apparent that only conscription could provide the necessary manpower, and moral cowardice for not accepting that the ensuing bloodbath was the result more of political than of military failure. No member of the Asquith government could claim ignorance as an excuse, least of all Winston, who knew the tactical pendulum had swung to the defensive and who in 1911, when Home Secretary, had circulated a memorandum (which had little to do with his departmental responsibilities, but was triggered by that summer's Agadir crisis) that accurately predicted the German army would march into France through Belgium in a wide flanking sweep that would be stopped and reversed on the fortieth day. This proved to be only a slight overestimate: Germany declared war on France on 3 August 1914, and the battle of the Marne was fought on 6–10 September.

Next in importance is his more individual responsibility for problems created by the post-war settlement and, as Chancellor of the Exchequer between 1925 and 1929, for economic policies that not only increased social tensions but left successor governments without the means to initiate the rapid military build-up he began to demand almost as soon as he was out of power. It is mitigation, but no defence, to argue that he took the advice of the leading figures in the field. He was one of the few British politicians who had the force of personality to jolt the Civil Service out of its rut, and when he did not do so it was because he concurred with the establishment. My own preoccupation with the sufferings of my grandfather's generation has unquestionably blurred my objectivity, but I believe the period 1914–29 to be one of compound betrayal of the British by their political leadership. Winston held high office for much of this time and consequently bears a heavy responsibility, but no politician or party emerges with much credit. Robert Rhodes James entitled his 1970 biography *Churchill: A Study in Failure, 1900–1939*, a verdict generally shared by later biographers. But which of his contemporaries can be judged wholly successful?

Winston considered the period 1929–39, when he was in his late fifties and early sixties, to be his years in the wilderness. But to what promised land would he have led his people had they chosen to follow him? In fact his opponents were more right than he was about most things, but like the hedgehog of the fable he knew one big thing, which turned out in the end to be the one that really mattered. I regard this period as being the moment when the character formed in a long and active life expressed itself as a commitment, above all, to a very British concept of proper behaviour. This point is not generally stressed in the books written about him by his countrymen. Happily, American authors are not so inhibited, and one of them has written the clearest expression of the central meaning of Winston's life: he passionately believed in decency, and that British influence in the world tended to promote it. Therefore compromise with Nazi Germany was impossible: what justification was there for the Empire and British power, if not to fight against Hitler and all he stood for?[23]

When very old and depressed, Winston lamented his inability to maintain the Empire and Britain's status as a great power. Those who call this failure ought, perhaps, to propose alternative policies that might have prevented the relative decline of British authority in a much enlarged world. The British Empire was the product of an unrepeatable combination of historical factors, and far from it being the case that Winston mortgaged Britain's future to wage World War II, in fact he spent a windfall inheritance to assure a future for values the civilized world regards as eternal.

State funerals have only been granted to seven men who were not members of the royal family: William Pitt the Elder in 1778, Lord Nelson and William Pitt the Younger in 1806, the Duke of Wellington in 1852, William Ewart Gladstone in 1898, Field Marshal Lord Roberts in 1914 and Sir Winston Churchill in 1965.[24] Wellington shares with Winston's great ancestor the Duke of Marlborough the distinction of having led mighty allied armies to victory; but not even the younger Pitt bears comparison with Winston as the inspirer of a great coalition of peoples. I had thought to close this introduction on a personal note, recalling my feelings when I watched Winston's funeral on television more than half a lifetime ago, with the London dockers, for so long his dogged political opponents, dipping their cranes in tribute as his coffin passed. But I cannot hope to improve on the words written by the Hungarian-American John Lukacs in his elegiac memoir of a cold, quiet and solemn day in London, 30 January 1965:

He loved life very much; and he made life possible for many of us because he had a very old, and very strong, belief in the possibilities of human decency and of human greatness . . . In the long and slow and sad music of humanity he once sounded an English and noble note which some of us were blessed to receive and to remember.[25]

CHAPTER ONE

FATHER TO THE MAN

1874–1895

There is an almost unsettling similarity between a photograph of Winston when he was seven years old and Yousuf Karsh's famous portrait of him taken in Canada on the last day of 1941, 60 years later. There he is, hand on hip, head thrust slightly forward and eyes challenging the camera. The main difference between the two is that the boy appears even more imperious than the statesman, who was outraged because Karsh had snatched the cigar from his lips just before snapping the shutter. The actions of historical figures are often attributed to adult motivation, but deeper answers are to be found in their inherited nature and earliest nurture. The 'wild words' of the Victorian poet Gerard Manley Hopkins are a sober fact—the child is the father to the man.

A mismatch between Winston's infant needs and the love and attention he received from his parents coloured the whole of his existence, but it has been too readily accepted that the imbalance was on the supply side. On the contrary, it is clear that his emotional demands were unlimited. Answering the question as to why people so often put up with his monumental egocentricity and forgave or even loved him for his lack of consideration, the distinguished psychiatrist Anthony Storr observed 'it is often true that men who demand and need a

23

great deal of attention from others are manifesting a kind of childish helplessness which evokes an appropriate response, however difficult they may be'.[1] Almost all who knew Winston well or worked closely with him commented, fondly or in exasperation, about his eternal boyishness. His was not the calculating seducer's charm but rather the beguiling appeal of a child, expecting affectionate compliance as though by right. He once said that all babies looked like him, but a truer statement might have been that all babies would wish to have lives like his: usually at the centre of a doting coterie, wishes anticipated and whims applauded. Life soon disabuses most children of this ambition, but some enter adulthood so convinced of their importance that they seldom have difficulty in persuading others to concur. This description fits Winston's adult personality too well to accept at face value his self-portrayal as the lonely child of distant and uncaring parents: it was far, far more complicated than that.

The 'poor little Winston' version of his childhood dates from 1930, when he published *My Early Life*. He was out of office following the 1929 general election in which the Labour Party, a powerful portent for the future but at that time little more than a vehicle for the social aspirations and economic grievances of the lower middle and industrial working classes, became the largest contingent in the House of Commons. It was also the first election since the 1928 Equal Franchise Act, which gave women the same voting rights as men. Winston was well aware that his career, launched with all the advantages of aristocratic birth and the benevolence of powerful men towards the son of a famously attractive mother, outraged the sensibilities of a newly enfranchised generation. A change of image was also advisable to overcome memories of his period as Home Secretary in 1910–11, when he was the particular target of suffragette hostility and was widely believed to have used troops against strikers in the Welsh town of Tonypandy. What better way than to reinvent himself as one who had triumphed over childhood adversity, while appealing to the maternal instinct?[2]

Even hostile biographers have accepted the spin put on his formative years by a man who cheerfully—and often—boasted that history would be kind to him because he intended to write it himself. He was more subtle than he is usually portrayed, more so even than the brilliantly devious President Franklin Delano Roosevelt (hereafter FDR), whose fondness for his great contemporary was tinged with the wariness of a master manipulator who knew that he himself was being played. FDR never let anyone know what he was thinking (his formidable wife declared that he did not think, he decided), whereas Winston appeared to reveal all in an avalanche of written and spoken argument, provoking others to show their hands while reserving his own final position. FDR found the technique extremely irritating. It gave rise to the celebrated incident when the polio-disabled President wheeled himself into his guest's room to find him stark naked. 'You see, Mr President', lisped the elderly cherub, 'I have nothing to hide from you.'[3] One suspects he had used the line before, probably after some domestic dispute with his wife Clementine; but how could anyone fail to be disarmed by it?

To the end of his days Winston retained the characteristics not of a deprived child, but of one excessively indulged; among these characteristics was a stubborn determination to have his own way, which, coupled with boyish enthusiasm, unfeigned kindness and an impish sense of humour, enabled him to ride out storms that would have sunk a less self-confident man. General Dwight D. Eisenhower, Allied Commander in Europe in 1944–5 and later President of the USA, recalled in his memoirs how 'if [Winston] accepted a decision unwillingly he would return again and again to the attack in an effort to have his own way, up to the very moment of execution. But once action was started he had a faculty for forgetting everything in his desire to get ahead, and invariably tried to provide British support in a greater degree than promised.'[4] So might his mother have written of many trials of will with her son, preserved for us in the reams of always frank and affectionate correspondence between them.

Winston may well have been conceived on his young parents' wedding night. Lord Randolph Spencer-Churchill (hereafter Lord Randolph to avoid confusion with Winston's son of the same name) was 25 and his wife Jeanette (née Jerome), known as Jennie, 20 when they were married at the British Embassy in Paris on 15 April 1874, and Winston was born seven and a half months later at Blenheim Palace, the country estate of his grand-father, the Duke of Marlborough. He was supposed to be born at his parents' home in London and nothing had been prepared at Blenheim for his birth, brought on when Jennie fell while accompanying the guns of a shooting party, followed by a rough ride in a pony carriage. Even this accident shed stardust on the newborn, for Blenheim remains one of the grandest of all British stately homes. Built to rival the magnificent Versailles residence of the 'Sun-King' Louis XIV, whose hopes for European hegemony were checked by John Churchill, the 1st Duke of Marlborough, at the battle of Blenheim in 1704, the palace was built within the Royal Manor of Woodstock, birthplace of Richard the Lionheart and of Edward the Black Prince, and where the home of Geoffrey Chaucer, the father of English literature, still stands. Blenheim no more brooked argument than did a company of British grenadiers, and, as Simon Jenkins has put it so well, 'was primarily intended not as a home but as a monument, symbol of British pride . . .'.5 It is the towering triumph of English Baroque, and the vision of its main front demands a sound-track to match, perhaps Henry Purcell's *Abdelazar* played very loudly indeed. Winston drew much of his sense of destiny from the potent aura of his fortuitous birthplace.

Before considering the environmental factors that shaped the infant Winston, we must look at the genetic endowment he brought to the equation. There can be little doubt that he was born with a predisposition to alcoholism, which is often associated with the sort of personality that finds fulfilment in story-telling. Another characteristic is a sense of apartness or insecurity that alcohol seems to resolve—while most people drink to enhance mood, some do so in order to feel what they believe to be 'normal'. The relationship between genetic endowment, personality and behaviour is complex and remains vigorously debated. None the less the vital importance attached to alcohol by the adult Winston deserves more than the anecdotal treatment it has been given, and the possible application to his character of conventional wisdom about the genetic component in substance dependency cannot be wholly dismissed. He also exhibited some symptoms of the neurological condition known as Asperger's Syndrome, in particular a pronounced lack of empathy, an apparent inability to read body language that could translate into rudeness, a preference for monologues over conversation, skin sensitivity expressed as a physiological need for silk undergarments, disorientation when his routine was disturbed, and an unusual intensity of determination to complete tasks, to the point that 'unfinished business' could prey on his mind to an obsessive degree.

Nor should we underestimate the crucial significance of the fact that he was the first fruit of a genuinely grand passion between two talented young people, who were themselves their parents' favourite children, and that for his first six years he was their only child. After meeting Jennie at a reception for the future Tsar Alexander III on board HMS *Ariadne*, the guard ship of the Cowes Regatta of August 1873, Lord Randolph fell in love with about as much thought for the consequences as Romeo upon meeting Juliet. He proposed and was accepted on their third meeting, but was then called away and obliged to continue his wooing by letters filled with the yearning of the hopelessly smitten:

my rooms and my things and my occupations here which I used to take such interest in are quite hateful to me now, all I can do is keep reading your letter and looking at your photographs and thinking thinking till I get quite stupid. I do not think dearest you have any idea of how much I love you, or what sacrifices I would not make to call you my own. My whole life and energies should be devoted to making you happy and protecting you from harm or wrong. Life should be to you one long summer day.[6]

Jennie replied as one would expect of a young woman sure of her worth, and as an American anxious that her future husband should not think her overly impressed by his family—which of course she was. Thus, while unattributably leaking news of the engagement to the *Court Journal*, in her first full letter to Lord Randolph, written in her usual breathless style and with her no less characteristic blithe indifference to internal coherence, she made a pre-emptive strike on any thought she might be marrying 'up':

Believe me, I consider you as free as if nothing had ever passed between us—and as I told you last night if your father and mother object in the least to our marriage—why cross them? Is it not much wiser to end it all before it is too late? . . . I cannot tell you how deeply hurt I am at the insinuation you gave me—as to your having heard something against my father—I was unable to answer you or defend him—as you did not choose to confide in

29

me—All I can say is that I love, admire and respect my father more than any man living . . . I wonder if you are very angry with this letter?—or will you not care? Forgive me—I really <u>cannot</u> break quite yet—for I feel I love you more than anything or person on earth— and that I am ready to do or say anything you like as long as you leave my family alone and not abuse it.[7]

The 7th Duke, Lord Randolph's father, was the first of the dynasty since its founder to play a significant role in public affairs. His Duchess was the daughter of the Marquess of Londonderry and great-niece of Lord Castlereagh, one of the greatest political figures of his generation. They were on poisonous terms with their erratic elder son George, Marquess of Blandford, and so all their hopes were invested in Lord Randolph, his younger brother. However, the Duke gave Lord Randolph only a modest marriage settlement of £1100 per annum (income only), thereby keeping the purse strings fastened tightly around his son's spirited neck.

Jennie was the favourite daughter of four born to the union of Leonard Jerome, himself the adored youngest of a large upstate New York farming family, and Clara (née Hall), an orphaned heiress. Leonard quickly made a fortune on the New York Stock Exchange, something he had to do several times thanks to spending and losing money faster than he made it. He entertained extravagantly, raced horses and yachts, and indulged a taste for music and female opera singers in a private theatre. Clara preferred to live in Paris,

Leonard in New York, but after Jennie informed her father of her lightning romance he reminded her that his marriage to her mother had also been a love match. Lord Randolph obviously adored her, Leonard reasoned, because: 'You are no heiress and it must have taken heaps of love to overcome an Englishman's prejudice against "those horrid Americans".'[8] Unusually, Leonard insisted on dividing Jennie's dowry (£50,000 in irrevocable trusts, producing an income of £2000 per annum) equally between the bride and groom. In today's money, the two marriage settlements produced an annual income in excess of £150,000—a great deal to us, but a pittance by the standards of their social set. Jennie was not the rich and empty-headed girl who traipses through some of the literature. She had exquisite taste, edited the short-lived literary magazine *The Anglo-Saxon Review*, and produced a play. As Winston candidly told her, they both liked the finer things in life and knew where to find them, even if they were uncertain whence the money would come to pay for them. One thing, however, shines clearly through their correspondence: a love which Jennie felt was unstinted, but which for Winston was never quite enough.

If the tale of parental distance Winston told in *My Early Life* is combined with a reading of his parents' letters to each other, the picture that emerges is one of superficially fond or narcissistic rather than indifferent parenting. Among the earliest references to him is one by Lord Randolph in a letter to Jennie in June 1876, when they were feverishly corresponding about a quarrel with the Prince of Wales which led to their being dropped by London society. 'I don't like this house without you it is awfully dull,' he wrote. 'The baby is very well. He came in to see me this afternoon and carried off the paper basket in triumph.'[9] When he and Jennie first fell in love, he wrote about his pug puppy in much the same terms. Perhaps of no less importance for Winston's development was that not long afterwards, to avoid humiliation for his son and daughter-in-law and to prevent a permanent breach with the Prince of Wales, the Duke of Marlborough accepted the office of Lord Lieutenant (essentially Viceroy) of Ireland, a post he had previously refused, and took his furious son with him as Private Secretary.

This period of exile meant that although, like all society couples, Winston's parents were not involved with the physical side of rearing their son, he probably saw more of them during the family's Irish sojourn in 1877–80, the time of his earliest memory, than he would have done had they spun through the social whirl of London. Winston recalled the period in a passage of great intensity, immediately preceding his more famous description of Jennie as 'a fairy princess: a radiant being possessed of limitless riches and power'. He remembered her 'in a riding habit, fitting like a skin and often beautifully spotted with mud. She and my father hunted continually on their large horses; and sometimes there were great scares because one or the other did not come back for many hours after they were expected.'[10] There are only two likely explanations for such absences, and had his parents' been occasioned by accidents Winston would surely have mentioned it.

Winston's description contains erotic overtones

that compel consideration of the Oedipus complex, however unfashionable the notion may now have become. In *Civilization and Its Discontents*, published the same year as *My Early Life*, the founder of psychiatry, Sigmund Freud, argued that all culture, civility and law was the product of the resolution of the psychosexual dilemma through which a boy passes between the ages of three and six, in which he wishes to emulate the mythical character who unknowingly killed his father and became his mother's lover. Freud's theory, developed in a series of books and extended essays beginning in 1900, is that the child's incestuous desire and concomitant murderous impulse make him feel guilty, and the result is the moral faculty called the super-ego. Freud believed the process was reprised in adolescence with regard to authority and could arise again when a parent died. Winston's comfortable adult relationship with Jennie, which he described as being like brother and sister, does not conform to the theory; none the less his father did die at a crucial moment in his life, and Winston did adopt a patriarchal tone in his subsequent correspondence with Jennie, who went on to marry two men the same age as, or younger than, her older son.

Another reason why Winston's adult character does not conform to the Oedipal pattern may be that as a child he, like most other children of his class, enjoyed the full-time attention of a mother surrogate in his nurse, Mrs Elizabeth Everest; her fond descriptions of Kent, her birthplace, gave him a burning desire to live there, an ambition finally realized when he bought his country home, Chartwell, in 1922. His pet name for her, which he continued to use until her death in 1895, was 'Woomany' or 'Woom', and one does not need to be a Freudian to observe that these are heavily weighted words. Winston wrote of Mrs Everest that she 'looked after me and tended all my wants. It was to her I poured out all my troubles, both now and in my schooldays.'[11] Perhaps not all of them: unmentioned in his memoirs was that he ceased to be an only child with the birth of his brother Jack in 1880, and that one of the reasons he was sent to boarding school was that he 'teased' the baby unmercifully.[12] It appears that he continued to do so when he came home for the school holidays. Jennie confessed in a letter to her sister in December 1884 that he was so ill-behaved she 'could not undertake to manage [him] without Everest—I am afraid even she can't do it'. The focus of his bad behaviour emerges from the resentful letter he wrote on 21 January 1885, upon returning to school: 'You must be happy without me, no screams from Jack or complaints. It must be heaven on earth.'[13]

It is clear from Winston's schoolboy letters to both his parents that he was used to being the centre of attention and saw no reason why that state of affairs should not have continued indefinitely. His frankly whining demands for visits from his mother should be read bearing in mind that it was usual for boys at boarding school to see their parents only in the holidays, and not even then if the parents were posted overseas. Winston was begging for more than the normal attention a boy of his age and social standing had a right to expect in those days.[14] This lack of restraint offended his very English father, and even his

American mother thought some of his letters unmanly. Even so, 50 years later Winston was still petulant about being sent away to school:

I was also miserable at the idea of being left alone among all these strangers in this great, fierce, formidable place. After all I was only seven [in fact the usual age for boys to go to preparatory school], and I had been so happy in my nursery with all my toys. I had such wonderful toys: a real steam engine, a magic lantern, and a collection of soldiers already nearly a thousand strong. Now it was all to be lessons. Seven or eight hours of lessons every day except half-holidays, and football and cricket in addition.[15]

If homesickness was normal, what happened afterwards was not. From the very start Winston would do only what interested him, and for the next 11 years he successfully resisted pressure from schools and parents alike to change his ways. He would not be pushed, and could be led only in a direction that was agreeable to him. In part this may have stemmed from some slight learning disabilities: in *My Early Life* he describes being taught to read in the manner a Special Needs teacher might employ today. He also inherited from his father a speech impediment, the 's' pronounced as 'sh' that stayed with him for life. In those days natural anomalies such as left-handedness were treated as correctable bad habits, and Winston's orotund pronunciation probably developed in the repetitive elocution lessons he took in his teens. His description of how his

35

teacher of English at Harrow brought the written language alive for him is also instructive:

> He took a fairly long sentence and broke it up into its components by means of black, red, blue and green inks. . . . Each had its colour and its bracket. It was a kind of drill. We did it almost daily. As I remained in the [lowest class] three times as long as anyone else, I had three times as much of it. I learned it thoroughly. Thus I got into my bones the essential structure of the ordinary British sentence—which is a noble thing.[16]

Winston's skill with the written word thus caught up with a precocious ability to marshal thoughts and speak them, a separate faculty which uses a different part of the brain. This talent was revealed in the deal he made with a sixth-former to compose English essays in exchange for the older pupil's help with his own Latin translations. Forty-two years later he recalled: 'I used to walk up and down the room dictating—just as I do now—and he sat in the corner and wrote it down longhand.'[17] The two were nearly discovered when the headmaster, impressed by one essay, eagerly summoned the sixth-former for further discussion, only to conclude a disappointingly one-sided conversation with the words, 'You seem to be better at written than at oral work.' Had the headmaster but known it, the opposite was the case of the true author, whose written words stride from the page with the cadences of speech. The pupil with whom Winston struck the deal may have been his future fellow politician Leopold Amery, who was only a year older but a sixth-former when Winston entered the third form at Harrow in 1888.

Winston was always physically small, growing to only five feet six inches, and his body was so narrow in the chest that, after scraping through the written entrance examination to the Royal Military College at Sandhurst on the third attempt, he almost failed the physical. He had frequent, often severe chest infections and also suffered concussion and internal injuries on a number of occasions, although not because of the clumsiness usually associated with the accident-prone. On the contrary, he had phenomenally good hand-to-eye coordination, excelling at gymnastics at preparatory school and winning the public schools fencing championship in 1892. He was among the best polo players during his time in India and continued to play, despite a permanently damaged right shoulder, until he was 52. Nor can he be said to have been unlucky: rather the opposite, for anyone less blessed by fortune would surely have died on one of the occasions when his Olympian disregard for danger came into sharp contact with the law of averages.

Winston was a frustrated product of the public school system. 'Public schools' were so called because for centuries the seriously wealthy had often had their children privately educated by tutors, and public schools were a cheaper alternative, originally patronized principally by the middle classes. From the time the pioneering Thomas Arnold (the essayist Matthew's father) was headmaster of Rugby, from 1828 to 1842, the public schools sought to inculcate team-playing, godliness, gentlemanly conduct and intellectual ability. Arnold brought mathematics and modern languages into the Rugby curriculum and grouped the boys into 'forms'—the word explicit as to their intention—but it was his innovative system of social control, based on the delegation of power to sixth-form prefects, that was most rapidly imitated by the other public schools.

In potent synergy with this transformation of secondary schooling, following the publication in 1853 of the Northcote-Trevelyan Report entitled *The Organization of the Permanent Civil Service*, the old system of patronage gave way grudgingly to recruitment and promotion on the basis of examinations, with a higher career track for university-educated clerks and a lower one for those with a good secondary education. While eminently successful in ensuring continuity and stability, the public schools and the new Civil Service expressed and reinforced a growing anti-commercial bias in the class previously defined by entrepreneurial activity, which, perhaps more than any other single factor, drained vitality from the British economy.

Winston was always mildly contemptuous of the public school ethic, and in later life spoke of Britain as 'a Laocoön strangled by old school ties'.[18] No amount of 'forming' was going to turn him into a lawyer or a civil servant; he would not or could not be shaped to fit the specifications, confronting him with the choice of either accepting the system's negative assessment of him or proving it wrong. There was no question which path he would take, and therein lies at least part of the explanation for his being for so long an anti-establishment figure, as well as one of the few

British ministers who so frequently put the fear of God into his permanent officials.

Winston was unhappy at school. It was not that he was stupid, as a close examination of his reports confirms. At his preparatory school in Ascot the headmaster acknowledged that he was very good at history and geography. However, he was certainly one of the worst-behaved boys in the school and a nuisance to everybody. Beaten for stealing sugar from the pantry, he took the headmaster's favourite straw hat and kicked it to bits, knowing very well that he would be flogged again. So it continued at Harrow, where he excelled in the few subjects that interested him. But the influence of school is often overstated. It cannot compete with or adequately substitute for family influence. Although the earliest years are definitive in anyone's life, it is also important to have an adult relationship with one's parents, merging into the role reversal that comes as they grow old and, with luck, can be loved as they are, not as totems of childish reverence or objects of adolescent rebellion. Winston was never granted this opportunity, and, as the following poignant passage in *My Early Life* reveals, his father's early death in 1895 engendered a lifelong sense of deprivation:

> . . . if ever I began to show the slightest idea of comradeship, he was immediately offended; and when once I suggested that I might help his private secretary to write some letters, he froze me into stone. I know now that this would have been only a passing phase. Had he lived another four or five years, he could not have done without me.[19]

39

Alas, some of the last words Lord Randolph wrote to his son were withering. 'Do not think', he wrote in August 1893, 'that I am going to take the trouble of writing you long letters after every folly & failure you commit & undergo. I shall not write again on these matters & you need not trouble to write any answer to this part of my letter, because I no longer attach the slightest weight to anything you may say about your own achievements & exploits.'[20] When Winston accidentally dropped a valuable pocket watch given him by his father into the Wish Stream, which still runs through the grounds of Sandhurst, he first dived for it, though it was a chilly April, and then had the stream dragged. When that failed he hired 23 men from the infantry detachment, who dug a new course for the stream, and finally he 'obtained the fire engine and pumped the pool dry and so obtained the watch'. Lord Randolph was not impressed, but Jennie immediately sent Winston £2 towards the £3 he had spent hiring men and engine. Fortunately his father soon recovered his temper, agreeing that 'the rough work of Sandhurst' was not suitable for such a fine watch and sending him a cheaper one. Historians (and I am no exception) are given to quoting the harsh passages of Lord Randolph's letters to his son, but the one about the watch, like so many others, ended: 'Ever your affte father Randolf SC'. There were also some encouraging signs. Winston, the butt of so many highly critical headmasters' reports, actually did well at Sandhurst, probably because, for once in his life, he could see the point in what he was doing. His conduct was described as 'good' and, having passed in 92nd in a list of 102, he passed out a very creditable 20th in a class of 130. But Lord Randolph was now too sick to take any pleasure from this radical improvement, and he died before Winston was commissioned into the cavalry. He had already told his son that this was precisely what he was to put 'out of your head altogether, at any rate during my lifetime', because of the expense involved. Scarcely was Lord Randolph buried at Bladon near the Blenheim estate than Winston embarked upon just that course of action of which he knew his father had strenuously disapproved.

About 55 years later Winston wrote an account of a dreamlike conversation with the spirit of his father, as it emerged from a portrait he was restoring. He quoted Lord Randolph as saying, 'I was never going to talk politics with a boy like you ever.' The hallucinatory interview ended with another dismissive comment from the spirit, all the more revealing for the self-vindication in its studied irony: 'Of course you are too old now to think about such things, but when I hear you talk I really wonder you didn't go into politics. You might have done a lot to help. You might even have made a name for yourself.'[21] That Winston should have been literally haunted by the memory of his father over half a century after his death is of more than anecdotal significance. The death of Lord Randolph in Winston's 21st year, the canonical age of manhood, and Winston's subsequent adoption of a proprietary attitude towards his youthful, attractive and sexually active mother, can fairly be assumed to have been among the most important facts of his life, which would colour every subsequent action.[22]

Lord Randolph's early death may also have marked his son in a more conscious but no less permanent way. Although his official biographer, Sir Martin Gilbert, reckons that he was not told the specifics at the time, Winston admitted later in life to believing the cause of his father's bouts of dementia and ugly death to have been general paralysis of the insane, the euphemism employed at that time to describe the dreadful final phase of syphilis.[23] Although this was the diagnosis of the specialist in charge of the case, syphilis is a highly contagious disease, which, had Lord Randolph suffered from it, would have manifested itself in his wife. That she did not develop the symptoms points to some other cause, probably a left-brain tumour.[24]

But Winston could not know this, and there appears to have been an abrupt change in his behaviour towards women at this time. Before, he had flirted and shown the usual interest, indeed on one occasion taking the lead in a 'riot' against the closure of a theatre where young bucks and 'ladies of the Empire' mingled.[25] But after Lord Randolph's death Winston's attitude towards the opposite sex became hesitant and almost excruciatingly chaste. His abstention from amorous adventures and his late marriage (he was 34) may have had a common cause in his belief that his father had been destroyed by erotic indulgence. If so, the redirection of sexual energy, what he called 'not wasting my essence in bed', may have been the most significant element in the complex inheritance left to Winston by his unfortunate father.

The overt example set by Lord Randolph in life was also influential. After returning from Ireland, he joined other young Tories to attack not only Gladstone's Liberal administration of 1880–5 but also their own comatose Conservative front bench. The rebels formed what came to be called the 'Fourth Party' (the other being the Irish Parliamentary Party) and in 1883 founded the Primrose League, which advocated a more populist conservatism to snatch the banners of social and political reform away from the Liberals. Elected chairman of the National Union of Conservative Associations in 1884, Lord Randolph resigned to avoid a split in the party; for the power and restraint he had demonstrated he was rewarded with the post of Secretary of State for India when Lord Salisbury formed a government after the 1885 elections.

Following further elections in 1886, Salisbury made Lord Randolph his Chancellor of the Exchequer and Leader of the House of Commons. Although Randolph showed tact and discretion in the House, he was never on good terms with all his Cabinet colleagues, and on 20 December 1886 he suddenly resigned, telling Salisbury that he could not concur with the naval and military demands made on the Treasury. He seems to have expected Salisbury to restore him to office on his own terms, but in fact the Prime Minister accepted the resignation and there was no outcry from the party faithful. That was the end of Lord Randolph's political career, more a self-destructive shooting star than the blazing meteor portrayed in his son's biography of him. Therein lies a tale, for although the book is generally regarded as a monument to filial loyalty, the political context of the time during which Winston wrote the two-volume *Lord*

Randolph Churchill, published in 1906, suggests less straightforward motives. On 18 February 1901 he ended his maiden speech to the House of Commons with the words: 'I cannot sit down without saying how very grateful I am for the kindness and patience with which the House has heard me, extended to me, I well know, not on my own account, but because of a certain splendid memory which many honourable members still preserve.' This was nonsense: the sons of old members were always given a sympathetic hearing in what was still a gentlemen's club. Winston was there on his own merits, if anything cursed by the comparisons that would inevitably be made between him and his father. Lord Randolph had been a far more naturally accomplished speaker, and by the time Winston entered the Commons many saw Lord Randolph's truncated career, in particular the miscalculation which ended it, through the prism of the dementia into which he lapsed at the end of his life. The phrase 'as undependable (or mad) as his father' was shaped and ready to be applied to Winston's words and actions. The son always sensed his father's unhappy ghost. When he accepted the office of Chancellor of the Exchequer in 1924 Winston told the Prime Minister that he 'should be proud to serve you in this splendid office', adding: 'I still have my father's robes as Chancellor.' They had been kept, in tissue paper and camphor, for the past 30 years.

In Chapter Three I return to the matters of political substance that may have been involved, but by the time Winston published his father's biography he had passed briskly through the 'Fourth Party' stage to an outright rupture with the

Conservative Party, crossing the house to sit with the opposition Liberals on 31 May 1904. Embarking on a biography of his father was a useful way of establishing a personal relationship with men who had been colleagues of Lord Randolph in his prime, and also to remind the Tory grandees that some within their own party felt that their treatment of his father had been shabby. The biography is marked by a patent concern not to offend those still active in politics, resulting in a balanced account of his father's career that did much to persuade doubters of Winston's maturity. But, no less obviously, it served to blunt charges of opportunism arising from his change in party allegiance by presenting a filial and ideological justification for it.

There is one final indication of an unhealthy influence exercised over Winston by Lord Randolph—or rather by the threatening image of him formed by his son. Until 1895 Winston's existence was a catalogue of illnesses. Some were life-threatening, such as a severe bout of pneumonia in March 1886 and, in January 1893, concussion and internal injuries after leaping from a bridge over a steep-sided valley at Alum Chine near Bournemouth during a game of tag with his brother Jack and a cousin, in the misplaced belief that he could grab a pine tree which would arrest his fall. But his schoolboy letters frequently complain of stomach pain and toothaches, often on the eve of examinations or other moments of stress, a tendency that continued through his time at the Royal Military College, Sandhurst. Although he remained mildly hypochondriac, the more obviously psychosomatic ailments disappeared when Lord Randolph died and Winston enjoyed generally good health until old age at last exacted a very belated price for a long life packed with alcohol, nicotine and cholesterol.

All of the factors considered so far may help us to understand Winston's character, but they do not explain it. The drawback to any psychological interpretation of someone no longer alive to refute it is that it is all too easy, post hoc, to attribute adult character traits to childhood formation. We are more than the sum of our genetic inheritance and of the influence upon us of our families, our schools and the broader society in which we grow up. We begin to learn from our experiences very early, and all of us will have vivid mental snapshots of apparently insignificant events that have remained with us when more obvious milestones have disappeared into the bland verges of memory. We can know what those events may have been in other people's lives if they volunteer the information, and in the case of Winston we are better served than most because after his father's biography he dictated all his books, correcting rather than rewriting them in typed draft. Thus the rise and fall of intensity in the language employed in *My Early Life* is a firm indicator of the power of the memories he is evoking.

Many aspects of Winston's behaviour around the time of his father's death were unlovable, chief among them prevailing on his newly widowed mother to finance his full participation in the activities of his expensive cavalry regiment, the 4th Queen's Own Hussars, entry into which Lord Randolph had strongly opposed because the family finances could not bear it. It is also shocking that after his old nurse Elizabeth Everest was dismissed by the dowager Duchess of Marlborough, with whom his parents were obliged to live because of their straitened circumstances, it did not occur to him to moderate his own financial demands in return for a small continuing payment to the woman he claimed to love so much. When, six months after Lord Randolph's death, Mrs Everest developed peritonitis and died, Winston typically charged to his mother the cost of the wreath he bought—though in the period 1906–11, when his finances were more robust, he paid for the upkeep of flowers at her grave.[26]

I confess to a deep sense of sadness when my enquiry led me to a close study of the documents in the *Companion* to the first volume of Winston's life, selected by his son Randolph. I defy anyone to like the young man who emerges from these letters, and most will find his unvarnished egomania and cynical exploitation of people who cared for him frankly detestable.[27] My sadness was for his son, so like Winston in so many ways, obliged to let the documents say what he himself could not. With due allowance made for what seems to have been a delayed adolescence, Winston devoted himself to advancing his own interests with a single-mindedness one can only admire with a hindsight conditioned by knowledge that he went on to do great things. Randolph would have needed to be supernaturally dispassionate not to have wondered how his own life might have turned out if his mother had been as devoted to him as Jennie was to Winston after the death of Lord Randolph. Instead, Clemmie continued to direct her best energies to a man who lived on to overshadow his only son so completely that the latter could never be more than a footnote. Whatever the younger Randolph's motives, he documented two episodes of behaviour so dishonourable that either might have curtailed Winston's career before it was fairly launched.[28]

The commanding officer of the 4th Hussars was John Brabazon, a 52-year-old veteran of several colonial wars and hanger-on to the Prince of Wales, who modelled himself on Lord Cardigan of Charge of the Light Brigade fame. The regiment's adjutant, and prime mover of the events that follow, was Captain Frederick de Moleyns. Some of the spiteful snobbery prevailing during Cardigan's command of the 11th Hussars in the 1840s was to be found in the 4th in the 1890s. Not long before Winston was gazetted to the regiment a subaltern called George Hodge had been driven out by a campaign of harassment, which had included being dunked in a horse trough. In April, less than two months after joining, Winston himself played a prominent part in the ostracism of Alan Bruce-Pryce, another new second lieutenant, on the alleged grounds that with an allowance of 'only' £500 a year (Winston's was £300) he was unfit to belong to a smart regiment, but really because de Moleyns had taken a dislike to him. Bruce-Pryce initially refused to leave, but after accepting an invitation to have a drink in the Sergeants' Mess at New Year 1896, he was charged with 'improperly associating with non-commissioned officers'. Faced with a court martial in which de Moleyns and the sergeant-major, who had tricked him, would have testified against him, Bruce-Pryce resigned.

The young man's father, most imprudently for

the successful barrister he was, wrote a complaint alleging the real reason for his son having been driven out was that he had rivalled Winston in shooting, fencing and riding while at Sandhurst, and 'incidentally that he knew too much about Mr Churchill', to wit 'gross immorality of the Oscar Wilde type'.[29] Served with a libel writ, he made an unreserved retraction and paid £400 damages. Winston had instructed that the money be given to charity, but his solicitor prevailed upon him to keep it. One doubts that he needed much persuading, given that he was constantly sliding into debt. The actionable words of the elder Bruce-Pryce no doubt echoed bitter comments made by his son, who clearly held Winston primarily responsible for what had happened to him.

Three weeks prior to informing Bruce-Pryce that he was not fit to serve in the 4th Hussars, Winston and his fellow subalterns had been involved in another murky affair, potentially far more damaging according to the rules of late Victorian society. The occasion was the annual Subalterns' Cup, a race over fences that attracted the sporting fraternity, and it was won by a 6–1 outsider with the heavily backed favourite coming in second. Winston, riding a friend's horse, came in third despite having promised his mother he would not race. Following an enquiry by the Stewards of the National Hunt, the race was declared null and void and all the horses involved were permanently banned from racing. Short of an outright accusation and consequent scandal, something from which the custodians of the Turf's sanctity might flinch even today, the verdict could not have been more clearly expressed. The balance of evidence so strongly implicated the subalterns in collusion to 'fix' the race that the usual whitewash would not stick.

During 1896 the Radical MP and journalist Henry Labouchère blew the lid off these scandals in the tabloid *Truth*, and the Hodge and Bruce-Pryce cases were raised in the House of Commons on 19 June. Winston was by then in India, and when the 22 October edition of *Truth* reached him he wrote in haste to Jennie:

> Mr Labouchère's last article in *Truth* is really too hot for words. I fail to see any other course than legal action. He distinctly says that five of us—mentioning my name—were implicated in a 'coup' to obtain money by malpractice on the Turf. You must not allow this to go unchallenged as it would be fatal to any future in public life for me. Indeed I daresay I should be exposed to attacks even on the grounds of having helped to turn out Bruce. This racing matter is however more serious.[30]

What may we conclude from these events, so utterly out of character with the rest of Winston's career, if entirely typical of the way Victorian society closed ranks in defence of its own members? In a biography uncompromisingly titled *Churchill: An Unruly Life*, Norman Rose convincingly argues that it was the result of a desire to be liked, to be accepted, something Winston had not known at school:

> Three days after the Subalterns' Challenge

Cup, he could note that 'Everybody in the regiment was awfully pleased at my riding . . . It has done me a lot of good here and I think I may say I am popular with everybody.' . . . The group of young blades with whom he associated set their own dubious standards. Churchill surrendered to them, hoping to break into their world.31

That year, 1895–6, was young Winston's *annus mirabilis*. He began it a callow youth begging for money in order to buy ever more expensive toys, and ended it having put aside childish things. Among those 'things' were the regiment and the young men who had led him into actions that almost betrayed his destiny. Following the passage cited above, he completed his instructions to Jennie with the words: 'Of course what you do must be done from my point of view alone and not with reference to the regiment—who have no ideas beyond soldiering and care nothing for the opinion of those who are not their friends.'32

He never ran with the pack again.

CHAPTER TWO

THE BUBBLE REPUTATION

1895–1901

If I had to select the one book that most clearly illustrates the development of Winston's adult character from the mid-1890s it would be the second part of the documentary companion to *Youth, 1874–1900*, the first volume of the massive official biography started by his son Randolph and finished by Martin Gilbert. It begins in September 1896 with Winston on his way to India at the start of his soldiering career, and ends in January 1901 with him about to take his seat in the Commons. In 1930 he recalled:

> From 1895 down to the present time of writing I have never had time to turn around. I could count almost on my fingers the days when I have nothing to do. An endless moving picture in which one was an actor. On the whole Great Fun! But the years 1895 to 1900 which are the staple of this story exceed in vividness, variety and exertion anything I have known—except of course the opening months of the Great War.[1]

What makes the volume in question stand out from all others is the intensely revealing nature of his correspondence with Jennie, continuing the passionately demanding tone of his schoolboy letters, until there came a moment when *she* needed *him*. At that point he revealed a cold selfishness that not even a doting mother could overlook. His initial reaction to her subsequent silence was that of a child who knows he is at fault but cannot bring himself to admit it. Thereafter maturity creeps in and each goes their own way, he to fame in the Boer War and she to marriage with a man only a few weeks older than Winston, thereby ending her physical relationship with the Prince of Wales, which she may just have prolonged in order to engage his influence on Winston's behalf.[2] As in the matter of bullying and horse-race fixing, I am struck by the fact that Randolph included every document he could find concerning the less savoury aspects of his father's dealings with Jennie, which reflect no credit on Winston whatever. Her tone was in general lovingly indulgent, but after he bounced a cheque in February 1897 she wrote to him in India as a mother rather than as a friend:

I *must* say it is *too* bad of you—indeed it is hardly honourable knowing as you do that you are dependent on me and that I give you the biggest allowance I *possibly can*, more than I can afford . . . As for your wild talk and scheme of coming home for a month, it is absolutely out of the question, not only on account of money, but for the sake of your reputation. They will say and with some reason that you can't stick at anything . . . I confess I am quite disheartened about you. You seem to have no real purpose in life and won't realize that for a man life means work, and hard work if you mean to succeed. Many

53

men at your age have to work for a living and support their mother.3

Winston ignored her and went ahead with his travel plans, although in a letter he indirectly suggested he was indeed hard at work, having read all twelve volumes of Macaulay, ten by Gibbon, as well as Rochefort's *Memoirs* and Plato's *Republic*. He later explained that he was working his way through the *Annual Register* (a record of parliamentary business), writing his opinions first, before reading the debates, in order 'to build up a scaffolding of logical and consistent views which will perhaps tend to the creation of a logical and consistent mind'.4 Instead it seems to have focused his mind on presentation as the essence of leadership, and the outcome was an unpublished essay entitled *The Scaffolding of Rhetoric* which began:

> Of all the talents bestowed upon men, none is more precious than the gift of oratory. He who enjoys it wields a power more durable than that of a great king. He is an independent force in the world. Abandoned by his party, betrayed by his friends, stripped of his offices, whoever can command this power is still formidable.5

While the reference to Lord Randolph is plain—he is also the thinly disguised hero of his son's only novel, *Savrola*, a melodrama written at this time— Winston also wrote of the hypnotic effect of rhythm in terms that defined the manner in which he prepared his speeches, in quasi-verse rather than essay form, for the rest of his life: 'The great

54

influence of sound on the human brain is well known. The sentences of the orator when he appeals to his art become long, rolling and sonorous. The peculiar balance of the phrases produces a cadence which resembles blank verse rather than prose.'6

But Winston's prose was not yet able to relieve the Churchills' money worries. At this time, early 1897, Jennie's finances were in so parlous a state that she needed to take out a large loan to consolidate her debts. The legal documents were sent to Winston, who learned that upon her death he would inherit the interest payments as well as an income of £1000 per annum from the settlement made on Jennie by her father at the time of her marriage to Lord Randolph. At first he treated the matter with what he thought was magnanimity, but which betrays resentment of past rebukes for his own profligacy:

Speaking frankly on the subject—there is no doubt that we are both you and I equally thoughtless—spendthrift and extravagant. We both know what is good—and we both like to have it. Arrangements for paying are left to the future . . . As long as I am dead sure and certain of an ultimate £1000 a year—I do not much care—as I could always make money on the press—and might marry. But at the same time there would be a limit. . . . I sympathize with all your extravagances—even more than you do with mine—it seems just as suicidal to me when you spend £200 on a ball dress as it does to you when I purchase a new polo pony for £100. And yet I feel that you ought to have the dress and I the polo pony. The pinch of the matter is we are damned poor.[7]

In a further exchange of letters, such as this one from the beginning of 1898, he wrote to demand that she make a settlement on him of £500 per annum. A more sensitive man would have perceived his mother's humiliation.

I need not say how painful it is to me to have to write in so formal a strain—or to take such precautions. But I am bound to protect myself in the future—as I do not wish to be left—should I survive you—in poverty. In three years from my father's death you have spent a quarter of our entire fortune in the world. I have also been extravagant: but my extravagances are a very small matter beside yours.[8]

'My father' had left nothing; the assets that remained were those that Leonard Jerome had wisely put beyond the reach of Lord Randolph. Winston's attitude was ungenerous and ungrateful, a reminder that his personal relationships throughout his life often corresponded very strictly with the degree to which someone served his interest. There is another point, remarked upon with reference to Field Marshal Haig by Norman Dixon in his seminal work on military psychology, that an obsessive personality loves to use other people's money but hates parting with his own.[9] Although he was himself the frequent beneficiary of others' hospitality and charity, there are very few examples of disinterested financial generosity in

Winston's life, and he was often offended when members of his personal staff asked for a pay rise. Just as Jennie should have been glad of the privilege of supporting the whims of her son, so his officials and domestic servants were supposed to feel rewarded by being of use to him. And they often were: Sir Edgar Williams, Oxford don and wartime senior intelligence officer wrote feelingly of the 'dutiful and bewitched contribution' made by those close to him.10

In 1898 he even belittled Jennie's string-pulling on his behalf. 'In Politics a man, I take it, gets on not so much by what he *does*, as by what he *is*,' he declared. 'It is not so much a question of brains as of character and originality. It is for these reasons that I would not allow others to suggest ideas and that I am somewhat impatient of advice as to my beginning in politics.' He went on to say that introductions and influence only got a man into the scales of public confidence, where he would be weighed. 'I should never care to bolster up a sham reputation and hold my position by disguising my personality. Of course—as you have known for some time—I believe in myself. If I did not I might perhaps take other views.'11 Such loftiness sat ill on a young man who, when Jennie remarried in 1900, appears to have hoped to obtain some financial benefit. In early 1901 when he had already been elected an MP, and in a letter in which he proudly announced having made £10,000 from writing and lectures in less than two years, he proposed that if she would relieve him of the payment of interest on her loan, 'I will not ask for any allowance whatever from you, until old Papa West decides to give you and G[eorge Cornwallis West, her new, much

57

younger second husband] more to live on.'[12]

It must, however, be remembered that under other circumstances Winston might have had time at university to develop his mind and to take stock of his possible place in the world, and there is something admirable about the manner in which he set about educating himself in the very unpromising surroundings of military life in India in the 1890s. This was the only period in his life devoted to systematic study, and he never again did any serious reading of political theory. The notes he wrote in the *Annual Register* for every year since his birth testify to an application sadly unmatched by originality of thought. In the volume for 1876 he outlined his ideas about education, suggesting that since most people 'were condemned to simple manual labour, too much education would excite desires which cannot be gratified and it will voice the desires in the language of discontent'.[13] The influence of Gibbon and Macaulay can be seen in all his writings, but works he commented on less influenced him just as much. One was Adam Smith's *The Wealth of Nations*, an early affirmation of the benefits of free trade, which informed his politics until the 1930s.

More lastingly, indeed at the very core of what Winston stood for, is the conservatism cogently expressed by Adam Smith's contemporary Edmund Burke. Winston made no reference to Burke and may have absorbed his philosophy indirectly from the works of others, but at times he wrote with a Burkean flavour bordering on direct quotation. For example, when writing to his old headmaster Winston argued against Christian proselytism in India, not for the usual reason that it risked provoking the masses, but because he believed each culture had developed the religion best suited to itself. He would not have supported any of the great religions when they first appeared, he declared, because their immediate result had been protracted bloodshed and misery. 'We regard the turmoil from a different standpoint', he continued. 'Other generations have paid the price—we enjoy the benefit. . . . But I should not have been prepared to pay the price then—nor do I approve of it being exacted—on a smaller scale—now.'[14] Compare this to what may be Burke's most famous dictum: 'I have no great opinion of that sublime abstract, metaphysic reversionary, contingent humanity which in *cold blood* can subject the *present time* and those whom we *daily see* and *converse with* to immediate calamities in favour of the *future and uncertain benefit* of persons who *only exist in idea.*'[15]

Winston was not a believer. 'I expect annihilation at death,' he wrote in March 1898. 'I am a materialist—to the tips of my fingers.'[16] Oxford, he wrote to his brother (echoing Gibbon), 'has long been the home of bigotry and intolerance and has defended more damnable errors and wicked notions than any other institution, with the exception of the [Roman] Catholic Church'.[17] However, he valued the Church as an institution, commenting after reading William Reade's *The Martyrdom of Man* that 'he may succeed in proving Christianity false. He completely fails to show that it is either wise or expedient to say so.'[18] More than that, he was passionately opposed to any system of belief built on the postulate that a 'new man' must be created: thus his hatred of Russian Communism

59

and German National Socialism. It was not that he entertained any high expectation of human nature, simply that he thought it immutable. He was by no means an unqualified libertarian, and again Burke might be said to have spoken for him when he wrote: 'The effect of liberty to individuals is, that they may do what they please: we ought to see what it will please them to do, before we risk congratulations.'[19]

All this mental development was taking place against a backcloth of intense reputation-making, to which the rest of this chapter is devoted. There is, however, one more aspect of his hardening personality that can be related closely to the father of intellectual conservatism. Winston always needed to 'be there', and this too was a hallowed Burkean principle:

> I must see with my own eyes, I must in a manner touch with my own hands, not only the fixed but the momentary circumstances, before I could venture to suggest any political project whatsoever. I must know the power and disposition to accept, to execute, to persevere. I must see the means of correcting the plan, where correctives would be wanted. I must see the things; I must see the men.[20]

Winston made no reference to his early intellectual development in *My Early Life*, which is too often taken as a factual reminiscence when it was written primarily with the purpose of advancing his political career. It presents part of the truth, but by no means the whole of it. The year 1930 was not one in which a defence of the ideas of Adam Smith, less still Edmund Burke, had any chance of evoking a favourable popular response. Instead, the middle-aged Winston sought to remind a fractious and disenchanted British public that he too was once young, and that the fires still burned:

> Twenty to twenty-five! These are the years! Don't be content with things as they are. 'The earth is yours and the fullness thereof'. Enter upon your inheritance, accept your responsibilities. . . . Don't take No for an answer. Never submit to failure. Do not be fobbed off with mere personal success or acceptance. You will make all kinds of mistakes; but as long as you are generous and true, and also fierce, you cannot hurt the world or even seriously distress her.[21]

During five months' leave in 1895, prior to his regiment's posting to India, Winston had obtained permission to go to Cuba as an observer of the counter-insurgency war being fought by the Spanish, and had also contracted with the *Daily Graphic* newspaper to provide occasional reports. He travelled via New York where he was the guest of Bourke Cockran, one of Jennie's oldest and most durable lovers, a prominent figure in the Democratic Party and a celebrated orator. Winston claimed he was much influenced by Cockran's style, although there is no evidence that he ever heard him speak. It is more likely that the older man took a fatherly interest in Winston, and that this helped fill the void left by the death of Lord Randolph. The experience of Cockran and New York was profound. Winston commented on the rude health and vigour of American life by comparison with 'enervated but well-bred' life in Britain. Accompanying a Spanish column in Cuba he came under fire for the first time on his twenty-first birthday, but the most abiding imprint of his trip was a taste for Havana cigars and his discovery of the midday siesta. The excursion also brought him to the public eye for the first time in Britain, with *The Times* sniffing pompously that 'spending a holiday in fighting other people's battles is rather an extraordinary proceeding even for a Churchill'.

Winston's regiment arrived in India in October 1896, and quickly entrained for Bangalore, the main military depot in southern India. He shared a bungalow with two brother officers and worked for only a few hours a day. Winston had enjoyed polo at Sandhurst, and now he played it well and often, reporting with glee that he expected the regiment's subalterns' team to beat the whole Bangalore garrison. He tried his hand at racing, too (significantly, wearing his father's old colours of chocolate and pink cap and sleeves), and although he did not do particularly well he found himself elected to the Turf Club in London, for which he had been proposed by his second cousin Charles, Marquess of Londonderry. As already mentioned, he read voraciously, and long afternoons in his bungalow helped define his stance as what he called a 'Tory Democrat', a phrase he had inherited from his father.

But although he took his military duties seriously—more than half a century later his old troop-sergeant was to remember that he brought rolls of foolscap and lots of coloured pencils to stables, and pestered the NCOs to go through the details of the manoeuvres they had carried out on exercise—the humdrum life of a cavalry officer in an Indian garrison at Britain's imperial apogee did not really suit him. And although he admired Rudyard Kipling (despite telling Jack in early 1897 that he had been spoiled by success) he never shared Kipling's deep understanding of, and affection for, India: Winston could never have written *Plain Tales from the Hills*. Yet Kipling's 'Recessional', written for Queen Victoria's Diamond Jubilee in 1897, struck a chord with him:

> Far-called, our navies melt away;
> On dune and headland sinks the fire:
> Lo, all our pomp of yesterday
> Is one with Nineveh and Tyre!
> Judge of the Nations, spare us yet,
> Lest we forget—lest we forget!

Nor could Winston face the prospect of crawling slowly up the clifflike eminence of the Army List: he was restlessly speculating on what he might do next, with politics already a warm favourite. He enjoyed two long leaves in England, paid three visits to Calcutta (each involving more than a week's travel) and went to Hyderabad with the polo team. Yet none of this would give him the springboard he needed to leave the army, and Jennie worked tirelessly on his behalf to get him posted on a campaign which would give him the chance to begin to inflate 'the bubble reputation' of Shakespeare's soldier. That opportunity came in 1897 when Major General Sir Bindon Blood (whose very name summons up an image of big moustaches and mahogany complexions) was sent to command the Malakand Field Force and suppress a rising on the North-West Frontier. At a social gathering both Jennie and Winston tried to persuade Blood to take the subaltern on to his staff, and thought they had achieved their aim. Yet on 17 August Winston told his mother that 'I have heard nothing more from Sir Bindon Blood. I cannot think he would willingly disappoint me and can only conclude that someone at headquarters has put a spoke in my wheel.' [22]

The Malakand operation came two years after a much more significant campaign, when the young ruler of the small state of Chitral, just north of the Malakand, had been besieged in his palace with a tiny British-Indian garrison until a storybook nick-of-time relief: the siege was likened by some to Gordon's at Khartoum in 1884–5.[23] It was during this earlier campaign that the Malakand Pass was stormed by troops under the command of Major General Sir Robert Low, accompanied by Francis Younghusband, formerly political officer at Chitral, then *The Times* correspondent and later the British envoy in an expedition sent to Nepal in 1904. His 1895 best-seller *The Relief of Chitral* was without a doubt the inspiration for the book Winston published in 1898, for Winston was already determined that he would not simply take part in the campaign but write about it too.

Although Blood told Winston in August that he had already appointed his staff and so 'have not been able to find a billet for you', he agreed that Winston could visit the front as a war correspondent and would be put on the strength of his force as soon as a vacancy appeared. At the end of the month Winston wrote to his brother Jack from the train carrying him northwards, admitting that he had no idea which paper he would actually write for. He was in camp in the Malakand in early September, and assured Jennie, who had arranged for his letters to be published in the *Daily Telegraph*:

I have faith in my star—that is that I am intended to do something in the world. If I am mistaken—what does it matter? My life has been a pleasant one and though I should regret to leave it—it would be a regret that perhaps I should never know. At any rate you will understand that I am bound for many reasons to risk something. Lord Fincastle [a serving officer and correspondent for *The Times*]—will get a Victoria Cross for his courage in a recent action [he rescued a wounded man under fire]—and though of course I do not aspire to that—I am inclined to think that my chance of getting attached [to the staff] would be improved by my behaviour. In any case—I mean to play this game out and if I lose it is obvious that I never could have won any other. The unpleasant contingency is of course a wound which would leave permanent effects and would while leaving me life—deprive me of all that makes life worth living. But all games have forfeits. Fortunately the odds are good.[24]

It soon became very evident that the game was a dangerous one. The tribesmen fought with fanatical courage, and mutilated British and Indian dead and wounded. In an early draft of his book

65

Map 1: THE NORTH-WEST FRONTIER (modern borders)

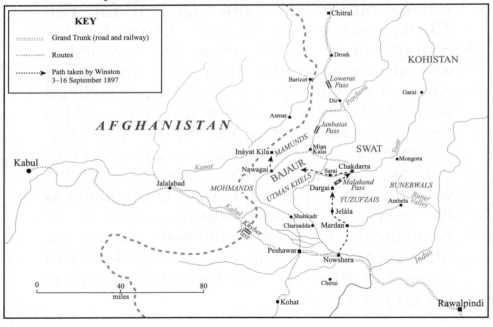

The Malakand Pass lay in tribal territories north of the Grand
Trunk Road, which connected Calcutta with Rawalpindi and
Peshawar. It was on a main route to Chitral, objective of the
1895 campaign. In September 1897 Churchill moved up the
pass from the military base of Nowshera.

(which no more survived publication then than we might expect it to now) Winston used words a million miles away from Kipling:

> These tribesmen are among the most miserable and brutal creatures of the earth. Their intelligence only enables them to be more cruel, more dangerous, more destructible *(sic)* than wild beasts. Their religion—fanatic though they are—is only respected when it incites to bloodshed and murder. Their habits are filthy; their morals cannot be alluded to. With every feeling of respect for the wide sentiment of human sympathy which characterises a Christian civilization, I find it impossible to come to any other conclusion than that, in proportion as these valleys are purged from the pernicious vermin that infest them, so will the happiness of humanity be increased, and the progress of mankind accelerated.[25]

Although Winston had already come under fire in Cuba, there was a world of difference in the level of danger that he encountered in the Malakand. And at least part of the risk was self-imposed.

> A subaltern . . . and I carried a wounded Sepoy [Indian soldier] for some distance and might perhaps, had there been any gallery, have received some notice . . . I felt no excitement and very little fear. All the excitement went out when things became really deadly. . . . I rode on my grey pony all along the skirmish line where everyone else

was lying down in cover. Foolish perhaps but I play for high stakes and given an audience there is no act too daring or too noble. Without the gallery things are different.[26]

Now attached to Blood's staff, he found himself with an Indian unit under very heavy pressure.

The Colonel said to me, 'The Buffs are no more than half a mile away. Go and tell them to hurry or we shall all be wiped out'. I had half turned to go on this errand, when a happy thought struck me. I saw in imagination the company overwhelmed and wiped out, and myself, an Orderly Officer to the Divisional General, arriving the sole survivor, breathless. 'I must have that order in writing, sir', I said. The Colonel looked surprised, fumbled in his tunic, produced his pocket-book and began to write.[27]

Then the Buffs came up anyway. In mortal danger, with the lives of the company in the balance, Winston was still concerned with how *he* might look in the eyes of others. Back in Bangalore after the campaign, which ended with the token surrender of numerous obsolete weapons and the destruction of forts and villages in the Malakand, he heard that he was to be Mentioned in Despatches.[28] He wrote:

To ride a grey pony along a skirmish line is not a common experience. But I had to play for high stakes and have been lucky to win. I did this three times, on the 18th, 23rd and

68

30th [September], but no one officially above me noticed it until the third time when poor Jeffreys—a nice man but a poor general—happened to see the white pony. Hence my good fortune. Bullets—to a philosopher, my dear Mamma—are not worth considering. Besides, I am so conceited I do not think the gods would create so potent a being for so prosaic an ending.[29]

He made his feelings clear in a letter to Jennie in December 1897, telling her: 'I am more ambitious for a reputation for personal courage than for anything else in the world.' And on the same day he told Jack: 'Being in many ways a coward—particularly at school—there is no ambition I cherish so keenly as to gain a reputation of personal courage.'[30] All in all, he felt that being under fire gave him 'quite a foundation for a political life'.[31] Yet he had reservations about the strategic logic of the campaign. He was not persuaded that the British were right to annex territory on the Frontier: 'Financially it is ruinous. Morally it is wicked. Militarily it is an open question, and politically it is a blunder.'[32] And he had seen that savagery was not one-sided: '. . . there is no doubt we are a very cruel people. At Malakand the Sikhs put a wounded man in the cinerator and burnt him alive.'[33]

The tribesmen torture the wounded and mutilate the dead. The troops never spare a single man who falls into their hands—whether he be wounded or not. The field hospitals and the sick convoys are the especial targets of the enemy and we destroy the tanks by which alone [water] for the summer can be obtained—and employ against them a bullet—the new Dum-Dum bullet—of which you may have heard—the shattering effects of which are simply appalling.[34]

Winston brought the campaign to a wider audience in *The Story of the Malakand Field Force*. Rushed into print in order to beat a book by Fincastle, it did so only at the cost of an appalling number of typographical errors: Winston noted 'about 200 misprints, blunders and mistakes'. This unhappy experience was the origin of his future insistence on doing all his rewriting and editing on the publisher's proof sheets—at his own expense. He regarded the publication of the book as 'the most noteworthy act of my life', and was delighted that 8500 copies were printed between March 1898 and January 1899. It did not simply make him money—although no more than the merest trickle compared with the golden torrent unleashed by his later works—but enabled him to play to a gallery that had not been present amongst the louring rocks of the Frontier.

With one campaign safely over, Winston, now even more discontented with the torpor of Bangalore, yearned for another. He told Jennie:

I know myself pretty well and am not blind to the tawdry and dismal side of my character but if there is one situation in which I do not feel ashamed of myself it is in the field. There I shall return at the first opportunity. . . . Now keep your eye on Egypt. It is much safer than the Frontier. At action on the 16th we lost 150 out of 1,000. We call it an *action*. At Firket [in the Sudan] they lost 45 out of 10,000. They call it a battle.[35]

The origins of the Sudan campaign of 1898 lay in a severe reverse incurred after the energetic and charismatic Major General Charles Gordon was sent to Khartoum in 1884 to contend with a great popular rising inspired by Muhammed Ahmad, known as the Mahdi (Expected Guide). The Mahdi's Dervish followers first defeated an Egyptian army under British leadership, and then went on to capture Khartoum and kill Gordon in January 1885. He was at once acclaimed as a Christian warrior-martyr, and the shock nearly brought down the government. A relief expedition had failed to reach Khartoum in time, and it was not until 1898 that an Anglo-Egyptian army under Horatio Herbert Kitchener, a dour and monkish Royal Engineer, was ready to attempt the reconquest of the Sudan.

Winston was desperately anxious to join the expedition, and pressed Jennie to work on 'all the people you know' to get him there. Kitchener, no lady's man, was immune to her charms, and Winston eventually took the extraordinary step of writing to the Prime Minister, Lord Salisbury, frankly admitting that he wanted to go 'first, because the capture of Khartoum will be a historic event; second, because I can, I anticipate, write a book about it which from a monetary, as well as from other points of view, will be useful to me'.[36] Eventually Winston got what he wanted. The War Office agreed to attach him as a supernumerary lieutenant to the 21st Lancers, although it added crisply that if he was killed or wounded no charge of any kind would fall on British army funds. Winston immediately applied for leave from his regiment, and set off for Egypt by such a circuitous route (albeit at the cost of travelling from Marseilles on 'a filthy tramp—manned by these detestable French sailors') that a refusal of leave would be unlikely to reach him before he joined the 21st in Cairo. Once again his luck held. He reported at Abbasiya barracks just too late to join a troop going south: the officer who went with it was killed at Omdurman, as Winston might have been had he commanded it.

Few of Winston's letters from the campaign survive, and he was so busy that he even found it hard to keep up to date with the despatches he had agreed to write for the *Morning Post*. For his account of the campaign we must rely on the two-volume *River War* (1899), its first edition occasionally critical of Kitchener, but its second, single-volume edition of 1902 more circumspect. After the campaign's decisive battle at Omdurman he told the future general Ian Hamilton, whose failure in Gallipoli in 1915 was to have such a marked effect on Winston's own career, that:

My remarks on the treatment of the [Dervish] wounded—again disgraceful—were repeated to him [Kitchener] and generally things have been a little unpleasant. He is a great general but he has yet to be accused of being a great gentleman. It is hard to throw stones at the rising sun and my personal dislike may have warped my judgement, but if I am not blinded

72

he has been on a certainty from start to finish and has had the devil's own luck to help him beside.[37]

The campaign was not only very carefully organized, with the Sudan Military Railway being constructed across the 385 miles of desert between Wadi Halfa and Atbara to enable Kitchener to bring his twenty-five thousand men within striking distance of Khartoum, but the Anglo-Egyptian army enjoyed a comfortable technological advantage with breech-loading infantry rifles and artillery, machine-guns and gunboats. As Hilaire Belloc put it in *The Modern Traveller* (1898):

> Whatever happens, we have got
> The Maxim gun, and they have not

Winston recognized that the battle of Omdurman, fought on 2 September 1898, was unrepeatable, and his description of it, taken here from *My Early Life*, shows how well his prose, well polished by then, could rise to such an occasion.

Nothing like the Battle of Omdurman will ever be seen again. It was the last in the long chain of those spectacular conflicts whose vivid and majestic splendour has done so much to invest war with glamour. Everything was visible to the naked eye. The armies marched and manoeuvred on the crisp surface of the desert plain through which the Nile wandered in broad reaches, now steel, now brass. Cavalry charged at full gallop in close order, and infantry or spearmen stood upright

73

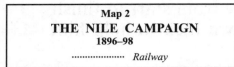

Map 2
THE NILE CAMPAIGN
1896–98

················· Railway

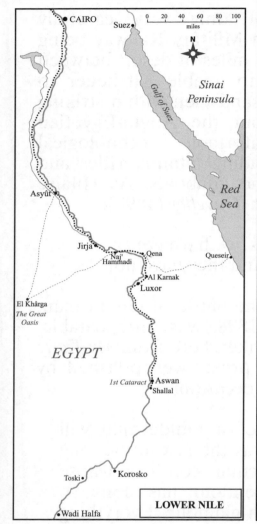

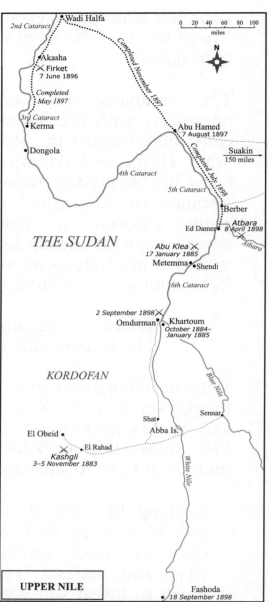

Kitchener avoided the long desert march which had impeded the 1884–5 Gordon relief expedition. The Sudan Military Railway reached Atbara, some 385 miles from Wadi Halfa, enabling him to bring his force within striking distance of Omdurman.

ranged in lines or masses to resist them. From the rocky hills which here and there flanked the great river the whole scene lay revealed in minute detail, curiously twisted, blurred and interspersed with phantom waters by the mirage. The finite and the concrete presented itself in the most keenly-chiselled forms, and then dissolved in a shimmer of unreality and illusion. Long streaks of gleaming water, where we know there was only desert, cut across the knees or the waists of marching troops. Batteries of artillery or long columns of cavalry emerged from a filmy world of uneven crystal on to the hard yellow-ochre sand, and took up their positions amid jagged red-black rocks with violet shadows. Over all the immense dome of the sky, dun to turquoise, turquoise to deepest blue, pierced by the flaming sun, weighed hard and heavy on marching necks and shoulders.[38]

Winston was no idle spectator. On 1 September it was he who delivered a message telling Kitchener that the Dervish army, vastly superior in numbers although grossly inferior in firepower, was coming on swiftly.

In an hour, if they continued their movement, the action must begin. All the results of many years of preparation and three years of war must stand upon the issue of the event. If there had been a miscalculation, if the expedition was not strong enough, or if any accident or misfortune such as are common in battles were to occur, then utter ruin would

75

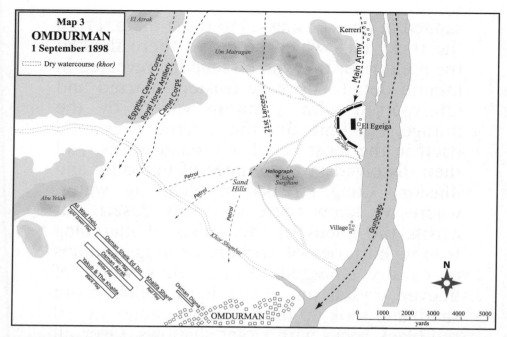

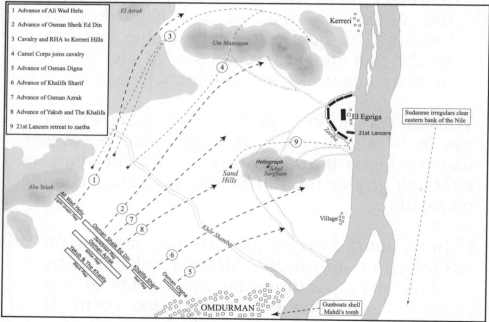

On 1 September 1897 Kitchener's army and
accompanying gunboats moved southwards down the
Nile to El Egeia, north of Omdurman (top). That
afternoon the Dervish army moved forward to threaten
Kitchener from the west (bottom).

descend upon the enterprise. The Sirdar [Kitchener] was very calm. His confidence had been communicated to his Staff. 'We want nothing better,' they said. 'Here is a good field of fire. They may as well come to-day as tomorrow. . . .'**39**

In fact the Khalifa, the Mahdi's successor as Dervish leader, delayed his attack until 2 September. The previous evening Kitchener had deployed five of his six brigades with their backs to the Nile, in a sweeping arc some 2000 yards long, with a *zariba* (thick thorn hedge) in front of the line in case the Dervishes attacked by night, and his gunboats ready to give supporting fire. When the Dervishes advanced at dawn they were shelled by Kitchener's artillery and then lacerated by rifles and machine-guns. It speaks volumes for their courage that they pressed on in the face of appalling casualties, although few of them got within 300 yards of the Anglo-Egyptian position.

At about 8.30 a.m. Colonel Martin, commanding officer of the 21st Lancers, was ordered to press the retreating Dervishes to prevent them from making for Omdurman, to the south. Winston was now back with the regiment, and found himself participating in an old-style cavalry charge.**40** The Lancers trotted in column from right to left across the front of a mass of Dervish infantry, at first believing that they were all spearmen. When many of the Dervishes dropped to their knees and opened fire, hitting some cavalrymen, the British officers at once recognized that they had only two alternatives: to wheel to the left and gallop off, returning later for the wounded ('a bad business', thought Winston), or right wheel into line and charge. Winston reported what happened next in his original despatch of 29 September:

The trumpet sounded 'right-wheel into line', and on the instant the regiment began to gallop in excellent order towards the riflemen. The distance was short, but before it was half covered it was evident that the riflemen were but a trifle compared to what lay behind. In a deep fold in the ground—completely concealed by its peculiar formation—a long, dense, white mass of men became visible. In length they were nearly equal to our front. They were about twelve deep. It was undoubtedly a complete surprise for us. What followed probably astonished them as much. I do not myself believe that they ever expected the cavalry to come on. The Lancers acknowledged the unexpected sight only by an increase in pace. A desire to have the necessary momentum to drive through so solid a line animated each man. But the whole affair was a matter of seconds. At full gallop and in the closest order the squadron struck the Dervish mass. The riflemen, who fired bravely to the last, were brushed head over heels in the khor [dry riverbed]. And with them the Lancers jumped actually on to the spears of the enemy, whose heads were scarcely level with the horses' knees.

It is very rarely that stubborn and unshaken infantry meet equally stubborn and unshaken cavalry. Usually, either the infantry run away and are cut down in flight, or they keep their heads and destroy nearly all the horsemen by their musketry. In this case two living walls crashed together with a mighty collision. The Dervishes stood their ground manfully. They tried to hamstring the horses. They fired their rifles, pressing the muzzles into the very bodies of their opponents. They cut bridle-reins and stirrup-leathers. They would not budge till they were knocked over. They stabbed and hacked with savage pertinacity. In fact, they tried every device of cool, determined men practiced in war and familiar with cavalry. Many horses pecked on landing and stumbled in the press, and the man that fell was pounced on by a dozen merciless foes.[41]

Winston began the charge carrying his sword, but, concerned that a sore shoulder would prevent him using it effectively, sheathed it as he rode forward and instead drew his new Mauser automatic pistol. Fortunately for him the Dervishes were only three deep where he crashed into the gully, and his impact knocked them 'AOT' (arse over tip) as he put it. As he emerged on the far side 'I pulled to a trot and rode up to individuals firing my pistol in their faces and killing several—3 for certain— 2 doubtful—one very doubtful'. The Lancers then dismounted and dispersed the Dervishes with carbine fire, but the episode had cost them one officer and 20 men killed, and four officers and 45 men wounded. It was not quite the battle's last act. When Kitchener ordered a general advance at 9 a.m. gaps appeared between his brigades and the Dervishes tried to exploit them, but were once

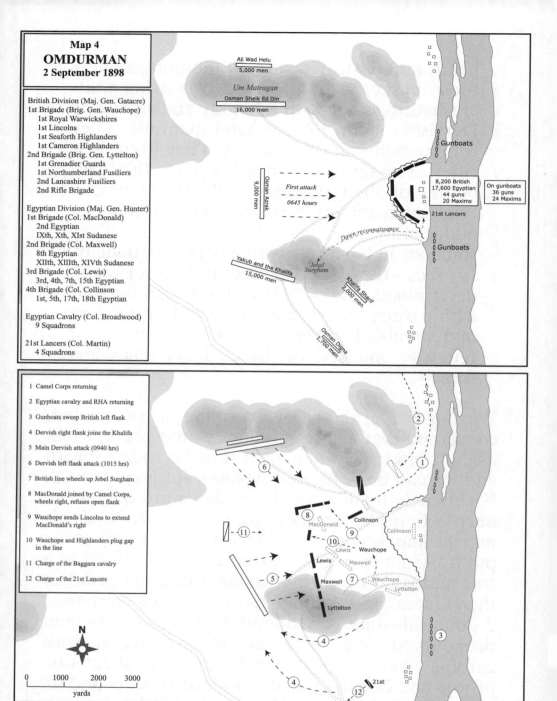

Map 4
OMDURMAN
2 September 1898

British Division (Maj. Gen. Gatacre)
1st Brigade (Brig. Gen. Wauchope)
  1st Royal Warwickshires
  1st Lincolns
  1st Seaforth Highlanders
  1st Cameron Highlanders
2nd Brigade (Brig. Gen. Lyttelton)
  1st Grenadier Guards
  1st Northumberland Fusiliers
  2nd Lancashire Fusiliers
  2nd Rifle Brigade

Egyptian Division (Maj. Gen. Hunter)
1st Brigade (Col. MacDonald)
  2nd Egyptian
  IXth, Xth, XIst Sudanese
2nd Brigade (Col. Maxwell)
  8th Egyptian
  XIIth, XIIIth, XIVth Sudanese
3rd Brigade (Col. Lewis)
  3rd, 4th, 7th, 15th Egyptian
4th Brigade (Col. Collinson
  1st, 5th, 17th, 18th Egyptian

Egyptian Cavalry (Col. Broadwood)
  9 Squadrons

21st Lancers (Col. Martin)
  4 Squadrons

Ali Wad Helu
5,000 men

Um Matragan
Osman Sheik Ed Din
16,000 men

Gunboats

Osman Azrak
9,000 men

First attack
0645 hours

8,200 British
17,600 Egyptian
44 guns
20 Maxims

On gunboats
36 guns
24 Maxims

21st Lancers

Zariba

Dawn reconnaissance

Yakub and the Khalifa
15,000 men

Jebel Surgham

Khalifa Sharif
2,000 men

Gunboats

Osman Digna
1,700 men

1 Camel Corps returning
2 Egyptian cavalry and RHA returning
3 Gunboats sweep British left flank
4 Dervish right flank joins the Khalifa
5 Main Dervish attack (0940 hrs)
6 Dervish left flank attack (1015 hrs)
7 British line wheels up Jebel Surgham
8 MacDonald joined by Camel Corps, wheels right, refuses open flank
9 Wauchope sends Lincolns to extend MacDonald's right
10 Wauchope and Highlanders plug gap in the line
11 Charge of the Baggara cavalry
12 Charge of the 21st Lancers

N

0   1000   2000   3000
yards

Collinson
MacDonald
Collinson
Lewis
Wauchope
Maxwell
Lewis
Maxwell
Wauchope
Lyttelton
Lyttelton

21st

On 2 September the Dervishes bravely attacked
Kitchener's brigades (top). As the fighting developed
(bottom) an attack by the Dervish left was thwarted by
the rapid movement of some of Kitchener's troops.
The Dervishes fell back and were charged by the 21st
Lancers, accompanied by Lieutenant Churchill.

again no match for well-directed firepower. In *My Early Life* Winston greatly expanded his account of the battle, no doubt thinking of his own tribulations in 1915, when so many of his erstwhile supporters deserted him as the Dardanelles campaign turned sour:

> In one respect a cavalry charge is very like ordinary life. So long as you are all right, firmly in your saddle, your horse in hand, and well armed, lots of enemies will give you a wide berth. But as soon as you have lost a stirrup, have a rein cut, have dropped your weapon, are wounded, or your horse is wounded, then is the moment when from all quarters enemies rush upon you.[42]

The campaign was full of portents. Kitchener and Churchill were to be Cabinet colleagues during World War I. And the day before Omdurman Winston, from the banks of the Nile, explained the land war to a young gunboat captain who tossed him a bottle of champagne by way of reward. It splashed into the shallows, and the grateful Winston waded in to retrieve it. The sailor was David Beatty, who was to command the battle-cruisers at Jutland in 1916 and would become one of Winston's naval heroes. Just before World War I, when Winston was First Lord of the Admiralty and Beatty a young admiral, Winston asked him what the Omdurman charge had looked like from his gunboat. 'It looked like plum duff: brown currants scattered about in a great deal of suet,' declared Beatty.[43]

The campaign and battle increased Winston's

own intense ambivalence about war. He first thought that he would have welcomed charging back through the gully *'pour la gloire'*, but was then grateful that further 'heroics' were off for the day. And the sight of dead Dervishes three days later brought the human cost of the whole business home to him.

> There was nothing *dulce et decorum* about the Dervish dead. Nothing of the dignity of unconquerable manhood. All was filthy corruption. Yet these were as brave men as ever walked the earth. The conviction was borne in on me that their claim beyond the grave in respect of a valiant death was as good as that which any of our countrymen could make. The thought may not be original. It was certainly most unwelcome.[44]

Winston was now anxious to return east to take part in the all-India polo tournament, but while he was in England pending his return he took the opportunity to make political speeches in Rotherhithe, Dover and Southsea. They were widely and favourably reported in the press, and not long after the polo tournament—won by Winston's team after a very hard-fought final—he at last decided to leave the army. As his son Randolph was to observe, the decision was 'courageous, even audacious'. He had not yet finished *The River War*, and had no idea that it would become a best-seller or be described by the *Daily Mail* in November 1899 as 'an astonishing triumph'. He was already moderately well known, with excellent political contacts, but had nothing approaching the offer of a parliamentary seat to fight, still less a safe one.

And then, almost miraculously, a seat turned up. The Oldham by-election of 6 July 1899 came about because, of the two sitting Conservative MPs, one had died and the other had resigned on account of ill-health. The local Tories invited Winston to stand to balance their ticket—the other candidate was James Mawdsley, general secretary of the Lancashire branch of the Amalgamated Association of Cotton Spinners. Alas, Oldham's large nonconformist population was outraged by the Conservative government's Clerical Tithes Bill, which awarded the Church of England support from local rates, and despite Winston's efforts to distance himself from the Bill both seats went to the Liberal candidates. What had looked like a glittering prize materializing at just the right minute had turned to ashes as he reached out to grasp it. Thirty years later Winston sourly observed, 'then came the recriminations which always follow every kind of defeat. Everyone threw the blame on me. I have noticed that they nearly always do, I suppose it is because they think I shall be able to bear it best.'[45]

A local newspaper observed that Winston took the blow well: 'He might have been defeated, but he was conscious that in this fight he had not been disgraced.'[46] Yet as one opportunity receded, another appeared. Although Britain had recognized the independence of the two Boer republics in South Africa, the Transvaal and the Orange Free State, the botched annexation of the Transvaal produced the first Boer War of 1880–1, which ended in ignominious British defeat. Over the years that followed, the prosperity of the adjoining British colonies of Natal and Cape Colony, and the large-scale influx of British workers into the Transvaal goldmines, threatened regional stability. These miners—*Uitlanders* to the Boers—did not enjoy the right to vote and complained bitterly about the discrimination they suffered. In 1895 an incursion into the Transvaal, the Jameson Raid, was made with the intention of provoking an *Uitlander* rising and consequent British intervention; however it was swiftly dealt with. The Boers purchased modern weapons in Europe and prepared their commandos, mounted militias led by elected officers, for an invasion they believed imminent. In Britain, too, there was a widespread feeling that war was in the offing, and when in September 1899 the Boers rejected a British compromise proposal for enfranchisement of the *Uitlanders* there seemed little hope of avoiding it. On 18 September Winston was approached by the proprietor of the *Daily Mail*, who asked him to act as his war correspondent. Winston at once told his friend Oliver Borthwick of the *Morning Post*, for whom he had worked before, and was immediately offered a salary of £250 a month (over £8000 in today's money) plus expenses, much the highest remuneration ever given to a war correspondent up to that time, and which did much to improve journalists' pay generally.

Winston accepted like a shot, and immediately set about preparing himself for another campaign. Never the man to rough it, he not only got his telescope and binoculars repaired but laid in five dozen bottles of assorted alcohol, including 18 of ten-year-old whisky and six of 'Very Old Eau de Vie'. He departed from Southampton aboard RMS *Dunottar Castle* on 14 October; the first shots of the war had been fired just two days before. Also aboard was General Sir Redvers Buller, who had won the VC fighting the Zulus in 1879 and was now off to South Africa as commander-in-chief. Winston reported that Buller was 'v amiable' and under the impression that nothing much would happen till he arrived. 'But I rather think', he told his mother, 'events will have taken the bit between their teeth.'[47]

Events had indeed moved swiftly. The Boers had struck before British reinforcements arrived, and were soon besieging Mafeking, Kimberley and Ladysmith. Winston found that Ladysmith had been invested when he tried to reach it by train. The line had been cut near Chieveley and he was reduced to camping, with the rest of the press corps, in the station yard at nearby Estcourt. They lived comfortably enough, and a fellow journalist recalled, with a mixture of irritation and admiration, that Winston persuaded a dinner guest, Colonel Charles Long, the garrison commander, not to withdraw his field guns from the town because it would encourage the Boers. One day Winston fortuitously ran into Captain Aylmer Haldane, a friend from his time on the Frontier, learned that Haldane had been ordered by Long to probe the line towards Ladysmith in an armoured train, and agreed to accompany him on his patrol the following morning, 15 November.

The disadvantages of the armoured train were already clear to many. Winston called it a 'forlorn military machine', which looked 'formidable and

85

impressive' but was in fact 'vulnerable and helpless'. Even Buller, not perhaps the brightest light in British military history, was to call the episode 'an inconceivable stupidity'.**48** The train had an obsolete muzzle-loading naval gun manned by four sailors from HMS *Tartar* on its first truck, then an armoured wagon full of Royal Dublin Fusiliers, then the engine and tender, then two more armoured trucks, one containing Dublin Fusiliers and the other members of the locally recruited Durban Light Infantry, and finally a breakdown gang on the rear truck. It clattered happily to Frere station and went on towards Chieveley where, as Haldane was warned by telephone, the Boers had occupied the station the night before: indeed, some were seen both ahead of the train and to the south of the track. Haldane accordingly ordered the train to reverse to Frere, but as it rounded the spur of a hill overlooking the line the Boers opened fire on it with artillery. The driver at once accelerated and the train ran down the gradient at high speed, only to crash into a boulder which the Boers had put on the line after the train had passed earlier. The impact derailed the breakdown truck and two armoured trucks which were now being pushed by the engine. The line was blocked, and the engine and wagons came under fire from Boer field guns and an automatic cannon known, from its distinctive sound, as a pom-pom.

Winston had been standing beside Haldane in the armoured wagon between the engine and the gun truck, and at once offered to help: they agreed that Haldane would try to keep down the Boer fire while Winston organized the clearing of the line.

The sailors pluckily brought their gun into action, but it was knocked over by a direct hit after firing only four rounds. Winston worked frantically under heavy and accurate fire. When the engine driver was wounded in the head, Winston assured him that he would be decorated for gallantry if he remained at his post and the man stuck it out courageously. Eventually the train butted its way past the derailed trucks, but the couplings connecting it to Haldane's wagon were broken or had been cut by a shell. The engine was crammed with wounded, and Haldane decided to send it off to safety. His men were now widely dispersed along the track and, to his consternation, he saw two of them wave white handkerchieves. As the men hesitated the Boers rushed in 'with equal daring and humanity', as Winston was to put it, and called upon them to surrender: Haldane and about 50 men were taken prisoner.

Winston was in the railway cutting a short distance from the train when the Boers surged in. Two of them, 'clad in dark flapping clothes, with slouch, storm-driven hats', were on the track and shot at him as he ran down the line. As he scrambled up the side of the cutting to escape he was confronted by a mounted Boer who galloped up, waving his hand and shouting. Winston reached for the Mauser pistol he had carried at Omdurman—as a correspondent he should not have been armed—but recalled with horror that he had left it in the engine cab so as to be able to work unencumbered. Consoling himself with the thought that the great Napoleon had said there was nothing dishonourable in surrender when one was alone and unarmed, Winston put his hands up. He was a prisoner of war.

The episode was dramatic enough in itself, but Winston did not leave it there. He later suggested that it was the Boer leader Louis Botha himself who had captured him, although it was in fact Field Cornet Sarel Oosthuisen. None the less, a lesser man might have been forgiven for shooting the breathless individual in quasi-uniform, who had so evidently inspired the defence, when he reached for what turned out to be a non-existent weapon.[49]

There was no doubt that Winston had behaved heroically. Captain Haldane, writing from their prison, the State Model School in Pretoria, on 30 November 1899, commended:

Mr Winston S. Churchill, whose valuable services have already been detailed in the text of this report, and whom, owing to the urgency of the circumstances, I formally placed on duty. I would point out that while engaged on the work of saving the engine, for which he was mainly responsible, he was frequently exposed to the full fire of the enemy. I cannot speak too highly of his gallant conduct.[50]

There was much talk of a VC, but Winston's case was fatally compromised by the fact that, in an effort to gain immediate release, he affirmed that he was a civilian and had always behaved as such. This allegation Haldane generously supported, certifying that Winston was 'unarmed and took no part in the defence of the train'.[51] The Boer authorities were not taken in, recognizing that Winston was not only a dangerous man but a potentially useful bargaining card: he would stay in prison. Winston had other ideas, and hatched an escape plan with Haldane and Brockie, a sergeant-major in the Natal Carabineers who had claimed to be an officer in order to pass a more comfortable imprisonment. They planned to climb the back wall of the prison yard when the sentries' backs were turned, and on the night of 12 December Winston managed to scramble over. No sooner had he done so than a sentry changed his position, making it impossible for the others to follow. Winston waited on the far side till it was clear that they could not join him, and then made off. Unsurprisingly, this incident became just as controversial as that of the armoured train. There were suggestions that he had abandoned his comrades, and in 1912 he successfully sued *Blackwood's Magazine* which had repeatedly attacked him on the score. It is impossible to prove the case beyond reasonable doubt. However, while I do not believe that Winston deliberately abandoned Haldane and Brockie, I cannot imagine him waiting too long on the far side of that wall.

His journey to safety was the stuff of novels. He jumped a train which took him to Witbank, some 75 miles east of Pretoria but still 200 miles short of the frontier with Portuguese East Africa. Winston knocked on the door of the local mine manager's house, discovered that he had fortuitously picked the one British household for miles around, and spent some time being sheltered in the mine before he could be smuggled on to a train which took him safely over the border to Lourenço Marques. There the British consul provided him with: 'A hot bath, clean clothes, an excellent dinner, means of

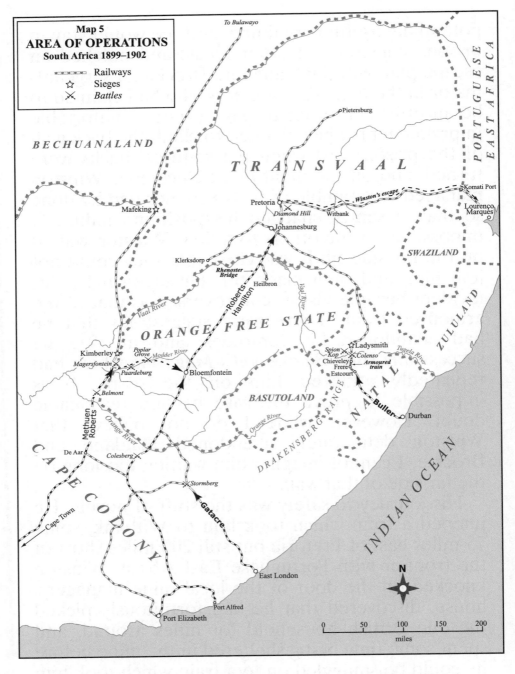

The opening of the Boer War saw the Boers besiege
Mafeking, Kimberley and Ladysmith. Churchill was
captured near Frere and imprisoned in Pretoria,
whence he escaped via Witbank. He then participated
in Buller's relief of Ladysmith, and was later at
Diamond Hill and the capture of Pretoria.

telegraphing, all I could want. . . .' From reading a weighty file of newspapers he discovered that the war was going badly for the British, with a 'Black Week' in December when Gatacre had been beaten at Stormberg, Methuen at Magersfontein and Buller at Colenso, 'staggering defeats, and casualties on a scale unknown to England since the Crimean War'.[52] The news made Winston eager to get back to the army; and his hosts, in a town full of Boer sympathizers, were no less anxious to see him safely away. He was quickly put aboard the *Induna* which took him to Durban, where he found that he had become famous overnight and was deluged with telegrams. Although one opined that: 'Best friends here hope you won't go making further ass of yourself', most were highly complimentary. One gentleman invited him to go shooting in central Asia, another included a poem written in his honour, and the Liberal electors of Oldham averred that, 'irrespective of politics', they would vote for him in future.

For the immediate future, though, Winston accepted a lieutenancy in the South African Light Horse, cheerfully sewed the pips to his epaulettes and stuck the regiment's jaunty plume in his slouch hat. It had been agreed that he could continue to act as a correspondent while acting in the ill-defined post of his regiment's assistant adjutant, and his despatches for the *Morning Post* provided an expectant public with vivid snapshots of the war. Some of these came from the heart. On 18 January 1900 Winston was with the South African Light Horse, at a farm called Acton Homes to the northwest of Spion Kop, when the cavalry cut off some retreating Boers. They fought on until their

91

commander, the 60-year-old Field Cornet de Mentz of the Heilbron Commando, had bled to death, loading and firing to the last. Winston found him lying dead:

> The stony face was grimly calm, but it bore the stamp of unutterable resolve; the look of a man who had thought it all out, and was quite certain his cause was just, and such a sober citizen might give his life for. . . . Further on lay our own two poor riflemen with their heads smashed like eggshells; and I suppose they had mothers or wives far away at the end of the deepsea cables. Ah, horrible war, amazing medley of the glorious and the squalid, the pitiful and the sublime, if modern men of light and leading saw your face closer simple folk would see it hardly ever.[53]

Later, when Winston reached Heilbron, he found that de Mentz's widow lived next door to his hotel, 'nursing her son who had been shot through the lungs in the same action. Let us hope he will recover, for he had a gallant sire.'[54]

With his knack for being in the path of the storm Winston was present at the battle of Spion Kop in late January 1901 when Buller, now replaced as commander-in-chief by Field Marshal Lord Roberts, but still in charge on the Natal front, botched another attempt to relieve Ladysmith. Winston was more forgiving of Buller than any modern historian would be. Spion Kop, its summit taken so easily but then held at shocking cost and to no purpose, is one of the most evocative battlefields in the world, with curved rows of white

92

stones marking the trench lines which now serve as mass graves for the men who held them. Winston rode up to the foot of the mountain, tethered his horse and climbed up to Brigadier General Talbot Coke on the spur below the crest, passing:

> Men [who] were staggering along alone or supported by comrades, or crawling on hands and knees, or carried on stretchers. Corpses lay here and there . . . I passed about two hundred while I was climbing up. There was, moreover, a small but steady leakage of unwounded men of all corps. Some of these cursed and swore. Others were utterly exhausted and fell on the hillside in a stupor. Others again seemed drunk, though they had had no liquor. Scores were sleeping heavily. Fighting was still proceeding, and stray bullets struck all over the ground, while the Maxim shells [from the infamous pom-poms] scourged the flanks of the hill and the sheltering infantry at regular intervals of a minute.[55]

A bullet snipped the feather from his hat. He went back down and then up to Three Tree Hill and reported what he had seen to Lieutenant General Sir Charles Warren, after which he was sent, by now at night, back up the hill to consult with Lieutenant Colonel Thorneycroft, commanding the troops there after the death of Major General Sir Edward Woodgate. Winston thought the position could have been held, but Thorneycroft was certain it could not. 'Better six good battalions safely down the hill than a mop-up in the morning,' he said. By the time Winston reached him with news that reinforcements were on their way, he had already begun to pull back. The episode, one of history's most striking examples of brave men being badly led, reflected very badly on Buller, and Winston himself noted that Buller only 'gripped the whole business in his strong hands' when organizing the withdrawal from the north bank of the Tugela.[56]

In mid-February, at Hussar Hill to the southeast of Colenso, Winston was walking along the prone and busily engaged skirmish line when he saw his brother Jack, for whom he had arranged a commission in the South African Light Horse, 'start in the quick, peculiar manner of the stricken man'. He had been hit in the leg in his first action. Winston emphasized this episode in *My Early Life*, for it was implicitly yet another proof that he was a man of destiny: Jack had been hit while lying down, while he was on his feet but unhurt. Jennie had meanwhile come south in the hospital ship *Maine*, paid for by £41,500 she had raised from American sympathizers, and Jack was her first patient. Winston was glad to see him 'honourably out of harm's way' for the moment.

Winston described one infantry attack in the face of heavy rifle fire that might almost come from World War I.

> Officers and men fell by scores on the narrowing ridge. Though assailed in front and flank by the hideous whispering Death, the survivors hurried obstinately onward, until their own artillery were forced to cease from firing, and it seemed that, in spite of bullets, flesh and blood would prevail. But at the last

supreme moment the weakness of the attack was shown. The Inniskillings had almost reached their goal. They were too few to effect their purpose; and when the Boers saw that the attack had withered they shot all the straighter, and several of the boldest leapt from their trenches and, running forward to meet the soldiers, discharged their magazines at the closest range. It was a scene of frantic blood and fury.[57]

He later observed the effect of indirect fire when a single gun dropped several shells among troops behind a hill. If it had been a battery, he mused,

the crowded infantry waiting in support would certainly have been driven out of the re-entrant with a frightful slaughter. Yet in European war there would not have been one but three or four batteries. I do not see how troops can be handled in masses under such conditions, even when in support and on reverse slopes. Future warfare must depend on the individual.[58]

After he joined Roberts' main force, Winston found himself facing death or capture yet again. He was with a party of Scouts commanded by Angus McNeill, an old Harrovian friend who had illustrated *The River War*, when some Boers beat them to a hilltop and opened fire. Winston's saddle turned as he tried to mount, and then his horse bolted. 'Suddenly, as I ran, I saw a Scout,' he wrote. 'He came from the left across my front; a tall man, with a skull and crossbones, on a pale horse. Death in Revelations, but life to me.' This was Trooper Clement Roberts of Montmorency's Scouts, and Winston vaulted up behind and so escaped certain death or wounding. The horse was hit as they galloped to safety. 'Never mind', said Winston, 'you've saved my life.' 'Ah', rejoined Trooper Roberts, 'but it's the horse I'm thinking about.'59

Winston closed his narrative circle by liberating his old prison camp in Pretoria, along with his cousin 'Sunny', then Captain the Duke of Marlborough of the Imperial Yeomanry.

> I raised my hat and cheered. The cry was instantly answered from within. What followed resembled the end of an Adelphi melodrama. The Duke of Marlborough called on the commandant to surrender forthwith. The prisoners rushed into the yard, some in uniform, some in flannels, hatless or coatless, but all violently excited.60

He had one last adventure with Ian Hamilton's column at Diamond Hill, east of Pretoria, where the Boer leader Botha with about seven thousand men was covering the railroad to Portuguese East Africa along which Kruger and his government escaped. Ian Hamilton recalled that Winston spotted a covered approach to the top of the plateau.

> He climbed this mountain as our scouts were trained to climb on the Indian frontier and ensconced himself in a niche not much more than a pistol shot below the Boer commandos—no mean feat of arms in broad

daylight and one showing a fine trust in the accuracy of our own guns. Had even half a dozen of the Burghers run twenty yards over the brow they could have knocked him off his perch with a volley of stones. Winston had the nerve to signal me with his handkerchief on a stick that this was the way up.

Hamilton described this act as 'conspicuous gallantry' and did indeed propose Winston for the VC, but Roberts and Kitchener, his chief of staff, would have nothing of it: Churchill had resigned his South African Light Horse commission and was only a press correspondent.[61]

As he was leaving South Africa, Winston had a last brush with the Boers. His train was halted at the Rhenoster River some 50 miles south of Pretoria, where Christian de Wet's commando had burned the bridge—and a huge accumulation of mail for the British army. Winston meditated on the eternal British propensity for being taken by surprise:

When we go to war our conceit costs us much in blood and honour. We are always absolutely sure that the enemy will not dare to attack us, and so certain that he will fly at our approach. I have scarcely seen an action in this war which officers of a certain class have not begun with an incredulous sniff . . . then suddenly—Bang!—and another glorious page is added to British military history.[62]

But by this time his prose was leavened by the sharp-eyed, sly humour that still makes some of his lighter writings a delight to read. His style had richly matured, as evidenced by his observations on a work gang of Basutos carrying a huge log to rebuild the bridge:

> The men moving it slowly forward on their shoulders as if they were the legs of a colossal black caterpillar; and as they moved a dusky fugleman at the rear sang solemnly:
> > Awa chowàchy: ehooka ehowee
> or words to that effect; to which the others chorused with the most extraordinary earnestness and conviction,
> > Azziz
> > Awa chowàchy: ehooka ehowee
> > Azziz
> and so on remorselessly, until at last they reached the edge of the chasm which their log was to span.[63]

The good luck which had looked after Winston so well in South Africa travelled back with him to England. When on the run following his escape in Pretoria he had been helped by the mining engineer Daniel Dewsnap, a native of Oldham. When Winston returned to Oldham in July 1900 he was greeted as a national hero, and addressed a capacity crowd in the Theatre Royal. When he mentioned the role of Dewsnap, 'this son of Oldham', the audience yelled, 'His wife's in the gallery.' The warm reception persuaded him to stand for Oldham again in the general election of October 1900, known as the 'Khaki Election'. It was a close call: the Liberals retained their overall majority, but enough Liberal voters had given

Churchill their second vote to get him elected as the second of the two MPs the town returned. It was a vote for him, not for the Conservative Party, and the peculiar circumstances with which he began his long career in the House of Commons certainly must have nurtured the highly independent spirit he took with him, as will be seen in Chapter Three.

CHAPTER THREE

THE TATTERED FLAG

1901–1911

The first ten years of Winston's life in politics bear comparison with the first decade of his existence. Just as babies are born with predispositions, so he was far from being a blank slate when he entered Parliament; but he did so with a more open mind than most. Both were periods of intense discovery during which he established behaviour patterns that were to persist throughout his career, and in which he tested an outstandingly independent personality. This was a period in which his orthodox Victorian belief in minimal government became modified by the seduction of exercising power in order to make the country stronger, and, it must be said, himself more prominent. In addition, the first decade of the twentieth century marked a fateful watershed during which the historic policy of keeping the affairs of the European mainland at arm's length was reversed, with profound and long-lasting results.

The English Channel had long permitted Britain, alone among the nations of Europe, to take as much or as little of international war as it chose. Along with relative immunity from foreign invasion came a greatly reduced need for strong central government and its attendant taxation, and the emergence of institutions designed to protect personal liberty by limiting the power of the executive. Winston's political trajectory peaked with him presiding over an administration that exercised almost total control over the life of the nation; but his first major speech, overtly an attack on a proposed doubling of the number of army corps from three to six, was in essence a highly traditionalist declaration in favour of strictly limited government. How he, and the country, went from one extreme to the other in less than 40 years is the story of how British society, still decidedly parochial at the turn of the century despite its world-wide influence and commitments, was transformed by international complications from which the Channel could no longer insulate it. Those clouds, however, were scarcely discernible on the horizon when Winston took his seat in Parliament in the month after Queen Victoria died, when the reassuring old certainties were still generally unquestioned.

He first addressed the Commons on 18 February 1901 to urge that magnanimity be shown to the defeated Boers, and thereafter looked for an opportunity to make a set-piece statement of principle. After trailing his ideas in an address to the Liverpool Conservative Association, he decided that the army proposals of William Brodrick, the Secretary of State for War and an old opponent of Lord Randolph, offered the appropriate target. When he rose to speak on 13 May he had already given the text of his hour-long speech to the *Morning Post*, a practice for which his father had been much criticized, and he began by quoting from Lord Randolph's 1886 resignation letter: 'I decline to be a party to encouraging the military and militant circle of the War Office and Admiralty

101

to join in the high and desperate stakes which other nations seem to be forced to risk.' These were 'wise words', affirmed Winston, 'and I am very glad the House has allowed me, after an interval of fifteen years, to lift again the tattered flag of retrenchment and economy'. There followed an acute prediction, poignantly ironic from one who was to be a member of the government that took the nation to war in 1914:

A European war cannot be anything but a cruel, heart-rending struggle, which, if we are ever to enjoy the bitter fruits of victory, must demand, perhaps for several years, the whole manhood of the nation, the entire suspension of peaceful industries, and the concentration to one end of every vital energy of the community [and] can only end in the ruin of the vanquished and the scarcely less fatal commercial dislocation and exhaustion of the conquerors. Democracy is more vindictive than Cabinets. The wars of peoples will be more terrible than the wars of kings. . . . The Secretary of State for War knows—none better than he—that [his proposed legislation] will not make us secure, and that if we went to war with any great Power his three Army Corps would scarcely serve as a vanguard. If we are hated, they will not make us loved. If we are in danger, they will not make us safe. They are enough to irritate; they are not enough to overawe. Yet, while they cannot make us invulnerable, they may very likely make us venturesome.

Given that his seat on the Conservative benches was barely warm, it was bold to attack the military spending proposals of a government led by Lord Salisbury, drawing attention to the fact that Lord Randolph's career had foundered over precisely the same issue. There was, however, less to it than met the eye, because Winston's main argument was that spending should be concentrated on the Royal Navy, as the guarantor both of territorial integrity and of the freedom of the seas upon which Britain's wealth and power as the world's premier trading nation depended. This put his intervention well within the boundaries of permissible dissent, and fully in tune with a national mood in favour of 'Splendid Isolation', in turn wedded to an overarching belief in Free Trade.[1] Merchant ships registered in Britain, which had long ago ceased to be self-sufficient in food, carried two-thirds of all international trade, much of it trans-shipped in British ports. Starting with the repeal of the tariff on imported grain in 1846, Britain had pursued a trade policy more faithful to David Ricardo's theory of comparative advantage than any country before or since.[2] But the speech was also designed to appeal to Salisbury, who was known to believe that 'the perils of change are so great, the promise of even the most hopeful theories is so often deceptive, that it is frequently the wiser part to uphold the existing state of things, if it can be done, even though in point of argument it should be utterly indefensible'.[3] It was Brodrick, not Winston, who was proposing change, and after Salisbury withdrew his support for the proposals the Secretary of War resigned and moved to the India Office. Winston had made his mark.

His position was also impeccably conservative when, in 1903, Joseph Chamberlain resigned as Colonial Secretary in order to launch his campaign for tariffs on goods produced outside the Empire ('Imperial Preference'). On 28 May, immediately following Chamberlain's speech to the Commons on the subject and in the absence of Herbert Asquith, who should have been present to reply for the Liberals, Winston rose to state that, if Chamberlain's proposals prospered, 'the old Conservative Party, with its religious convictions and constitutional principles, will disappear, and a new party will arise, rich, materialistic and secular, whose opinions will turn on tariffs and who will cause the lobbies to be crowded with the touts of protected industries'. Winston had received a thorough indoctrination in Ricardian orthodoxy from Sir Francis Mowatt, Permanent Secretary to the Treasury between 1894 and 1903, and he spoke with the enthusiasm of the newly enlightened.

Winston's early years in Parliament must inevitably be seen as a preamble to his defection to the Liberal Party on 31 May 1904. He was unquestionably hungry for office and the move was certainly well timed, for the long period of Tory ascendancy was coming to an end. Although he argued, with justice, that the Conservative Party under Salisbury's nephew and successor Arthur Balfour moved away from him, not vice versa, he had also made himself an intolerable nuisance. It is most unlikely that Balfour, even had he wished to, could have prevented his defection by offering him a government post, because Winston had staked out a position of principle from which he could not retreat. The day before he crossed the floor of the

House he wrote to Lord Hugh Cecil, a fellow dissident but, as Lord Salisbury's son and Balfour's cousin, precluded by family loyalty from following his friend:

What a wrench it is to me to break with all that glittering hierarchy and how carefully one must organize one's system of thought to be utterly independent of it. The worst of it is that as the Free Trade issue subsides, it leaves my personal ambitions naked and stranded on the beach—and they are ugly and unsatisfactory by themselves, though nothing but an advantage when borne forward with the flood of a great outside cause.[4]

The Free Trade issue did not subside, however, and it led to Balfour's resignation at the end of 1905, followed by a landslide victory for the Liberals under Sir Henry Campbell-Bannerman in the general election of January–February 1906.[5] Winston threw himself into the election with vigour and was rewarded with the post of Under Secretary of State for the Colonies in the new administration. A fair assessment of this period in Winston's life must overcome the lingering legacy of the sneering tone that coloured the first wave of revisionist biographies, written soon after his death. While in general they were a healthy reaction against his epic efforts to rewrite history in his own favour, they also betrayed the distaste felt by those grown to maturity in a time of limited possibilities, and dimly flickering hope, for an earlier age when horizons seemed unbounded. The following passage is representative:

youth and ambition are regarded with suspicion in England. Activity and energy are hardly less suspect. Young men who tackle problems with ardour, unafraid of committing errors and prepared to accept these as the necessary price for great advances, tend to be regarded with much concern . . . It is always safest in England, particularly for young men, to do nothing save by . . . stealth and guile; the safest course of all is to do nothing whatever, and thereby acquire a reputation for shrewdness and soundness.[6]

This tells us more about the experience of the author, Senior Clerk in the House of Commons till 1964 and Conservative MP for Cambridge from 1976 to 1992, than it does about the milieu in which Winston served his apprenticeship. By the time Winston died distrust of those 'too clever by half' was a fact of British political life, but it was not always so. Today an ambitious young person can achieve fame far more easily in other fields, but a century ago those seeking public prominence had few other outlets for their talents. Although politics is now a relatively well-paid occupation to which many MPs bring little outside experience, when Winston entered it only office-holders received salaries.[7] Therefore those who sought election were either financially secure in their own right or were possessed of talents that individual or collective patrons believed worth subsidizing. As a result, party discipline was attenuated and debate in Parliament was not only more substantive but also considerably more entertaining. For a 'young man in a hurry', the phrase applied in turn to Lord Randolph and his son, it was vital to convince his party leader that it was better to have him inside the tent of patronage and power than clawing at it from without.

John Lukacs writes of the British as 'an unrhetorical and unintellectual people', but this is another allegedly national characteristic of more recent vintage.[8] When Winston entered politics rhetoric was prized as the art of using language to persuade or influence others, and leading politicians considered it part of their duty to educate the electorate. His first major published collection of speeches consisted of those made to working-class voters in the manufacturing towns of Manchester, Preston, Southport, Liverpool, Bolton, Burnley, Oldham and Crewe in 1909, and they contain no indication that he over-simplified issues or otherwise talked down to his audience.[9] Nor, partisan vituperation always excepted, did he resort to the demagoguery of which his opponents accused him.[10] On the contrary, he argued the case for Free Trade and social reform alike in a tone that most people today would find intolerably lofty.

But it was in Parliament that intellect allied with eloquence was most influential, for it was still considered, in practice as well as in theory, to be the highest court in the land. Winston never wavered in his confidence that the process of Common Law, that weighty accretion of precedents deriving from issues contested in open court, was evidently superior to abstract reasoning as a means of arriving at workable solutions. He shared Lord Salisbury's High Victorian belief about 'the proved futility of theorists to whatever school they might belong; the worthlessness of forecasts based on logical calculation; the evil which has repeatedly been wrought by the best intended policies; the hopeless incongruity between aim and result which dominates history'.[11] Winston's eyes were opened to the impersonal nature of the adversarial system when, as a teenager in the gallery of the Commons, he witnessed what he thought was a furious personal exchange between his father and another MP, 'and I was astonished when only a few minutes later, [the other MP] made his way up to where I sat and with a beaming smile introduced himself to me, and asked me what I thought of it all'.[12]

One of his few real friends in maturity was Frederick (F.E.) Smith, later Lord Birkenhead, a brilliant King's Counsel of relatively modest origins whom Winston described, in words that could as easily have been written of himself, as 'a robust, pugnacious personality, trampling his way across the battlefields of life, seizing its prizes as they fell, and exulting in his prowess'.[13] In 1911 the two men founded the Other Club, a dining society whose members—MPs and peers of all parties and leading figures from other walks of life—would meet every fortnight, while Parliament was in session, in the Pinafore Room at the Savoy Hotel. Although the rules famously declared that it was not intended to 'interfere with the rancour and asperity of Party politics', it was formed at a time when political temperatures were running dangerously high and was obviously designed to reinforce collegiality among the warring advocates.[14]

Winston's faith in the adversarial system, as

characteristic of politics as it was of law, led him to argue whatever cause he adopted to the full extent of his ability and, if the verdict went against him, to move on to other matters. As he grew in age and authority he moved on less and less willingly, but he would still give way to a sound argument, if stoutly maintained, and generally did so with good grace. When in the minority he followed his father's dictum that 'the duty of the opposition is to oppose'; when in power he expected his opponents to come at him just as hard, and harboured no animosity towards them for doing so. He was never able to understand why some of the victims of his well-honed barbs took it all so personally: he had a hide like a rhinoceros, and no sympathy for the thin-skinned. The result was a pragmatic approach to policy formulation singularly free of doctrinaire ideological commitments beyond a general commitment to liberty. His official biographer concluded that Winston's political philosophy:

> was based on the preservation and protection of individual freedom and a decent way of life, if necessary by means of State aid and power; on the protection of the individual against the misuse of State power; on the pursuit of political compromise and the middle way, in order both to maintain and to improve the existing framework of Parliamentary democracy; on the protection of small States against the aggression of more powerful States; and on the linking together of all democratic States to protect themselves from the curse and calamity of war.[15]

Unfortunately, these views outline a framework of society and the role of government to which all save libertarian fundamentalists or utopian socialists might subscribe. The devil, as usual, is in the detail: the planks, as it were, that must be nailed to the ribs of the vessel. There is rarely likely to be consensus on what constitutes a 'decent way of life' or 'misuse of State power', still less on how they may be assured on the one hand and prevented on the other.

Some might see Free Trade as a dogma to which Winston subscribed, but that is to misunderstand its attraction to one of a conservative temperament, which is that it put the temptation to manipulate trade for corrupt or partisan purposes out of political reach. Although the words were actually written by Lord Acton in 1887, it had long been a principle of British political thought that 'power tends to corrupt and absolute power corrupts absolutely'. First the example and then the threat posed by the German Reich caused Winston, along with the rest of the political elite, to abandon the commitment to limited government that had defined British history. The German Chancellor Otto von Bismarck, the apostle of 'blood and iron', was also the architect of a welfare state not matched in Britain before the late 1940s. Like Bismarck's short, sharp wars, his welfare provisions were a means to the end of unifying Germany under a strong central government. A desire to balance the growing power of the continental giant explains the apparent contradiction between the 'tattered flag of retrenchment and economy' Winston raised in 1901, and the social reforms he advocated in 1908–11.

Rational analysis was never enough to convince Winston, however. In late 1906 he proclaimed that 'man is at once a unique being and a gregarious animal. For some purposes he must be a collectivist, for others he will for all time remain an individualist.' This is not, on the face of it, a surprising sentiment from one who had served in the army. But he went on to declare that 'the whole tendency of civilization is, however, towards the multiplication of the collective functions of society', and to call for the state to 'embark on various novel and adventurous experiments' in order to establish 'minimum standards of life and labour'.[16] This was a remarkable turnabout by one who had defected from the party into which he was born in opposition to state interference with the free market. There is no evidence that he underwent an intellectual conversion; indeed, someone who tried to convert him commented on his 'capacity for quick appreciation and rapid execution of new ideas, whilst hardly comprehending the philosophy beneath them'.[17] Instead, he was probably emotionally engaged not so much by the plight of the poor as by the prospect of a noble and rewarding role for himself, triggering a messianic zeal that was never far from the surface. 'Why have I always been kept safe within a hair's breadth of death except to do something like this?' he asked a fellow Liberal MP.[18]

Winston's first taste of office as the Liberal spokesman for colonial affairs in the House of Commons (his titular chief being in the Lords) was marked by the 'hands on' vigour that characterized his performance of public duties, and gave him the material for another book designed to raise his

111

public profile while improving his bank balance.[19] Joe Chamberlain's policy of aggressive imperialism was reversed and a generous political settlement reconciled the defeated Boers to a South African Union, at the expense of the native population and the Indian immigrant community. The settlement laid up trouble for the future both in South Africa and in India, but it succeeded in its immediate aim, which was to take the heat out of the imperial issue in order to permit the government to concentrate on domestic reforms. This was entirely in keeping with Winston's view that the purpose of Empire was to strengthen Britain's international standing, something he believed to be self-evidently in the interest of associated or subject peoples.[20] He was lucky to have, in Lord Elgin, an indulgent boss who appreciated that colts must stretch their legs. But in terms of his political development the period he spent at the Colonial Office was a preamble to his first Cabinet post, in which for the only time in his career he was consciously devoted to an overhaul of the institutional structure of Britain.

In 1908, when Herbert Henry Asquith succeeded the dying Campbell-Bannerman as Liberal Prime Minister, he made David Lloyd George, the populist Welsh MP, his Chancellor of the Exchequer and promoted Winston to the Cabinet to replace Lloyd George as President of the Board of Trade. The two men now formed a most unlikely alliance. In late 1901, writing to the Birmingham Conservatives to chide them for a bloody riot that had prevented Lloyd George from speaking at the Town Hall, Winston wrote: 'Personally, I think Lloyd George a vulgar, chattering little cad . . . '.[21] It is unlikely that his assessment ever really changed, although after Lloyd George's death 44 years later Winston composed a moving eulogy which reads in part:

> Most people are unconscious of how much their lives have been shaped by the laws for which Lloyd George was responsible. Health Insurance and Old Age Pensions were the first large-scale State-conscious efforts to set a balustrade along the crowded causeway of the people's life, and without pulling down the structures of society to fasten a lid over the abyss into which vast numbers used to fall, generation after generation, uncared-for and indeed unnoticed.[22]

The new measures required a substantial increase in revenue, at a time when extra money also had to be found to provide for the massive re-equipment of the Royal Navy. This had become necessary after the launching of the fast, big-gunned HMS *Dreadnought* in 1906, which had rendered all other battleships obsolete and created an opportunity for the German Empire to build a fleet that might challenge British naval supremacy. Lloyd George and Winston threw in their lot with the League of Liberals against Aggression and Militarism (the 'Lambs'), to which a majority of Liberal MPs belonged, and argued for a reduction in the battleship-building programme. Asquith saw it as a minor trial of strength, commenting that it would not become an issue over which either man would resign because 'Lloyd George has no principles and Winston no convictions'.[23] The Admiralty wanted to lay down six battleships, Lloyd George said there could only be money for four, and then the Tory press caught wind of the controversy and the slogan 'We want eight and we won't wait' was born. As Winston later recalled, 'A curious and characteristic solution was reached. The Admiralty had demanded six ships: the economists offered four and we finally compromised on eight.' But, he conceded, 'Although the Chancellor [Lloyd George] and I were right in the narrow sense we were absolutely wrong in relation to the deep tides of destiny. The greatest credit is due to the First Lord of the Admiralty for the resolute and courageous manner in which he fought his case and withstood his Party on this occasion.'[24]

In April 1909 Lloyd George announced what became known as the 'People's Budget', which imposed significantly increased rates of income tax, raised death duty on estates worth more than £1 million by a third (to 15 per cent) and increased duty on property transfers, tobacco and spirits. There was bipartisan recognition of the pressing need for extra revenue, and these measures alone would not have been enough to provoke the Lords into breaking with a long precedent by which revenue matters were the *de facto* prerogative of the elected house. Not *de jure*, however, and the customary civilities did not extend to a raft of proposed new taxes on land, designed to decrease the value of ownership without penalizing productive use. The Tory-dominated 'House of Landlords' rejected the Budget outright, precipitating the most serious constitutional crisis since the Glorious Revolution of 1688.

Overlooked in the ensuing verbiage of class confrontation was the fact that there were many large landowners in the Liberal Party and that the Budget was in some ways only incidentally provocative. The package as a whole bears the mark of Treasury orthodoxy, seeking a self-regulating mechanism that, once in place, would require a minimum of tinkering to achieve policy objectives, in this case to capture an equitable share of the national wealth arising from land, capital and labour alike. Lloyd George was not equal to the task of presenting the Treasury case and Asquith's daughter, in the gallery, felt that his four-and-a-half-hour speech 'was read so badly that to some he gave the impression that he did not himself understand it'.[25] He bears the main responsibility for letting the intellectual argument go by default, confident that he could ride a wave of levelling sentiment. He misread the electorate, however, and although mythology has it that 'the people' triumphed over the evil aristocrats, the social engineering aspects of the land taxes were to be abandoned in the final compromise over the Budget, never to return in their pristine form.[26]

Winston fully understood the technical argument in favour of the land taxes, although again for coherently conservative reasons, declaring the 'best way to make private property secure and respected is to bring the processes by which it is gained into harmony with the general interests of the public'.[27] His efforts to improve the lot of the poor have been branded 'paternalism', as if the term could not be applied with equal justice to any redistributive measure by any ruling elite, be it ever so proletarian. Yet he was acutely aware that charity, however uplifting to the donor, risks locking the recipient into dependency. I suspect the

115

true reason why his efforts have been denigrated is the belief that otherwise sound policy was vitiated by personal ambition, so inextricably woven into so much of what Winston did. He set out his motives bluntly in 1909, illustrating the seamless continuity among his patrician, imperialist and social reforming impulses:

> the greatest danger to the British Empire and the British people is not to be found among the enormous fleets and armies of the European Continent, nor in the solemn problems of Hindustan; it is not the 'Yellow Peril' or the 'Black Peril' nor any danger in the wide circuit of colonial and foreign affairs. No, it is here in our midst, close at home, close at hand in the growing cities of England and Scotland, and in the dwindling and cramped villages of our denuded countryside. It is there you will find the seeds of Imperial ruin and national decay—the unnatural gap between the rich and poor, the divorce of the people from the land, the want of proper discipline and training in our youth, the exploitation of boy labour, the physical degeneration which seems to follow so swiftly on civilized poverty, the awful jumbles of an obsolete Poor Law, the horrid havoc of the liquor traffic, the constant insecurity in the means of subsistence and employment which breaks the heart of many a sober, hard-working man, the absence of any established minimum standard of life and comfort among the workers, and, at the other end, the swift increase of vulgar, joyless luxury—here are

116

the enemies of Britain. Beware lest they shatter the foundations of her power.28

The similarity between Winston's views and those of Theodore Roosevelt, President of the USA in 1901–9, is striking.29 The British equivalent of the Progressivism with which the first Roosevelt is associated was Fabianism (the common denominator might best be described as 'efficientism'), and the influence of the leading Fabians Beatrice and Sidney Webb on the policies Winston advocated at this time reveals a common approach to social problems in Britain, and towards what the French had dubbed the 'civilizing mission' of Empire in the wider world.30 Accustomed as we are to the modern great divide between the free market postulates of classical Liberalism and the socialist aspirations of the Fabians, it is intriguing to find the two tendencies working so closely together a century ago.

The first generation of technocrats had a deep and lasting influence on British history. A representative biography is that of William Beveridge, appointed by Winston in 1909 to be the first director of the national system of Labour Exchanges, based on the highly successful model created by Bismarck in Germany. Beveridge was an adviser to Lloyd George in the preparation of the National Insurance Act of 1911, and later director of the London School of Economics (founded by the Webbs in 1895), before being appointed master of University College, Oxford, by the Conservative Prime Minister Neville Chamberlain. In 1942, at the invitation of Ernest Bevin, the trade union leader and Minister of Labour in Winston's wartime government, he produced the *Report on Social Insurance and Allied Services*, which Winston accepted in principle and on which the post-war Welfare State was based. Beveridge ended his career as the Liberal leader in the House of Lords.

Winston once described socialist society as the rule of officials who would 'look upon humanity through innumerable grilles and pigeon holes and over innumerable counters',[31] but the narrow, regimented world whose prospect so appalled him came appreciably nearer when he and Lloyd George chose to centralize the administration of the new social legislation. What might have happened if in February 1908 Asquith had left Winston at the head of the Local Government Board, a post he had already accepted, instead of switching him to the Board of Trade? Of the two, there is no doubt that Local Government was by far the most in need of Winston's energy. Many of the anti-poverty measures he sponsored might have been more effectively implemented at the county and municipal levels. But against that stood the grim history of local administration of the 1834 Poor Law, an inequitable blot on the record of the Victorian era which Lloyd George was determined to eradicate, although in fact he was unable to do so and the two systems coexisted chaotically for a further 20 years. For many pressing reasons, including the need to compete with the Labour Party for the votes of the industrial working class and to catch up with Germany, the Liberals missed what proved to be the last opportunity to reform and revitalize the layer of government that had been their historic source of strength. The result was that within a generation they lost most of it to the Conservatives and the Labour Party, and with it any hope of rebuilding the Liberal Party into a major player at the national level.[32]

The Liberal Party took its first step towards oblivion when Asquith yielded to King Edward VII's request to call a general election, although by law he was not required to do so before 1913,[33] instead of insisting that the monarch should use the threat of creating enough new peers to overcome the Tory veto in the House of Lords, as Edward's successor George V was to do in 1911. Consequently the election of January–February 1910 was fought as a referendum on 'Who rules?' Unfortunately for the Liberals, they did not win a significantly greater number of votes than they had in 1906, while the Tory vote recovered strongly, leaving the two main parties tied and the balance held by Labour and the Irish Nationalists.[34] A compromise Budget was passed in April, but Asquith was determined to curtail the power of the Lords within an omnibus Parliament Bill. The death of the King in May was followed by a six-month political truce, but Asquith went to the country again in December, to achieve no change amid a markedly lower turn-out.[35] Following the first election, in which he was in demand as a speaker all over the country, Winston wrote to Asquith asking for greater recognition and suggested either the Admiralty or the Home Office. His request met with approval, for Asquith judged 'that the close reasoning of his speeches [unlike Lloyd George's] was that of a real statesman'.[36] On 14 February 1910, aged 35, Winston became the youngest Home Secretary since Robert Peel in 1822, who had gone on to become Prime Minister 12 years later. Few in 1910, least of all Winston himself, doubted he would reach the top of the greasy pole at least as quickly as his great predecessor.

In the interest of thematic continuity I have galloped past the event with which Winston ended *My Early Life*, going from a conversation with Joe Chamberlain in 1902 to 'The End' in a superb rhetorical swoop: 'Events were soon to arise in the fiscal sphere which were to plunge me into new struggles and absorb my thoughts and energies at least until September 1908, when I married and lived happily ever afterwards.' Clementine Hozier was 11 years younger than Winston and no 'catch' in either financial or political terms. She was probably the biological daughter of a man other than the one married to her mother at the time of her birth, and, given that Blanche Hozier was among the fastest of a very fast set, it is difficult to be sure who the father was. After Winston and Clemmie met for the second time at a dinner in March 1908 (their first encounter in 1904 had been inauspicious, with Winston staring at her in uncharacteristic silence), they started to exchange letters. So began one of the great political marriages, and for once there was truth in the cliché that behind every great man there is a great woman. Blanche and Jennie had been very close, and equally lively, at the time Clemmie was born, and the desire of both children to have a private life as unlike their parents' as possible was perhaps the true foundation of a marriage singularly free of scandal. Clemmie had a discreet affair in 1935 during an irresistibly romantic cruise in the Far East, but there is no credible evidence that

120

Winston ever even contemplated adultery.

In their lifelong correspondence—they were often apart and even wrote notes to each other when at home together—one exchange captures what might, other things not being equal, have been a fatal incompatibility. It came in the six months during which he commanded a battalion of Royal Scots Fusiliers on the Western Front in World War I, when she was desperately concerned for his safety and he was no less desperate to get back into the political game. He bombarded her with instructions to make contacts and take soundings until at last she wearied of it and wrote:

> The facts you mention in support of your immediate return are weighty and well expressed, but it would be better if they were stated by others than yourself . . . . My Darling these grave public anxieties are very wearing—When next I see you I hope there will be a little time for us both alone—We are still young and Time flies stealing love away and leaving only friendship which is very peaceful but not stimulating or warming.

Winston's prompt reply may be the most revealing thing he ever wrote, combining a belated awareness that he had caused offence without either knowing exactly how (a plight shared by so many husbands), or more particularly what he should do to make amends. He began by mentioning that he had been wandering around in No Man's Land again, something she had begged him not to do, and even forgot her birthday. But in the end he found the right words:

121

Oh my darling do not write of 'friendship' to me—I love you more each month that passes and feel the need of you and all your beauty. My precious charming Clemmie—I too feel sometimes the longing for rest and peace . . . would it not be delicious to go for a few weeks to some lovely spot . . . far from the clash of arms and the bray of Parliaments? We know each other so well now and could play better than we ever could. Sometimes also I think I would not mind stopping living very much—I am so devoured by egoism that I would like to have another soul in another world and meet you in another setting, and pay you all the love and honour of the great romances.[37]

Clemmie bore him five children, Diana (1909–63), Randolph (1911–68), Sarah (1914–82), Marigold (1918–21) and Mary (b. 1922). Mary, born to fill the void left by the death of the adored baby Marigold, seems to have been the only one who ever warmed to her mother, whose life was so fully taken up with taking care of her talented but in many ways infantile husband that she had little energy left for coping with the vital needs of her children. The three eldest became obstreperous drunks, and Diana killed herself at a time when Clemmie was in hospital receiving electrotherapy for 'nervous prostration', something to which she was prone throughout her married life. There is always a price to pay for greatness, and the great seldom pay it all themselves. Tolstoy wrote that 'all happy families resemble one another, each unhappy family is unhappy in its own way', and I cannot hope to do justice here to the domestic environment Clemmie built around Winston. Clearly it was damagingly dysfunctional to the children, but it gave him the love and moral support he needed, and for this the world has reason to be grateful.[38]

As Home Secretary Winston now enjoyed a salary of £5000 (approximately £200,000 today) and wrote no more for publication until 1923. His office was in the sumptuous Home and Colonial Office building in Whitehall, now occupied by the Foreign Office, just two minutes' walk from Downing Street and five from the House. In those halcyon days senior politicians walked to nearby appointments or took taxis to ones further away: the disdainful high-speed official cavalcade was a thing of the future. Winston, always something of a dandy, was a familiar sight in his morning coat and silk hat, and it was noticeable that his civil uniform, then worn by ministers on the most formal occasions, seemed to have more gold lace (and of course more medals) than anyone else's. Always a fastidious man, Winston bathed at least once a day and exuded the mingled odours of clean linen, cigar smoke and Penhaligon's citrussy 'Blenheim Bouquet' cologne. He was every inch the young man who had arrived.

The Home Office is notoriously more likely to harm than to enhance reputations because it is responsible for so much that directly affects the citizen. Winston's legacy was one of intelligent and humane liberalization, making it all the more astonishing that he is remembered chiefly for alleged hostility to women's suffrage and a bias against trade unionism. The Mines Act of 1911, praised by the Labour Party as 'a boon to our mining community', was a response to the appalling safety record of the country's largest industry, which in 1910 alone suffered colliery disasters costing the lives of 132 miners in Cumberland and 320 in Lancashire.[39] The Shops Bill of the same year courageously sought to regulate the country's largest employers of labour, who were also mainly supporters of the Liberal Party. Consequently, what Winston called 'a mere piece of salvage from the wreck' became law, although it is in the nature of British politics that once a pinhole has been made in the dyke of vested interest the steady flow of precedent eventually widens the breach. Lastly, Winston took the lead in steering through the Commons the second part of the National Insurance Act, dealing with unemployment insurance and prepared at the Board of Trade under his direction. This was his most treasured achievement at the Home Office.

These were impressive results, especially since Winston's 21 months at the Home Office covered the period of the resolution of the Budget impasse and the political truce after the death of Edward VII, followed by renewed obstruction of normal business until the passage of Asquith's Parliament Act. The legislative agenda was too crowded with a backlog of business for him also to obtain a place for a thorough-going Criminal Justice Bill, but in its absence he did a great deal to modernize the system through administrative action. The list of reforms is long, but all addressed problems with which Home Secretaries have continued to wrestle ever since: the inappropriateness of custodial sentences for minor crimes; the waste of human potential involved in the premature incarceration of juvenile offenders; the failure of rehabilitation in prison and the problem of recidivism; and so on. Since the basic problems are so hard to change, Winston's words on the subject are likely to remain eternally valid:

> The mood and temper of the public in regard to the treatment of crime and criminals is one of the most unfailing tests of the civilization of any country. A calm and dispassionate recognition of the rights of the accused against the State, a constant heart-searching by all charged with the duty of punishment, a desire and eagerness to rehabilitate in the world of industry all those who have paid their dues in the hard coinage of punishment, tireless efforts towards the discovery of curative and regenerating processes, and an unfaltering faith that there is a treasure, if only you can find it, in the heart of every man—these are the symbols which in the treatment of crime and criminals mark and measure the stored-up strength of a nation, and are the sign and proof of the living virtue in it.[40]

Winston's commutation of about half the death sentences brought before him for ratification was neither more lenient nor more severe than that of any other Home Secretary during the first half of the twentieth century.[41] Roy Jenkins asserts that Winston believed death to be preferable to permanent incarceration. On the contrary, when Violet Asquith (later Lady Violet Bonham Carter) expressed this sentiment he burst out: 'Never abandon life! There is a way out of everything except death.'[42] Largely because of his duty to review all capital cases he looked back on his period at the Home Office with no fondness, but he does not appear to have lost any sleep over his decisions. Not so the Foreign Secretary, Edward Grey, who deputized for Winston when he went on holiday in August 1910 and, after confirming two death sentences, wrote, 'I think this part of your job is beastly and on the night before the two men were hung I kept meditating on the sort of night they were having, till I felt as if I ought not to let them hang unless I went to be hung too.'[43]

Winston's tenure at the Home Office is not remembered for his eloquently expressed liberal instincts and the practical reforms arising from them, however, but for the occasions when he was compelled to act as the chief law enforcement officer. He had been a particular target of the campaign for women's suffrage launched in 1909 by the Women's Social and Political Union (WPSU), led by Emmeline Pankhurst and her daughters Sylvia and Christabel, even before he became Home Secretary; once he assumed the office, he became the Great Satan.[44] The WPSU was an upper middle-class association with little concern for the plight of working women, whose older organizations such as the Women's Trade Union League and the Women's Industrial Council focused on bread-and-butter issues. And the cold political fact that Winston and his colleagues had to wrestle with was that the extension of the franchise to middle-class women would have been a huge electoral gift to the Conservative Party. It did not bring out the best in Winston and in April 1912, apropos the sinking of the *Titanic*, he wrote revealingly to Clemmie:

> The story is a good one. The strict observance of the great traditions of the sea towards women and children reflects nothing but honour upon our civilisation. Even I hope it may mollify some of the young unmarried lady teachers who are so bitter in their sex antagonism, and think men so base and vile . . . I cannot help feeling proud of our race and its traditions as proved by this event.[45]

Any anthology of indelible stains includes the one the Labour Party splashed on Winston about an alleged massacre of strikers in South Wales in November 1910. A walk-out by twenty-five thousand miners in the Rhondda and Aberdare valleys over pay differentials exploded into violence in the town of Tonypandy during the night of 7 November and continued for several days. Sixty-three shops were looted and two men died in confused circumstances before police reinforcements sent by Churchill from London arrived at the scene and, in combination with the local constabulary, restored order with the vigorous but non-lethal use of their heavy, rolled-up waterproof capes. The local Chief Constable had appealed directly to the Army Southern Command and troops were advancing from their barracks on Salisbury Plain until Winston stopped them. He eventually authorized a detachment of cavalry to advance to Pontypridd, commanding the entrance to both valleys, and a detachment of infantry to go into the Rhondda, but the troops were never used directly against the strikers. Indeed, General Sir Nevil Macready, who had military responsibility for the episode (and later served as commissioner of the Metropolitan Police), wrote that 'it was entirely due to Mr Churchill's forethought . . . that bloodshed was avoided'. And if subsequent legend has accused him of brutality, many contemporaries in fact thought him too lenient. On 9 November the *Daily Express* denounced Winston's measured response and his appeal to the miners for calm as 'the last word in a policy of shameful neglect and poltroonery which may cost the country dear'.

On the morning of 3 January 1911, as he recalled in *Thoughts and Adventures*, he was in his bath when news came that a gang of Latvian anarchists in a house at 100 Sidney Street in Stepney, in the East End, had shot a policeman dead and wounded two others, and that the officer in command of the operation had appealed for troops. The criminals had killed two policemen and wounded another nearly a month earlier, when the tunnel they were digging into a jeweller's shop was discovered, and Winston had attended the funerals. He immediately authorized a detachment of Scots Guards based at the Tower of London to go to the aid of the civil power, but could not resist the temptation to hurry to the scene himself, arriving just after midday in a top hat and an overcoat with an astrakhan collar, and appearing in the newspaper headlines and even the primitive newsreels of the day. Twenty-one years later he was unrepentant: 'It was not for me to interfere with those who were in charge on the spot', he wrote, but

128

my position of authority, far above them all, attracted inevitably to itself direct responsibility. I saw now that I should have done much better to have remained quietly in my office. On the other hand, it was impossible to get into one's car and drive away while matters stood in such great uncertainty, and, moreover, were extremely interesting.[46]

The house caught light and Winston ordered the fire brigade to let it burn until there was no great likelihood of the inhabitants still being alive, after which he signalled to the firemen to fight the blaze and then led the police in a rush to the door. Two charred bodies were found but the leader of the gang, known as Peter the Painter, either escaped or had not been there in the first place.

The Tory press, of course, assaulted him for bringing his office into disrepute, but Winston pointed out that two months previously they had attacked him for taking a detached view of matters in the Rhondda valley. Even among those inclined to support him, however, the Siege of Sidney Street watered a seed of doubt about his sense of proportion. Some years later A.G. Gardiner, the great Liberal editor of the *Daily News*, captured the essence of this unease in one of his trademark, acid-etched pen-portraits:

He is always unconsciously playing a part—an heroic part. . . . He sees himself moving through the smoke of battle—triumphant, terrible, his brow clothed in thunder, his legions looking to him for victory, and not looking in vain . . . It is not make-believe, it is not insincerity; it is that in this fervid and picturesque imagination there are always great deeds afoot, with himself cast by destiny in the Agamemnon role. Hence the portentous gravity that sits on his youthful shoulders so oddly, those impressive postures and tremendous silences, the body flung wearily in the chair, the head resting gloomily in the hand, the abstracted look.[47]

Although it was not his intention, by making himself the story Winston distracted public attention from the combination of immigration and crime that remains the bane of liberal Home Secretaries to this day. London was the home from home for terrorists from other countries, and Peter the Painter's gang had broken the unwritten rule against soiling the safe haven which even the Georgian revolutionary Josif Dzhugashvili (better known as Stalin) had respected during a long stay in 1907. Several biographers have asserted that the incident confirmed a general view within the political establishment that Winston was inclined to shoot from the hip, and that this was the reason why the Prime Minister moved him to the Admiralty in October 1911. But we should not judge too hastily, for it would be a damning comment on Asquith's own judgement had he moved someone he believed to be lacking in discretion to take control of what was then the most powerful war-making—or peace-keeping—institution in the world, the Royal Navy. On the contrary, Asquith, weary of constant political crises, increasingly delegated his parliamentary duties to Winston. There was another reason why he did so, particularly in the evenings when the Commons was at its fullest and its members at their most aggressive. It would be kindest to say that he enjoyed a drink, and, as Winston confided to Clemmie on 22 April 1911, this usually extended to three or four:

> On Thursday night the P.M. was very bad: and I squirmed with embarrassment. He could hardly speak: and many people noticed his condition. He continues most persistent and benevolent, and entrusts me with everything after dinner. Up till that time he is at his best—but thereafter! It is an awful pity and only the persistent freemasonry [48] of the House of Commons prevents a scandal. I like the old boy and admire both his intellect and his character. But what risks to run. We only got him away the other night just before Balfour began the negotiations which I conducted, but which otherwise would have fallen to him—with disastrous consequences. [49]

However, Winston's continuing usefulness at the Home Office was doubtful following his performance during the sweltering hot summer of 1911, when the trade unions, emboldened by full employment, set out to recover lost rights and to demand a bigger slice of the growing economic pie. This is another perennial in democratic societies: unequal prosperity tends to breed discontent, and people feel the pain of loss far more acutely than they appreciate compensating gains. It is pointless to lament the apparent popular ingratitude that invariably overwhelms reforming governments, because, although they may successfully abolish historic injustices, an increasingly demanding attitude among the governed is the natural by-product of heightened expectations. In 1911 the populist rhetoric of Lloyd George and Winston came home to roost, and neither man was to espouse such socially radical measures in public again.

Industrial unrest began in June with rapidly successful strikes for better pay by seamen and firemen, but sympathetic strikes among dockers and railwaymen gathered a momentum of their own and moved rapidly towards a coordinated strike. Winston noted with alarm that 'a new force has arisen in trade unionism, whereby the power of the old leaders has proved quite ineffective, and the sympathetic strike on a wide scale is prominent. Shipping, coal, railways, dockers etc. etc. are all uniting and breaking out at once.'[50] His analysis was correct: although syndicalism had long been powerful in France, where it was the founding principle of the Confédération Générale du Travail, the ideology of united direct action by organized labour to bring about a social and political revolution had only recently taken root in Britain. It was in 1910 that Tom Mann had published the first number of *Industrial Syndicalist*. However, the vocabulary of syndicalism had been rapidly adopted by labour militants whose real targets were the established trade union bosses, and during the summer of 1911 there was a lot of rhetorical posturing and street violence which

132

Winston could not have ignored had he wished to—and he did not.

He was, however, in a constitutional bind. By law he was obliged to await a request from local authorities to deploy troops, but since such requests came only when the police had already been defeated it was likely that, when soldiers with no training in crowd control came up against mobs emboldened by success against the unarmed police, bloodshed would ensue. This is precisely what happened in Liverpool, when in response to an appeal by the Lord Mayor Winston arranged with the Admiralty to send in HMS *Antrim*, whose Marines shot into a hostile crowd of dockers on 14 August, fortunately only wounding eight of them. In London Winston personally met the leader of the dockers and defused the situation, but on the 15th the railway unions called for a national strike. In the cities there were already food shortages, which in themselves increased the risk of rioting, and on the 19th Winston alerted fifty thousand troops and unilaterally declared that 'the Army Regulation which requires a requisition for troops from a civil authority is suspended'.[51]

To suggest that any of this was done without the express permission of Asquith is absurd, and there is likewise little doubt that Lloyd George and Winston, with the agreement of the Prime Minister, played 'good cop, bad cop' with both the railwaymen and their employers. Emphasizing the greater threat posed by the militants, as Winston had already done to defuse the situation in the London docks, Lloyd George persuaded the railway companies to recognize their unions, the proximate cause of the strike. Meanwhile Winston massed troops in Hyde Park and called the syndicalists' bluff by directing the army to secure all the railway stations in Manchester, the only actual exercise of the powers he had assumed by the suspension of normal procedures. By 20 August the danger of a general strike was past, and Labour Party leaders felt free to denounce the bad cop. It was a smokescreen, as was the belated trumpeting by the Liberal press about civil liberties. All were equally relieved that someone had taken the initiative to restore order, perhaps most of all the trade union leaders whose authority had been most directly challenged.

It is as well to emphasize the eternal nature of the problems Winston tried to deal with during this, the only period in his career when he was directly concerned with purely domestic issues. As was suggested earlier, they are not readily subject to solution because the relationship between civil liberties, social justice, general welfare and international imperatives is so fluid and complex. In Chapter Five I shall take the Liberal government of which Winston was a prominent member sternly to task for committing the nation to a course of action for which it was militarily unprepared. But the verdict on its efforts to adapt the institutions of government in order to cope with changing social realities is far more favourable. No nation has ever undergone a similar non-violent transformation with such negligible economic dislocation or erosion of civil liberties. On the domestic front, at least, Asquith and his talented ministers not only did the best they could, but also all that was realistically achievable.

That Winston came out of this period with his

skill as a reformer buried under accusations that he was anti-labour is a triumph of propaganda over reality. It had little to do with his actions and much to do with his being a duke's grandson. Lloyd George, corrupt in office and persistently lecherous in private life, attacked socialism no less vehemently; but he was redeemed, in the eyes of so many, by his relatively humble birth. The lack of logic in judging a man by his origins rather than his deeds could not be more clearly illustrated.

Gladstone's national speaking tour prior to the 1880 general election was the first exercise in mass consciousness-raising in British history, and the public performances of Winston and Lloyd George in 1908–11 were in that tradition. It remains something of a mystery why the broadening of the franchise in the 1920s was accompanied by such a steep decline in the quality of public speaking, although loss of respect for the political elite certainly played a part. In this context, Winston's 'radical decade' can perhaps be seen as the last opportunity for rhetorical cavalry charges before the debate settled into the trench warfare of class-based ideology, accompanied by what he described as 'a crudeness and dullness . . . brought into the discussion of every question which can already be sharply contrasted with the tenseness of Victorian debates, and the strict control then exerted by the House of Commons over the Executive'.[52] Written in the era of Stanley Baldwin and modern party management, this was a belated recognition that the issues on which Winston cut his political teeth had ceased to occupy the mainstream of British politics.

Chief among these was Free Trade, which has

recovered much of its lustre today but in Winston's lifetime went from being the guarantor of stable, low prices behind which the Liberals and the Labour movement were united both before and after World War I, to being a source of employment-damaging mental rigidity in the late 1920s, until abandoned at the start of the ruinously protectionist 1930s and through the long subsidization of failure that followed. All economic theories are based on assumptions about human nature. The free market presupposes that individuals will perceive the advantage to their own interests of fairly conducted competition, socialism that competition is never fair and therefore can be neither efficient nor humane. During a century characterized by international tension and punctuated by all-consuming wars, British governments persisted beyond reason first with one and then the other until their failure became apparent. The pendulum now appears to be settling down somewhere between the two, inclining towards individual liberty. This was where Winston's instincts positioned him, and if we substitute 'New Labour' for 'Liberalism', the following extract from a speech he gave to the electors of Dundee in 1908 becomes remarkably topical:

Socialism seeks to pull down wealth; Liberalism seeks to raise up poverty. Socialism would destroy private interests; Liberalism would preserve private interests . . . by reconciling them with public right. Socialism would kill enterprise; Liberalism would rescue enterprise from the trammels of

136

privilege and preference. Socialism assails the pre-eminence of the individual; Liberalism seeks, and shall seek more in the future, to build up a minimum standard for the mass. Socialism exalts the rule; Liberalism exalts the man. Socialism attacks capitalism; Liberalism attacks monopoly.[53]

CHAPTER FOUR

FIRST LORD

1911–1915 AND 1939–1940

Although Winston tells us so in *The World Crisis*, it is hard to believe that Asquith made him a firm offer of the Admiralty in 1908, still less that Winston refused it and accepted the Board of Trade instead.[1] Asquith may have flicked the prospect over Winston's nose in order to see if he would rise to the fly, but it was not a job for a young man with limited departmental experience. When finally appointed First Lord three and a half years later Winston thought it 'the biggest thing that has ever come my way—the chance I should have chosen before all others'.[2] He moved along Whitehall to the imposing building with its anchor-topped portico designed by Thomas Ripley in 1723, which had housed the Board of Admiralty since 1726. Winston's sense of history cannot but have been stirred by the board room, with its wind-dial above the fireplace so that in Nelson's time their Lordships could see whether the French fleet might be likely to try to break through the blockade that day. He enjoyed comfortable (and, no less to the point, free) accommodation in Admiralty House, just behind the main building.

Winston served two stints as First Lord of the Admiralty—political head of the Royal Navy—the first including the run-up to World War I and the early years of that conflict, and the second

138

An imperious, but very young, Winston in his sailor suit at the age of seven.

This famous portrait by Youssuf Karsh taken in Canada in December 1941 perfectly captured the bulldog image of the determined wartime leader. Winston's expression was actually a reaction to the photographer confiscating his cigar for the picture.

Winston's mother, the American heiress Jennie Jerome, later Lady Randolph Churchill, shown here in a photograph taken in about 1880.

Winston's father, Lord Randolph Churchill, Conservative politician and briefly Chancellor of the Exchequer, photographed *circa* 1880.

Sept. 3

Dear Papa,

I am very glad to be able to write to you on this extremely smart paper. On Friday I left London by the 12.20 & got down here in time for lunch. Since then I have had little or nothing to do. Yesterday there was a drill at 10 o'clock for an hour & to day there has been a parade & church.

The first 3 days are devoted chiefly to being measured

A letter Winston wrote to his father from Sandhurst on 3 September 1893. 'Dear Papa, I am very glad to be able to write to you on this extremely smart paper. On Friday I left London by the 12.20 and got down here in time for lunch. Since then I have had little or nothing to do. Yesterday there was a drill at 10 o'clock for an hour & today there has been a parade & church.'

Winston as a second lieutenant in the full dress uniform of the 4th Queen's Own Hussars at Aldershot in 1895. Lord Randolph had tried to steer Winston away from the cavalry, whose costly uniform and high living expenses made it an unwise choice for a young man of limited means.

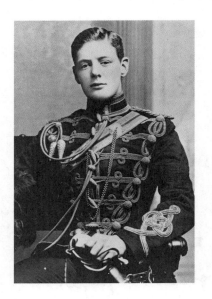

ABOVE Standing out from the crowd. A sullen Winston, in something very close to military uniform, just after his capture by the Boers near Frere in South Africa on 15 November 1899.

RIGHT Wanted—dead or alive. The Boers issued a poster offering a £25 reward for Winston's capture after his escape from prison in Pretoria.

ABOVE A large and enthusiastic crowd greeted Winston on his arrival in Durban after his escape from Boer custody.

RIGHT Winston with Kaiser Wilhelm II at military manoeuvres in Germany in 1909. Winston retained an almost lifelong affection for uniforms, and here he is dressed as an officer in the Queen's Own Oxfordshire Hussars, a Yeomanry (Territorial cavalry) unit.

ABOVE Winston's fondness for dressing up extended to the civil uniform worn by ministers and senior officials on formal occasions. Here he is returning in a taxi after attending a Convocation of Clergy to the King.

LEFT Winston with David Lloyd George in 1910, the year he became Home Secretary. The two men were very close political associates at this time, working together under the Prime Minister, Herbert Asquith, whose daughter Violet maintained that Winston 'was to learn the language of Radicalism' from Lloyd George.

ABOVE Winston at the Siege of Sidney Street in 1911.
Home Secretary at the time, he went to a house in the
East End of London where police and soldiers had
cornered an anarchist gang. Images like this helped give
the impression that Winston was not a safe pair of hands
for delicate matters.

LEFT Winston
accompanied by
his wife
Clementine and
General Sir
Bruce Hamilton
during
manoeuvres on
Salisbury Plain.
Clemmie
provided Winston
with unfailing
support during
his long and
tempestuous
career.

Winston, his brother Jack (second from right) and
Lieutenant General Sir Ian Hamilton in Buckingham
during manoeuvres in 1913. The brave and charming
Hamilton commanded the Gallipoli landings in 1916. His
failure led to Winston's fall from power.

Winston was an early advocate of air power, and learned
to fly before World War I. This photograph shows him in
front of a Royal Flying Corps aircraft in 1914.

comprising the first nine months of World War II. I will consider these two episodes in this chapter, and look at Winston's further political involvement in World War I, and his time in uniform on the Western Front, in Chapter Five.

The Royal Navy was the principal instrument of British geopolitical power, where the salty spirits of Drake, Blake, Hawke, Rodney, Jervis and Nelson loomed to remind their descendants why Britain had not been invaded since 1066. When Winston took office in October 1911 the navy was involved in the largest re-equipment programme in its history, its supremacy seriously challenged for the first time in a century not only by Germany but also by the USA. Along with the erosion of the Royal Navy's absolute numerical superiority came doubts (in fact, all too well founded) that it still enjoyed a qualitative advantage over its potential enemies. And although the navy's shipbuilding programme went far towards checking this quantitative and qualitative decline, its ethos remained decidedly pre-modern.

If Winston emerged from his spell at the Home Office with a reputation for being a bull in a china shop, why would Asquith have appointed him to such a sensitive and high-profile post? The most obvious explanation, a constant throughout Winston's career, is that the central dilemma for any Prime Minister is how to nurture scarce talent without at the same time encouraging a potential rival. Winston had no personal following in the Liberal Party and, once detached from his alliance with Lloyd George, posed no threat to Asquith's authority. It is also likely that Asquith thought Winston's complete lack of diffidence would be well suited to the job of asserting political control over by far the largest-spending department, at a time when the Liberal government needed to fund its social programme and also to modernize the army. The Liberals had inherited the cost of a revolution in capital ship design begun by the turbine-engined, big-gunned HMS *Dreadnought*, which rendered the existing battle fleet obsolete. This tied the Asquith government's hands in a number of ways, while simultaneously raising the barrier of technological mystique around the navy and saturating its capacity to absorb innovation. Winston's task was to obtain value for money (that *leitmotiv* in defence policy) from what Arthur Marder, the great American historian of the Royal Navy, has described as 'a drowsy, inefficient, moth-eaten organism'.[3]

This, Winston's first spell at the Admiralty, is of particular interest in the evolution of his personality because the political momentum that carried him to the office was to be so drastically diminished by the circumstances in which he left it that he was obliged to spend the next quarter-century trying to repair the damage. The experience was not only the most severe test of character that he ever endured, but was also genuinely formative in a way that does not occur in most people's adult lives.[4] Perhaps because one can readily imagine him playing with model warships in his bath he did not entirely fulfil Asquith's expectations of getting a political grip on spendthrift sailors, and rapidly became captivated by the romance of the senior service: the gamekeeper soon took to poaching. In mitigation, it is hard to imagine that anyone could have resisted the allure of the largest fleet in the world and of the citadels of steel with which it was being equipped during his tenure. One of Winston's last speeches about the navy, in 1948, lamented that not even *Warspite*, with battle honours stretching from Jutland to D-Day, was spared the scrapyard torch.[5]

The period 1911–15 was also the only occasion in his career when he was required to change the way a government department worked within the constraints of peacetime; it therefore provides the clearest answer to a criticism frequently levelled against him, that although he was energetic and gifted he was none the less an amateur in an increasingly professional world. The charge begs a much larger issue framed by the trade union leader Clive Jenkins, self-styled 'organizer of the middle classes', who commented in 1977 that the fault line running through British society from top to bottom was poor management. Charles de Gaulle judged that Winston's greatest strength was his ability to 'stir the dull English dough', but a systems analyst might ask whether his efforts produced lasting, institutional changes. A generally admiring assessment concludes that Winston had 'more influence on the condition of the Royal Navy in two world wars than any other civilian', but the author recognizes that there was little competition.[6] The unasked question is whether or not Winston transformed the culture of the Royal Navy, and the simple answer is that he fell far short. Whether any other politician could have done better poses a larger question to which I shall return.

He did, however, carry off the lordly manner

with panache. The first of the new battleships launched during his tenure, *Centurion*, was christened by Clemmie, and the *Benbow* later by Jennie. Two others were to be named *Marlborough* and *Ramillies* in honour of his ancestor, the 1st Duke. Among the perks of his new job was the aptly named luxury steam yacht *Enchantress*, in which he visited all naval coastal establishments, every important warship and many lesser vessels as well, often with only minimal warning. The Second Sea Lord, Sir John Jellicoe, termed it 'meddling', and in 1912 Rear Admiral Sir Lewis Bayly, aboard HMS *Lion*, warned him that 'on any repetition of his inquisitorial methods he would turn him off the ship. Winston took his drubbing very well.'[7] For a few years the yacht took the place of Blenheim Palace as his preferred PR venue. Thus an invitation to dine on board served to heal the wounds left by *The River War* on Field Marshal Kitchener, and he was able to call in splendid style on Lloyd George at his home on the Lleyn peninsula in northwest Wales. The yacht also gave him priceless personal time with the Asquith family on a Mediterranean cruise in 1912, serving as a more than adequate substitute for the country house he yearned for, with the added attraction, to one with no secure private income, of being paid for entirely by the navy. The reverse side of this borrowed magnificence was more than a hint of *folie de grandeur* in a squabble with King George V over Winston's wish to name one of the new battleships after Oliver Cromwell (the King, a sailor himself, also objected to William Pitt as a possible name because there was a 'danger of the men giving the ship nicknames of ill-conditioned words rhyming with it'). At the end of this bickering Winston snidely drew attention to the cost of the royal yacht. Clearly, he did not believe that the adage about people in glass houses applied to him.[8]

Although he was closely associated with Lloyd George's opposition to increased naval expenditure in 1909, it will be remembered that Winston's first major speech to the Commons, on 13 May 1901, had been open-ended in its commitment to the Royal Navy. He did not know, when he spoke, that behind the scenes the threat posed by Admiral Alfred von Tirpitz's Navy Laws of 1898 and 1900 had begun to overshadow all other foreign policy considerations. The huge fleet projected by these laws was clearly aimed at Britain. In 1902 the then First Lord, the Earl of Selborne, had minuted his Cabinet colleagues that 'the great naval expenditure on which Germany has embarked involves a deliberate diminution of the military strength which Germany might otherwise have attained in relation to France and Russia'.[9] Public awareness was not far behind, and in 1903 Erskine Childers published his best-seller *The Riddle of the Sands*, which portrayed a German invasion attempt. While other countries of course bear some responsibility, German nationalism and expansionism, coupled with contempt for international treaties, played a leading role in the origins of both the world wars that gutted the nations of Europe and, after centuries of being the driving force of world affairs, reduced them to minor players after 1945.[10]

The German Navy Law of 1900 projected a High Seas Fleet of 34 battleships by 1920. The building and launching of *Dreadnought* in the astoundingly brief period of one year served as a bold demonstration of British superiority both in technology and in construction capacity, calculated to exercise a deterrent effect. Instead, the rivalry quickened and the supplementary German Navy Law of 1908 projected a new figure of 58 capital ships by 1920. In 1912, when the German-educated British War Minister Richard Haldane made a good faith visit to Berlin to propose a moratorium on battleship-building, he found his overture was taken as a sign of weakness. Kaiser Wilhelm II believed his navy would 'bring the English to their senses through sheer fright', after which they would 'submit to the inevitable and we shall become the best friends in the world'.[11] It was unrealistic to believe that the shipyard of the world would permit itself to be outbuilt, and the millions who subscribed to Tirpitz's Navy League and its publications, which stridently pronounced the inevitability of war with Britain, did not appreciate that they were assailing an interest which was vital to Britain but not to Germany.

If one had to choose a single episode to sum up the dilemma British statesmen were unable to resolve before both world wars, a good choice would be the uproar in Germany when, during the Haldane mission, Winston stated publicly that 'the British navy is to us a necessity and, from some points of view, the German navy is to them more in the nature of a luxury'.[12] In Germany the (deliberate) mistranslation of this as *Luxusflotte*, suggesting that Tirpitz's fleet was a sensual indulgence, stoked the fire of public outrage. Appeasers condemned Winston's speech as

152

provocative, but Asquith thought it a 'plain statement of an obvious truth' and Haldane judged it to have been a useful intervention which strengthened his hand in negotiations with the Germans.13

The verdict on re-equipment during Winston's tenure of the Admiralty is mixed. His predecessor, Reginald McKenna, had already done much of the hard work. The move from 13.5-inch to 15-inch for the main armament of the new *Queen Elizabeth* class and the decision to convert from coal-fired to oil-fired propulsion were technical decisions for which momentum already existed. But this is not to belittle Winston's achievement in sustaining it and winning funds for the innovations, increasing the naval estimates from £39 million to over £50 million. In particular his initiative to buy a controlling share in the Anglo-Persian Oil Company was a rare example of a highly profitable investment by a British government. However, other technical choices made during his time at the Admiralty were less far-sighted. In the field of capital ships, the '*R*' class was a retrograde design based on a false dichotomy between speed and protection convincingly resolved by the *Queen Elizabeth*s. In 1914–15 the lightly armoured battle-cruiser concept was revived with the conversion of *Repulse* and *Renown*, followed in 1915–16 by *Hood*, names redolent with tragedy in the annals of the Royal Navy. Outright follies were the lightweight *Glorious*, *Courageous* and *Furious*, shallow-draft vessels intended for shore bombardment in support of land operations in the Baltic, which proved structurally too weak to fire their main armament and were eventually converted into aircraft carriers.[14]

These decisions betrayed a powerful influence over Winston exerted by the recently retired (in January 1911, to widespread relief) First Sea Lord, Admiral of the Fleet 'Jacky' Fisher, one of the most controversial figures in a service that has thrown up more than its fair share of flamboyant personalities. *Dreadnought* was a natural outcome of improvements in propulsion and steel technology, certain to be built sooner or later even if Britain did not take the lead. Not so the battle-cruisers, a concept that can be attributed entirely to Fisher. Laid down in the same fiscal year as *Dreadnought*, they were originally sold to the government as being essential to keep Britain's trading routes open by hunting down enemy commerce raiders, and for this, had they been deployed around the world, there were more than enough in service or laid down by 1911. Instead, they were concentrated in home waters as adjuncts to the battle fleet. For the purpose of protecting the seaways, *Repulse*, *Renown* and *Hood* were blatantly surplus to requirements by the time they were laid down, and three more *Queen Elizabeth*s would have been a far better investment. The *Courageous* class was an even more unconscionable waste of resources because it corresponded to a concept firmly rejected by the Committee of Imperial Defence before the war. This was Fisher's belief that the army was just another missile to be delivered by the navy, an unrealistic approach to European warfare ever since railways had made it possible for troops to reach an invasion site faster by land than they could by sea, and in any case strategically misplaced in view of the government's

154

increasing interest in sending direct military support to France. On the other side the Germans suspended work even on battleships they had already launched in 1914 because their addition to the fleet would not offset British numerical preponderance, a calculation they might have made to infinitely greater advantage many years earlier. If Fisher's obsessions bordered on the irrational, the same can be said with greater justice about the costly steel albatross that Tirpitz hung around Germany's neck.[15]

It is easy to see why the volcanic Fisher appealed to Winston. As a behind-the-scenes adviser the old man (he was born in 1841) permitted Winston to present a knowledgeable façade to his admirals and to the Commons, while once war broke out Fisher's proven ability to galvanize the navy made him irresistibly attractive. Winston had set up a staff organization, but in 1914 the navy was still unshakeably committed to the leader principle. Winston did not disagree in theory, but felt he should be the leader. Failing that, he wanted a First Sea Lord as restless and imaginative as himself. Winston's recall of Fisher was a catastrophic decision from the point of view of his own immediate career prospects, but the most remarkable aspect of an extremely odd partnership is that neither man believed in his heart what his mind told him was true. The Royal Navy had always been a python, not a cobra. Its function was to shut down the enemy's overseas trade while defending its own, to that end keeping an enemy fleet bottled up. This it did even during World War I, and although at Jutland on 31 May 1916 the Grand Fleet failed to win the Trafalgar-like victory expected of it, Tirpitz's High Seas Fleet never ventured out in force again and Germany eventually turned to unrestricted submarine warfare. This helped to bring the USA into the war on the Allied side, and demonstrated just how much more vulnerable Britain was than Germany to the interruption of overseas trade.

Yet if Jutland was a strategic victory for the British, at the tactical and technical level its implications were sobering. The German range-finding system, although inferior overall to the British director system, was better at obtaining the initial range. This proved fatal to the British battle-cruisers in the first phase of the battle, when *Indefatigable* and *Queen Mary* blew up and the flagship *Lion* nearly shared their fate. To compensate for chronic inaccuracy resulting from a lack of live firing facilities at the battle-cruiser base of Rosyth, Vice Admiral Sir David Beatty had encouraged a cult of rapid firing which led to safety measures being ignored. Too much ready-to-use cordite was stored inside the turrets and anti-flash doors were kept open. It was this (a practice common to both fleets), and not any structural defect, that the Germans had corrected after their own battle-cruisers were mauled at the Dogger Bank battle in January 1915.[16] It was also identified in the Royal Navy's own post-Jutland analysis, along with serious flaws in the reporting and signalling procedures of the battle-cruiser squadron. The report was suppressed by the then First Sea Lord Admiral Sir John Jellicoe, and inadequate armour was blamed instead. Jellicoe had commanded the Grand Fleet at Jutland, but the cover-up served mainly to protect the reputation of Beatty, who succeeded him in command of the fleet in 1916 and was to be First Sea Lord from 1919 to 1927. There was nothing seriously 'wrong with our bloody ships today', as Beatty put it when *Queen Mary* blew up: the faults were in him and were magnified by systemic failure.[17]

Overall, therefore, the Royal Navy enjoyed a sufficient advantage in numbers and weight of fire to compensate for its organizational weaknesses. Yet it was these last that Winston had, at least in part, been appointed to correct. Furthermore, he had rescued Beatty from half pay by appointing him Secretary to the First Lord in 1912, thence to command of the battle-cruiser squadron in 1913. It was fair return for that bottle of champagne on the eve of Omdurman. For failing to detect the glaring logical flaw in Fisher's changing justification for the battle-cruisers, and then appointing a *beau sabreur* to command them, Winston bears some responsibility for the fact that greater material losses obscured the reality of strategic victory at Jutland.

Winston and his devotees made much of the fleet being ready in August 1914, in the sense of being mobilized and at its war stations when war was declared. As the responsible minister he was certainly entitled to that credit, and Kitchener told him, when he was acrimoniously removed from office, that: 'There is one thing, at least, they can never take away from you. When the war began, the fleet was ready.' But for the same reason Winston cannot avoid a share of blame for the blunders with which the navy started the war. The first and most fateful happened right at the outset, when the German battle-cruiser *Goeben* and the light cruiser *Breslau* escaped from the British Mediterranean fleet and sailed into Constantinople harbour, where they were reflagged as *Sultan Yavuz Selim* and *Middili*. Simultaneously Winston ordered two battleships nearing completion in British yards to be seized from their Turkish crews, a measure that should have been, but was not, accompanied by an immediate offer of compensation to the Turkish government, at this stage still officially neutral. That said, it is likely that Turkey would have declared for the Central Powers sooner or later. The 'Young Turk' officers who had seized power in 1908 aspired to the German model in most things, and the Turkish army was permeated with German advisers. None the less, the 11-inch guns of a warship manned by German sailors wearing fezes in Constantinople harbour were an eloquent argument against procrastination, and, after failing to respond to Allied ultimata, Turkey entered the war on 31 October 1914.[18]

Winston's part in this debacle went beyond simple departmental responsibility. Signals in his own handwriting, which were not passed through the war staff, were fatally ambiguous and contributed to the confusion that permitted the German warships to escape. The immediate court martial of Rear Admiral Sir Thomas Troubridge for not attacking when he had the chance flew in the face of one of the signals, which clearly stated that British ships were not 'at this stage to be brought into action against superior forces, except in combination with the French'.[19] Although these ambiguous Admiralty orders, which led to a debate over what 'superior forces' actually constituted, ensured Troubridge's acquittal, his career was broken and he never received another seagoing command.

If the intention of pillorying Troubridge was to 'encourage the others', as Voltaire explained the execution of Rear Admiral John Byng in 1757, it was to have sinister consequences. On 1 November, off Coronel on the coast of Chile, Rear Admiral Sir Christopher Cradock's squadron of old armoured cruisers attacked a superior force under the command of Vice Admiral Graf von Spee, including the armoured cruisers *Scharnhorst* and *Gneisenau*. Cradock's squadron was sunk with the loss of all 1600 men on board. On 1 October Winston had minuted the War Staff that 'it would be best for the British ships to keep within supporting distance of one another, and to postpone the cruise along the West Coast until the present uncertainty about the *Scharnhorst* and *Gneisenau* is cleared up'.[20] The words 'Rear Admiral Cradock should be instructed that . . .' would have made this an executive order, and Winston should have known that nothing less was likely to bring it to the urgent attention of the First Sea Lord. In fact, one of the first actions taken by Fisher on his return to the Admiralty was to send the big battle-cruiser *Princess Royal* to cover the Panama Canal, and her smaller sisters *Inflexible* and *Invincible* to the Falkland Islands to cover Cape Horn. These performed as designed when Spee's squadron approached the islands on 8 December, and duly sank *Scharnhorst* and *Gneisenau*, albeit with the staggering expenditure of 1174 12-inch shells.

On 18 September Winston had penned another

prescient but non-executive minute about three older cruisers patrolling the Dutch coast for no clearly discernible purpose: '. . . these cruisers ought not to continue on this beat. The risk to such ships is not justified by any services they can render.' On 22 September *Cressy*, *Hogue* and *Aboukir* (their names redolent of happier times in British naval and military history) were all sunk by *U-9* with the loss of 1460 men, many of them cadets and reservists. The failure of the staff was complete: it had ignored the warnings of seagoing officers who called the three cruisers 'the live-bait squadron' and, following the tragedy, did not order all ships to zigzag and maintain speed at all times.

German submarines continued to do serious damage. On 15 October *U-9* was in action again, sinking the cruiser *Hawke* with the loss of over 500 lives, and on the 27th *U-27* sank *Hermes*, the navy's only seaplane carrier. On New Year's Day 1915 the pre-dreadnought battleship *Formidable* developed engine trouble off the Dorset coast and was left to make her own way back to port. *U-24* sank the crippled, unescorted ship with the loss of 550 men. Overall, it is impossible to resist the conclusion that the Admiralty War Staff was not up to its job. Winston's personal interventions sometimes made matters worse, but more often failed to shake the staff from its torpor. We need look no further for the reason why when Winston returned to the Admiralty in 1939 for his second term as First Lord he brought a supply of specially printed red tags marked 'Action This Day'.

Lest too bleak a picture emerge, mention must be made of an outstandingly bold raid into the Gulf of Heligoland, the backyard of the German navy where the Elbe and Weser rivers and the western end of the strategic Kiel Canal feed into the North Sea. On 28 August a trap was sprung by converging British forces including a squadron of battle-cruisers commanded by Beatty, which sank three German light cruisers and badly damaged three more. Serious 'friendly fire' losses were only narrowly avoided, and a more complete victory was not gained, because of atrocious staff work. 'Several awkward embarrassments followed from this,' Churchill wrote many years later. 'However fortune was steady and the initial surprise, together with the resolute offensive, carried us safely through.'[21] Admiral Gretton comments that 'the remarkable feature of the official papers is the complete lack of self-criticism by the War Staff'.[22] Another success veiling a near-disaster was the action at the Dogger Bank on 24 January when the Admiralty's newly acquired signals intelligence section permitted Beatty with five battle-cruisers to pounce on Admiral Hipper with three, accompanied by the hybrid heavy cruiser *Blücher*.[23] Battle damage to the British flagship, bad signalling and lack of initiative among subordinate commanders resulted in an overkill of the hapless *Blücher*, while the other three escaped.

Winston was more personally to blame for the Grand Fleet being forced to move from its designated base at Scapa Flow in the Orkneys, where it was open to submarine attack, after war had been declared. He had decided that the current flowing through the narrow entrance by which he entered the anchorage in the Admiralty yacht *Enchantress* was too strong for a submarine to negotiate; what he did not know was that there

161

was another, broader channel.[24] Early recognition that Scapa Flow's vulnerability to submarine attack made it unsuitable for use as the Grand Fleet's base, or firm direction on appropriate anti-submarine measures would have helped, but neither were forthcoming. When the Grand Fleet moved to Lough Swilly, an alternative base in Northern Ireland, the dreadnought *Audacious* struck a mine and sank, happily without loss of life. Scapa Flow remained vulnerable even in World War II, and on 14 October 1939 *U-47* daringly entered it to sink the battleship *Royal Oak* with the loss of 833 of her crew.

In *The World Crisis* Winston sneered at Admiral Jellicoe for 'deducting any ship which had any defect however temporary' while crediting the Germans with more 'than we now know they had, or were then thought likely to have'.[25] The loss to a single mine of one of the *Orion/King George V* class, the backbone of the Grand Fleet, betrayed structural flaws that should also have preyed on the mind of the First Lord, particularly as the newly joined *Iron Duke* class was suffering from serious teething problems. The sinking of *Audacious* was not admitted until after the war because the margin of superiority over hostile fleets was well below the margin believed to be essential.[26] One must conclude that Winston coldly maligned Jellicoe because to do otherwise would have required an admission that the navy was far from 'ready' in 1914.

While it may be argued that Winston was let down by subordinates, he had been a minister long enough to know that simply pulling a lever did not necessarily result in action. If the First Sea Lord (Admiral Prince Louis of Battenberg, until replaced by Fisher on 30 October 1914), his staff and the area commanders involved in these disasters can be faulted for not doing their jobs properly, then by the same token their civilian master can justly be criticized for his failure to set priorities and to ensure they were implemented. As regards *Goeben* he compounded his failure to think things through by intervening directly at the operational level, when the whole point of the reorganization of the Admiralty was that all such directives should have come from the First Sea Lord and his staff. Finally, the massacre at Coronel (for it was nothing less) cannot be wholly divorced from the fact that Winston left the Admiralty during October 1914 to become personally involved in the defence of Antwerp, when, rather like Stephen Leacock's Lord Ronald, he flung himself upon his horse and rode off madly in all directions.[27] Even Winston's partisans in the navy were alarmed by what they saw as grandstanding at a time when so much was at stake in his own bailiwick.[28]

As so often when dealing with this protean man, one would judge him more kindly if it were not that his own version of events laid a false trail away from his lapses to concentrate attention elsewhere.[29] Whether or not the port of Antwerp fell sooner or later to the German armies that had just swept across Belgium was not his responsibility; what should have been attracting his attention was that the ships and men of the Royal Navy abroad and at home were needlessly exposed to danger. Instead, Winston rushed an ad hoc division consisting of Royal Marines and two recently formed brigades of untrained naval volunteers to reinforce the Belgian defenders of Antwerp; much of this Naval Division would end up interned in the Netherlands for the rest of the war. When Winston joined them in early October he sent a signal to Asquith which read in part: 'I am willing to resign my office and undertake command of relieving and defensive forces assigned to Antwerp in conjunction with the Belgian Army, provided I am given necessary military rank and authority, and full powers of commander of a detached force in the field.'[30] This was greeted in Cabinet with 'Homeric laughter', although Kitchener, appointed Secretary of State for War on 3 August, expressed an apparently sincere willingness to give him the rank of lieutenant general. But Asquith sharply ordered Winston back to London.

One has to walk a fine line in assessing the Antwerp initiative. Militarily, as is suggested by Kitchener's approval, it was worth making a relatively small commitment to increase German concerns for their exposed northern flank. It covered the retreat of the Belgian field army and may have helped the Allies win the race for Dunkirk, although the regular infantry division and the cavalry division sent by Kitchener to Ostend and Zeebrugge at this time were probably the decisive factor. The fact that all these troop movements (and, indeed, the main British Expeditionary Force's move to France) were carried out without the interference of the German navy also infers a proper performance of the duties assigned to the Royal Navy in pre-war planning, and the Heligoland battle had played a major role in securing moral dominance over the German surface fleet. Winston's personal fearlessness, too, was an inspiration to the confused young men of the Naval Division. But it was not his job to be there, and his offer to surrender control over the largest military force available to Britain in order to take command of a certainly doomed defence is a damning comment on his sense of proportion. Winston was a gambler, the antithesis of a chess player. Indeed, his favourite games were roulette and backgammon, where a quick assessment of the odds allied to blind chance can lead to instant gratification. There are undoubtedly moments in even the largest battles when resolute action by a small number may tip the balance. Antwerp was not one of them. Unfortunately this was something that Winston was never able to accept in his heart, whatever his mind and his pen might say.

During his ten wartime months at the Admiralty, Winston was responsible for some solid achievements. Although the idea of a caterpillar-tracked armoured combat vehicle came from the official journalist to the British army, Colonel Ernest Swinton (later Professor of Military History at Oxford), and was first adopted by Colonel Maurice Hankey, Secretary to the Committee of Imperial Defence, Winston put Admiralty money into what was, for that reason, originally designated a 'land ship'. He remained heavily enthused with the project even after he left the government and deserves the credit he claimed for the development of the tank.[31] The same can be said for the development of military aviation, where again the early and judicious employment of Admiralty resources enabled the Royal Navy to accept responsibility for the aerial defence of Britain in

1914. As a result:

> the Royal Naval Air Service, when it was absorbed by the Royal Air Force in 1918, was the largest and most efficient air force in the world. By his active encouragement and forthright methods Churchill cut red tape, dispelled mistrust and helped to produce miracles. He must be credited with a considerable share in a remarkable achievement.[32]

But sadly the energy and fiscal sleight of hand Winston employed to overcome departmental rivalries and institutional conservatism in the advancement of projects that actively engaged his interest was not in evidence for more vital matters that did not, such as the defences and shore facilities at Scapa Flow and Rosyth. He had a quick but superficial intelligence, which at times did not distinguish between the vital and the circumstantial. Such evidence of deep strategic thinking as emerges from *The World Crisis* tends to take the form of post hoc justification for initiatives either aborted or which failed at the practical level. Far and away the most significant of the latter was the attempt to force the narrow straits known as the Dardanelles with the aim of getting British ships through to Constantinople and securing a Turkish surrender. It began as a purely naval operation in March 1915, expanded to amphibious landings in April and dragged on at the expense of 265,000 Allied casualties, 46,000 of them fatal, until the final evacuation in January 1916. In mid-May 1915 it precipitated the resignation of Fisher followed by Winston's removal from the Admiralty and from the central direction of the war. After his death Clemmie confided in Martin Gilbert, 'the Dardanelles haunted him for the rest of his life. He always believed in it. When he left the Admiralty he thought he was finished. I thought he would never get over the Dardanelles; I thought he would die of grief.'[33]

The result has been that a relatively minor episode in a cataclysmic war has received disproportionate attention from historians, when its deeper significance lies in its effect on a man who would later achieve the eminence he aspired to, and in the distrust of his judgement that was to doom other major operations in a later, even greater war. Part of the responsibility for this lay with Winston, who protested far too much. *The World Crisis* did not pretend to be a work of history.[34] It was originally intended to set the record straight on his time at the Admiralty and on the Dardanelles (the first two volumes), and Winston specifically disclaimed 'the position of the historian. It is not for me with my record and special point of view to pronounce a final conclusion. That must be left to others and to other times.'[35] But the broad scope of the work, and above all its selective reproduction of documents that would otherwise have been subject to the 50-year rule, renders the disclaimer moot. It fully merited Stanley Baldwin's jibe, in 1929, that Winston had written a five-volume autobiography and called it the history of the world.[36] There is a limit to how much egomania even a well-inclined biographer can stomach, and I regret that *The World Crisis* exceeds my own appetite.

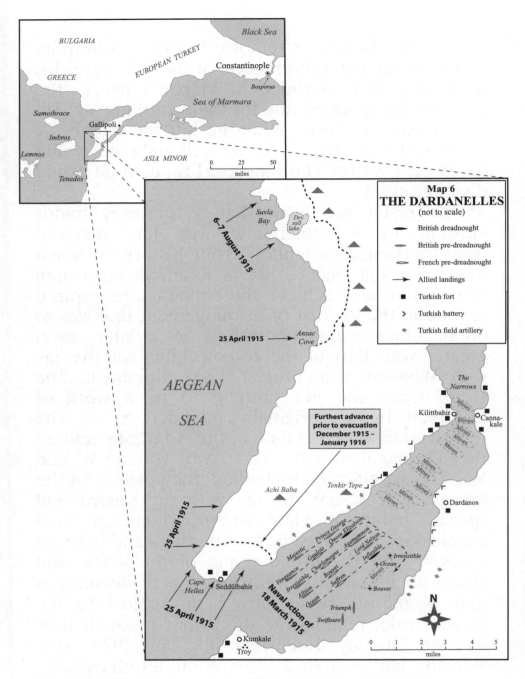

The Gallipoli campaign originated in an Allied attempt to force the Dardanelles and reach Constantinople and the Black Sea (top). After the failure of a naval attack troops were landed at Cape Helles and Anzac Cove on 25 April, and at Suvla Bay on 6–7 August but failed to seize the peninsula (bottom).

Michael Howard characteristically cut to the heart of the matter when he wrote, 'few historians would now claim that any help reaching Russia as a result of defeating Turkey could have turned the scale on the Eastern Front: the problems of the Russian Army, and the Russian Imperial regime, were too deep-rooted to be solved by short-term material or financial help'.[37] It is also worth pondering whence, in view of the serious shortages being experienced by the Allies on the Western Front, this material assistance was meant to have come. In retrospect, the strategic case for the advance on Constantinople via the Dardanelles was flawed. But at the time it seemed to offer an attractive alternative to what was already being seen as stalemate on the Western Front. On 29 December 1914 Winston wrote to Asquith that 'some alternative' must be found to 'sending our armies to chew barbed wire in Flanders'.[38] After the war Major General Sir Charles Calwell, author of *Small Wars* (1896) and *Military Operations and Maritime Preponderance* (1905), which are still considered relevant in staff colleges today, wrote of his experiences after being recalled from retirement in 1914 to serve as Director of Military Operations and Intelligence. He judged that peripheral operations were irresistibly attractive to politicians because it is in their nature to gravitate 'towards what they imagine to be the line of least resistance'. The peripheral strategy advocated by Winston, Lloyd George and others rested on

the fallacy that the Western Front represented the enemy's strongest point. It was, on the contrary, the enemy's weakest point, because

169

this front was from its geographical position the one where British and French troops could most easily be assembled, and it was the one on which a serious defeat to the enemy necessarily threatened that enemy with grave, if not irretrievable, disaster.[39]

The Dardanelles fiasco amply illustrated that you cannot 'muddle through' a major undertaking in the face of a determined enemy. I do not generally subscribe to the view that World War I generals were donkeys, but there were more long ears and plaintive brays at Gallipoli than I care to admit. Leaving aside the cascade of errors in appreciation, planning and execution that characterized the land operations, for which Winston was blameless, let us look instead at the preceding naval assault, for which he was partly responsible. There was an early bombardment, alerting the Turks to the danger that an attempt might be made on the Dardanelles and enabling them to reinforce the straits, although it was indeed a puzzle to them and their German advisers that any sane person would wish to sail through 28 miles of narrow water with both banks in hostile hands. The operation was posited on the belief that Turkish resistance would collapse if a fleet broke through to the Sea of Marmara and brought Constantinople under threat of bombardment. But if it did not the fleet could find its line of retreat cut off, and end up as little more than unneeded reinforcements for the Russian Black Sea Fleet.[40]

On 18 March the attempt to storm the straits by ships alone ran into a newly laid string of mines after a successful penetration of 9 miles, as far as

Dardanos. The French pre-dreadnought *Bouvet* was lost catastrophically with 660 men, followed to the bottom more sedately, and thus at less human cost, by her British equivalents *Irresistible* and *Ocean*. *Suffren* and *Gaulois*, two other old French battleships, were seriously damaged, as was the battle-cruiser *Inflexible*, which had no business being there. Nor, in the rapidly changing opinion of Jacky Fisher, should the brand-new *Queen Elizabeth* have been exposed to such danger. The story after this is usually told as one of Fisher betraying Winston, but in fact it was the other way around. Fisher, who had been enthusiastic for the venture when Winston was still hesitant, had always conceived of it as a combined operation. He was persuaded to try the 'ships alone' approach by an assurance that, if serious resistance were encountered, the whole operation could more easily be cancelled if there were no troops ashore. What is more, Winston had sold the plan to the Cabinet as though speaking for a unanimous Admiralty, and Fisher did not feel he could contradict him. He did, however, write to Asquith to express his misgivings, and after he walked out of a Cabinet meeting on 28 January Lloyd George hastened after him to persuade him not to resign. Asquith did not circulate Fisher's memorandum, and Lloyd George made light of his too frequent threats of resignation, so although technically the Cabinet was not properly informed, the members who mattered were fully aware of what Winston was up to.

Winston nagged Fisher and other senior officers until they gave way. The then Captain William 'Blinker' Hall, Director of Naval Intelligence, recalled after an exhausting session 'the odd feeling that although it would be wholly against my will, I should in a very short while be agreeing with everything he said'. He began to mutter his own name until at last Winston asked him what he was saying. 'I'm saying that my name is Hall because if I listen to you much longer I shall be convinced that it's Brown.'[41] To his credit, Winston laughed and let the matter drop. But although he might win the arguments by attrition he failed to persuade, and matters came to a head after *Goliath*, another old battleship, was lost with 570 men to an attack by a Turkish torpedo boat in the straits on 13 May. Two days later, on receipt of a proposal from Churchill to send more ships to the Dardanelles than they had agreed the previous evening, Fisher at last resigned and told Andrew Bonar Law, the leader of the Conservatives, why he was doing so.[42] At the same time reports in *The Times* of a shell shortage on the Western Front presaged a major scandal, and Asquith received a letter from the young Venetia Stanley, with whom he had been infatuated for five years, telling him that she intended to marry Edwin Montagu, once Asquith's Parliamentary Private Secretary and now in the Cabinet as Chancellor of the Duchy of Lancaster (essentially a Minister without Portfolio). Asquith was shattered, and his indulgent tolerance of Winston finally evaporated.

Winston struggled desperately to cling on to office, and was deeply shocked to find how vehemently he was disliked on both sides of the House. Between 18 and 21 May he wrote five letters to Asquith pleading to remain in the government, to which Clemmie added a personal note containing the much-quoted words: 'Winston may in your eyes and in those with whom he has to work have faults but he has the supreme quality which I venture to say very few of your present or future Cabinet possess, the power, the imagination, the deadliness to fight Germany.'[43] Asquith thought her intervention (which sounds so Churchillian that we may suspect Winston's hand in it) the work of a 'maniac', and added contemptuously that 'the situation for Churchill has no other meaning than his own prospects'.[44]

This was the pot calling the kettle black with a vengeance, for Asquith himself was no more able to rise above the misery of his rejection by Venetia Stanley than he had proved capable of responding to the challenge of war. In a half-hearted gesture in the direction of forming a national coalition, whose prime purpose was to shore up his own position, Asquith brought in the Conservatives Arthur Balfour at the Admiralty, Bonar Law as Colonial Secretary and Austen Chamberlain at the India Office, moved Lloyd George to create a new Ministry of Munitions and replaced him at the Exchequer with Reginald McKenna, giving the Home Office to the Solicitor General Sir John Simon, the last two being Asquith loyalists who had been urging him to dump Winston. A last spiteful flourish was to sack Montagu and give Winston the powerless Duchy of Lancaster, enabling a cartoonist to depict Winston enquiring where Lancaster was and what a duchy might be.

Admiral Gretton's summary of Winston's first spell at the Admiralty concludes 'that *someone* had to take action to provide the imagination so lacking, to inculcate the spirit of the offensive and

173

above all, to build up an efficient machine for the direction of operations'.[45] But although Winston had had three peacetime years at the head of an intensely hierarchical institution to prepare it for war he signally failed to 'build up an efficient machine for the direction of operations', not least by his dependence on Fisher, who was averse to the whole idea of a staff. As to inculcating the spirit of the offensive, Winston repeatedly intervened to prevent Fisher sacking senior officers who had failed the test of combat; this was in contrast to his own vindictiveness towards Troubridge, whose disgrace served to conceal Winston's share of responsibility for the escape of *Goeben* and *Breslau*. Nor was Clemmie's assessment of Winston's deadliness wholly correct: the Dardanelles operation was actually a flinch away from the harsh reality of the Western Front, not a strike at the jugular.

The case for the defence rests heavily on the argument that anyone else would have done worse. We cannot know, just as we cannot know whether the German High Seas Fleet might have prevailed had it sought a trial of strength in 1914, when all except two of the ships with which it fought Jutland were in service and when the British Grand Fleet had fled the submarine menace to Lough Swilly, lacked the *Queen Elizabeth* class and the '*R*' class, and had ships of doubtful battle-worthiness in the *Iron Duke* and vessels of the *Orion* and *King George V* classes. 'What ifs' are two-edged: it is pointless to speculate about what might have happened if only the errors committed by one side had been avoided.[46]

The poor performance of the entire British political elite in war and in the wasted peace that followed is the subject of Chapter Five. To draw the line under Winston's first venture into military management, a comparison with the work of Richard Haldane at the War Office in 1906–12 is instructive. Haldane came to the job after the Boer War had woken the army to its deficiencies and in the wake of a number of failed initiatives by his Conservative predecessors. The idea of a Committee of Imperial Defence (CID) had been accepted in 1902; in 1904, after the publication of a damning report on the conduct of the war, a bipartisan committee named for its chairman, Viscount Esher, recommended the creation of a General Staff as well as the creation of a secretariat for a CID chaired by the Prime Minister and including the Foreign and Colonial Secretaries and the Chancellor of the Exchequer. Under Haldane, in September 1906 a Special Army Order defined the remit of the General Staff as 'to advise on the strategical distribution of the army, to supervise the education of officers, and the training and preparation of the army for war, to study military schemes, offensive and defensive, to collect and collate military intelligence, to direct the general policy in army matters, and to secure continuity of action in the execution of that policy'. It is as well to ponder why the need for such an organization had not been recognized long before.[47]

Having done so, it will be better appreciated what a towering mountain Asquith asked Winston to climb at the Admiralty, which had not been shaken by defeat in battle, had not been scrutinized by the Esher Committee and regarded itself as independent of and equal in status to the CID. Haldane's process of reorganization was eight years

175

old in 1914, but even so its products were badly buckled by the heat of war. Much of what Winston might have instituted in a mere three years would have suffered the same fate. The Britain of those days was a pre-modern society, and its military institutions faithfully reflected the nexus from which they sprang and which they existed to protect. This said, Winston clearly fell between the two stools of directive control and order command. He neither set clear priorities, leaving it to his subordinates to implement his orders according to their judgement, nor did he ensure that operations were conducted exactly as he wished—something he certainly had the energy and application to do if he had only concentrated on matters that fell within his ministerial competence. In a word he dabbled in this and that, never doing any one thing thoroughly and inclined to ignore the trees of his particular duty in favour of the wood of grand policy.

This was a function not of his character but of the intoxication of power, for when, having decided to return to the army, he took command of the 6th Royal Scots Fusiliers on the Western Front at the beginning of 1916 he showed a real mastery of leadership:

> After a very brief period he had accelerated the morale of officers and men to an almost unbelievable degree. It was sheer personality. We laughed at a lot of things he did, but there were many other things we did not laugh at for we knew they were sound. He had a unique approach which did wonders to us. He let everyone under his command see that he

was responsible, from the very moment he arrived, that they understood not only what they were supposed to do, but why they had to do it. No detail of our daily life was too small for him to ignore. He overlooked nothing. Instead of a quick glance at what was being done he would stop and talk with everyone and probe to the bottom of every activity. I have never known an officer take such pains to inspire confidence or to gain confidence; indeed he inspired confidence in gaining it.[48]

Even making allowance for the fact that this is the impression of an 18-year-old lieutenant recalled over half a century later in the light of Winston's subsequent apotheosis, it rings true and demands an explanation for the failure of these qualities to infuse the Admiralty with his spirit in 1911–15. The answer is twofold: first, the practical power of a battalion commander over his officers and men is vastly greater than that of a minister over his department; second, winning the affection and trust of young men whose lives depend on you is a very different proposition to persuading old men that the way they have always done things is obsolete. Martin Gilbert has dispelled one of the most cherished myths concerning Winston's involvement with the navy: it seems he never snorted that its traditions were 'rum, sodomy—and the lash'. Gilbert has also found no trace of the signal 'Winston is back', allegedly sent around the fleet when he returned to the Admiralty at the beginning of World War II, though Arthur Marder asserts otherwise.[49] Winston was a traditionalist, and while in 1939, at the start of his second term as

First Lord, he was an improvement on his immediate predecessor (James, Earl Stanhope, inevitably known as 'No Hope'), the Admiralty was naturally inclined to reserve judgement on a man the term 'loose cannon on the deck' might have been coined to describe.

Winston served at the Admiralty again for only a short spell, between September that year and May 1940 when he became Prime Minister, and it is worth departing from strict chronology to link this second tour of duty with his previous one. The links were strong, but not generally helpful. Throughout World War II the Royal Navy paid a heavy price for the baggage of resentments and operational misconceptions which, coexisting bizarrely with a profound appreciation of what had gone wrong at the level of political direction, he brought with him from his experience of World War I. One of the least true encomiums in Sir John Wheeler-Bennett's collection of short memoirs by officials who worked with Winston is the breathtaking assertion by Lord Bridges, Secretary to the Cabinet throughout the war, that 'I cannot recollect a single minister, serving officer or civil servant who was removed from office because he stood up to Churchill.'[50] He could be vindictive towards those who thwarted him, and the only reason more heads did not roll was that most of those close to him were aware of it and adjusted their behaviour accordingly. Admirals, annoyingly masters of their own domain and given to the very blunt speech Winston is supposed to have admired, attracted his particular ire. The First Sea Lord, Sir Dudley Pound, rapidly discovered that 'standing up to Churchill' in naval matters brought out the worst in him; he therefore adopted the prudent habit of agreeing in principle and then letting evidence accumulate of the practical impossibility of Winston's wilder schemes. When Pound died in harness in October 1943 he was succeeded by Sir Andrew Cunningham, lately commander-in-chief Mediterranean, who resolutely blocked Winston's impractical schemes with a good deal less subtlety. Richard Ollard, whose invaluable *Fisher and Cunningham: A Study of the Personalities of the Churchill Era* is gentler than he might have been to Winston, mildly comments that 'the ghost of Jacky Fisher and the nightmare of his own dismissal haunted his mind'.[51]

The legacy of an undigested past was plain in Winston's first initiative on his return to the Admiralty on the outbreak of World War II. This was a revival, code-named Catherine, of Fisher's pet project for a charge into the Baltic to mount an invasion of Germany—wildly impractical even in 1914 and frankly insane in 1939, when the Luftwaffe would have sunk every ship.[52] In fairness, with the exception of the Japanese Admiral Yamamoto and perhaps a few others there was not, before the war and in some cases well into it, any senior naval officer in any of the world's navies who would have disagreed with the following, written by Winston in 1937:

I do not myself believe that well-built modern warships properly defended by armour and anti-aircraft guns, especially when steaming in company, are likely to fall prey to hostile aircraft. Battleships which are built to withstand the plunging fire of the heaviest cannon should be able to endure the bombs of aeroplanes. . . . This and many other features have led the British Admiralty and all the other Admiralties to believe that the battleship, and the power to draw out a superior line, still constitute the only trustworthy foundations of sea power. This, if true, is of the highest importance to the British Empire and the United States, each of which possesses a battle fleet superior to the present battle fleet strength of all the other Naval Powers combined.[53]

However, Winston's refusal to recognize the vulnerability of warships to air attack was maintained in denial of much contrary evidence during the war. And his willingness to put the navy in harm's way was directly responsible for the loss of *Prince of Wales* and *Repulse* off the coast of Malaya on 10 December 1941.

It must also be noted that he had a blind spot about the true nature of anti-submarine warfare, despite recognizing that the U-boats alone brought Britain perilously close to outright defeat in 1917 and 1943. In 1937 he had written, 'the technical discoveries since the war have placed the submarine in a position of far less strength and far greater danger than was apparent even at the moment when the U-boat warfare was decisively mastered'.[54] Even in 1939, belatedly realizing how bare the anti-submarine cupboard had become, he could still write:

The U-boats . . . would be a serious inconvenience and injury to British commerce in case of war. But the methods of dealing with submersible craft have been developed out of all measure, and provided the British flotillas and anti-submarine craft are multiplied on high priority and a large scale, there is no reason to believe that the U-boat will be a decisive weapon.[55]

In *The World Crisis* he claimed for Lloyd George the credit for forcing the Admiralty to adopt the convoy system, an argument of dubious merit but given some weight by the fact that the Admiralty did not, as it should have done, at once revert to a system employed with success in past wars with maritime powers.[56] This makes it all the more remarkable that, after returning to the Admiralty in 1939, Winston argued for the relaxation of convoy discipline to free up escorts to act as hunter-killer groups. Admiral Gretton selects a telling footnote from *The Second World War* to demonstrate that

he never understood the functions of the support groups that were [eventually] formed in late 1942 and early 1943. They were intended to strengthen the escort of convoys . . . or, when *accurate* intelligence of a U-boat was known, to seek it out and destroy it. Support groups never aimlessly swept the ocean; they were kept in positions from which they could best reinforce convoys, and it was near convoys that they scored their greatest successes.[57]

In September 1939 the aircraft carriers *Ark Royal*

and *Courageous* were involved in a so-called anti-submarine sweep west-southwest of Ireland. The U-boats found them instead. On the 14th only malfunctioning German torpedoes saved *Ark Royal* from *U-39*, which was sunk by her escorts, but on the 17th *Courageous* was successfully attacked by *U-29* and lost with 518 men. The *déjà vu* of the circumstances in which *Royal Oak* was lost at Scapa Flow in October has already been noted, and a further echo of 1914 came when the fleet flagship *Nelson* was disabled by a mine when entering the alternative base at Loch Ewe. On 8 June 1940 the aircraft carrier *Glorious* and her escorting destroyers were sunk in the Norwegian Sea, with the loss of over 1500 men, by the German battle-cruisers *Gneisenau* and *Scharnhorst*.[58] This episode and the ensuing cover-up, maintained indefinitely in the teeth of overwhelming proof to the contrary, was the inspiration for *Ministries of Deceptions* by Tim Slessor, whose father was among those killed.

There is a macabre symmetry about the life and death of *Courageous* and *Glorious*: both were laid down as hybrid battle-cruisers during the Winston/Fisher regime at the Admiralty; both were converted to carry aircraft, the weapon with which Winston is most associated; and both were needlessly exposed to danger and lost when he was again First Lord. It is ironic (and proof, if any more were needed, that Winston was lucky) that the Norwegian campaign, of which the loss of *Glorious* was an almost unbearably apt coda, precipitated a political crisis that ended with him becoming Prime Minister.

Winston had pressed the government to take offensive action against Germany during the

'Phoney War'. One of his pet schemes, codenamed Operation Royal Marine was to float mines down the Rhine River. He was also anxious to intervene in the Baltic or Scandinavia, primarily to check Germany's import of Swedish iron ore, and in December he told the War Cabinet that stopping iron ore traffic from Sweden, across Norway and down through Norwegian territorial waters would rank as 'a major offensive operation of the war'. But both Sweden and Norway were neutral, and there was every chance that Germany would strive to pre-empt an Allied move. Although Winston's proposal was turned down, it was followed by a lengthy period of discussion, and by February 1940 there was widespread support for a landing in the Norwegian port of Narvik to seize the ore fields and then help the Finns, whose struggle against Russia was reaching its climax.

In mid-February Winston ordered HMS *Cossack* to board the German submarine supply ship *Altmark* in Norwegian waters and free the British prisoners aboard her. The operation's success gave an enormous fillip to his popularity, and Martin Gilbert observed that it 'marked a high point of Churchill's work as First Lord'. It also encouraged the French and British to amble ahead with their plans to invade Norway: commanders were appointed in early March, and a decision to land there followed soon afterwards. In one sense this was already too late, for the Finns asked the Russians for terms on 13 March. At the end of the month the Allied Supreme War Council agreed that Norwegian territorial waters would be mined on 5 April, and that a landing would follow.

These plans, shot through with the infirmity of

purpose that so characterized Allied activities at this stage in the war, failed miserably. The Germans pre-empted them, invading both Denmark and Norway, and although the Norwegians fought back stoutly, sinking several warships, when Allied troops eventually landed they were hammered by the Luftwaffe. Only at Narvik was there real success. The ten German destroyers that had taken a mountain division there were all sunk, and the Allies eventually secured the port, though they evacuated it in June.

This lacklustre campaign was crisply summarized by Major General Hastings 'Pug' Ismay, Secretary to the Committee of Imperial Defence at the time, and from May 1940 the indispensable chief of staff to Winston as Minister of Defence:

> The worst shortcomings of the First World War, as exemplified by the conduct of the Dardanelles campaign, were faithfully repeated. The Chief of Naval Staff and the Chief of the Imperial General Staff acted with sturdy independence. They appointed their respective commanders without consultation with each other; and, worse still, they gave directives to these commanders without harmonizing them. Thereafter they continued to issue separate orders to them.[59]

True as far as it goes, this assessment skirts the matter of Winston's close involvement, although perhaps Ismay judged the comparison with the Dardanelles to be sufficient. Piers Mackesy, like Slessor a son with a close personal reason to dig to

184

the bottom of the matter, accurately described Winston's account of one part of the Norwegian campaign, in Volume II of *The Second World War*, as 'cast in a framework of factual inaccuracy, of careful innuendo, and of inconsistencies'.[60] Stephen Roskill extends that to the entire operation, underlining at every step how Winston's understanding of naval operations had stuck fast in 1915.[61] Arthur Marder concluded that 'there can be no dispute about Churchill's strong influence on the inept overall strategy' or about his responsibility for constant changes of plan affecting not only the fleet but the overall conduct of combined operations.[62] Roskill disagreed with Marder only in the matter of whether the interventions that disrupted naval operations and undermined the chain of command can be attributed to 'the Admiralty', when there is abundant evidence that they were the personal initiatives of Winston, unmediated by the staff for whose genesis he claimed credit in *The World Crisis*, but whose functioning existence in 1939–40 he seems to have regarded as of no consequence.

There was a bright lining to the otherwise dark cloud of the Norwegian campaign: the German navy came out in force and suffered crippling losses. A heavy cruiser, two light cruisers, a gunnery training ship, ten modern destroyers, three minesweepers, eight U-boats, three torpedo boats, 11 transports and four fleet auxiliaries were sunk. Two battle-cruisers, a heavy cruiser, a pocket battleship, a light cruiser, a gunnery training ship and two transports were severely damaged and another transport captured. The operational German surface fleet at the end of the campaign was reduced to three cruisers, three destroyers and 19 torpedo boats. British and other Allied losses were also heavy, but as a proportion of the forces available the Germans suffered a naval defeat almost on a par with losses inflicted on the Allies in the Japanese sweep of the East Indies in 1941–2, and as a result there could be no question of the Germans contesting control of the Channel in combined operations following the fall of France in May–June 1940.

I had no idea when embarking on the research for this chapter that a narrow focus on Winston's involvement with the navy would produce such a catalogue of deception designed to divert attention from so many stubbornly maintained errors, often stemming from overweening conceit. We all carry the memory of past mistakes, which, if we are honest with ourselves, can prove the foundations of wisdom. The harmful ones are those that we dare not look at plainly: these may lead to an edifice of denial that can distort our future behaviour. There are strong indications that Winston's experience at the Admiralty in 1914–15 helped define the attitudes he maintained towards his admirals and the employment of sea power during World War II; those attitudes were, respectively, petulant and unsound. The errors and omissions in *The World Crisis* may perhaps be excused as personal propaganda employed to maintain a public stature that, in the end, proved redemptive. But the same cannot be said for the distortions of the truth in *The Second World War*, which largely ignored the chronic social, economic and military-doctrinal backwardness that diminished Britain's contribution to the war.

CHAPTER FIVE

THE GREAT BETRAYAL

1914–1929

The Roman military writer Vegetius advised his countrymen that if they wished for peace, they should prepare for war. Almost two thousand years later, on two occasions separated by a mere quarter-century, the rulers of the largest empire the world has ever seen committed the peoples they governed to major wars for which they were neither physically nor mentally prepared. Following World War I the British rapidly discarded the alliances and the military organization that had won them eminence, and with them the means to fight another world war. Domestically, the self-destruction of the Liberal Party left the field to the Conservatives, themselves in search of an identity, and a Labour movement promoted prematurely into the role of principal opposition party. The policy-making vacuum was filled by officials who were overwhelmingly Liberal in sympathy, and so, although the Tories were overtly the dominant party between the world wars, in practice both foreign and domestic agendas fell between the stools of libertarian 'old' and statist 'new' liberalism. Ineffectual though British public policy during this period may seem, democratically elected rulers in other industrialized societies enjoyed no better success, and some performed so dismally that they lost control of events and were replaced by authoritarian regimes.

As a leading figure in the Liberal government that took the country to war in 1914 Winston shares responsibility for committing a small all-volunteer army to battle amid conscript behemoths, and for persisting in voluntary recruiting until 1916; the result was that the human cost of the war fell disproportionately on the most public-spirited. The reason for this can be traced to December 1905 when the Conservative Foreign Secretary, Lord Lansdowne, authorized secret talks between British and French army staffs. Following the Liberal electoral landslide a month later Lansdowne's successor Sir Edward Grey, with the concurrence of both parties' leaders, Campbell-Bannerman and Asquith, gave permission for the talks to continue without seeking Cabinet approval. This was the root of British involvement in World War I. Many further steps down the slippery slope, and without a formal commitment ever having been made, Asquith's government felt honour-bound to send the British army to fight alongside the French against German aggression. There was also a geopolitical imperative: both the Conservative and Liberal leaders, with the German battleship-building programme in mind, saw this clearly. However, Grey and Asquith made no effort to win support for a policy pursued behind the backs of their supporters. In one sense they were fortunate that the Germans did indeed violate Belgian neutrality in 1914, providing a credible *casus belli*.

Winston was privy to the negotiations with France by September 1911 at the latest, but neither their substance nor their secrecy appears to have perturbed him. He should have remembered his own words in 1901 about Brodrick's proposal for a British Expeditionary Force, which 'would scarcely serve as a vanguard' in a war with a great land power: it could contribute nothing to national security but would 'very likely make us venturesome'. So it proved. Only large-scale preparation for a land war and a public commitment to fight alongside the French might have exercised a deterrent effect on the German General Staff. Since such preparations were politically impossible, then in all conscience the French and the Russians should have been told that they must choose to fight, or not, with the assurance only of traditional British naval and financial support; this might have deterred them. Once war was joined it meant Haldane's regulars, regular reservists and the part-time Territorials, who together might have provided the cadres for a greatly expanded fighting force, were sacrificed to buy time while an army of millions was extemporized. On the one hand, the story of the British army in World War I is indeed the triumphant tale of the forging of the greatest citizen army in the nation's history. But it is also true, on the other, that this army's agonizing learning curve would be charted by far fewer crosses if its staggering expansion had been properly prepared for. There was a wide gap between the implications of foreign policy and the abilities of defence policy, and for that politicians, not military leaders, were primarily to blame. However, those politicians anxious to evade their own responsibility for the outbreak and duration of World War I, Winston among them, penned

189

memoirs that heaped the blame on the generals.

Whatever we may say about the old ruling class of Britain, that narrow segment of which Winston himself was so much a part, it went to its death with courage. Thirty-two peerages and 35 baronetcies became extinct in 1914–20, not all as a result of the war, although some 300 peers or their eldest sons (of 1500 who served) were killed or died as a result of war service. The 1914–15 battlefields of Flanders have some cause to be regarded as the cemetery of the pre-war aristocracy.[1] The gentry were heavily concentrated in the Territorials and, although they were specifically excluded from service abroad, in 1914 the great majority voted to go overseas and in the process suffered dreadful losses: 47 heirs to peerages were killed in action before the end of the year. Double death duties levied when a father and heir died soon after each other crippled many landed estates, and 25 per cent of land in England and Wales changed hands in 1918–21. Another, probably more significant, change was the decline in the participation of the gentry in public life. With so many of the sons who traditionally stood for Parliament still serving in the armed forces, the candidates for the 1918 election tended to be older men with backgrounds in business. The character of politics changed so greatly thereafter that the squirearchy never really got back into it.[2]

Winston himself, a regular cavalry officer early in his life and then a Territorial (in the Queen's Own Oxfordshire Hussars) after the Boer War, ran the risks that distinguished his class and generation. Just as he had begun to make his reputation in war, when his career faltered after the Dardanelles fiasco he sought to recoup himself

190

by again leading men in battle and therefore volunteered for service in his Territorial rank of major. In the interval between losing office and volunteering he had not spoken in the House and showed all the symptoms of his 'black dog' depressions, from which not even painting, taken up specifically to relax his fevered brain, could free him. He had had to move out of Admiralty House and now rented the delightful Hoe Farm, near Godalming in Surrey, a precursor, though on a much smaller scale, to Chartwell. But he could not bear to look and feel irrelevant to the war. Winston was on good terms with the commander-in-chief of the British Expeditionary Force, Field Marshal Sir John French, who had enjoyed his hospitality aboard *Enchantress*. On 18 November 1915 he was staying in a château near French's headquarters at St-Omer in northern France when the field marshal offered him command of a brigade, then consisting of four infantry battalions with an overall strength of some four thousand men. Winston asked to be attached to a front-line unit to gain experience first, and was duly posted to 2nd Battalion The Grenadier Guards, still tangibly 'old army' and commanded by that grenadier of grenadiers, Lieutenant Colonel 'Ma' Jeffreys, near Neuve Chapelle.[3]

The attachment began inauspiciously. Jeffreys drily pointed out that they 'were not at all consulted' in the matter of Winston's posting. He had arrived with a mass of impedimenta and was curtly informed that most of it would be left behind in billets: for his first tour of duty in the trenches his servant managed to secure his shaving gear and a spare pair of socks. However, his hosts soon

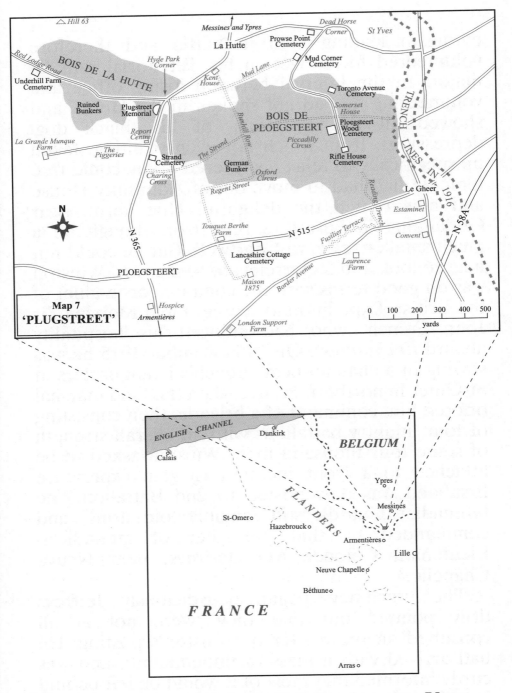

The Ploegsteert sector lay in Belgium between Ypres and Armentières (bottom). During Churchill's time in command of 6th Royal Scots Fusiliers his headquarters was in Laurence Farm, south of Ploegsteert Wood (top). Lancashire Cottage Cemetery contains the graves of several of his soldiers.

realized that Winston genuinely wished to be treated as the infantry officer he now was rather than the politician he had been, and relations improved. But it was hard for his seniors not to remember that they had an ex-Cabinet minister under them and on 25 November he was summoned by his corps commander, not the sort of man who routinely sought meetings with the average major. Winston walked three dangerous miles only to discover that shelling had driven the general away. He then retraced his steps to find that his dugout had been demolished by a shell and an orderly had been killed. 'Now I see from this how vain it is to worry about things,' he told Clemmie. 'It is all chance or destiny and our wayward footsteps are best planted without too much caution.'4

French knew that he was about to be replaced, but still hoped to give Winston a brigade. Winston optimistically ordered his brigadier general's uniform, but never got the chance to wear it. His enemies in the Commons searchingly enquired just how much front-line experience Major Churchill had, and on 18 December French showed him a letter from Asquith saying that the appointment 'might cause some criticism', but adding, 'perhaps you might give him a battalion'. Winston told Clemmie how much he resented the 'almost contemptuous indifference of this note . . .' General Sir Douglas Haig, French's successor, agreed to give him a battalion, and on 5 January 1916 Winston took command of 6th Battalion The Royal Scots Fusiliers, which had been badly mauled at the battle of Loos the previous September and was now in the Ploegsteert sector, just north of the

Franco-Belgian border. He arrived in 'Plugstreet' with his bath and water-heater, and at once got off on the wrong foot with his officers, telling them: 'Gentlemen, I am now your Commanding Officer. Those who support me I will look after. Those who go against me I will break.'5 He had decidedly mixed feelings about his battalion, telling Clemmie that it was 'pathetic. The young officers are small middle class Scotsmen—very brave and willing and intelligent, but of course all quite new to soldiering. All the senior and all the professionals have fallen.'6

Winston spent five months in command and, despite his inauspicious start, was an unqualified success as CO. It was very much in his gregarious nature to try to make his officers a band of brothers. He organized a regimental dinner soon after taking over, and soon asked Clemmie to send him sufficient food to ensure that he could always entertain. He wanted 'large slabs of corned beef: stilton cheeses: cream: hams: sardines:—dried fruits: you might almost try a big beef steak pie: but not tinned grouse or fancy tinned things'.7 His eye for detail paid off. On one occasion he saw that a soldier was limping, and at once asked him why this was so. When the man said that he needed new boots, Winston immediately wrote a note to the soldier's company quartermaster sergeant ordering him to issue a pair forthwith. His courage never flickered. He frequently went out into No Man's Land with his second-in-command, Archie Sinclair, gleefully reporting on 15 February 1916:

Went out in front of our own parapet into the No man's land and prowled about looking at

194

our wire and visiting our listening posts. This is always exciting. Last night two of my officer patrols went right up to the German wire and cut large strands of it as trophies. This will only make them more vigilant. Can you imagine such a silly thing.[8]

Winston's famous luck held out. He was enjoying a post-prandial cup of coffee in Laurence Farm when a shell crashed in but failed to explode, and on another occasion the Hospice in Plugstreet, a favourite haunt, was hit by several shells when he was 150 yards away in brigade headquarters. He was fortunate, too, in his times of arrival and departure. He served at the front between Loos and the Somme, his time in command a relatively peaceful period sandwiched between two big battles. Having gone some small way towards expiating his guilt for the Dardanelles in the public eye, and rather further to proving to himself that he could still do it, Winston decided to go back into politics. Here, too, he was lucky. His own battalion was to be amalgamated with another, and the other commanding officer was senior to him. Lieutenant Colonel Churchill could become Mr Churchill again with a clear conscience.

Winston's participation in this lamentable period may not sparkle, but it does at times gleam against a generally dull political background. British policy between the wars reflected a loss of national self-confidence of which World War I was the catalyst, not the principal cause. What the war did above all was to confront the British middle class, for the first time, with an invoice of blood and treasure for that exercise of great power in which it had once exulted, but from which now it shrank in horror. For the rank and file, military service was in many ways an improvement on what they had known in civilian life, notably in nutrition, clothing and medical care, while the danger of sudden death or injury and the sights and sounds of warfare often made less impression on them than on those brought up in more sheltered surroundings. If the middle and upper classes were shamed by exposure to the wretched physical condition of the working class, the camaraderie of the trenches, which made such an impression on so many young middle-class men, hid from them the deep antagonism that lay at the root of the 'British disease', which no amount of anxious ministration by government could cure for the rest of the century.

The rancorous gulf between management and labour in British industry was so wide that it had misled one London resident, Karl Marx, into perceiving it as part of an inevitable historical process in *Das Kapital*, first published in English in 1887 as *Capital: A Critique of Political Economy*. In fact British social and economic development was unique because the country had industrialized so greatly in advance of any other. Obsolete working practices resulted in stagnant productivity and discouraged investment, until international competitiveness could only be maintained by squeezing labour costs or by subsidies paid, through taxation, by the less diseased parts of the economy. The effect on British foreign and defence policies was direct, immutable and lasting.[9]

The 'great betrayal' of the title of this chapter lay neither in social and economic trends which politicians, for all their promises to the contrary, could do little to change, nor in the poor choices from limited options, that they made in the 1930s, but in the process by which those options became sharply limited. This was so closely a product of the contradictions that led to the self-destruction of the Liberal Party as to be almost indistinguishable from it. Modern British politics emerged from the eclipse of 'old' liberalism as a doctrine and as a political organization. The messianic 'new' liberalism persisted, to become the banner of the Labour Party and in time to achieve virtual thought control in the universities and the civil service. Its devotees, dubbed 'New Jerusalemers' by Correlli Barnett, had much in common with the spiritual heirs of the Progressive Era of the first two decades of the twentieth century in the USA, described as 'True Believers' by Eric Hoffer and as 'The Anointed' by Thomas Sowell.

The Asquith government's decision to go to war in 1914 alienated some of the support on which his parliamentary majority depended and divided his party, leaving him too politically weak to introduce the measures necessary to fight it properly. It affronted moderate Irish Nationalists whose Home Rule Bill was suspended for the duration, and alienated much of the Labour Party and the progressive wing of the Liberal Party itself. Asquith's austere arrogance defined this stage of the Liberal debacle, as Lloyd George's opportunism was to define the next. Winston's acute pen-portrait of Asquith captures the hauteur which did much to poison British politics before, during and after World War I:

if, as was inevitable in the rough and tumble

197

of life, he was forced to submit and bow to the opinion of others, to the force of events, to the passions of the hour, it was often with barely concealed repugnance and disdain. If one is to select his greatest characteristic, this massive finality stands forth, for good or ill, above and beyond all others.[10]

Having put himself in the hands of his political opponents, Asquith proceeded to treat them as if they did not exist and excluded them from the direction of the war until the crisis in 1915, which ended with Winston tossed to the wolves and the Conservatives grudgingly granted the Cabinet representation their support merited. After that, and especially after the belated introduction of conscription alienated yet more traditional Liberal support, Asquith's survival depended on the Tories and Lloyd George being unable to overcome their mutual antipathy. As Minister of Munitions and then War Minister, Lloyd George built up a personal slush fund large enough to permit him to operate as a political force in his own right for many years after the war, and in due course he felt strong enough to make a deal with the Tories to replace Asquith.[11] The contempt felt by British generals for the 'frocks' (from frock coats), as they called the politicians, was more justified than it has been comfortable for many historians to admit. When the future Tory leader Stanley Baldwin commented that among the MPs elected in 1918 there were many 'hard faced men who have done well out of the war', he failed to mention that a lot of them had been drawn to politics by the mutually profitable associations they had formed with wartime politicians.[12]

Although Winston cannot be absolved of his share in collective responsibility for a lacklustre period in British politics, he ran the departments entrusted to him with characteristic energy. As Minister for Munitions during the last year of Lloyd George's wartime coalition government he contributed significantly to the prompt recovery of the British army from the German offensives of 1918 and the relentless advance that followed, ending in an armistice on terms amounting to German surrender. As Minister of War and Air after the general election of 1918 he helped avert widespread mutiny by a sensible and humane direction of demobilization, and then provided much of the political will for a ruthless campaign that encouraged the directors of a highly effective terrorist insurgency in Ireland to come to the negotiating table—in London. As Colonial Secretary in 1921–2 he initiated a policy of imperial policing using air power, which was probably the best that could have been done to match greatly increased liabilities with sharply reduced resources.

Throughout this time Winston was in power solely through the grace and favour of Lloyd George. In 1910 he had been able to demand high office by virtue of his drawing power as a speaker, but after the war his voice no longer found popular resonance, nor his opinions much weight beyond what the Prime Minister might privately afford them. This was unfortunate at one level, for Winston was one of the few politicians who still believed it his duty to lead public opinion; but at another level it was a necessary discipline for a man always inclined to speak from the heart. For

199

example, he believed that after the enemy knew himself well beaten, the victors should show magnanimity and goodwill.[13] He saw it as enlightened self-interest, as he made plain in an article he wrote in 1919 after the Treaty of Versailles had been imposed on a nation soon to convince itself that it had not been honestly beaten but rather stabbed in the back by its own 'frocks':

> The reconstruction of the economic life of Germany is essential to our own peace and prosperity. We do not want a land of broken, scheming, disbanded armies, putting their hand to the sword because they cannot find the spade or the hammer. The power of Britain to guide Germany into a safe channel of development and pacific recovery is considerable. We do not know how great is our power for good these days. It is a considerable opportunity in our hands. Do not let us miss it. Our safety depends on it.[14]

This was a pure expression of liberalism, judged by posterity to have been superior to the 'foot on the neck' policy adopted at Versailles, which could only have worked if consistently pursued by the victorious Allies acting in concert. But was it any more realistic? The war had not changed the fact that the Germans were in general better fed, better housed, better educated and worked in better managed, more modern factories and offices served by superior communications. It had diminished neither Germany's dominant geopolitical position in Europe, nor the social attitudes that had been the greatest single cause of

200

the war. In *Ordinary Men: Reserve Police Battalion 101 and the Final Solution in Poland*, Christopher Browning quotes a middle-aged German, not even a member of the Nazi Party and one whose personality was formed long before the rise of Hitler, saying that he and his fellows believed that 'whatever serves the state is right, whatever harms the state is wrong'. This state was a formidable antagonist, and it is far from self-evident that it was in Britain's interest to help it to recover more quickly, or that the German people would have consented to be guided into a 'safe channel' by Britain.

On a smaller but more poignant scale, the chronic failure of British politicians to answer the Irish Question might also have shaken Winston's faith in the power of enlightened self-interest. At times both British and American politicians have sought domestic advantage by playing the Irish card. But feeding the fire throughout has been an indifference in London towards issues that matter very greatly to the Irish, as exemplified by Winston's extended metaphor, used during the debate that led to the creation of the Irish Free State in 1922, which has answering echoes even today:

The differences [in 1914] had been narrowed down, not merely to the counties of Fermanagh and Tyrone, but to parishes and groups of parishes inside the areas of Fermanagh and Tyrone, and yet, even when the differences had been so narrowed down, the problem appeared to be as insuperable as ever, and neither side would agree to reach

201

any conclusion. Then came the Great War: every institution, almost, in the world was strained. Great Empires have been overturned. The whole map of Europe has been changed. The position of countries has been violently altered. The modes of thought of men, the whole outlook on affairs, the grouping of parties, all have encountered violent and tremendous changes in the deluge of the world. But as the deluge subsides and the waters fall short, we see the dreary steeples of Fermanagh and Tyrone emerging once again. The integrity of their quarrel is one of the few institutions that has been unaltered in the cataclysm which has swept the world.[15]

In 1929, writing the fifth volume of *The World Crisis*, Winston piously hoped 'that British political leaders will never again allow themselves to be goaded and spurred and driven by each other or by their followers into the excess of partisanship which on both sides disgraced the year 1914'.[16] Four volumes earlier, however, he was more forthright: 'I have always urged fighting wars and other contentions with might and main till overwhelming victory, and then offering the hand of friendship to the vanquished.'[17] Earlier still, at Bradford on 14 March 1914, his natural pugnacity found memorably menacing expression when, in a speech previously approved by Asquith, he envisaged imposing Home Rule and a united Ireland on a reluctant (and heavily armed) North:

This is the issue—whether the civil and

202

Parliamentary government in these realms is to be beaten down by the menace of armed force . . . if all the loose, wanton and reckless chatter we have been forced to listen to, these many months, is in the end to disclose a sinister and revolutionary purpose, then I can only say to you: Let us go forward together and put these grave matters to the proof.

Winston's involvement in the Irish drama, leading for Asquith before the war and for Lloyd George after it, illustrates that once he was embarked on a course of action it was his natural predilection to see it through to a conclusion. Unlike Asquith, he was obviously prepared to force the issue on Home Rule in 1914, and if Lloyd George's nerve had not failed he would certainly have done his best to crush the post-war IRA insurgency. What he learned from these episodes was that infirmity of purpose harvested all the political damage without the reward of a clear result. It was whimsical of him to write that 'those who can win a war well can rarely make a good peace, and those who could make a good peace would never have won the war. It would perhaps be pressing the argument too far to suggest that I could do both.'[18] He did both very well in 1920–2, employing counter-terror to raise the costs to the IRA to such a degree that Michael Collins, the charismatic Irish guerrilla leader, was on the point of ordering a ceasefire. Then, despite dealing from a position of less strength than he had hoped, his strong man-to-man rapport with Collins in the negotiations that followed salvaged a workable agreement where others might have bickered their way into further conflict. Both, of course, knew that they had been put in the firing line by weaker men who reserved the right to repudiate their efforts, which is just what Eamon de Valera did to Collins. Before he was killed in an ambush by fellow Irishmen, Collins sent a last word to 'tell Winston we could not have done it without him'.

Clemmie was right about Winston's deadliness in one respect, which is that he had no qualms about how many, or by what means, casualties were inflicted in war.[19] As Minister of Munitions he had placed particular emphasis on the mass production of gas shells; as War Minister he urged the declaration of martial law in Ireland to permit the taking of hostages for summary execution, and he took a very broad view of the methods employed by his creation the 'Black and Tans', ex-servicemen recruited in 1920 to support the Royal Irish Constabulary under uncompromising rules of engagement set out by one of their commanders:

> If the persons approaching carry their hands in their pockets, or are in any way suspicious-looking, shoot them down. You may make mistakes occasionally and innocent persons may be shot, but that cannot be helped, and you are bound to get the right parties some time. The more you shoot, the better I will like you, and I assure you no policeman will get into trouble for shooting any man.[20]

Winston's reservations about slaughter were the product of a cool military appreciation of whether or not it was effective. His celebrated condemnation of Brigadier General Reginald Dyer for firing on an unarmed crowd of Sikhs gathered to protest against earlier acts of repression at Amritsar in India in April 1919 included the phrase 'frightfulness is not a remedy known to the British pharmacopoeia'.[21] Yet he backed the blockade of the Central Powers in World War I and the bombing of German cities in World War II. In the context of India, however, where a few thousand held sway over millions, Winston rightly pointed out that British authority 'has never stood on the basis of physical force alone, and it would be fatal to the British Empire if we were to try to base ourselves only upon it'.[22] In Ireland, however, he was perfectly prepared to be harsh. The premise for Collins' insurgency had been that the British would not be as ruthless as he was himself, and Winston was astounded when Lloyd George abruptly abandoned a policy that was doing the IRA real damage.

Winston's 'pharmacopoeia' statement came in a passage actually devoted to salvaging the moral arguments he had used in favour of armed intervention to overthrow the Bolsheviks, the Communists who had seized power in Russia in 1917. The time may be ripe to admit that Winston was right to wish to do so, if wholly wrong to believe that the will to do so existed in war-weary 1919. Even after the Russian Communist regime had collapsed in the late twentieth century amid abundant evidence of its essentially life-denying nature, Roy Jenkins thought it 'extravagant' of Winston to have written of 'a poisoned Russia, an infected Russia, a plague-bearing Russia; a Russia of armed hordes smiting not only with bayonet and cannon, but accompanied and preceded by swarms

205

of typhus-bearing vermin which slew the bodies of men, and political doctrines which destroyed the health and even the soul of nations'.[23] The fact that the Leninist state was to be instrumental in the defeat of another genocidal tyranny in 1941–5 makes it no less of a blot on the pages of history, nor does it mitigate the guilt of those Western intellectuals whose allegiance to it involved the suppression of their intelligence. Jenkins still found it hard to admit that its legacy was as evil as Hitler's, and hence to agree that Winston's eloquent hatred of one was as justified as that of the other. Winston's own anti-Communism never wavered. He had famously compared Lenin's arrival in Russia to that of a plague bacillus, and tended to see the hand of Moscow behind many difficulties, both domestic and international, in the 1920s. He attributed the General Strike of 1926 and also unrest in China to Russian influence.

The 1920s were a time of extreme flux that does not lend itself to easy divisions into 'left' and 'right'. Patriotism generally trumped political affiliation during the war, only to become a devalued concept in the years that followed. The socialist parties of Europe generally supported the war and in due course suffered electorally for doing so, except in Britain where the split in the Liberal Party permitted the Labour Party to make the greatest proportional gain from the 1918 Representation of the People Act, which extended the franchise to all men over 21 (19 if they had served in the war) and women over 30. Its share of the popular vote went from 7 per cent in 1910 to 21 per cent of double the number of votes in 1918.[24] Uniquely, Labour was also well placed to benefit from the mood of anti-war revulsion in 1922 because it was once more under the leadership of Ramsay MacDonald, whose pacifism had led to his resignation as leader of the party in 1914 in order to found the Union of Democratic Control (UDC) with the progressive Liberals who resigned from Asquith's Cabinet. The UDC manifesto demanded that in future foreign policy should be subject to parliamentary oversight, that after the war an organization must be set up to prevent armed conflict, and that the eventual peace terms should neither humiliate the defeated nations nor create artificial frontiers.

The UDC Liberal MPs lost their seats in the 1918 general election and most joined the Labour Party, the new political alignment impinging very directly on Winston's career when he lost his own seat at Dundee in 1922. In five previous elections he had held it with declining majorities while the indefatigable Edwin Scrymgeour, an Independent Prohibitionist in a notoriously hard-drinking constituency, increased his vote from 650 votes in 1908 to 32,000 in the 1922 general election.[25] The leading Labour candidate was Edmund Morel, the leading light of the UDC, who had been jailed for six months in late 1917 on trumped-up charges under the draconian Defence of the Realm Act, and who now won 30,000 votes.[26] It was a two-member constituency, but Winston, with just over 20,000 votes did not even come third: he came fourth behind his National (Lloyd George) Liberal running mate, while the Asquith Liberal and the Communist candidates brought up the rear.

After the rejection of his party in the 1945 election Clemmie suggested it might be a blessing in disguise, to which he replied, 'At the moment it's certainly very well disguised.'27 She may easily have said the same in November 1922. Winston was recovering from an emergency appendectomy when Lloyd George resigned following a Conservative revolt led by Leo (Leopold) Amery, probably the boy Winston had helped with his work at Harrow.28 Winston sent Clemmie along with several of his friends, the lawyer F.E. Smith (by now Lord Birkenhead) among them, to represent him to the electors of Dundee. They did not receive a warm reception. Birkenhead was drunk and made a fool of himself at a first meeting with the party faithful on 5 November, and local women spat on Clemmie, unwisely wearing pearls, at a public meeting in a working-class ward on 6 November. When Winston appeared five days later neither his visibly weak condition nor his many campaign medals, which he proudly wore on Armistice Day, won him any sympathy, and he was compelled to abandon an address at the Drill Hall in the face of exceptionally violent heckling.29 It is evident that he and the cosmopolitan circle in which he moved had completely misread the mood of the country and defeat at Dundee, followed by a further defeat at West Leicester in the general election of December 1923, imposed a much-needed pause for reflection.30

Winston later wrote, 'in a twinkling of an eye I found myself without an office, without a seat, without a party, and without an appendix',31 but failed to add that all of them had become infected. His letters to Clemmie reveal rising impatience with Lloyd George, but never a word about the outright sale of honours to raise money for party funds. There can be no doubt that Winston was well aware of what was going on, not least because his cousin Freddie Guest, the Liberal Coalition Whip from 1917, was Lloyd George's fixer in the matter.32 The Churchills moved in with the Guests between changes of residence in 1909 and again in 1920, Winston made Freddie one of his Parliamentary Private Secretaries in 1910, it was Guest who engineered the secret session of the Commons on 10 May 1917 that marked Winston's return to the front rank, and in 1921 Winston passed the Air Ministry to his cousin when splitting it off from his own War Ministry. In the dock of history Winston is guilty by association with the sleaziness of the post-war government. The strong odour of corruption emanating from his extended family never bothered him, and David Cannadine has charitably proposed 'family piety' as an explanation.33 This may be one reason, although usefulness is a safer guide than sentiment for most of Winston's social relationships. At the core, his tolerance of political malfeasance was of a piece with his views on 'frightfulness'. What mattered was whether or not it was effective. Thus his judgement on Lloyd George:

He never in the days when I knew him best thought of giving *himself* satisfaction by what he said. He had no partiality for fine phrases, he thought only and constantly of the effect produced upon other persons. . . . He was the greatest master of the art of getting things done and of putting things through that I ever knew; in fact no British politician in my day has possessed half his competence as a mover of men and affairs.34

Being out of Parliament permitted Winston to distance himself from the dispute within the acrimoniously divided Liberal Party and to emancipate himself painlessly from his patron. But more than that, the scalding class hatred showered on Clemmie in Dundee revealed the bankruptcy of 'new' liberalism. The battle lines had been redrawn, and whether he liked it or not—and the evidence is that he liked it no more than Clemmie, who voted Liberal for the rest of her life—he was on the Tory side of the divide. As in 1904 his colours remained the same; what changed was their place in an altered spectrum. In 1918 he was still a radical, urging the nationalization of the railways and a swingeing levy on wartime profits, a remarkably naïve suggestion to make to Lloyd George;[35] but when he returned to power as Chancellor of the Exchequer in 1924–9 he was formally responsible for a doctrinaire financial orthodoxy that precluded government activism. As will be seen, there was less to this than many commentators have made of it; but the ferocious reverse snobbery he encountered in Dundee and later in Leicester cannot have failed to leave its mark. No matter what he might do on the social front his motives would be questioned, and his privileged birth would be held against him by those he sought to benefit. He had no part to play in the emerging left of ineffectual moralizing, vengeful envy, intellectual arrogance and troglodyte proletarianism.

In the 18 months prior to the Dundee defeat several deeply significant events in Winston's private life may have at last imparted permanent form to his adult personality. His mother died on 29 June 1921 and in October he exceeded his father's life span, each of incalculable significance to him and together a definitive break with the past. Jennie tripped and broke her left ankle on 29 May, three days short of the third anniversary of her third marriage, to a man named Montagu Porch who was three years younger than Winston. It was a simple fracture but two weeks later gangrene set in and her leg was amputated above the knee. A further two weeks later the stitches in her femoral artery gave way and she began to bleed profusely. Winston hurried over in his pyjamas as soon as he was informed, but by the time he arrived she was already in a coma and she died soon afterwards. She was 67. He described the scene in a letter to a friend:

> I wish you could have seen her as she lay at rest—after all the sunshine and storm of life was over. Very beautiful and splendid she looked. Since the morning with its pangs, thirty years had fallen from her brow. She recalled to me the countenance I had admired as a child when she was in her heyday and the old brilliant world of the eighties and nineties seemed to come back.**36**

In April Clemmie's much-loved brother Bill, for whom Winston also felt great affection, had shot himself for no reason the family was able to establish; and in August a further link with the past was severed with the death of Winston's faithful manservant Thomas Walden, who had worked for Lord Randolph and accompanied Winston to

South Africa. But all these paled beside the death from septicaemia on 23 August of the Churchills' youngest child, Marigold, their adored three-year-old 'Duckadilly'. The stoicism for which the British were once famed mutes the written record of their grief, and Mary, the replacement child born on 15 September 1922, grew up not knowing the identity of the little girl whose photograph stood on her mother's dressing table for the rest of her life.

Amid so much personal tragedy, Winston's arrival at the forty-seventh birthday his father failed to attain was a milestone. Throughout his early life Winston had been driven by the conviction that he would die as young as Lord Randolph, hag-ridden by the fear that for his family it was 'forty and finished'.[37] This is what lay behind the cold-blooded courage he displayed under enemy fire, and was certainly a key element in the anguish he felt when his career was interrupted by the Dardanelles. For most people, the infamous 'mid-life crisis' is in part recognition that death has become nearer than birth, but for Winston the thought that he might not, after all, be destined for an early grave may have precipitated a quite different psychological process. Possibly as a result of his reconsidering the time available for his life's work signs of longer-term calculation begin to appear for the first time, notably in the new image he shaped for himself in the later volumes of *The World Crisis* and in *My Early Life*. It should never be forgotten that from an early age he had felt himself to be a man of destiny. The conviction remained with him, and may have led him to conclude that it had been a mistake to try to force the pace. It could also explain why he refrained from the customary plotting and alliance-making of the ambitious politician—although this might have been in honour of his family motto, the Spanish *Fiel Pero Desdichado* (Faithful but Unfortunate).

Mary was not the only new beginning in 1922, although the other permanent feature to enter Winston's life was a gift from the past. His formidable Londonderry grandmother had bequeathed Garron Towers, an estate producing £4000 a year in Northern Ireland, to Winston as the contingent beneficiary should his cousin Lord Henry Vane-Tempest die without issue. This he helpfully did in a railway accident in January 1921, and in July 1922 Winston committed the revenues from Garron Towers—and much more—to the purchase and almost complete rebuilding of Chartwell Manor in Kent, only 25 miles from Westminster but set in 80 acres overlooking its own valley, with a matchless view over the quintessentially English Weald of Kent. Clemmie felt that the purchase of Chartwell and Winston's concealment of the enormous cost he knew it would involve was the sole occasion during their marriage when he actively deceived her. Her youngest daughter recalled that Clemmie 'tried very hard to love the place that so enthralled Winston. She worked like a Trojan to make it the home and haven for us all that he dreamed of. But it never acquired for her the nature of a venture shared; rather it was an extra duty, gallantly undertaken and doggedly carried through.'[38]

Winston's defeat at Dundee within six months of embarking upon the Chartwell project made 1923 the closest thing to a fallow year in his life so far, extended into 1924 by defeat at West Leicester,

213

where his car was stoned and spat upon by Labour supporters even though it was a town with a tradition of Lib-Lab cooperation. When Stanley Baldwin emerged to replace the spent Bonar Law as leader of the Conservative Party and Prime Minister he decided to call a general election on the issue of tariff protection for British industry, which had split the Tories in 1906 and was the only cause capable of uniting the opposition. The trade union bosses had not yet perceived how protection would serve their interest and shared with both Liberal factions a commitment to Free Trade to keep the cost of living down. Despite this, Winston found that Labour was still determined to hang the Dardanelles around his neck, with Antwerp added for good measure, and when the election was followed by the first Labour government with the support of the Liberals a break became inevitable. After standing as an 'Independent and Anti-Socialist' in a by-election in the Abbey division of Westminster in March 1924 and finishing a very close second to the official Conservative, he then won Epping as a 'Constitutionalist' with the backing of the local Conservative Association in the general election of October 1924.[39] As, at last, a formal Conservative, he was to hold Epping in 1929,[40] 1931 and 1935, and the part which became Woodford, after the constituency was split, in 1945, 1950, 1951, 1955 and 1959. He never paid much attention to constituency matters but, despite a wobble in 1938–9, the same can be said of the Conservatives of Epping and Woodford as of his family: they gave him the backing he needed to be fully himself in the place where he belonged, and deserve our gratitude.

Return to the Conservative fold brought an immediate reward when Baldwin granted him the opportunity to don Lord Randolph's lovingly preserved robes as Chancellor of the Exchequer, which he was to wear for the next four and a half years. It is a daunting challenge to assess his performance of this duty, not least because, while he upheld the principles of classical economics that had guided Britain through its period of greatest growth, the alternative mechanism proposed by his strongest critic, John Maynard Keynes, assumed totemic status after World War II. It was not difficult for rulers and their clients to choose between a doctrine that concentrated ever-greater power in their hands and another that regarded government as at best a light-handed arbiter in the interplay of natural forces. The political attractions of Keynesianism have kept it alive despite proof of its corrupting effect on society and its failure as an economic doctrine, although the reasons are not all cynical. Keynes regarded himself as a philosopher, not as an economist.[41] His *General Theory of Employment, Interest and Money*, published in 1935–6, argued that in an economic downturn there was no wage so low that it could eliminate unemployment, and accordingly it was wicked to put the onus on the unemployed to find work. His answer was to maintain a high level of aggregate demand through spending by public agencies, which we now know leads to a growth in parasitism accompanied by inflation. But nobody knew it at the time, and even now the moral argument tends to trump the realities.

Keynes leaped to prominence in 1920 with the publication of *The Economic Consequences of the*

215

Peace, his swingeing criticism of the confiscatory aspects of the Treaty of Versailles. Without denying that the war had been caused by the 'insane delusion and reckless self-regard' of the German people, which had 'overturned the foundations on which we all lived and built', he castigated the terms imposed on Germany as likely to complete the ruin by mopping up liquidity and causing a severe contraction in international trade. The book was published first in New York because Keynes's prescription was that the USA should relax its repayment demands on Britain, permitting Britain to do the same for France, and so on down the chain of indebtedness. Alas, the USA was neither willing nor ready to play an international role commensurate with its power. Between 1921 and 1929 Presidents Warren Harding and Calvin Coolidge presided over administrations distinguished by the Siamese twins of tariff protection and corruption, and their view on international debt was summed up by Coolidge's laconic comment, 'They hired the money, didn't they?'

Not even the most ardent hagiographer would argue that Winston had much feeling for numbers. His personal finances trembled on the brink of disaster for much of his life, the history he wrote lacks an economic dimension, and his youthful struggle with mathematics illustrates a deep-seated aversion to any subject he could not talk his way around:

> figures were tied into all sorts of tangles and did things to one another which it was extremely difficult to forecast with complete

accuracy. . . . If it was not right it was wrong. It was not any use being 'nearly right'. In some cases these figures got into debt with one another: you had to borrow one or carry one, and afterwards you had to pay back the one you had borrowed. These complications cast a steadily gathering shadow over my daily life.[42]

They did not in 1924–5, however. Winston unhesitatingly challenged the received wisdom of the senior officials at the Treasury and the Bank of England, who were by any measure of continuous influence the true rulers of Britain between the wars and beyond.[43] These included Montagu Norman, Governor of the Bank of England 1920–44; Otto Niemeyer, who was Controller of Finance at the Treasury 1921–7, Chairman of the Financial Committee of the League of Nations 1927–38, Controller of the Bank of England 1927–38 and a director until 1952; Ralph Hawtrey, who in 41 years at the Treasury acquired an international reputation on a par with Niemeyer's; Warren Fisher, Permanent Secretary to the Treasury and *de facto* head of the Civil Service 1919–39; and his deputy and successor Horace Wilson (until 1942 when Winston dumped him), who was Permanent Secretary at the Ministry of Labour 1921–30, Chief Government Industrial Adviser 1930–9 and, when seconded to the Prime Minister's office in 1935–9, played a key role in Neville Chamberlain's policy of appeasement.[44]

Britain had long adhered to the Gold Standard, in which the standard unit of account was a fixed weight of gold, for which banknotes could be redeemed. In the latter part of the nineteenth century it was widely adopted across the world. This system was challenged by World War I, and Britain was compelled to end its adherence to the Gold Standard, which meant that Bank of England notes could no longer be converted to gold. Combatants printed more and more money which could not be redeemed in gold, contributing to widespread inflation. After the war, most conservative economists in Britain argued that a return to the Gold Standard at the values of 1914 would drive down inflation and ultimately restore stability.

Roy Jenkins' chapter on this period of Winston's life coolly dismembers one of the most treasured myths of the British left, namely that the restoration of sterling to the Gold Standard in 1925 at pre-war parity was a smack in the face of the working class by the Tories and employers.[45] It was instead an effort to 'knave-proof' the economy, in the words of John Bradbury, the key man in the People's Budget of 1909 and in devising the welfare provisions it was drawn up to fund, who as Permanent Secretary at the Treasury in 1913–19 had managed the successful financing of the war. Winston tried to force a debate by bringing together Bradbury and Niemeyer with the two leading opponents of the scheme, Keynes and Winston's old rival in the Asquith Cabinet Reginald McKenna, now chairman of the Midland Bank. Every man present was a Liberal. McKenna and Keynes had no answers to the arguments of the Treasury heavyweights, and conceded that Winston had no choice in the matter.[46] This did not stop Keynes writing *The Economic Consequences of Mr Churchill*, a pamphlet published by Leonard and

Virginia Woolf in 1925, which set out the Tory stab hypothesis when Keynes knew that the leaders of the Labour Party were no less devoted to the idea of a self-regulating economy. Claiming moral high ground for arguments that had failed the test of the possible was to become typical of the Bloomsbury group and its many self-regarding successors.[47]

The real Tory policy was the protection of home industries against competition by way of import controls, seen both by Joe Chamberlain in 1903 and by Baldwin in 1923 as a means of winning the votes of organized labour. In later times, of course, it became indelibly associated with trade unions seeking to maintain their membership at the expense of the wider population, in which the Tory Party was content to indulge them. The granting of autonomy to the Bank of England in 1997 was a major step towards the restoration of the politician-proof economy desired by Bradbury, perceived as the essential underpinning for Free Trade, itself the principal instrument of creative destruction in any economy, clearing the dead wood to let new shoots emerge and as such the mortal enemy of 'the forces of conservatism'.[48] This was the crux of the matter, and the orthodoxy for which intervening generations of historians, following Keynes's lead, excoriated Winston now looks more like the radicalism one would have expected of him. Regrettably, the uncompetitive 'dead wood' included large chunks of every major industry in the country, but Winston's faith in the genius of the British people was such that he was sure the new growth would be rapid and vigorous.

We might now disagree with this confidence, but we should at least recognize that the optimism

219

which characterized Winston illuminated his time at the Treasury. It is also to his credit that he accepted the desirability of limiting the political elite's ability to manipulate the economy for partisan or personal benefit. But beyond these considerations, he could only concur with the Whitehall mandarins because the peculiarity of Britain as a great power was that it rested on naval supremacy, imperial possessions and financial hegemony.[49] The USA now had a fleet equal to the Royal Navy and Japan's was stronger than anything Britain could send to the Far East, but he believed an attack on British interests by either was highly unlikely, and an alliance between them impossible, while the British merchant fleet was still larger than the rest of the world's put together. The imperial possessions were still, in the 1920s, seemingly secure, so, for one unalterably convinced that British power was a force for good in the world, to see off the challenge of Wall Street to London as the world's financial clearing house was the only statesmanlike option.

Finally, nobody apart from Keynes and a few others questioned the peace-enhancing effects of Free Trade. The Christian socialist Philip Snowden, son of a weaver devoted to the raising of living standards among the working class, and Winston's predecessor and successor as Chancellor in the Labour governments of 1924 and 1929–31, was no less devoted to Free Trade as a moral imperative. Snowden lifted the last rag of wartime protection in 1924 and went down in 1931 with the Gold Standard nailed to his mast. Furthermore, it was not the function of the Treasury to deal with social matters. Other departments were

220

responsible for unemployment relief, financing public works and giving incentives to exporters. Monetary policy was the business of the Bank of England and industrial matters were the responsibility of the Board of Trade and Ministry of Labour. It was the job of the Chancellor to control public expenditure, and any likely candidate for Winston's place at that time would have seen it as his duty to the country and to humanity to balance the budget and to facilitate Free Trade.[50]

A good deal of humanity, too, characterized Winston's approach to labour relations. In the summer of 1925 he did much to avert trouble with the miners by trying to curb the mine-owners. In 1926, however, when a miners' strike extended to a General Strike, it touched the nerve which always jerked him into an extreme response when he believed that the fundamentals of parliamentary democracy were threatened. After overseeing the government's response during a period when Baldwin, in what Roy Jenkins calls 'exhausted lassitude', had retired to Aix-les-Bains, Winston then ran the government's principal propaganda organ, the *British Gazette*, from the *Morning Post*'s offices in Aldwych. It was a characteristically Winstonian performance. He wrote some copy himself, then tweaked the commas and full stops of that written by others before going down to the machine room to show the staff there how to work their presses. But although he was well to the fore in breaking the strike, in his attempts to make the mine-owners give ground over pay and conditions he was far ahead of most of his Cabinet colleagues.

A year after the Conservatives lost power to the

221

Labour Party Winston delivered the Romanes lecture at Oxford in June 1930. In it he set out the classical economic concepts by which he had lived and which had guided Britain to greatness since Victorian times, sadly commenting 'we can see clearly that they do not correspond to what is going on now'. These concepts were:

Free imports, irrespective of what other countries may do and heedless of the consequences to any particular native industry or interest. Ruthless direct taxation for the repayment of debt without regard to the effects of such taxation upon individuals or their enterprise or initiative. Rigorous economy in all forms of expenditure whether social or military. Stern assertion of the rights of the creditor, national or private, and full and effectual discharge of all liabilities. Profound distrust of State-stimulated industry in all its forms, or of State borrowing for the purpose of creating employment. Absolute reliance upon private enterprise, unfettered and unfavoured by the State.

It is bitterly poignant that Winston's dynamic performance of his departmental duties in pursuit of what were regarded as unquestionably laudable ends should have caused him to be the agent of the very military unpreparedness against which he was to rage so furiously for the next ten years. Perhaps that is the reason why the following passage did not appear in the published version of *The Gathering Storm*, the first volume of his history of the Second World War.

We shall hear in succeeding generations a lot of talk about the pacific virtues we displayed; how we exhausted every expedient; how we flaunted a magnificent patience; how we never lost our heads or were carried away by fear or excitement; how we turned the second cheek to the smiter seven times or more. Some historians will urge that admiration should be given to a Government of honourable high-minded men who bore provocation with exemplary forbearance and piled up to their credit all the Christian virtues, especially those which command electioneering popularity. . . . I hope it will also be written how hard all this was upon the ordinary common folk who fill the casualty lists. Under-represented in Government and Parliamentary institutions, they confide their safety to the Ministers and the Prime Minister of the day. They have just cause of complaint if their guides or rulers so mismanage their affairs that in the end they are thrust into the worst of wars with the worst of chances.[51]

Following World War II the Labour government, technically insolvent and facing enormous internal pressure to slash defence expenditure, nevertheless maintained conscription and a British Army on the Rhine, soon to be equipped with one of the best battle tanks of the time; scrapped the battleships and concentrated naval research and development on anti-submarine warfare; re-equipped the RAF with jet fighters and committed the funds necessary to develop nuclear weapons and the V-bombers to deliver them. It entered into a permanent defence association with the Allies with whom Britain had fought the war, and threw itself whole-heartedly into the new United Nations organization. These were all perceived as so self-evidently in the national interest that only the tub-thumping Aneurin Bevan and a coterie of 'progressives' opposed them. Furthermore, these policies were pursued at a time when a comprehensive effort was under way to raise British standards in health, housing and education. It was an heroic if in some respects misguided endeavour directed by patriotic and public-spirited politicians who did not let their commitment to a vision of how society should be get in the way of doing all they could to make the one they inherited as equitable and secure as possible.

There was, in principle, no reason why similar policies could not have been pursued after World War I, without the constraints of national bankruptcy or the doctrinaire worm in the apple of the 1945–51 'revolution'. Not one of them was. It was an achingly lost opportunity, a squandering of the sacrifice made by the tens of thousands killed and crippled, and a contumacious breach of the promise made to provide the survivors with 'homes fit for heroes'. Perhaps worst of all, a wilful refusal to learn from the failure of deterrence that occurred in 1914 and the strategic lessons of the war itself meant the country was obliged to scale the same blood-daubed learning curve again 20 years later. Britain's power for good at home and abroad in 1945 was a fraction of what it had been in 1918, and responsibility for this and all the other failures of public trust lies with the party and the

224

governments led by Asquith and Lloyd George. Liberal Britain did not die a natural death: it was murdered.

Something else died as well. It is mere casuistry to say that Lloyd George's outright sale of honours was only a difference of degree from existing practice: as the enabler of a cabal of war profiteers, he had sold the government's honour long before he put a price tag on titles. The spirit of the young men who volunteered to serve their country, or who willingly accepted the obligation to 'do their bit', was diminished even among those whose lives were spared. There is probably nothing so pernicious to the health of a society than for people to feel they have been tricked, that their better sentiments have been exploited and that the opportunities they have foregone for the greater good have been appropriated by others for personal gain. Although I was writing about World War II, the following words are as pungently applicable to the aftermath of the earlier conflict: 'Worse, perhaps, was that those who loyally abstained from black marketeering, bought War Bonds and paid their taxes, saw that those who had not done so prospered unpunished. Not the least casualty of the war was the corrosion of the minimum social solidarity without which civilisation is just a word.'52

Much as I wish that it were not so, Winston belongs in the dock of history along with so many of his colleagues. Of course there are mitigating circumstances. If others had matched his energy and commitment the war would have been prosecuted with a greater use of mechanical energy and less human loss. Complaining of the

225

inadequate field communications and the lack of light railways to serve the front, he wrote that 'this war is one of mechanics and brains and mere sacrifice of brave and devoted infantry is no substitute and never will be. By God I would make them skip if I had the power—even for a month.'[53] There is no reason to doubt it. He proposed radical measures after the war as well, and a levy on war profits would have done much to reconcile public opinion. But leaving aside his public writings, which served a propaganda purpose to which I shall return in Chapter Six, the more damning indictment of him as an individual emerges from his private correspondence, in which he unfailingly aligned the national interest with his own. A passage in one of the letters he wrote to Clemmie from Plugstreet, in which he enclosed an adamantine photograph of Archie Sinclair and himself, stands out: 'It is odd to think of you at Walmer now.[54] I remember so well being there at the end of February last, when all was hope at the Dardanelles and I looked forward to a very wide sphere of triumphant activity. Everything is changed now—only the old block [Asquith] continues solid and supine.'[55] In fact only Winston's personal circumstances had changed. Everything else was as before, and as he had found richly enjoyable before the curtailment of his ambition.

A similar thought struck me as I stood in Lancashire Cottage cemetery, just behind the field containing the well-head that marks the site of Laurence Farm, his 1916 headquarters at Plugstreet. I admire him enormously for serving in the infantry on the Western Front. But he left the front because it suited him, and he wanted to get back into politics. Over 5 million of his countrymen did not have that option.

CHAPTER SIX

CLIMACTERIC

1929–1935

In a somewhat premature political obituary published in 1931, the author decried Winston as an opportunist who never did anything thoroughly.[1] It has already been seen how, for Winston's critics, any stick will do to beat him. It is in their characters, not his, that explanation should be sought. His failings as a politician were the reverse side of his greatness as a statesman: he was protean where most people can only sustain a narrow expertise, brave where most are timid, decisive where most dither, strong where most are weak, diligent where most are casual, a brilliant manager of his own time where most are disorganized. In sum, he had all the manly virtues set out in 'If', Rudyard Kipling's High Victorian catechism, save a total disregard for the stricture against looking too good or talking too wise, which in a democracy are often unpardonable offences.[2]

If, in Robert Rhodes James's phrase, Winston's career before 1940 was indeed a study in failure, it was failure of a very odd sort. Winston had occupied every major office of state except No 10 and the Foreign Office and was usually the most dominant figure in Cabinet, at times rivalling the Prime Minister. Therein lies another rich vein for revisionism, as it is remarkable how often the strength of his personality has been singled out for criticism, as though it was something he should have muted for the greater good. Yet it is a principle of Cabinet government that the national interest emerges from competition among its members, with the Prime Minister as the arbiter. Thus, to take one small example, Winston has been blamed for excessively severe cuts in defence spending after World War I and also for vetoing the creation of a single Ministry of Defence. As Chairman of the Review Committee for the massive spending cuts of 1921 (known as the 'Geddes Axe' after the man appointed by Lloyd George to chair a committee of businessmen charged with identifying where savings might be made), Winston opposed the creation of a single ministry mainly because it was part of a package to cut defence spending far below pre-war levels.[3] He fought his corner and halved the defence cuts, some of which were made in education and housing instead. We may now judge this outcome to be undesirable, but if the ministers responsible for the social programmes failed to sway a Prime Minister as well inclined to their cause as Lloyd George, then the fault was at least in part theirs. Had Winston been one of them, and had there been someone less dynamic at the War Office, no doubt military spending would have taken a bigger hit—but those were not the cards he was dealt.

Winston is often criticized for by-passing the chain of command to 'interfere' at the operational level, as though the intervening ranks would have got it right had he not done so. The generals wasted much of the money Winston saved from the Geddes Axe on 'getting back to real soldiering' after the harsh encounter with reality in 1914–18.

Would it have been 'interfering' of Winston, had he remained at the War Office, to have taken the drastic action necessary to shake up the military hierarchy? In 1925–6 he used his position as Chancellor to force his old friend Admiral Beatty, then First Sea Lord, to justify every penny of the naval estimates, just as Lloyd George had forced Winston to do in 1913–14. Beatty wrote, 'it takes a good deal out of me when dealing with a man of his calibre with a very quick brain. A false step, remark or even gesture is immediately fastened upon, so I have to keep my wits about me.'[4] It was quite like war, he might have added. Unfortunately the adversarial method, in this case, failed because the matter at issue (the type and equipment of cruisers for the protection of trade routes) betrayed a fixation with surface warfare that should not have survived the experience of the U-boat offensive in 1917. The cruiser issue was driven by the USA, which was ranting about the need for naval parity to ensure that it could force the British blockade in any future conflict (a war with Britain and the USA on opposing sides was seen as a possibility), and ignored the proven need for large numbers of escort vessels to protect Britain's lifelines from the far more likely submarine threat.[5] In lieu of the longed-for battleships, cruisers were seen as assertive, escorts as passive, making it almost as much of a psychosexual as a purely technical matter.[6] Roskill does not mince words on the subject:

For the shortage of convoy escorts . . . the Admiralty must bear direct responsibility, and there can be little excuse . . . in 1939 the Navy was unprepared psychologically as well as materially for an attack on trade. There was no 'doctrine' of convoy defence, no tactics had been evolved, the potential escort commander had no guidance and historians had paid little attention to the tragic story of trade protection. The importance of aircraft in the defence of convoys against U-boat attack had been entirely forgotten, and here the Air Ministry was no less at fault.[7]

'Fortress Singapore' was Britain's principal naval base in the Far East, built at considerable cost in the 1930s and lost to a Japanese attack down the Malay peninsula in early 1942. Its sad saga is among the more prominent totems in the cult of blaming Winston for the shortcomings of others. As Minister of War he saved the funding for the project from the Geddes Axe, but demanded that the service chiefs present him with a coherent case for the base's defence. They did not. As Chancellor he repeated the same demand and found the same deficiency. Nor can the sovereign governments of Australia and New Zealand, and the British administrators of Burma, India and Malaya be wholly absolved for their passivity in a matter that affected them so very directly.[8] In the absence of agreement among the services, Warren Fisher at the Treasury imposed the customary worst-of-all-worlds solution, and the project was neither wholly abandoned nor properly funded.[9]

The most telling count against Winston lies not in his deportment as a minister, but in the writing he did in order to burnish his political stature. In keeping with his distrust of ideology he did not

231

believe consistency was a virtue in politics, therefore to quote an earlier Winston against a later when the circumstances had changed is often otiose.[10] By the 1930s, however, there is reason to believe he was hoist by a 1920s' petard he had helped to ignite. In July 1915 he thought he would be going to the Dardanelles and wrote a letter to Clemmie, which was to be opened in the event of his death, in which he asked her to vindicate his memory.[11] The first two volumes of *The World Crisis* performed that task. Everything thereafter, to a greater or lesser degree, served not only to make enough money to guarantee his personal autonomy—for which, given the ambient political amorality and the opportunities for corrupt enrichment open to him, he deserves great honour—but also to project a new and improved Winston Churchill and to shape his posthumous monument. One passage, seeking to invest his brief experience of the Western Front with a philosophical depth which, it is clear from his private correspondence, was notably absent, is particularly cynical:

As in the shades of a November evening, I for the first time led a platoon of Grenadiers across the sopping fields . . . the conviction came into my mind with absolute assurance that the simple soldiers and their regimental officers, armed with their cause, would by their virtues in the end retrieve the mistakes and ignorances of Staffs and Cabinets, of Admirals, Generals and politicians— including, no doubt, many of my own.[12]

While certainly an accurate assessment of how a war is won, the distancing phrase 'no doubt' robs the statement of sincerity. The Royal Scots Fusiliers whom he did lead, if not into the assault at least in trench warfare, were not grand enough for this self-portrait. The passage captures his lack of emotional engagement with the reality of the war better even than his self-centred correspondence with Clemmie. One may argue that detachment is necessary in a commander who must send men to be killed, but surely here was a moment when, after a decade of reflection, he might have expressed a little genuine humility.

In the conjoined Volumes III and IV, published in 1927, Winston blatantly recast himself from the hawk he had been to the dove he now wished to seem, leading Keynes to praise the book as 'a tractate against war—more effective than the work of a pacifist would be'. At a time when it was open season on Western Front generals, Winston gleefully joined in the hunt. He quoted from a letter written by General Sir Henry Rawlinson during the battle of Passchendaele of August–November 1917 ('I confess I stick to it more because I see nothing better, and because my instinct prompts me to stick to it, than because of any good arguments by which I can support it'), in order to comment austerely that 'these are terrible words when used to sustain the sacrifice of nearly four hundred thousand men'.[13]

I do not seek to belittle the special horror of a battle where thousands vanished without leaving a trace beyond leaving names incised on the memorial at Tyne Cot. British and Empire casualties during the battle were a still appalling

260,000 against about the same number of Germans (although these figures remain disputed), making it a grimly successful exercise of attrition by the Allies with their greater manpower resources. Earlier in the year General Nivelle had broken the spirit of his own French army with hideous losses during the Chemin des Dames offensive, and it was left to the British army to maintain the pressure on the Germans. Winston knew this perfectly well, and in 1918 he attacked an article written during the battle by Lord Lansdowne, the same man who had lit the long fuse to Britain's commitment to the land war in 1905, in which he called for peace negotiations in order to save what was left of European civilization. Winston replied that the war was a conflict between Christian civilization and scientific barbarism. 'Germany must be beaten,' he wrote. 'Germany must know she is beaten; Germany must feel she is beaten. Her defeat must be expressed in terms and facts which will, for all time, deter others from emulating her crimes, and will safeguard us against their repetition.'[14]

Finally, in *The Aftermath*, published in 1929, Winston expressed the apocalyptic vision that made the unilateral pacifism against which he was to inveigh for much of the next decade seem the only sensible or indeed sane policy in the eyes of millions no less patriotic than he:

Mankind has never been in this position before. Without having improved appreciably in virtue or enjoying wiser guidance, it has got into its hands for the first time the tools with which it can accomplish its own extermination. That is the point in human destinies to which all the glories and toils of men have at last led them . . . Death stands at attention, obedient, expectant, ready to serve, ready to shear away the people *en masse* ready, if called upon, to pulverize, without hope of repair, what is left of civilization. He awaits only the word of command. He awaits it from a frail, bewildered being, long his victim, now—for one occasion only—his Master.[15]

Declaring war to be unthinkable does not make it less likely. These were not the passionate words of a callow young man, but the considered view of a man in his mid-fifties who had for many years held high office and whose readers had every reason to believe would know more than they about the development of arms technology. It was also unhistorical: only the scale and duration of World War I distinguished its trenches, saps, mines, bombardments and assaults from the siege warfare of earlier times, while as a proportion of the European population then living the human losses of the Thirty Years War (1618–48) may not have been exceeded even in World War II. In addition to his share of responsibility for the collective errors and omissions of public policy already discussed, as an influential author and commentator Winston contributed significantly to swelling the mood of terrified denial against which he was to struggle in vain throughout the 1930s.

In fairness, Winston never dreamed that a British government would one day disarm unilaterally in the hope of setting a good example to militaristic dictators. His view was that although 'the story of the human race is war',[16] the costs and consequences had risen to the point where a determined effort must be made to change the narrative. But his efforts to do so could be unsubtle. 'Shall We All Commit Suicide?' he demanded in 1924,[17] an evergreen money-spinner for a journalist but irresponsible from a statesman. Here again, though, it should be borne in mind that he had a large establishment to maintain, that he did not collect the directorships and government sinecures that are the modern equivalent of pre-1884 Reform Act pocket and rotten boroughs, and lastly that even the worthy Homer nods off sometimes. Winston's literary output was prodigious, the more so considering it was only his secondary occupation, and in general the views expressed over time were internally coherent. He was the highest-paid commentator of his time, on a range of subjects ranging from high policy to the trivial, and the men who paid him were not in the business of giving away money.

The 'climacteric' of the chapter title was not Winston's but society's. The country had a 'change of life' at this time, and although it is not an analogy I dare pursue too far, in one respect it is exact: British culture became decreasingly fertile, drawing into itself and away from engagement in the wider world. It was not a sudden or dramatic change, rather it was a period when the adventurousness that had long characterized the British faded at many levels. The 'horrid respectability' and 'little, finite, systematic routine' that Dickens had denounced in 1842 was now the social norm. The economy was structurally stagnant, a dreary sameness characterized so much domestic architecture, writing became more navel-gazing, painting increasingly derivative and the performing arts more dominated by the recycling of past glories. Lastly, an unhealthy if understandable rejection of the immediate past manifested itself firstly in the National Trust, an admirable institution in its way, but one which encouraged a sentimental myth of a pre-industrial Eden, and secondly in the Bloomsbury Group, no less devoted to denigrating the values of Victorian England in order to applaud its own cleverness.[18] Both trends were inimical and the latter frankly hostile to Winston's Burkean view that 'it is this union of past and present, this golden chain, never yet broken, because no undue strain is placed upon it, that has constituted the peculiar merit and sovereign quality of English national life'.[19]

None of these developments can be reduced to a simple dichotomy between 'progressive' and 'conservative', still less between 'socialist' and 'capitalist', with the Labour Party representing a brave new dawn, but the legacy of scholars who believed this unquestioningly still lies heavy on public discourse. Labour did not even win a majority of the working-class vote until 1945, by which time its leaders had gained experience in office and the apparent success of a centrally planned and directed economy during World War II had given its programme credibility. Before that, Baldwin and the Conservatives won a relative majority in the seven elections between the wars and an absolute majority in all but two because they best expressed the national mood, of which a dominant characteristic was fear of social demotion across a spectrum ranging from the skilled working

237

class to the royal family. In the static view of society then prevailing, any gain by one group, however needy, was perceived as necessarily being at the expense of another.

The organized working-class equivalent was what economists call the 'lump of labour fallacy', the belief that there is only a fixed amount of work to be done and that any increase in productivity therefore reduces the number of available jobs. Such attitudes are greatly strengthened in an economic downturn and lead to demands for protection. If the public no longer believes the economy can create new jobs it will demand that old jobs should be preserved from overseas competitors, and political parties will bow to this demand. Nor should it be thought that progressive opinion offered any viable alternative. In the USA, for instance, not for nothing was part of FDR's New Deal called 'social security'—it was designed above all to reassure the lower middle class, a wise move given the political form the fears of that class eventually took in Germany. The progressive ideal was always bureaucratic oligarchy, and it became associated with proletarianism in Britain mainly by historical accident.

Winston's own faith in the free market was severely shaken by the loss of his savings (£300,000 in today's money, along with over 30 billion dollars in the paper wealth of the USA) in the Wall Street Crash of October–November 1929. He was in New York on 'Black Tuesday', 29 October, and claimed that one of the many stockbroker suicides tumbled past his hotel window. Worse was to follow. With a series of ill-considered acts the US government turned the bursting of a speculative bubble into a full-blown economic depression at home, while leading a Gadarene rush into beggar-my-neighbour protectionism that throttled international trade and rolled the consequences across the globe. The tough attitude that US financiers had adopted towards war debt came home to roost as debtor nations, denied the credit that was all that had kept the payments merry-go-round going, and no longer able to earn a surplus through trade, erected their own tariff barriers and eventually defaulted.

The effects in Britain, second only to the USA as a creditor and still the world's premier trading nation, were brutal.[20] By the end of 1930 exports had fallen by 50 per cent and unemployment had risen from around a million to 2.5 million, about 20 per cent of the workforce, at a time when government revenues were tumbling. Under pressure from its Liberal allies, Ramsay MacDonald's Labour administration set up a committee to review the state of public finances, which in July 1931 recommended cuts in public-sector wages and in payments to the unemployed. The Chancellor, Philip Snowden, fully accepted the findings of the commission but the great majority of his party in Parliament and in the country furiously opposed it. Happily, few followed the lead of Oswald Mosley, who resigned as Chancellor of the Duchy of Lancaster in 1930 following the rejection of his own proposals that the government should take control of banking and exports, and increase government spending to boost purchasing power. Seeking to emulate Mussolini, who had seized power in Italy in the early 1920s, Mosley now abandoned the Labour Party to form the New Party and later the British Union of Fascists.

Amid the flight of investors and a run on gold, on 24 August MacDonald and his senior colleagues formed a National Government with the other parties.21 Promptly expelled by the Labour Party and denounced by Lloyd George, who hoped that his moment might have come again, MacDonald called a general election which saw Labour reduced to a rump and the Conservatives become the party of government in all but name.22 Treasury orthodoxy continued to prevail under the new Chancellor, Neville Chamberlain, with public sector wages and unemployment payments reduced and income tax raised by 10 per cent. The fixed exchange rate was defended by raising the lending rate to 6 per cent, and by the end of 1931 unemployment had reached 3 million. Then came as sudden a reversal as there has ever been among the mandarins, who floated the pound and let it fall by 30 per cent against the dollar. This stopped the run on gold and an immediate improvement in the balance of trade was followed by a reduction in the interest rate, which laid the ground for an overall recovery led by a house-building boom in the southeast and rapid growth in non-traditional manufacturing, also mainly in the south and the south Midlands. Even agriculture, for so long the poor relation in the British economy, enjoyed the first upturn in its fortunes for nearly a century. Not so the mining, steel, shipbuilding and textile industries, and unemployment remained crushingly high in Scotland, Wales, Northern Ireland and the north of England.

In an attempt to breathe life back into the traditional pillars of the economy, the coffin of classical Liberalism was nailed shut with the

240

introduction of a general tariff, again at 10 per cent, on all imports except those from the Empire, which did not harbour competing industries. Thus Joe Chamberlain's son at last introduced the Empire Preference scheme with which his father had split the Conservative Party 30 years earlier. The effects on British competitiveness were, in the long run, just as harmful as classical theory predicted. But as Keynes quipped, 'in the long run we are all dead', and the mandarins deserve credit for abandoning lofty detachment in order to respond to the immediate crisis, showing greater courage than their peers in the USA while remaining more mindful of their international obligations. As a result they became even more influential at a time when politicians were desperate to do the right thing but had no idea quite what it might be.

It is not remarkable, against this backdrop, that the first of Winston's two campaigns to rally public opinion behind him during this period was a flop. Cut loose from the certainties of the age into which he had been born, he had no reliable compass to guide him through uncharted seas.[23] Unable to take the lead in economic matters, he chose to break with Baldwin over the issue of Conservative support for a Labour initiative to grant (very limited) self-government to India, something far from people's immediate concerns. For public consumption his view was that 'India is a geographical term. It is no more a united nation than the Equator.'[24] His true concern was spelled out in correspondence with the Marquess of Linlithgow (a dynamic but frustrated Viceroy of India in 1936–43), chairman of a committee set up in 1933 to tackle the issue, which Winston refused to join.

The mild and vague Liberalism of the early years of the twentieth century, the surge of fantastic hopes and illusions that followed the armistice of the Great War have already been superseded by a violent reaction against Parliamentary and electioneering procedure and by the establishment of dictatorships real or veiled in almost every country. Moreover the loss of our external connections, the shrinkage in foreign trade and shipping brings the surplus population of Britain within measurable distance of utter ruin. We are entering a period when the struggle for self-preservation is going to present itself with great intenseness to thickly populated industrial countries. It is unsound reasoning therefore to suppose that England alone among the nations will be willing to part with her control over a great dependency like India . . . In my view England is now entering a new period of struggle and fighting for its life, and the crux of it will be not only the retention of India but a much stronger assertion of commercial rights. As long as we are sure that we press no claim on India which is not in their real interest we are justified in using our undoubted power for their welfare and for our own.[25]

Linlithgow replied that falling birthrates in conjunction with increasing demand for primary and manufactured goods rendered this position obsolete, and that Winston was 'hanging, hairy, from a branch, while you splutter the atavistic shibboleths of an age destined by some to retreat into the forgotten past'.[26] It must have been galling for Winston to be lectured by a rather younger Tory peer from the podium of Liberal imperialism where he himself had stood for so long, especially since both knew that population and production factors could only take effect over a very long period. Linlithgow's vision depended on a peaceful, orderly future in which there would be time for incremental changes to work, Winston's was of a world rapidly becoming more dangerous, in which a hole in the dyke, however small, would soon let through a torrent. While there can be no doubt that the Raj was doomed as soon as the native peoples began to defy its authority, in the light of the European cataclysm that followed a mere five years later it is difficult to argue that Winston was entirely wrong.[27]

He saw the issue as a didactic tool to raise public consciousness about how much depended on British power, which it never occurred to him could be anything other than a force for stability, order and hence for good in the world. Indian autonomy would reduce that power significantly in the long term, but there can be little doubt that Winston opposed it mainly to draw attention to something he saw as a far more immediate threat, namely that 'the leaders of the Conservative Party, and particularly Baldwin . . . were small and mediocre figures whose indifference to Britain's decline also made them contemptible'.[28] His campaign failed at both levels: the Tory die-hards who shared his view that it was the beginning of a slippery slope which would end in independence, and Labour members who were furious that it did not go much further, together summoned up only 112 votes against 386 when the India Bill was finally voted into law in June 1935. Having lost, Winston invited Ghanshyam Das Birla, a wealthy Indian businessman, close associate of Gandhi and lobbyist for the Bill, to Chartwell. Winston grandly declared that Gandhi had risen high in his esteem for having spoken out in defence of the lowest members of Indian society, the Untouchables—something he should have known Gandhi had been doing since the beginning of his civil disobedience campaign. His parting words, relayed by Birla to Gandhi and the leaders of the Congress Party, were:

> I am genuinely sympathetic towards India. I have got real fears about the future. India, I feel is a burden on us. We have to maintain an army and for the sake of India we have to maintain Singapore and Near East strength. If India could look after herself we would be delighted. After all the span of life is very small and I would not be too selfish. I would be only too delighted if the reforms are a success. I have all along felt that there were fifty Indias. But you have got the thing now; make it a success and if you do I will advocate your getting much more.[29]

It was eloquent, moving, and patently insincere. Winston cared about Britain, and about India only in so far as it served British interests. Having fought the good fight, he now had to cut away the detritus of a lost struggle to free himself for the next, and in his concession speech to the Commons he quoted Lord Salisbury's words following the Reform Bill of 1867: 'It is the duty of every Englishman, and of every English party to accept a political defeat cordially, and to lend their best endeavours to secure the success, or to neutralize the evil, of the principles to which they have been forced to succumb.'[30]

Although for clarity's sake presented sequentially here, Winston's opposition to the India Bill and his increasing concern about the Nazis' rise to power in Germany overlapped considerably, and it is entirely possible that his farewell words to Birla reflected a heightened awareness that Britain could either pursue a policy of active imperialism or make a significant contribution to the balance of military power in Europe, but not both. Even at the height of British power this had always been the latent strategic dichotomy; yet now, when reduced circumstances and greater dangers should have made it impossible to continue evading the issue, the evil genius of British politics expressed itself in a prolonged argument over air power as a deterrent, in terms very similar to the debate over battleships before 1914. There was only one certain way to ensure that the coast across the Channel did not fall into German hands, and that was a large, well-equipped army committed to a military alliance with France to defend the Low Countries.[31] Such preparation would also have rapidly resolved the twin problems of idle industrial capacity and unemployment, as it did in Germany. The rulers of Britain chose to ignore the failure of deterrence in

1914 along with ample warning that Germany was determined first to undermine and then to reverse the verdict of 1918.

Almost alone, Winston saw that Nazi Germany was unappeasable; as a result he emerged from a decade of dither with the prestige to lead the nation in the war that followed. But there are few indications that he had learned the lessons of 1914 any better than the rest. He shared the traditional British view that a large standing army was unnecessary, and did not demand extra escort vessels or funding for development and manufacture of armoured vehicles when U-boats and tanks were rolling off the German production lines. His focus on air power was probably less concerned with military preparedness than with highlighting the character weakness of the men in government. People might not care about the Empire, but it was reasonable to suppose that the prospect of being bombed would concentrate their minds. It did, but neither soon enough nor strongly enough to bring about renewal at the top. The years that followed confirmed the centrality of the character issue. Even after the MacDonald/ Baldwin administration timidly committed to rearmament, it lacked the courage of what were never whole-hearted convictions. Winston had to be guarded in his comments about the leader of his own party, but his contempt for MacDonald overflowed in his attack on the Labour leader's proposals for unilateral disarmament:

I remember, when I was a child, being taken to the celebrated Barnum's Circus, which contained an exhibition of freaks and monstrosities, but the exhibit on the programme which I most desired to see was the one described as 'The Boneless Wonder'. My parents judged that that spectacle would be too revolting and demoralizing for my youthful eye, and I have waited fifty years to see the Boneless Wonder sitting on the Treasury Bench.32

There were many constraints on Winston's freedom of expression, but the greatest was that he had occupied high office for most of the past 25 years, the last five under Baldwin. Personal animus against his benefactor not only offended against contemporary standards of correct behaviour, but also called into question Winston's own character and judgement: why had he only discovered how unsuited Baldwin was to lead the country after the Conservatives lost the 1929 election? He also had to be wary of attacking policies that could be presented as the continuation of measures he had advocated when in office, and underlying it all was the gulf that always opens under the feet of a politician who wishes to disavow positions once strongly held without frankly admitting they were misconceived. Winston may have reinvented himself to his own satisfaction, and one should never underestimate the truism that to persuade others one must first convince oneself, but during the period 1929–35 he encountered the problem familiar to actors seeking to break with type-casting. The old Winston was out of fashion, but the new Winston failed to attract a loyal following in Parliament and, despite support from Lord Rothermere of the *Daily Mail* group and Lord

Beaverbrook of the *Daily Express*, in the country as well.

That they were important employers of Winston the journalist does not mean they could tell Winston the politician what to do—nobody could—but the apparent conflict of interest laid him open to damaging innuendo.[33] That was as far as his detractors dared to go, while he lived, since he sued for libel whenever his integrity was questioned in print. Given the copious paper trail left by Winston himself, and the zeal of those anxious to expose his feet of clay, it is reasonable to suppose that any corrupt dealings he might have had would by now be public knowledge. He was not venal and accepted favours from the rich as though by right. The surest and swiftest way to be banished from Winston's consideration was to presume that any service done for him implied a reciprocal obligation.[34] In this as in many other respects he was regal in outlook, and at the end of his political life he refused a dukedom in part because it would have represented a step down from the eminence he had won for himself. Machiavelli might have found him a touch soft-hearted, but he had the makings of a Renaissance prince.

I have been a military historian all my working life, and neither glory in war nor believe it inevitable. However, it should be self-evident that peace can only be assured by a correct balance of carrot and stick, and that it is incumbent on those who wish for peace to be strong enough to impose it on those who flagrantly disturb it. In the face of aggression, principled pacifism requires a level of physical courage that most people (myself, I am sure, amongst them) do not possess. Gandhi was a

248

stretcher-bearer at Spion Kop in the Boer War, carrying out a mission of mercy that also honours the memory of hundreds of extraordinarily brave conscientious objectors in both world wars. The most decorated other rank in World War I was Bill Coltman, who belonged to a nonconformist sect which opposed the taking of human life: he won the Victoria Cross, Distinguished Conduct Medal and bar and Military Medal and bar serving as a stretcher-bearer on the Western Front. One may disagree with, but not question, a faith so convincingly displayed. Unilateral disarmament presumes that the result of surrendering to those who do not follow your example cannot be worse than resisting them. It follows that whatever the arguments in favour of disarmament before the Nazis took power in Germany, to persist in them after that time was to accept for oneself and posterity a steep descent into night and fog. This is not wisdom after the event: it was written on the walls from the moment Hitler became Chancellor of Germany on 30 January 1933.

Cognitive dissonance is the technical term for the psychological friction produced by maintaining two or more incompatible beliefs at the same time. Among those enveloped in it at this time was the high-minded first governor general of the BBC, Sir John Reith, who had taken it upon himself to deny the microphone to Winston over India and continued to do so over German rearmament, mirroring the government's fear that it would offend the Nazis. It was not until 16 November 1934 that Winston was able to address the nation and to lay out the alternatives whose hard edges the government was determined to blur (the full text of this crucial and much-quoted speech is in Appendix A):

> I am afraid that if you look intently at what is moving towards Great Britain, you will see that the only choice open is the old grim choice our forebears had to face, namely whether we shall submit or whether we shall prepare. Whether we shall submit to the will of a stronger nation or whether we shall prepare to defend our rights, our liberties and indeed our lives. If we submit, our submission should be timely. If we prepare, our preparations should not be too late. Submission will entail at the very least the passing and distribution of the British Empire and the acceptance by our people of whatever future may be in store for small countries like Norway, Sweden, Denmark, Holland, Belgium and Switzerland, within and under a Teutonic domination of Europe.

This was indeed the stark choice, and the reason why Winston came to feel undying contempt for MacDonald and Baldwin, but felt respect for Neville Chamberlain even after he persuaded the French to abandon their treaty commitment to the Czechs and signed a humiliating joint communiqué with Hitler at Munich in 1938. Like his predecessors, Chamberlain believed war would lead to the destruction of British cities and the decimation of her youth. Unlike them, he faced the moral issue squarely and took upon himself the historical opprobrium for deceiving the public and sacrificing the interests of other peoples in order, he hoped, to spare his own.[35] In a word he led, and Winston forgave the choice made because of the moral courage displayed. MacDonald and Baldwin, in contrast, holding a far stronger hand vis-à-vis Germany in 1933, fudged the moral choice. For this they were applauded across the land, from the humblest dwelling to Buckingham Palace, where as late as 1935 the usually subdued King George V blazed out at Lloyd George: 'I will not have another war. *I will not.* The last one was none of my doing and if there were another one and we are threatened with being brought into it, I will go to Trafalgar Square and wave a red flag myself sooner than allow this country to be brought in.'[36]

The red flag reference points to one of the saddest aspects of this wretched time, which is that until August 1935 it was an article of faith in a Labour Party led by the uncompromising pacifist George Lansbury that to rearm in competition with another major power was a certain step towards war.[37] Then, in belated response to the destruction of the German Communist Party, the Seventh Congress of the Communist International (Comintern) announced the desirability of anti-Fascist unity among Communists, socialists (previously 'social-fascists') and the progressive bourgeoisie.[38] When, after this, assorted leftists began to cluster around Winston, it is unsurprising that he took a sardonic view of his new-found popularity among people who had spent the past 25 years denouncing him. Nor was he likely to believe his hand strengthened by the support of people who required a lead from Moscow in order to admit the danger posed by the Nazi regime.

Before the Comintern announcement, in

251

another passage from his November 1934 broadcast Winston identified the evil at the core of that danger and repudiated the idea that mere equality of military strength was enough, for which he was denounced as a provocateur and a warmonger both by the British left and by the Nazis. Bearers of bad news are seldom popular, but after the suppression in Germany of even the Christian Trades Union Federation, the passage of vilely anti-semitic laws and the 'Roehm Purge' of 30 June 1934, when the leaders of Hitler's own Brownshirts were murdered in cold blood to curtail the organization's ambitions, he could be excused for wondering what he had said that could possibly be construed as news. Churchill's American biographer William Manchester also wonders how this could not have been obvious to everyone. Winston's collected speeches of 1932–8, published as *Arms and the Covenant* in Britain, bore the title *While England Slept* in the USA, and in 1940 John Kennedy, a student at Harvard whose Anglophobe Irish father was at that time US ambassador to Britain, presented a thesis later published as *Why England Slept*. But was any country awake? The belief that World War I had been caused by secret diplomacy and what was later to be dubbed the military-industrial complex was widespread on both sides of the Atlantic, but more so in the USA because it was overlaid with the conviction that the 'City on a Hill' had been dragged into the war by the cunning British.[39]

Following the primacy given to economic factors, British defence policy was posited on the belief that, since a rapid military solution was no longer possible, war had become a test of economic staying power. From this arose the belief that any measure taken to improve military preparedness which distorted the normal development of the economy or incurred debt would reduce the country's ability to prevail in the prolonged economic and financial struggle to come. Ordnance factories had been run down, former military suppliers long ago converted to civilian work, and it was firmly believed that large-scale rearmament could not be pursued without diverting industrial capacity from non-military economic activities that were the real sinews of war. Lord Halifax, Baldwin's War Secretary, asked: 'Are we in fact to judge the situation so serious that everything has to give way to military reconditioning of our Defence Forces? Such a conclusion, in fact, appears to me to rest on premises not only of the inevitability but to a certain degree of certainty as to the early imminence of war, which I am not prepared to accept.'[40]

Winston did not question the conventional wisdom, and below the political-tactical reasons for his emphasis on air power lay a legitimate military-strategic argument that air power could act directly against the enemy's economic base. He was a pioneer of military aviation and, as already seen, under his aegis the Royal Naval Air Service (RNAS) rivalled the Royal Flying Corps (RFC).[41] At the end of World War I he fell under the spell of Sir Hugh Trenchard, RFC commander in France for much of the war, almost as completely as he had been in thrall to Admiral Fisher at the beginning. Trenchard was the foremost apostle of 'strategic' bombing, the name he gave to air attack against enemy productive capacity, in part to differentiate it from 'tactical' bombing in support of ground forces on the battlefield or to hamper the movement of enemy reinforcements and supplies, but also because he believed a sufficient mass of heavy bombers could by itself win the war.[42] In June 1918 he became the first commander of the amalgamated RFC and RNAS. The Royal Air Force (RAF) was therefore from its inception devoted to the idea that it had rendered the other services obsolete except for the purpose of consolidating a victory over an enemy whose capacity and, no less importantly, whose will to resist had been shattered by aerial bombardment. As Sir Maurice Dean points out in *The Royal Air Force and Two World Wars*, only the concept of strategic bombing as a war-winner in its own right provided a compelling reason for the creation and continuing existence of an independent RAF.

In the spring of 1918 Winston declared that victory would be won by whoever 'possessed the power to drop not five tons but five hundred tons of bombs each night on the cities and manufacturing establishments of its opponents'.[43] As Minister of War and Air he made Trenchard Chief of the Air Staff in February 1919, a post he was to hold until 1929. Both at the War Office and at the Colonial Office Winston worked closely with Trenchard in the development of the concept of imperial policing using air power and armoured car columns, and in the first suppression of a native revolt from the air—against the Kurds in Iraq. Winston argued strenuously in favour of employing air-dropped 'asphyxiating bombs calculated to cause disablement of some kind but not death . . . for use in preliminary operations against turbulent

254

tribes'.[44] There were no such munitions in existence—but there were thousands of tons of lethal gas shells to hand, easily convertible into bombs, and it is as well for his own and Britain's historical reputation that Winston was over-ruled in Cabinet.[45] This, therefore, is the true context for Winston's rearmament campaign, and explains why Baldwin, who sometimes committed the cardinal sin of actually saying what he meant, defined the terms of the debate in a loudly cheered speech to the Commons on 10 November 1932:

> I think it is well for the man in the street to realize that there is no power on earth that can protect him from being bombed. Whatever people may tell him, the bomber will always get through . . . The only defence is in offence, which means you have to kill more women and children more quickly than the enemy if you want to save yourselves. . . . That is the question for the young men far more than it is for us. When the next war comes and European civilization is wiped out, as it will be and by no force more than that force, then do not let them lay the blame upon the old men. Let them remember that they principally and they alone are responsible for the terrors that have fallen on the earth.[46]

There is no reason to doubt that gas featured high on Baldwin's mental list of the terrors that would fall on the earth. The cryptic closing comment on 'young men' is intriguing, and suggests that Baldwin was wrestling with the paradox that those who opposed spending on expensive conventional

255

weapons were in effect forcing governments to rely on the cheaper but infinitely deadlier option of air power. Churchill's reply chided him for his 'fatalism, and perhaps even helplessness'.[47] Ministers were responsible for the defence of the country and the Dominions, he said, and had a duty to do it properly if only to guarantee 'that strong and unassailable neutrality from which we must never be drawn except by the heart and the conscience of the nation'.[48] He did not, however, believe that Baldwin's fears were exaggerated. On 30 July 1934, supporting an amendment to the address which said that 'the state of our national defences, and especially of our air defences, is no longer adequate to secure the peace, safety and freedom of Your Majesty's faithful subjects', Winston said that a week or ten days of bombing would kill thirty to forty thousand Londoners and drive 4–5 million out of the city. He also stated that new incendiary bombs would go right through buildings, igniting each floor as they went, and claimed that the only deterrent to such an attack was a bomber force at least the equal of that of the Luftwaffe. In an article in the *Sunday Chronicle* of 28 July 1935, he declared 'another Great War would cost us our wealth, our freedom, and our culture, and cast what we have slowly garnered of human enlightenment, tolerance, and dignity to different packs of ravening wolves'.[49]

No great exercise of historical imagination is required to re-create the atmosphere of the time, and many readers will recall similar arguments over NATO and nuclear weapons from the 1950s until the fall of the USSR. The major difference was that throughout the Cold War the side most reluctant to initiate hostilities enjoyed preponderance, and so deterrence worked. It might not have done so, for the risk of fatal miscalculation was always present, but war is and always has been hell for those directly involved in it. From time immemorial these have included civilians unfortunate enough to live where combatants chose to do battle, and there was nothing new about a besieged fortress being bombarded or starved into submission. Aerial bombardment simply extended the boundaries of the battlefield; it did not make its realities any harsher.50 Winston sought to concentrate British minds on the fact that the opening of the aerial dimension raised the strong possibility that the British people might become as well acquainted with those dreadful realities as the inhabitants of the European mainland already were:

> For the first time in centuries we are not fully equipped to repel or retaliate for an invasion. For an island people that is astonishing. Panic indeed! The position is the other way round. We are the incredulous, indifferent children of centuries of security behind the shield of the Royal Navy, not yet able to wake up to the woefully transformed conditions of the modern world.51

This was charitable. The truth of the matter was that the British were wide awake to the threat and extremely anxious for it to be directed elsewhere. Churchill condemned the 'habit of saying smooth things and uttering pious platitudes and sentiments to gain applause' which he believed 'more

257

pronounced now than it has ever been in my experience', but he was not inclined to 'tell the truth to the British people' because they really were not, at that time, as tough and robust as he wished they were.[52] Robert Graves's *Goodbye to All That* (1929), Erich Maria Remarque's *All Quiet on the Western Front* (translated in 1930), Siegfried Sassoon's *Memoirs of an Infantry Officer* (1930) and R. C. Sherriff's haunting play *Journey's End* (first performed in January 1929) are still in print today, still being performed. They were required reading for my own, post-World War II generation and there has probably never been a constellation of works that has affected the British public longer or more profoundly: I have argued elsewhere that our understanding of World War I is hamstrung because we generally come to it as literature, not as history.[53] Of course there had never before been a war that snatched sensitive and literate men from their quieter environment and plunged them deep into the world of random death and systematic destruction. To those spared the horrors they read about it was easy to vote, as the undergraduates at the Oxford Union did in February 1933, by 275 votes to 178 in favour of the motion 'that this House will in no circumstances fight for King and Country'. Randolph, Winston's son, spoke against the motion when it was debated again in March, only to be defeated by 750 votes to 138. This was duly noted in Berlin, where, as Winston predicted, Nazi lips curled in contempt at the apparent decadence of the British elite.

There is no way of knowing how much the episode weighed in Hitler's later calculations, and it is entirely possible he formed his opinion that

Britain would never fight from observation of leading figures of British society, including the Prince of Wales and Lloyd George, who came to visit him. But the strident rejection of patriotism by the most privileged youth of Britain can only have confirmed his view that the liberal democracies were husks with no *virtù* left in them. Any doubts on that score were surely allayed when, on

25 October 1933, the previously safe Conservative seat of East Fulham fell to John Wilmot, the Labour candidate, with a swing of 26 per cent. Wilmot stood as an outright pacifist, declaring that he would close every recruiting station and disband the army and air force, and that he wished Britain would 'give a lead to the whole world by initiating immediately a policy of general disarmament'.[54] Roy Jenkins rightly points out that East Fulham returned to the Tory fold in 1935 and that Wilmot proved robust in defence matters during the rest of his political career, but the election thoroughly rattled Baldwin, with terrible consequences.

The foreign repercussions of domestic politics are always difficult to assess, but I do not believe it chauvinist to suggest that Britain may well be the country whose temperament is least easy to gauge from the actions of its politicians and the headlines of its press. These constitute the written record, leavened by the observations of people who by the very act of keeping a daily diary are registering a particular kind of self-regard. We cannot know what moved the electors to vote for Wilmot in 1933 and to discard him in 1935, but it is reasonable to suppose that the sudden change from outright pacifism to a call for all progressive forces to unite in arms against Fascism had something to do with it. In truth the Labour Party was never as utopian as its public utterances seemed to indicate—for example, Labour MPs called for Britain to take the lead against Japanese aggression in China, which, as Winston pointed out, would 'have added the cold, unforgetting, unforgiving hostility of Japan to all these other serious preoccupations'.55 After East Fulham, it seemed that pacifism offered Labour its best chance of recovering from the electoral debacle of 1931, but then came the Seventh Congress of the Comintern and suddenly it was a case of the emperor's new clothes. In France and Spain the call for anti-Fascist unity gave rise to Popular Front governments, followed in Spain by civil war and in France by the first of many rightist conspiracies by shadowy figures known generically as *cagoulards*. In Britain it robbed the only substantial opposition party of momentum in the run-up to the 1935 election.56 The result was that Baldwin's men, tired by their struggle to cope with the effects of the world-wide depression, had no credible alternative to keep them on their toes.

The period 1933–5 was later and most unwisely described as the years of aircraft development that 'the locusts have eaten'. The opinion was that of Sir Thomas Inskip, the pacifist appointed to a newly created Ministry of Defence Coordination by Baldwin in March 1936 following Hitler's militarization of the Rhineland (thus breaking the terms of the Treaty of Versailles, although, as will be seen in Chapter Seven, the Nazis could do so with impunity). The exchange between Winston and Baldwin that followed wrote the epitaph for those years. Winston had muted his criticism of the government during 1935 in the expectation that once Baldwin had a renewed mandate there would be prompt action to regain lost ground. The appointment of Inskip to the post whose creation Winston had urged and for which he himself was clearly the best qualified was a slap in the face, but he kept his powder dry until Inskip's 'locust years' comment opened the door in November. The issue here, it must be noted, was not aircraft production but the hold put even on research and development. The motives for the choice of Inskip had been craven, both Baldwin and Chamberlain agreeing that the appointment of anyone more vigorous, Winston in particular, would make Hitler angry.[57] Inhibited by the certainty that any attack on Inskip would be open to the childish but always effective jeer that he was simply a frustrated office-seeker, Winston laid a thunderous charge on the entire House for its complicity:

> Two things, I confess, have staggered me, after a long Parliamentary experience, in these Debates. The first has been the dangers that have so swiftly come upon us in a few years, and have been transforming our position and the whole outlook of the world. Secondly, I have been staggered by the failure of the House of Commons to react effectively against these dangers. That, I am bound to say, I never expected. I never would have believed that we should have been allowed to go on getting into this plight, month by month and year by year, and that even the Government's own confession of error would

have produced no concentration of Parliamentary opinion and force capable of lifting our efforts to the level of emergency. I say that unless the House resolves to find out the truth for itself it will have committed an act of abdication of duty without parallel in its long history.[58]

Baldwin's reply doomed his historical reputation. Prior to the debate he had spoken in private along much the same lines to a deputation of Conservative back-benchers led by Winston, explaining that the East Fulham election result had tied his hands until the renewed mandate won in November 1935. He asked for understanding of the government's current situation, trying to catch up for the years, as he saw them, unavoidably lost to the electoral realities then prevailing.[59] Winston did not mention this meeting in his memoirs and, as a practical politician, may have grudgingly accepted Baldwin's reasoning—after all, to let in Labour at that time was to condemn the country to debilitating social strife as well as an even weaker position on rearmament. What he could not forgive was that Baldwin then said the same thing in open session, opening with the words: 'I put before the House my own views with appalling frankness.' In *The Gathering Storm* Winston commented that the speech 'carried naked truth about his motives into indecency', and the index lists Baldwin's speech under 'confesses to putting party before country'. It was not the nakedness Winston objected to, but its shameless exposure to the public gaze. Baldwin's words speak for themselves as an admission of lack of confidence both in his own capacity and in the heart of the British people:

> My position as the leader of a great party was not an altogether comfortable one. I asked myself what chance was there . . . within the next year or two of that feeling being so changed that the country would give a mandate for rearmament? Supposing I had gone to the country and said that Germany was rearming and that we must rearm, does anybody think that this pacific country would have rallied to that cry at that moment? I can think of nothing that would have made the loss of the election from my point of view more certain . . . [by delaying] we got from the country, with a large majority, a mandate for doing a thing that no one, twelve months before, would have believed possible. **60**

The significance of the statement does not lie primarily in the calculation of electoral advantage and low opinion of the public it revealed, but in the fact that these words were spoken a year after the election, when Britain was still not geared up to meet the German threat. Atop every other consideration it was an outright falsehood, as neither Baldwin nor his successor Chamberlain believed Britain either could or should match German rearmament. Baldwin was playing with words to conceal his true intentions, and Winston knew words better than any man alive. From their pulse he could sense the health of the man who spoke them, and so knew Baldwin to be morally infirm. The mood of the country may or may not have been as Baldwin saw it, but we will never know because he chose not to put it to the test. Winston was right; it was indeed a matter of character, and perhaps the saddest thing about Baldwin's statement was that he was unaware how inadequate it revealed his own to be.

CHAPTER SEVEN

IN THE WINGS

1936–1940

One of the saddest statistics of World War II is that, until mid-1942 at the earliest, the human and financial cost to the Commonwealth of the bombing campaign against Germany outweighed the damage it had inflicted, and during that time no Luftwaffe fighter squadron was withdrawn from any other theatre to defend the homeland. Before that, German bombers and fighters never intended for long-range operations came close to establishing air supremacy over southern England during the Battle of Britain, at one point obliging the RAF to commit every fighter in its inventory. During the damaging night-bombing Blitz that followed, the Luftwaffe suffered losses minor by comparison to those of the RAF's Bomber Command later in the war because pre-war British planning was dominated by the principle that attack was the best defence. The resources of Fighter Command, barely sufficient to blunt the daylight assault, had been built up over the doctrinaire objections of the Air Staff, and little provision made to combat night-bombing. Thus Germany, which had never entertained the doctrine of strategic bombing (against factories, docks and so forth), almost succeeded where Britain failed, and in the process revealed the hollowness of the theory of deterrence upon which

Winston based his campaign for rearmament during the 1930s.

The performance data and the dates of design and production of the aircraft deployed by Britain and Germany speak for themselves. The two 'strategic' bombers with which the RAF entered the war were the twin-engined Handley Page Hampden and the Vickers Wellington, developed in response to a September 1932 Air Ministry specification. Prototypes flew within a week of each other in June 1936, a modified specification followed in August and the new bombers began entering service in December 1937. They had a top speed of around 255 mph and a range of 1500 miles with a bomb-load of 4000–4500lb. In 1934, panicked by the long lead-time before the Hampden and Wellington would be operational, the Air Ministry issued a specification for a cheaper, lower-performance bomber also able to fly troops to trouble spots in the Empire and then support them from the air. The Armstrong Whitworth Whitley first flew in March 1936 and entered service in early 1937. It had a top speed of less than 200 mph and a range of 1500 miles with a bomb-load of 3400lb, and a design flaw which ensured that the aircraft flew in a nose-down attitude that degraded its already poor performance. Winston's emphasis on numbers entitles him to be considered the political godfather of this truly dreadful aircraft.

The Germans never put a 'strategic' bomber into service. All their bombers were optimized for what the RAF called 'tactical' bombing (to aid one's own ground forces or impede those of the enemy), and the mainstays in 1940 were two dual-purpose types designed when the Germans were still paying lip-service to the Treaty of Versailles prohibition on military aircraft. The Dornier Do-17 first flew in 1934 as a mail carrier prototype, and three years later entered service as a bomber with a maximum speed of 265 mph and a range of 750 miles carrying 2200lb of bombs. After the Heinkel He-III's first flight as a passenger prototype in 1935 it went through 15 variants before entering service as a bomber in 1938, with a maximum speed of 270 mph and a range of 760 miles with a 5500lb bomb-load. A third type was purpose-built in response to a January 1936 specification, which it greatly exceeded. The Junkers Ju-88 first flew in December 1936 and began to enter service at the end of 1939; it had a maximum speed of 285 mph and a range of 1050 miles with 5500lb of bombs. Thus it was not until after the outbreak of war that Germany possessed a bomber in service capable, unmodified, of attacking deep into England from German soil.[1]

The Germans believed the Trenchard doctrine to be unsound, and the Nazi Air Ministry in fact leaked grossly inflated statistics of their aircraft production to encourage British over-commitment to the bomber.[2] They did not believe British bombers would always get through, because of the long German lead in the development of radar. Initiated in 1928, by the mid-1930s two functional sets had been produced which between them permitted the early detection of attacking aircraft and, as the range closed, the determination of their exact range and height. Code-named Freya and Würzburg, these remained in effective service throughout the war. Britain did not start

267

developing a similar capability before 1934, and the Chain Home radar stations that proved decisive in 1940 were primitive by comparison.[3] Fortunately the technology was sufficiently developed by 1936 to permit Air Marshal Sir Hugh Dowding to prevail over RAF orthodoxy in time to develop a coherent system of air defence, for which his service superiors never forgave him. This led to the astonishing ingratitude of his compulsory retirement immediately following the vindication of his policy in the Battle of Britain.[4]

The main British 'tactical' bomber in 1939 was the single-engined Fairey Battle, product of an Air Ministry specification issued in early 1933. The production prototype flew in March 1936, but design changes and the addition of a third crew member had degraded performance to the point where senior officers favoured abandoning the project. It could carry 1000lb of bombs at 200 mph for nearly 1200 miles—speed was sacrificed to obtain an exaggerated range for a supposedly 'tactical' bomber. The Battle did little more than provide target practice for enemy fighters, but 2200 were delivered before production ceased in October 1940. The Bristol Blenheim emerged from a design ordered by Lord Rothermere, owner of the *Daily Mail*, to compete with the American twin-engined Douglas DC1. The prototype, named 'Britain First', flew in April 1935 and Rothermere donated it to the RAF. By then Bristol had developed a version with the same range and payload as the Battle, only 70 mph faster. The Air Ministry first issued a specification for an aircraft with similar performance and then, bureaucratic face saved, ordered the type into production in parallel with the Battle, which it outclassed in every respect including the vital factor of openness to improvement thanks to freedom at the design stage from the limitations of excessively detailed specifications.5

The aircraft that best illustrated the weakness in the Air Ministry's philosophy and rigid procurement methods were the heavy bombers, which alone held out the prospect of realizing Trenchard's dream. The Short Stirling was the first, a cut-down version of the Sunderland flying boat produced in response to a December 1936 specification for an aircraft capable of carrying 14,000lb of bombs or 100 soldiers in the transport mode, with a range of 3000 miles. Among several other detailed requirements was that to fit into all existing hangars the wingspan could not exceed 100 feet. The Sunderland had a wingspan of 114 feet, which could easily have been accommodated by the 125-foot doors of the most common domestic hangar, but even after other restrictions were dropped this one was maintained.6 The Stirling entered service in May 1941, but after suffering appalling losses in the main force role was relegated to secondary operations in 1943. The smaller, better-performing Handley Page Halifax and Avro Lancaster emerged from designs originally produced in response to a 1936 Air Ministry requirement for a twin-engine bomber to carry more than 8000lb over 2000 miles, and were built around a powerful engine under development that never lived up to expectations. The result of the 1936 requirement had been the Avro Manchester, an under-powered widow-maker even more notorious than the Stirling, of which fortunately only 200 of the 1200 ordered by the Air Ministry were built. Independently, the design teams at Handley Page, which dropped out of the original competition, and at Avro developed four-engined versions using the dependable Rolls-Royce Merlin, so the undistinguished Manchester did at least sire illustrious progeny.[7]

Winston was a strident abetter of the Trenchardians in the Air Ministry, and the only question is whether he was deceived or self-deluded by the same rejection of 'passive' methods that distorted his understanding of anti-submarine warfare. If he was misled, the finger points at the man who exercised more direct influence over him than any other in his adult life. Professor (of Experimental Philosophy at Oxford) Frederick Lindemann became a regular house-guest at Chartwell in the early 1930s and remained Winston's closest friend and confidant until his death in 1957. The full extent of Lindemann's impact on British scientific and technical development, through Winston, is almost incalculable, but the basis for their long and close association was his personal bravery, the *sine qua non* of Winston's esteem.[8] Lindemann had been director of the Air Force Physical Laboratory during World War I and, in person, proved his theory of how a pilot should recover from a spin, until then usually a fatal occurrence in flight. Born in Germany of an Anglo-German father, he was none the less a fierce Germanophobe who unsuccessfully contested the Oxford University seat in Parliament as an anti-appeasement candidate in 1935 and 1937.[9] During World War II he supplied spurious technical justification for the policy of 'area bombing'. This was in fact the only option left for a Bomber Command unable to operate by day or to bomb with real precision by night, and was far more attractive than we might now wish to admit to an embattled nation with no other means of bringing the realities of war home to the German people.

The slip between the cup of the Trenchard doctrine and the lip of making it effective against German industrial power was that the size of the bomber force required was unthinkably larger than anything Britain could afford in peacetime, and the slow build-up during the war gave time for the Germans to develop counter-measures. Added to this, British aircraft manufacturing was not immune from the classist rancour and managerial amateurism that was ultimately to lead to de-industrialization.[10] As proved post-war, these problems were not susceptible to political solutions, not least because it was already clear in the 1930s that the machinery of government which would implement any solution was itself a major part of the problem. The procurement system in which Winston insisted that the rulers of Britain should deposit their faith was deeply flawed, something he admitted only partially and belatedly in an April 1938 article on 'Britain's Deficiencies in Aircraft Manufacture':

[Manufacturers] complain that no broad layout of the British aircraft industry was made at the beginning of the expansion; that orders were given, and are given, piecemeal, in little packets; that they have never been able to prepare their works for mass

271

production; that designs are repeatedly altered, to the delay of production, and that very often there is a gaping void between the execution of one contract and the assignment of another.[11]

In September he posed the key question in 'Is Air-Power Decisive?' He argued that the experience of the Spanish Civil War, which would end in 1939, showed how aerial bombardment was not sufficiently accurate to be decisive against properly handled and defended warships—a frequent theme in his writing for many years—and he also doubted its effectiveness against field fortifications, in disrupting supply lines or even against arms factories. As for attacks on the civilian population, the psychological effects had been the opposite of what was expected:

> So far from producing panic and a wish to surrender, they have aroused a spirit of furious and unyielding resistance among all classes. . . . I, therefore, remain convinced that where the strength of the air forces is equal, the side which consumes its energy upon slaughter of the civilian population is likely to encounter surprising disappointments.

But what of the thirty to forty thousand Londoners killed and the 4–5 million driven out of the city that he had predicted in 1934? One can almost hear him clearing his throat, and pausing to consider how to square the circle before continuing:

All these considerations might be vitiated by a

very much larger number of aircraft operating against much larger targets. I must, therefore, add, to avoid misunderstanding, that none of the conclusions I have tried to draw from the Spanish civil war in the slightest degree diminishes the need for Great Britain, with her special dangers and vulnerabilities, to acquire at the earliest possible moment an air force at least equal to that of any other Power within striking distance of her shores.[12]

If, however, 'strategic' bombing could only be effective against enemy civilians and was constrained to act solely as a symmetrical deterrent, the prospect of it being employed in Europe in any circumstance other than retaliation for all-out war was negligible. Thus it could not serve to uphold Britain's obligations as the guarantor of the principles of the Locarno Treaties signed in December 1925, by which Britain, France and Italy in combination with the new states of central and eastern Europe sought to secure the post-war territorial settlement in return for normalizing relations with Germany. The principal treaty was a non-aggression pact among Germany, France and Belgium, which Britain and Italy undertook to guarantee. Germany also signed arbitration agreements with France, Belgium, Poland and Czechoslovakia to submit any disputes to neutral and binding arbitration. France signed two further treaties with Poland and Czechoslovakia confirming pledges of mutual assistance in the event of conflict with Germany. Although not a formal part of the agreements, the 'spirit of Locarno' led to Germany's admission to the League of Nations in September 1926 and the phased withdrawal, completed in June 1930, of Allied troops from the Rhineland.

Historians agree with Winston that the Anglo-German Naval Treaty of June 1935 was the moment when Baldwin openly scuttled the principles not only of the Locarno Treaties, which his own Foreign Secretary had negotiated in 1925, but of the Treaty of Versailles itself. Winston later wrote that after Hitler announced the introduction of conscription in May 1935, MacDonald's 'last and best' foreign policy act before he resigned was the 'Stresa Front' of France, Italy and Britain against Nazi repudiation of international agreements. 'However,' he wrote,

> on June 18 the Anglo-German Naval Agreement was signed, and Europe was astonished to learn that the British government had made a private bargain for themselves with Nazi Germany which completely stultified the agreement of the three allied Powers at Stresa, and made the latest declaration of the Council of the League of Nations ridiculous.[13]

It also, he continued, sanctioned German naval supremacy in the Baltic with obvious consequences for the outlook of the Scandinavian countries— and, he might have added, the Soviet Union.

Thus when Hitler repudiated Locarno by sending troops into the demilitarized Rhineland in March 1936, against the advice of his military commanders, the Naval Treaty had told him he had nothing to fear from the nebulous guarantee

Britain had given France. He also calculated, correctly, that the French would not move because of their related decision in 1930 to build fortifications along their border with Germany (and Italy). The expense of the Maginot Line precluded the development of the mobile strike force that was necessary to make good France's own Locarno commitments. If 1933–5 were the 'locust years' for Britain's armaments programme, they were years consumed by the concrete and steel Moloch along only a part of France's eastern frontiers. Any German government might have exploited the strategic imbalance created by the defensive posture of the powers that had defeated and humiliated it in 1918–19; for Hitler the opportunity was irresistible.[14] Winston quoted him to that effect in an article he wrote in March 1939:

> History [Hitler had written in *Mein Kampf*] teaches us that nations which have once given way before the threat of arms without being forced to do so will accept the greatest humiliations and exactions rather than make a fresh appeal to force. He who has obtained such an advantage will, if he is clever, only make his fresh demands in small doses. When dealing with a nation which has lost all force of character owing to its having given way spontaneously, he will be entitled to expect that his fresh but piecemeal demands will not be considered worth resisting by the nation from which they are made.[15]

Locked into a static defensive scheme, and into a strategy of blockade and bombardment aimed at the civilian population of Germany which could not be justified to the British people except in retaliation for an attack on their own cities, French and British governments were paralysed during the 1930s by the logic of military choices to which they were committed before the Nazi threat loomed on their horizon. There is no indication in any of Winston's published or private writings that he appreciated how greatly British options were narrowed by neglecting the army in favour of an air force built on a theory tested only against tribesmen.

Perhaps Winston was right to despise Baldwin more than any other public figure, but a review of the field is not reassuring. From left to right the air crackled with static about the need to create a 'New Man' in a 'New World Order'. As far as Winston was concerned both government and opposition were equally culpable, and it is fair to see his passage through the 1930s as that of a battleship sailing among a fleet of lesser vessels, firing to left and right without fear or favour as their counterblasts bounced off his armour. He was the only person left in public life who believed that institutions evolved over centuries could surmount the challenges of the twentieth century, and that was because he alone believed the British were still capable of greatness.

Winston was, however, baffled and not a little hurt by the ambient mediocrity. As a professional politician he regretted the disappearance of flash and fire from the Commons, which he felt was symptomatic. In an article mildly critical of the game of musical chairs played in the French Chamber of Deputies, he attributed the contrast with the House of Commons in part to the fact that 'in the British Parliament, there is a marked and felt dearth of men of high ability. In France, there is a plethora'.16 In another article, looking down from the plateau he felt Britain had attained '10,000 feet above', he commented that it was

> pleasing to look back over the plains and morasses through which our path has lain in the past, and remember in tradition the great years of pilgrimage. Then [the dwellers in the lowlands] point to the frowning crag, their venerated 'El Capitan' or 'Il Duce' casting its majestic shadow in the evening light; and ask whether we have anything like that up there. We certainly have not.17

His meaning is clear: a nation might be fortunate to produce a great leader, but most unfortunate to need one.

Winston's admiration for Mussolini seemed surprisingly uncritical. During a visit in 1927 he was fulsome: 'If I had been an Italian, I am sure I should have been wholeheartedly with you from start to finish in your triumphant struggle against the bestial appetites and passions of Leninism,' he wrote in the text he prepared before the interview. 'But in England we have not yet had to face this danger in the same deadly form. We have our own way of doing things.'18 Although he was laying it on with a trowel to obtain an agreement on debt repayment, these were dangerous words and led Mussolini to assume that under no circumstances would Winston make common cause with the Soviet Union. As late as 1937 Winston could still

277

write, with reference to the Italian invasion of Abyssinia: 'It would be dangerous folly for the British people to underrate the enduring position in world history which Mussolini will hold; or the amazing qualities of courage, comprehension, self-control and perseverance which he exemplifies.'[19] Again, his words were coloured by a desire not to drive Mussolini into Hitler's arms, which he correctly judged would be the result of the policy of ineffectual sanctions pursued by Anthony Eden, Baldwin's Foreign Secretary. Finally in May 1940, after becoming Prime Minister, Winston tried once more to appeal to Mussolini's vanity, and received an insulting reply. A perceptive analysis of the two personalities concludes:

> The bilateral misunderstanding was at its climax. Churchill had always believed he was dealing with a dictator interested in making gains from his actions; a political gambler, but one interested in victory; a man who used rhetoric, as he himself did, to put a certain complexion on things, to create an atmosphere, not to say anything politically decisive. He was a professional politician . . . having relations with a ruling class who had a tradition in this field. The Duce was just the opposite . . . Mussolini bound himself to the image of 'the man of Providence' and assumed a line of action, not having in mind results, but what he supposed to be the duty of a man of providence arriving at a historical turning point. So he spoke of 'honour' and obligation to act as Britain did at the top of the international game.[20]

278

There was never any ambivalence in Winston's attitude towards dictators. He thought them undesirable, while recognizing that circumstances in a given country at a particular time made them preferable to revolution. A devout believer in an ideal House of Commons, he was aware that while it was a good forum for the sort of politics he loved, it was not well adapted to the task of delivering the economic and social demands of mass democracy.[21] He did not regard those demands as necessarily legitimate, and indeed saw the intrusion of ill-informed public opinion in high matters of state as partially responsible for the fact that 'the grand and victorious summits which the British Empire won in the war' had been lost in the years that followed it. 'The compass has been damaged,' he wrote. 'The charts are out of date. The crew have to take it in turns to be captain; and every captain before every movement of the helm has to take a ballot not only of the crew but of an ever-increasing number of passengers.'[22] His response, worth considering again today, is that the ruling elite must justify itself by trying harder to educate, to inspire and to lead.

The Spanish Civil War was to acquire posthumous status as a rehearsal for World War II, and Winston's reputation as an anti-appeaser is open to attack for his support of a Franco-British policy of non-intervention, which denied a democratically elected government the support to which it was entitled in the face of armed rebellion. Unfortunately the election of a Popular Front government in Madrid was accompanied by widespread disorder, something that always

279

brought out the authoritarian in Winston, with assassinations by paramilitary police loyal to the government, which he believed cancelled any legitimacy arising from what had been a very evenly divided election between implacably hostile coalitions.23 By the time the Soviet Union, Italy and Germany were drawn into the conflict, massacres perpetrated by both sides had turned his support for non-intervention into a 'plague on both your houses':

I have tried very sincerely to adopt a neutral attitude of mind in the Spanish quarrel; I refuse to become a partisan of either side. I will not pretend that, if I had to choose between Communism and Nazi-ism, I would choose Communism. I hope not to be called upon to survive in the world under a Government of either of these dispensations. It is not a question of opposing Nazi-ism or Communism, but of opposing tyranny in whatever form it presents itself . . . I cannot feel any enthusiasm for these rival creeds. I feel unbounded sorrow and sympathy for the victims, but to give a decisive punch either way, without making sure that the result would not be to make ourselves responsible for a subsequent catalogue of foul atrocities, would be a responsibility which no one in the House ought willingly to accept.24

Bearing in mind that Winston cared little for the rights and wrongs of the internal politics of any country except in so far as they might affect British interests, the relaxed view he took of the triumph of Fascism in Italy and of something very similar in Spain can be simply explained: both countries were peninsulas surrounded by waters dominated by the Royal Navy, and he judged that Britain could contain either or both, unilaterally if necessary. He was right: British forces overwhelmed the Italians in Africa and the Mediterranean after they came into the war in 1940, while Generalissimo Franco prudently remained neutral. When, in April 1941, Winston spoke of Mussolini as 'this whipped jackal . . . frisking up by the side of the German tiger with yelps not only of appetite—that could be understood—but even of triumph', the lash of his contempt was nerved by the recollection of his demeaning and wasted praise.[25]

Winston's attitude to Hitler, in contrast, was always deadly serious. From the moment he became Chancellor of Germany he was invested with the authority of his formidable nation, and there was no flattery in Winston's 1935 assessment of him: 'Adolf Hitler was the child of the rage and grief of a mighty empire and race which had suffered overwhelming defeat in war. He it was who exorcised the spirit of despair from the German mind by substituting the not less baleful but far less morbid spirit of revenge.'[26] A later passage from the same article, where Winston wrote that 'the world lives on hopes that the worst is over, and that we may yet live to see Hitler a gentler figure in a happier age', is often cited to support the argument that Winston accepted the logic of appeasement. He did, but solely from a position of strength. The full text makes it clear that he did not share the hopes of the world—for which we should read those of his party and a large

281

majority of his countrymen—because 'meanwhile, the great wheels revolve; the rifles, the cannon, the tanks, the shot and shell, the air-bombs, the poison gas cylinders, the aeroplanes, the submarines, and now the beginnings of a fleet flow in ever-broadening streams from the already largely war-mobilized arsenals and factories of Germany'.27

He was profoundly and fortunately mistaken on the last point. Germany was not 'largely war-mobilized' and would not be until 1943, and the belief that the Reich was fully stretched as early as 1935 was an error of strategic appreciation shared by most of the proponents and critics of appeasement. Thus Winston in January 1937:

> Judged by every standard Germany is bankrupt. In the next two or three years, perhaps in a much shorter period, she will either be forced to reduce sensibly her outlay upon armament, or be tempted to some desperate venture. If the decision of Germany is to plunge the whole world into war . . . [it] would spell the ruin of such civilization as Europe has been able to build up and preserve.28

Unfortunately for Europe Hitler had found in Hjalmar Schacht, President of the Reichsbank in 1923–30, not only a supremely well-connected fundraiser who made the Nazis' rise to power possible and who persuaded President Hindenburg to appoint Hitler as Chancellor in 1933, but also a man whose financial ruthlessness and pioneering development of what the British call Keynesian economics enabled Nazi Germany to have both

282

guns and butter in a seemingly never-ending supply.[29] In September 1936 Hitler created a Four-Year Plan Office under Hermann Goering, head of the Luftwaffe and Prime Minister of Prussia, to put the entire economy on a war footing—by 1941. Goering failed in this as he did in most enterprises entrusted to him, but he did force Schacht out of the planning of the war economy. Schacht believed that the novice Goering would unleash uncontrollable inflation, and engineered his own dismissal from the Reichsbank in January 1939 to evade the blame.[30] If the miracle-worker had lost faith in his creation, it is understandable that the British Treasury was also convinced that the Nazi economic edifice was fragile. Schacht had built more strongly than he realized, however, and Goering's incompetence perversely delayed economic melt-down until the conquests of 1940 rendered the prospect irrelevant in a continent-wide command economy.

In September 1937 Winston again wrote about Hitler, in a clearly placatory tone that at first glance sits extremely ill with his image as the mortal foe of Nazism:

> To feel deep concern about the armed power of Germany is in no way derogatory to Germany. On the contrary, it is a tribute to the wonderful and terrible strength that Germany exerted in the Great War, when almost single-handed she fought almost all the world and nearly beat them. Naturally, when a people who have shown such magnificent military qualities are arming night and day, its neighbours, who bear the scars of previous

283

conflicts, must be anxious and ought to be vigilant. One may dislike Hitler's system and yet admire his patriotic achievement. If our country were defeated I hope we should find a champion as indomitable to restore our courage and lead us back to our place among the nations.[31]

Winston knew his articles were read carefully by Joachim von Ribbentrop, the German ambassador in London, and this was manifestly insincere flattery. The statement is significant not for what it said but because he felt it necessary to write something to rebut the widespread criticism, in Britain, that he was anti-German. However, for 70 years Prussia/Germany had offered its neighbours a choice of capitulation either with or without war. Since both the Soviet Union and the USA were for the moment out of the equation, the choice for Britain was between pre-emptive submission or a far higher level of preparation for war than in 1914. Because the alternatives were so unpalatably stark, magical thinking conjured up a third way, based on the belief that the Germans must share Anglo-French popular revulsion against war. Hitler was the problem, so this theory ran, and if the German people were reassured that their desire for unification with ethnic Germans across the borders created at Versailles would not be thwarted, then support for Hitler would collapse along with his artificial economy.

Winston did not believe Hitler to be unrepresentative, but as a politician he could not ignore, still less dismiss, a hope so many of his countrymen clung to, even though the policy

ABOVE Men of the King's Own Scottish Borderers going over the top at Helles, Gallipoli, on 4 June 1915. Clementine later confided that 'the Dardanelles haunted [Winston] for the rest of his life. He always believed in it. When he left the Admiralty he thought he was finished. I thought he would never get over the Dardanelles; I thought he would die of grief.'

RIGHT Winston as lieutenant colonel commanding 6th Royal Scots Fusiliers at Armentières, 11 February 1916. On the left is his second-in-command, Archibald Sinclair, later Liberal leader and a member of Winston's War Cabinet. Winston is wearing a French steel helmet, still preserved at Chartwell.

Winston's beloved Chartwell. This house in Kent, which he bought in 1922, remained the family home until his death. The dining room (the long windows at the lower right) offers charming views in three directions.

Winston, unable to walk because of his recent appendix operation, is carried in a chair during his 1922 election campaign in Dundee. Neither his visibly weakened state nor the determined support of Clemmie enabled him to retain his seat.

Winston laying bricks for a new cottage on the Chartwell estate on September 1928. According to the *Daily Sketch*, in which this picture appeared the following day, Churchill could lay a brick a minute.

Winston in a carriage at a Queen's University Belfast Rag in 1926. At the age of 51 he was still lively and gregarious. He played his last game of polo in Malta the following year.

Winston was a very keen swimmer. In *My Early Life* he described an episode when his swimming ability enabled him to save his brother's life. Here he is seen leaving the water at Deauville in 1927.

Chancellor of the Exchequer in Stanley Baldwin's government, Winston carries the despatch box on his way to the House of Commons to present his Budget on 29 April 1929.

A Churchill family photograph with Charlie Chaplin (right) taken at Chartwell in July 1931. From left to right: Tom Mitford (Clementine's cousin and the only brother of the Mitford sisters – he died during World War II), Winston, Freddie Birkenhead, Clementine, Diana and Randolph junior

Winston was taken ill with paratyphoid fever on 27 September 1932. He is seen here being stretchered out of London's Beaumont Street Nursing Home on 10 October.

RIGHT Winston striding down Whitehall with Lord Halifax, the Foreign Secretary, at his side on 29 March 1938, less than three weeks after the German annexation of Austria. Halifax was later appointed British ambassador to the United States of America.

BELOW A photograph from *Picture Post* showing Winston working on *The History of the English-Speaking Peoples* in his study at Chartwell on 25 February 1939. He liked to see his books in proof at an early stage, and then worked on them at this specially designed desk.

Winston on England's south coast in 1940 with Vice Admiral Sir Bertram Ramsay, who masterminded the Dunkirk evacuation and was later Allied naval commander on D-Day.

Winston inspecting the crew of a Wellington bomber during a visit to a British airfield on 6 June 1941.

Churchill visiting dock workers at Liverpool on 28 September 1941. The city had suffered heavy bombing. According to the official army caption, Winston asked 'Are you managing to get plenty of food?' 'Aye, sir! We're doing grand, thank you,' came the reply.

The Churchills visiting a bomb-site in Bristol on 14 April 1941, following a heavy German air raid on the city two days earlier. The man to the left (leaning backwards) is Walter Thompson, the detective who accompanied Winston on trips at home and abroad during the war. The hatless man standing behind Winston and to the right of Clementine is the American ambassador to Great Britain, J. Gilbert Winant.

involved securing peace of mind for the appeasers at the expense of the sacrifice of the interests of others.[32] Nor, given his attitude towards Japanese, Italian and German aggression in China, Abyssinia and Spain respectively, was he in a position to condemn the concomitant moral cowardice of justifying appeasement by arguing that the sacrificial victims deserved their fate. He had no objection to throwing other peoples to the wolves if it genuinely helped the British sledge to reach safety. All he demanded was that none should be discarded if they could help defend the sledge, which should itself be equipped with sufficient firepower to keep the wolves at bay if all else failed. With regard to international relations, the philosopher Thomas Hobbes could be said to have spoken for him in 1651 in *Leviathan*:

> For the laws of nature . . . of themselves, without the terror of some power to cause them to be observed, are contrary to our natural passions, that carry us to partiality, pride, revenge, and the like. And covenants without the sword are but words, and of no strength to secure a man at all. Therefore, notwithstanding the laws of nature, if there be no power erected, or not great enough for our security, every man will—and may lawfully— rely on his own strength and art for caution against all other men.[33]

From this came the title *Arms and the Covenant* for the collection of speeches he had delivered between May 1932 and March 1938, mainly to the Commons, that was published in 1938. The 'covenant' in question was the founding document of the League of Nations, something Winston, together with the Foreign Office establishment, regarded as a useful adjunct to, but no substitute for, traditional 'balance of power' diplomacy. Although the speeches are a treasure-trove of quotes these are diluted by tens of thousands of less memorable words and their cumulative effect is stupefying. Winston became a long-winded bore, and his habit of leaving the Chamber after speaking made other MPs less inclined to give him a respectful hearing. However, even he was not so thick-skinned that he could fail to notice his colleagues pointedly trooping out when he rose to speak.

Few men have been so conscious of making history as Winston, or have devoted so much time and thought to the written record. George Washington and Napoleon Bonaparte spring to mind, but neither of them actually wrote the histories in which they played the leading role. When Winston jovially declared that history would be kind to him because he intended to write it himself, he was diverting attention from the extent that he had already done so—in the archives. Anyone contemplating the mountain of documentation Winston left for historians to pick over must conclude that some of it was generated with posterity in mind. In an October 1939 broadcast he said, 'I cannot forecast to you the action of Russia. It is a riddle wrapped in a mystery inside an enigma.' So was he, further enclosed in the double bluff of seeming to be an open book. How much of this was the product of conscious calculation is less easy to say.

Winston was never as much 'in the wilderness' as

294

his memoirs suggest. Martin Gilbert affirms that the information on British policy he received officially from ministers and informally from civil servants gave him 'a unique position in British public life for someone without Cabinet office'.[34] The best-known of his sources was Desmond Morton, who survived being shot through the heart in 1916 and met Winston when serving on Field Marshal Haig's staff in 1917. Morton lived near Chartwell and was a frequent guest. As head of the Industrial Intelligence Centre (IIC), set up in 1929 'to discover and report the plans for manufacture of armaments and war stores in foreign countries', in 1931 he obtained permission from the then Prime Minister, MacDonald, renewed by Baldwin and Chamberlain, to share IIC intelligence with Winston. It could not be otherwise—the nature of the information alone would have revealed Morton as Winston's informant, and the fact that he was not sacked is sufficient proof that he had political clearance. Other sources were the traditional leaks from heads of department who disagreed with government policy, no doubt discounted to a degree by Winston who as an experienced minister knew very well how the Whitehall game was played.[35]

The primacy of Morton's raw data in the formulation of Winston's campaign for Britain to match a non-existent threat of German strategic bombing raises the question of 'intelligence failure' so beloved of journalists. There are never sufficient resources to explore all avenues of enquiry, so political direction will define where the spotlight of intelligence is pointed. In this case, it illuminated disinformation crafted by the Nazi Air Ministry to coincide with what the British government expected but dreaded, and what the RAF wanted to believe. Probably the original intention was simply to make Britain hesitant about threatening to use force at a time when Germany was vulnerable, but, as already seen, the consequences for British diplomacy, defence strategy and allocation of resources were far-ranging.

More intriguing, in its way, is the fact that all three Prime Ministers during the 1930s wanted Winston to be as well informed as they were on the subject of German rearmament. Clearly this was not simply professional courtesy. They wanted something from him in return, and this may have been to do precisely what he did: to beat the warning drum when they could not, and to be the hard man they could point to as the alternative to their accommodating selves in dealings with the Germans. Sadly, they were dealing with people on whom finesse was wasted. The Nazi hierarchy saw only weakness in the exclusion from power of the only man in British public life who seemed capable of calling a spade a spade. The stratagem, if such it was, worked better in the domestic sphere. With home-grown extremists of left and right a tiny minority and the Labour Party reduced to irrelevance, Winston alone provided the foil to make steady increases in defence expenditure seem both reasonable and restrained.

Pursuing the hypothesis further, Winston was also useful to the Tory Prime Ministers in attacking manifestations of racial and nationalist extremism among the right-wingers of their own party. His leadership of the backwoodsmen over the India question gave him an authority Baldwin and

Chamberlain lacked in that quarter, and their role as party leaders made it impossible to speak to their MPs with the necessary directness and severity. Winston liked nothing better, and concentrated his fire on those who attacked France without regard for the fact that without it Britain would be powerless in Europe. In June 1937 he explained the strategic calculation wittily but explicitly:

> Many countries, not excluding our own, are apt to regard the French as a vain, volatile, fanciful, hysterical nation. As a matter of fact they are one of the most grim, sober, unsentimental and tenacious races in the world . . . The British are good at paying taxes, but detest drill. The French do not mind drill, but avoid taxes. Both nations can still fight, if they are convinced there is no other way of surviving; but in such case France would have a small surplus and Britain a small army.[36]

Finally, in April 1938 he addressed those on both sides of the Channel whose language and behaviour were endangering the Entente, with a contemptuous slap at those of his erstwhile followers who denigrated the French as a means of expressing their own pro-German sympathies:

> I wonder whether the French people realise how bitter and persistent is the pro-German propaganda in this island? The strongest point, repeatedly made, is that France is on the verge of collapse. She is portrayed as

about to go down the same bloody sewer Spain has done. All the 'Heil Hitler' brigade in London society exploit and gloat over what they are pleased to call 'the Parliamentary impotence of the French democracy'. Thus the amusing game in which French politicians rejoice is turned in deadly fashion to their detriment—and to our common danger.[37]

Winston's earlier hostility towards the Soviet Union became a liability in the face of a resurgent Germany. Eating his own words was never a problem, but finding some reason to say anything positive about Stalin's dictatorship strained the limits of sophistry. As it happens, his solution permits us simultaneously to examine the conundrum that Winston, one of Britain's most forthright Zionists, often wrote about Jews using terms that jar on modern sensibility. Such language was considered unremarkable at the time, but his comment on the liquidation of the Bolshevik Old Guard in the show trials of 1936 revealed something else. He took the opportunity to gloat over the execution of 'the heroes of the British Socialist Party' such as Zinoviev and Kamenev. Noting that the victims were nearly all Jews, he continued:

Evidently the Nationalist elements represented by Stalin and the Soviet armies are developing the same prejudices against the Chosen People as are so painfully evident in Germany. Here again extremes meet, and meet on a common platform of hate and cruelty. . . . Clearly Soviet Russia has moved decidedly away from Communism . . . It may well be that Russia in her old guise of personal despotism may have more points in contact with the West than the evangelists of the Third International. At any rate it will be less hard to understand. This is in fact less a manifestation of world propaganda than an act of self-preservation by a community which fears, and has reason to fear, the sharp German sword.[38]

Anti-Bolshevism was the trump card played by the Zionist leader Chaim Weizmann to get the Foreign Secretary, Arthur Balfour, to declare, in a letter to Lord Rothschild of November 1917, that

His Majesty's Government view with favour the establishment in Palestine of a national home for the Jewish people, and will use their best endeavours to facilitate the achievement of this object, it being clearly understood that nothing shall be done which may prejudice the civil and religious rights of existing non-Jewish communities in Palestine, or the rights and political status enjoyed by Jews in any other country.

For the *realpolitik* behind this, however, the key document is an article written by Winston in 1920:

Zionism offers the third sphere to the political conceptions of the Jewish race. In violent contrast to international communism, Zionism has already become a factor in the political convulsions of Russia, as a powerful

299

competing influence in Bolshevik circles with the international communistic system. Nothing could be more significant than the fury with which Trotsky has attacked the Zionists generally, and Dr Weizmann in particular. The cruel penetration of his mind leaves him in no doubt that his schemes of a world-wide communistic State under Jewish domination are directly thwarted and hindered by this new ideal, which directs the energies and the hopes of Jews in every land towards a simpler, a truer, and a far more attainable goal. The struggle which is now beginning between the Zionist and Bolshevik Jews is little less than a struggle for the soul of the Jewish people.[39]

The article began with the words 'no thoughtful man can doubt the fact that [the Jews] are beyond all question the most formidable and the most remarkable race which has ever appeared in the world', and went on to say that the internationalist malevolence of the Jewish Bolsheviks was the result of generations of rejection and persecution in countries that should have been happy to have them. He saw the Jewish homeland as a poultice to draw the poison distilled into an admirable race by the evil inflicted on them by others. In seeking simultaneously to redress a historic wrong and to defuse a current menace the Balfour Declaration laid the basis for another problem that haunts us today, and this necessarily obscures the fact that at the time this statement of intent was seen to be both pragmatic and principled, the Edwardian *beau idéal* of public policy-making.

Returning to the 1936 article, the key phrase was 'Russia in her old guise of personal despotism may have more points in contact with the West than the evangelists of the Third International.' This was an acute observation. Stalin's 'anti-cosmopolitanism' led him to exterminate the highly successful Comintern cadres who in every Western country had recruited 'moles', some of whom reached places of great influence, particularly in the USA. Nor should we forget the 'Famous Five' Cambridge undergraduates whose activities resulted in a British publishing cottage industry in the later twentieth century.[40] From this time onwards Winston was inclined to believe that 'communism' had become a front for Great Russian imperialism, no less a threat to British interests than it had been in the days of the Great Game along the North-West Frontier of India.

There was, perhaps, just a chance that the course of history might have been altered in 1936, when Winston became the cynosure of an all-party Focus Group formed to support his view that Nazi Germany must be dealt with from a position of strength. Prominent members of the group included Sir Norman Angell, founder member of the Union of Democratic Control, leading light of the related League of Nations Union, vehement opponent of World War I and winner of the Nobel Peace Prize in 1933; Sir Walter Citrine, the general secretary of the Trades Union Congress; Sylvia Pankhurst, the suffragette; Archibald Sinclair, Winston's old second-in-command at Plugstreet and now leader of the Liberal Party; Lady Violet Bonham Carter (née Asquith); and Labour MPs Hugh Dalton and Philip Noel-Baker. Progressives all, many of them had spent half a lifetime denouncing Winston as a reactionary. He had not changed his views on social matters in the slightest; it was they who had suddenly realized the danger in arguing about the shape of the future in the face of a present threat to everything they valued. Glad of the support though he was, Winston had no faith in extra-parliamentary pressure groups. This, and personal animosity towards Baldwin which was by now almost beyond the limit of his ability to control, led him to commit the most clumsy intervention in a Commons debate of his whole career: it drew a repudiation that would have sunk a lesser man.

The issue was the desire of the as yet uncrowned King Edward VIII to marry his long-time mistress Wallis Simpson, a woman with a colourful past and a complaisant husband from whom she was not yet divorced. His attempt was manifestly unwise, but there is a strong case for arguing that Edward's pro-German stance and his subsequent behaviour during the first year of the war meant that it was as well for the monarchy that he sidelined himself.[41] Winston got involved in the imbroglio as the King's champion at the last minute, when the only politically possible outcome, abdication, was apparent to everyone, including Edward. By so doing he brought together in one package everything about himself that aroused distrust and anger in others. Bumbling into the Chamber in the middle of an emollient explanation by Baldwin, which actually answered the points made by Winston in a press release the previous day, his intemperate interruption was drowned out in a display of near-unanimous rejection tinged with hatred. Recording an interview with Bob Boothby, one of Winston's few followers, William Manchester summed it up:

> They had brooded over Churchill's recitation of alarming facts, resenting his insistence that they face the growing danger. As events vindicated him, that exasperation grew. Now, when he was clearly in the wrong, they made him the target of their chagrin. In raging at him they were raging at the prospect of another great conflict, one they did not deserve and for which, as they saw it, they bore no responsibility.[42]

Monday 13 December 1936 marks the lowest ebb of Winston's political career. It killed the momentum of the Focus Group, and it ruled him out of consideration for ministerial office when Neville Chamberlain became Prime Minister following Baldwin's resignation at the peak of his own popularity in May 1937. Winston later described John Foster Dulles, US Secretary of State from 1953 to 1959, as 'the only case I know of a bull who carries his own china shop around with him', but on this occasion he was the bull and the china shop was entirely of his own creation. During 1937 his financial situation was more than usually precarious—he even contemplated selling Chartwell—and his literary output positively industrial.[43] But he was severely chastened, and his political influence was negligible during Chamberlain's first year as Prime Minister, when opportunities to engage more closely with the Italians, the Americans and the Russians were spurned in pursuit of Chamberlain's tightly focused vision of bilateral deals with the dictators. This exclusion of alternatives, in due course, was to lead to the abandonment of Czechoslovakia at Munich in September 1938: arguably the nadir of British diplomacy and moral authority.

The most common apology for Chamberlain is that he was buying time for British rearmament. This does not stand up to scrutiny: the relative military strength of Britain and France declined vis-à-vis Germany in 1938–9 and Chamberlain knew it would. Appeasement was a strategy devised by Sir Horace Wilson, chief industrial adviser to the government since 1930 and from 1935 seconded to the Prime Minister's office. It was fostered by the calculation that Goering's wasteful Four Year Plan would puncture Schacht's miracle, which Schacht himself believed was likely to happen in early 1939. Wilson was also well placed to appreciate that British industry was not responding to the stimulus of additional government spending with anything like German vigour. In May 1938 he prodded the crux of the matter, which was no longer whether or not Britain should rearm in the face of the German threat, but why the country was doing it so slowly:

We are now in our third year of openly avowed rearmament. Why is it, if all is going well, there are so many deficiencies? Why, for instance, are the Guards drilling with flags instead of machine guns? Why is it that our small Territorial Army is in a rudimentary condition? Is that all according to schedule? Why should it be impossible to equip the

304

Territorial Army simultaneously with the Regular Army? It would have been a paltry task for British industry, which is more flexible and fertile than German industry in every sphere except munitions. . . . If Germany is able to produce in these three years equipment and armament of every kind for its Air Force and for sixty or seventy divisions of the regular Army, how is it that we have been unable to furnish our humble, modest military forces with what is necessary? If you had given the contract to Selfridge or to the Army and Navy stores, I believe that you would have had the stuff today.[44]

The answer was that British industry was not more flexible and fertile, and was chronically less productive to boot. Wilson and Chamberlain lacked any real feel for military matters, which in itself inclined them away from armed confrontation, but they did understand money and trade, which had always been the basis of British power. They therefore played to the country's strength, as they saw it, and did so in secrecy because they believed that public opinion, which they regarded as incorrigibly ignorant and dangerously volatile, would not stand for it. They would not have disagreed with the comment made by the 'American Eagle' Charles Lindbergh, following a visit in April 1938, that 'the assets in the English character lie in confidence rather than ability; tenacity rather than strength; and determination rather than intelligence . . . It is necessary to realize that England is composed of a great mass of slow, somewhat stupid and indifferent people, and a small group of geniuses.'⁴⁵ The Prime Minister and his chief adviser considered themselves among the latter, and if Hitler's regime had collapsed as they expected history might have agreed with them.

As already noted, Winston too believed the growth in German power was unsustainable, but his whole being revolted against a policy whose moral costs he felt to be unbearable. Hitler's demand for the Sudetenland, where the majority of the *Volksdeutsche* (ethnic Germans) in Czechoslovakia lived but which also contained the fortified mountains that constituted the country's main defences, came down, as most things did in his opinion, to a trial of wills. His generals told him that an invasion was out of the question, but as he commented when they were inspecting the abandoned defences together later in the year, 'It's not the guns, it's the men behind them.'

Winston had hoped that Czechoslovakia would play the role of 'heroic little Belgium' in 1914 by providing an unequivocal *casus belli* to unite British public opinion:

Three days before Britain entered the Great War, four members out of five in the cabinet and nine out of ten in the House of Commons would have been found inveterately opposed to our intervention upon the Continent. Four days later these proportions were reversed. It was not argument or reflection that produced this change of view. People simply would not believe that Germany would really attack France and Belgium. But when [Germany did] everyone knew instinctively where they stood and what we ought to do. An episode like the trampling-down of Czechoslovakia . . . would change the whole current of human ideas and would eventually draw upon the aggressor a wrath which would in the end involve all the greatest nations of the world.[46]

He could not imagine that Chamberlain would make submission to Hitler and then induce the French to renege on their treaty obligations. In a cold footnote added later to an article published on 15 September 1938, he noted that on that day Chamberlain flew to see Hitler at his mountain retreat in Berchtesgaden and 'in accord with Monsieur Daladier [the French Premier], adopted the policy of appeasement embodied in the agreement of Munich (September 28th). The Czechoslovak Government were induced to yield themselves without resistance . . . to deliver up the fortress-line upon which their power to defend themselves against further aggression depended.'[47]

Daladier flew back to Paris feeling ashamed, and was flabbergasted to be greeted as a conquering hero. *'Les cons!'* he commented of the cheering crowd. Not so Chamberlain, who accepted the adulation as richly deserved and read out the meaningless phrases to which Hitler had set his hand: Anglo-German relations were of the 'first importance for the two countries and for Europe'; the Anglo-German Naval Treaty and the Munich Agreement were 'symbolic of the desire of the two peoples never to go to war with one another again'; German and British ministers were to use 'the method of consultation . . . to continue our efforts to remove possible sources of difference, and thus

307

to contribute to assure the peace of Europe'. Hitler had not given him anything not already implicit in the existence of diplomatic relations between the countries. Yet this was the paper Chamberlain waved with the words: 'My good friends, this is the second time in our history that there has come back from Germany to Downing Street peace with honour. I believe it is peace in our time.'[48]

A week later Winston rose to deliver what may have been the most powerful speech of his career. Men who had refused to join him in sending a warning telegram to Chamberlain before Munich had none the less criticized the agreement during the preceding days of debate: Alfred Duff Cooper, Chamberlain's First Lord of the Admiralty, who resigned; Anthony Eden, who had resigned as Foreign Secretary nine months previously; Clement Attlee, the leader of the Labour Party; Archibald Sinclair for the Liberals; Leo Amery and Harold Macmillan for the uneasy Conservatives. Amid desultory heckling, mainly from the gadfly Nancy, Lady Astor,[49] Winston opened by saying 'the most unpopular and most unwelcome thing . . . We have sustained a total and unmitigated defeat.' The terms obtained, he asserted, could have been reached through ordinary diplomatic channels, and 'I believe the Czechs, left to themselves and told they were going to get no help from the Western powers, would have been able to get better terms than they have got.' It was not warmongering to have demanded a firm policy, he said:

Between submission and immediate war there was this third alternative, which gave hope not only of peace but of justice. It is quite true

308

that such a policy in order to succeed demanded that Britain should declare straight out and a long time beforehand that she would, with others, join to defend Czechoslovakia against an unprovoked aggression. His Majesty's Government refused to give that guarantee when it could have saved the situation, yet in the end they gave it when it was too late, and now, for the future, they renew it when they have not the slightest power to make it good. All is over. Silent, mournful, abandoned, broken, Czechoslovakia recedes into the darkness. She has suffered in every respect by her association with the Western democracies and with the League of Nations. . . . She has suffered in particular from her association with France, under whose guidance and policy she has been actuated for so long.

He did not begrudge 'our loyal, brave people' their 'natural, spontaneous outburst of joy and relief', he continued. He was not addressing a public gathering, he was calling the House to account for its stewardship of British sovereignty. The people should know the truth:

They should know that there has been gross neglect and deficiency in our defences; they should know that we have sustained a defeat without a war, the consequences of which will travel far with us along our road; they should know that we have passed an awful milestone in our history, when the whole equilibrium of Europe has been deranged, and that the terrible words have for the time been pronounced against the Western democracies: 'Thou art weighed in the balance and found wanting.' And do not suppose that this is the end. This is only the beginning of the reckoning. This is the first sip—the first foretaste of a bitter cup which will be offered to us year by year—unless—by a supreme recovery of our moral health and martial vigour, we arise and take our stand for freedom, as in the olden time.[50]

In the months that followed Winston was twice threatened with de-selection by his constituency party and treated like a bearer of a contagious disease by the ambitious men of his own party, young and old alike. When it seemed possible that Chamberlain might call for a general election to obtain a personal mandate, he warned:

If there is an election in the near future it will be a very strange and unhappy one. It is not so much a question of who wins or loses, but what happens to the country. I have never seen it divided as it is today. The division does not follow exactly the regular groupings of party, but it cuts very deep, and will sever many ties and friendships.[51]

The psychological misjudgement of Munich became apparent on 15 March 1939, when Hitler drove into Prague at the head of his troops. Chamberlain had thought Hitler would appreciate the advantages of leaving him with some 'face', but the man could barely wait to occupy the rest of

Czechoslovakia and to crow over the ease with which the French and the British had been fobbed off. Even now, Chamberlain felt he could move only hesitantly towards preparation for war. He had promised not to introduce conscription in peacetime, and in May the Military Training Act merely called up two hundred thousand men for militia service, after which they would pass to the Territorials or the Reserves. The Labour Party, even at this late stage, denounced it, remarkably, not for being pathetically inadequate but for being excessively warlike. Winston kept his own counsel, but took the opportunity to express pride in the greatly improved physical health of new recruits compared to the situation in 1914: 'What a vindication all this has been for our social services and those who have worked for them! There is no more far-seeing investment for a nation than to put milk, food and education into young children'.[52]

Proper conscription was not introduced until the National Service (Armed Forces) Act was passed on the eve of war that September. Meanwhile Chamberlain issued defence guarantees to Poland, Romania and Greece. As Winston commented in the Commons, neither the Polish nor the Romanian 'assurances had any military value except within the framework of a general agreement with Russia'.[53] This was not forthcoming in part because the Poles and Romanians feared Stalin as much as they did Hitler, in part because Chamberlain and the Foreign Secretary, Lord Halifax, committed the diplomatic blunder of not making their public declarations of guarantees contingent upon the parties accepting a general strategy of containment,

311

and to an even greater extent because Stalin was not interested. At the Party Congress on 10 March 1939 he spoke of 'warmongers who are accustomed to have others pull the chestnuts out of the fire for them' and his own intention to stay out of the new imperialist war.

Thus Chamberlain's contempt for traditional diplomacy had convinced Stalin that the only possible explanation for Munich was a desire by the Western powers to encourage Hitler to strike east. Without Soviet support the guarantees given to Poland and Romania were of solely symbolic value, and by now Hitler knew it. Why Chamberlain and Halifax should have thought Hitler would believe they were really serious is a puzzle in view of signals of continuing appeasement, such as a refusal to intervene to prevent the transfer of £6 million worth of Czech gold from London to German-occupied Prague by the Bank for International Settlements.[54] But this time they did actually mean it, and believed that a deal with the Soviet Union was unnecessary because Hitler would shrink from war with France and Britain while his eastern flank was menaced by a mortal ideological enemy. This confidence soon evaporated. On 19 August the Germans and the Russians signed a comprehensive trade agreement, followed on the 23rd by a non-aggression pact whose secret clauses agreed the partition of much of eastern Europe. Poland was to be divided between the two nations, the Russians were to have Finland, Estonia, Latvia and Bessarabia, with Lithuania added later, and the Nazis everything to the west. Barely a week later Germany attacked Poland. France and Britain declared war on

3 September and on the 17th the Russians joined the attack on Poland to secure their share of the spoils.

In the end it took the invasion of Poland as well as the rape of Czechoslovakia to achieve what the German attack on Belgium in 1914 had done almost overnight. It would be pleasant to record that the occupation of Prague brought Britain's rulers a heightened awareness of their responsibility, but in fact politics continued as usual up to and well into the war. Chamberlain does not appear to have considered resigning and there was no pressure from his party for him to do so. In July the *Daily Mail* and the *Daily Telegraph* led a campaign demanding that Winston be included in the government, but Chamberlain 'did not feel he would gain sufficiently from Winston's ideas and advice to counterbalance the irritation and disturbance that would inevitably be caused'.[55] The Labour opposition was diffident and went through the motions: everyone seemed intent on the strict observance of routine, as though normality could somehow be preserved by ritual. So life continued, with men diminished by the scale of the moment clinging to mundane certainties, in an effort to postpone as long as possible the moment when theories would be put to the test, when words must give way to deeds, and posturing to purposeful action.

Michael Foot and his two co-authors glibly proclaimed Chamberlain and his ministers *Guilty Men* in a book that first appeared in 1940, but he and his political associates would have denounced earlier or greater preparations for war. In September 1939 Britain was ready—to fight a long, slow, low-intensity war, the only kind in which the

313

financial weapon might eventually prevail and from which it could hope to emerge with its international standing intact. In France the large and Moscow-subservient Communist Party denounced the war and urged its members to desert from the army, while German Communists in exile pronounced the Western Allies worse than Hitler.

In contrast, the Communist Party of Great Britain came close to extinction after it adopted a policy of 'revolutionary defeatism'. The only social group in which fear predominated was the metropolitan elite. On 3 June 1940, having barely outmanoevred the capitulationists in his party, Winston commented that defeatism 'isn't in the workshop, it's all the upper middle class'.[56] There was nothing approaching the patriotic enthusiasm of 1914 among the working class—only a weary and bitter mood of 'here we go again', coupled with a cold determination that there should not be a third round. And appeasement was at last discredited among senior officials. Sir Robert Vansittart, who as Permanent Under Secretary at the Foreign Office was one of Winston's most assiduous informal sources throughout the 1930s, and whom Chamberlain had moved aside before Munich, summed it up crisply in November 1939:

It is abundantly plain that we are fighting not only Hitlerism; we are fighting Germany. We are fighting a country which has already cost the world a great deal more than it is worth, and not only our cooperation with France but our own security and existence make it imperative that we should have better security for the future this time than the last.[57]

CHAPTER EIGHT

CENTRE STAGE

1940–1942

The events of May 1940 and the two years that followed are the most studied in the entire history of Britain.[1] Winston's memoirs placed the fateful moment when Chamberlain had to choose between him and Halifax on the 10th, as the Wehrmacht crashed into Holland and Belgium and the Battle of France was about to begin, but that was dramatic licence. The meeting actually took place on the 9th, the day when both Chamberlain and the French Prime Minister, Paul Reynaud, separately found they lacked the political support to continue. Thus the political bankruptcy of the two Allied governments came 24 hours before the nullity of their military leadership began to be exposed. It does not bear thinking what would have happened had Chamberlain still been in place during the collapse of France. As it was, Halifax was the Conservative Party's (and King George VI's) first choice of successor, and the Labour Party was willing to serve under him in a coalition government. Fortunately Halifax ruled himself out because as a peer he would not have been able to defend his government in the Commons. That role would have fallen to Winston, making Halifax's position doubly anomalous, and he had the good sense to realize it.

Winston was also the only man with the

experience and moral authority necessary to impart some dynamism to the war effort. This is not hindsight: it was widely recognized at the time. After nine months of 'Phoney War' conscription was still not fully implemented and over a million men remained unemployed.[2] Factories continued to work peacetime hours and armaments production burbled on at a leisurely pre-war pace.[3] The canonical version of events, most cogently expressed by John Colville, Assistant Private Secretary to Winston in 1940–1, is that the new Prime Minister promptly infused Whitehall and Westminster with a sense of dynamic common purpose.[4] This might have applied to those nearest Winston, but Andrew Roberts has shown that a strong faction in the Conservative Party and its allies in the Civil Service, which he deftly dubs the Respectable Tendency, was unreconciled: 'despite Colville's assertion that after fourteen days of Churchill's leadership the Establishment had coalesced behind Churchill, it is clear that the Respectable Tendency actually spent fourteen months putting Party before country, and love of intrigue before both'.[5]

If the public heaved a collective sigh of relief to know someone was at last in charge, it found no echo among those supposed to represent their will in the place Winston regarded as the temple of democracy, for which all his great speeches were crafted and to which, in the first instance, most were addressed. On the day he first entered the Commons as Prime Minister it was Chamberlain, not he, who received a standing ovation from the Tories. The Labour members, even though they had received posts in his government that exceeded

316

their supply of able men, were caught on the flypaper of their martyrology and buzzed perfunctorily. Even among the generally well-disposed Liberals, Lloyd George coldly calculated that the country would turn to him when Winston failed. As late as 1942 he was still conspiring with a group that included future Prime Ministers Harold Macmillan and Alec Douglas Home, to replace Winston.

Lloyd George refused several invitations to join the National Government, possibly because he was piqued to note that Winston's blueprint for taking control of the war effort used his own performance in 1916 as the negative example. Winston was determined to avoid becoming the captive of the opposition. Having few dependable friends, he could not afford to turn the passive ill will of the Respectable Tendency into active enmity, so 'he took every care to make sure the change-over was done in a way which showed consideration for the outgoing Prime Minister and the other Ministers who left the Government'.[6] He behaved impeccably towards Chamberlain, permitting him to stay in 10 Downing Street for a month while he himself remained at Admiralty House, and even took the time to be courteous to Baldwin. He opposed any scapegoating of the 'men of Munich', asked Attlee and Sinclair to restrain their followers, slapped down an attempt by Amery to generate an 'under-secretaries' plot' (reminiscent of the one he himself had led in 1922, which toppled Lloyd George), and summoned Cecil King, editor of the *Daily Mirror*, to warn him that if he continued his attacks on Chamberlain's men Winston's administration would fall and be replaced by a government of capitulationists. He deplored any inquest into the past as 'a foolish and pernicious process. There are too many in it. Let each man search his conscience and search his speeches. I frequently search mine.'[7]

Chamberlain was terminally sick, but served on in the War Cabinet until ill health forced him to retire. Winston had to watch his back even after succeeding him as leader of the Conservative Party in early October 1940, while the act of consolidating his political base offended the more partisan Labour MPs, particularly the Welsh class warrior Aneurin Bevan who spent the rest of the war heckling him.[8] After Hitler invaded the Soviet Union the following year Bevan was among those convinced that Winston secretly wanted Russia to be defeated and clamoured, in defiance of overwhelming military logic, for an early cross-Channel invasion. Most historians have dwelt on the dull defeatism of the extreme right while drawing a charitable veil over the stridently anti-patriotic policies espoused by the left. Both are equally understandable in their historical context, and equally lamentable in the glare of hindsight. Bevan's real target, of course, was the Labour Party leadership, which did indeed put country before party and proved a loyal coalition partner. Indeed, Labour leaders were surprised to find that the ogre of Tonypandy and the General Strike was very far from being a reactionary. Thus Herbert Morrison, Attlee's unsuccessful rival for the leadership of the party in 1935 and Winston's robust Home Secretary, observed in May 1942: 'He is full of sympathy, you know, for the ordinary British man and woman, and doesn't like inflicting hardship on

318

them. He's the old benevolent Tory squire who does all he can for the people—provided always that they are good obedient people and loyally recognise his position, and theirs.'9

Anyone less like a Tory squire than the cosmopolitan Winston is hard to imagine, and Morrison's attempt to cram him into that straitjacket was a harbinger of the way the Labour Party was to deal with Winston post-war: a great man, but trapped behind the times by age and class. With possibly unconscious irony, Paul Addison puts his finger on the core conceit:

> Whether dealing with problems of discipline and morale in the Army, or the conditions of the civilian population, Churchill's views were distinctly old-fashioned. He . . . never understood the incorporation of the liberal intelligentsia in the war effort. Nor, of course, did he see the British people through their eyes, as a people aspiring to a welfare state under the management of enlightened experts and planners.10

Colville wrote that Winston 'pretended to a ruthlessness which was entirely foreign to his nature and, while the thunder and lightning could be terrifying, they could not disguise the humanity and the sympathy for those in distress which were the solid basis of his character'.11 Although he moved swiftly to equip the government with almost unlimited powers of repression by the imposition of Defence Regulation 18B on 22 May 1940, he was opposed to restrictions on the populace 'for its own good'. Winston also appreciated that civilians responded positively to being in the front line and should be treated as soldiers, not nibbled to death by bureaucrats. He knew that it was power, not class, that set him apart. 'When one is in office', he remarked, 'one has no idea how damnable things can feel to the ordinary rank and file of the public.'[12] In his mind there was little connection between morale and promises of better social conditions after the war, still less the ethical and spiritual justifications that so exercised progressives on both sides of the Atlantic. When he intervened in domestic policy it was to emphasize food, rest, transport and, above all, fairness. Everything else he regarded as matters to be dealt with post-war.

Rationing was the principal means of expressing fairness. The common standard of living was set at about the level of a skilled blue-collar worker, an appreciable gain for a large proportion of the population, which during the war was clothed and fed better than ever before.[13] Unfortunately the regime was contaminated by niggling measures designed to harass the better off, whose assets had already been appropriated and whose incomes were heavily taxed. 'Everything save conscience can now be conscripted in this country', wrote the great American reporter and Anglophile Ed Murrow. Consciences not proving stern enough, profits were officially banned and the result was a black market, leading to 'food wardens' and an increase in official intrusiveness that eroded the solidarity between people and state in whose name the measures were decreed. Winston's instincts were against this, as they were against repressive acts in general. It is unlikely that he ever knew the extent to which the war was used to justify gratuitous bureaucratic tyranny, and clearly he did not suspect what a permanent feature it would become. The great paradox of his public life is that in defence of freedom he presided over the greatest and most irrevocable shift of power from the citizen to the state in British history.[14]

He could not, while rallying the nation to face the Nazi threat, permit himself the luxury of disputing the methodology of fairness with the generally well-intentioned Labour leaders, not least because they were his firmest supporters in the struggle. Many years later, after serving as deputy Prime Minister during the war, beating Winston in the 1945 general election and being beaten by him in turn in 1951, Clem Attlee judged that 'Without Churchill, Britain might have been defeated. I do not say we would have been defeated. But we might have been. He was so perfectly suited to fill a particular need; the need was so vital; and the absence of anybody of his quality was so blatant that one cannot imagine what would have happened if he had not been there.'[15] This came from a man wounded at Gallipoli and repeatedly hurt by some of Winston's most cruel invective.[16] The sub-text to Attlee's encomium is that Britain, with Winston, *could not* be defeated. Pride, conceit, delusion—call it what you will—this was his principal gift to the nation. The void of quality he filled may be the least carefully examined feature of what the nation has been happy to accept as its finest hour. It was certainly Winston's. As he explained at the end of *The Gathering Storm*, the first volume of his *History of the Second World War*, the call to form a government answered the central question of his life:

> I was conscious of a profound sense of relief.
> At last I had the authority to give directions
> over the whole scene. I felt as if I were
> walking with destiny, and that all my past life
> had been but a preparation for this hour and
> this trial. Ten years in the political wilderness
> had freed me from ordinary party
> antagonisms. My warnings over the last six
> years had been so numerous, so detailed, and
> were now so terribly vindicated, that no one
> could gainsay me. I could not be reproached
> either for making the war or with want of
> preparation for it. I thought I knew a good
> deal about it all, and I was sure I should not
> fail. Therefore, although impatient for the
> morning, I slept soundly and had no need for
> cheering dreams. Facts are better than
> dreams.

Yet at the beginning dreams were all he had to
enable him to breathe beneath an avalanche of
facts so harsh that to continue the struggle required
willing suspension of disbelief. He was not alone in
this. Once it became apparent that France was
collapsing, but before the unexpected success of
the evacuation from Dunkirk, Winston demanded
an assessment of the military prospects from the
Chiefs of Staff of the three armed forces. Major
General Hastings 'Pug' Ismay, head of the small
defence staff that was the indispensable handling
machine for all Winston's contacts with the services
throughout the war, recalled that the report was:

a curious document. The first twelve paragraphs were devoted to showing that the enemy had the whip hand in almost every sphere, and the summing-up set out in the thirteenth and final paragraph seemed somewhat inconsistent: 'Our conclusion is that, *prima facie*, Germany has most of the cards; but the real test is whether the morale of our fighting personnel and civil population will counterbalance the numerical and material advantages which Germany enjoys. We believe it will.[17]

Ismay was a quintessential cartilage to Winston's vertebrae throughout the war.[18] Because his memoirs are so restrained they tend to be ignored today in favour of the diaries of General Sir Alan Brooke, later Field Marshal Lord Alanbrooke, who also had to contend with the Prime Minister's sometimes ill-directed dynamism and was often, in the privacy of his diary, scathing about him. Brooke was Commander Home Forces from June 1940 until December 1941, when Winston appointed him Chief of the Imperial General Staff (CIGS).[19] But of the two, Ismay was better placed to see the whole picture across the full span of Winston's strategic direction. He did not share Brooke's dislike for politics and politicians, and if his account stresses the positive too much for modern tastes, that is no more than one might expect from a man who facilitated the pounding optimism of the master he was proud to serve.

It is said that no man is a hero to his servant, but a very wide range of officials, a breed not noted for genuine deference, admired Winston.[20] Of them

323

all, Ismay was the most alike to Winston in spirit, and the bond between them was sealed in a conversation on 12 June 1940 after their penultimate conference with the demoralized French leaders. When Winston commented, 'It seems we fight alone', Ismay replied that he was glad of it and that 'We'll win the Battle of Britain.' Winston gave him the sharp look of one who knows a resonant phrase when he hears it, then said, 'You and I will be dead in three months' time', to which Ismay replied, 'Quite possibly, but we'll have a hell of a good time those last seven days.'[21]

It is wise to be cautious of an account written in the glow of a successful outcome, and even Ismay's memoirs do not hesitate to point out occasions where Winston's own history of the war departed from the objective truth. Ismay's judgement of the mood of the nation was not drawn solely from the Whitehall milieu, but also from outsiders such as Ernest Bevin, head of the powerful Transport and General Workers' Union and Winston's Minister of Labour, reflected in the following anecdote:

> Shortly after the fall of France, Mr Bevin had to address a somewhat restive audience of trade unionists. He started off by saying that although things looked bleak, the Government, on the advice of the military experts, had decided to carry on the fight. Whereupon a voice from the front row shouted, 'We'd knock your bleedin' 'ead off, Ernie, if you'd decided anything else.'[22]

Following an unprecedented all-party tribute from both Houses of Parliament on his eightieth birthday in November 1954, Winston's gracious reply added the last of the many entries under his name in countless books of quotations:

I was very glad that Mr Attlee described my speeches in the war as expressing the will not only of Parliament but of the whole nation. Their will was resolute and remorseless and, as it proved, unconquerable. It fell to me to express it, and if I found the right words, you must remember that I have always earned my living by my pen and by my tongue. It was a nation and a race dwelling all round the globe that had the lion heart. I had the luck to be called upon to give the roar.

This was not false modesty; following the 'Finest Hour' speech, delivered on the 125th anniversary of the battle of Waterloo on 18 June 1940, Ismay was amazed to note that Winston genuinely believed he was simply expressing the will of the people: 'I had never attributed to him the quality of humility, and it struck me as odd that he failed to realise that the upsurge of the national spirit was largely his own creation. The great qualities of the British race had seemed almost dormant until he had aroused them. The people then saw themselves as he portrayed them.'[23] Winston's determination not to behave as Lloyd George had done in 1916 was also essential if he wished to command the respect as well as the obedience of the armed services. Loyalty may be a flaw in a politician, but soldiers live by it. Like courage, it is a mental conditioning born of practice and every person has a finite amount of it. In *Anatomy of Courage* (1945)

Winston's doctor, Lord Moran, called it a 'habit', a moral quality nurtured by making the right choices in undemanding times because it cannot be invoked from nothing in an emergency. In a memorandum of 8 October 1942 to Sir Edward Bridges, Secretary to the Cabinet, Winston said he rated 'the capacity of a man to give a useful opinion on any question connected with war' to be first, courage and ability; second, real experience under fire; third and last, staff studies and seniority.[24]

Unfortunately, men with good war records did not necessarily have the 'bottom' he considered the foundation for all other human qualities. Anthony Eden, Winston's Foreign Secretary from late 1940 and long-frustrated heir apparent, was crippled by survivor guilt from being the only field officer of his battalion neither killed nor wounded at Delville Wood in 1916. He wished for a strong foreign policy but shrank from its cost, and his obsession with defeating Italy may have been a compensation for an unconfessed fear of confronting Germany. Even among those who remained brave, the after-effects of World War I could be pernicious. The brave and charming Field Marshal Lord Harding, severely wounded in January 1943 when leading 7th Armoured Division from the front, thereafter Chief of Staff to Winston's favourite general, the debonair but indolent Field Marshal Earl Alexander, told me that senior commanders of his generation consciously strove not to follow the example of World War I predecessors. This was, in part, a triumph of 1930s anti-war propaganda, for no fewer than 78 British generals were killed and more than twice that number wounded during that war. Their successors were sometimes over-anxious to spare their men, and as a result many of them lacked what the influential military thinker Major General J.F.C. Fuller described as 'the brutality essential in war'.[25]

Brooke lamented a shortage of real leaders, attributing it to 'the cream of the manhood having been lost in the First World War'.[26] The truth is that British officer casualties were proportionately higher than German in both wars because more was required of them, their men often lacking the combat instincts so evident in their opponents. There is nothing remarkable or demeaning about this. The last successful invasion of Britain had taken place in 1066, the last major war on British soil had ended in 1651, and with the exception of the world conflicts all the rest of Britain's wars have been fought by small volunteer expeditionary forces. The history of Germany, in contrast, was one of almost continuous invasion and counter-invasion involving ever-larger conscript armies, and it became a unified nation under the leadership of Prussia, the German state most perfectly defined by war. In *A Genius for War*, Trevor Dupuy summarized his extensive statistical research of World War II combat effectiveness in sobering terms:

> On a man for man basis the German ground soldiers consistently inflicted casualties at about a 50 per cent higher rate than they incurred from the opposing British and American troops under all circumstances. This was true when they were attacking and when they were defending, when they had

327

local numerical superiority and when, as was usually the case, they were outnumbered, when they had local air superiority and when they did not, when they won and when they lost.[27]

Any analysis of Winston's performance as a war leader that does not start from the premise that Allied armies could only hope to prevail in major engagements when they enjoyed substantial numerical superiority in all arms cannot arrive at valid conclusions. It will also underestimate the scale of his achievement. He knew Germany was an economic and military superpower and that Britain, alone, was not. Although the resources of the Empire and the USA helped to redress the quantitative imbalance, only absolute preponderance could overcome embarrassingly superior German operational skill. In his recent *The Dictators: Hitler's Germany and Stalin's Russia*, Richard Overy argues that, contrary to general belief, German manpower and industry were indeed organized for a long war by 1940. The doubt remains whether this was the result of Nazi direction or an almost natural condition in a country created by war. The Germans placed greater confidence in their subordinates, and vice versa.[28] The results were evident in factories as well as in battle. One wonders if even Winston would have been daunted by his task had he known that German manpower was only briefly and partially mobilized in 1940, and that the Wehrmacht won the Battle of France with fewer men, tanks, aircraft, artillery and motor transport than the French, Belgians and British.

Despite the best efforts of Bevin at a Ministry of Labour pullulating with worker-friendly planners, the chronic inability of British industry to raise output proportionate to increased inputs remained unchanged. It proved impossible to increase productivity by cash incentives and greater use of machine tools because the craft unions would not allow it, and because workers in other industries threatened to strike if their wages fell behind in a 'league table' from which the notion of productivity was fiercely excluded. Workers in key industries still downed tools over 'who does what', quality control was negligible, and some equipment delivered to the armed forces required overhaul by military fitters before it could be used. This was despite a greatly heightened sense of patriotism and with strikes in theory suspended for the duration, under a government enjoying the full cooperation of the Trades Union Council and its political arm, the Labour Party.

There seemed to be no way, in liberty, to compete with Germany; yet if the competition were lost, liberty itself would be forfeit. Winston could not change the underlying social and economic realities, but his long experience of the machinery of government permitted him to wring greater efficiency from it than any Prime Minister before or since—indeed, greater efficiency than most of those who worked in it believed possible. Diarists like Brooke or the gadfly Henry 'Chips' Channon might refer to him as 'The Dictator', but in fact Winston's authority rested on his refusal to exercise arbitrary power. Sir Leslie Rowan, later his Principal Private Secretary, noted that the first instruction he gave upon becoming Prime Minister was that no order from him was to be regarded as valid unless it was in writing, thus imposing discipline on himself and giving certainty to others. The moral power of Winston's administration lay in his creation of a structure that permitted him to impart his energy to all aspects of the war effort, but which also, by design, placed limits on him.

Within the constraints he devised for his own impulsiveness, Winston was determined to prevent the abdication of political direction that had permitted the Central Powers to dictate strategy to the Entente during World War I. His War Cabinet excluded the service ministers, and with the King's blessing, but without a vote in Parliament, he created the post of Minister of Defence for himself. 'I had made no legal or constitutional change,' he recalled. 'I had been careful not to define my rights or duties.'[29] The service ministers, later joined by the Foreign Secretary, formed the Defence Committee (Operations) chaired by the deputy Prime Minister, Attlee. Winston himself chaired a separate Defence Committee (Supplies). Although the Chiefs of Staff always accompanied their ministers, their own deliberations took place in a subordinate committee, also often presided over by Winston. Under them in turn were the Joint Planning Board and the Joint Intelligence Sub-Committee.[30] At every level Winston sought to encourage inter-service cooperation, if not with great success certainly in marked contrast to the adversarial empire-building FDR encouraged among the US armed forces.[31]

Although other ministers and committees were left to get on with their jobs, Winston distrusted the Foreign Office both because he believed it to be

330

compromised by Chamberlain's appointments and because its house style grated on him.[32] 'The ideas set forth appear to me to err in trying to be too clever', he wrote on a draft despatch, 'and to enter into refinements of policy unsuited to the tragic simplicity and grandeur of the times and the issues at stake.'[33] He conducted foreign policy himself, supplemented by off-the-record contacts through the Secret Intelligence Service (SIS). The extent and vital importance of purely oral communications is the great bugbear of historical research, bound as it is to the paper trail. Winston insisted that all executive orders should be in writing, but in certain key areas we not only have no way of establishing the truth but in some cases will never know even the subject headings. It is a measure of how little importance Winston attached to formal diplomatic channels that he sent Halifax to the Washington Embassy and Sir Stafford Cripps, a standard-bearer of the left, to Moscow. Cripps was the nephew of the Fabian Beatrice Webb and, like her, convinced that planning by a self-anointed elite was the answer to nature's regrettable untidiness.[34] Cripps was expelled from the Labour Party in 1939 because of his adamant advocacy of a Popular Front linking Labour with the Communists, a strategy pressed by Moscow, and Attlee considered it poetic justice to expose him to the realities of Stalin's rule, as well as convenient to have him far away.

One can perhaps make too much of Winston's antipathy towards the Foreign Office—it may have been no more than a recognition that war is, as the great strategist Clausewitz put it, 'a continuation of policy with the admixture of other means', which

331

did not include the skills of professional diplomats. In truth he had little time for mandarins of any kind. Colville once asked him which he disliked most, the Foreign Office or the Treasury—'The War Office,' he growled.35 The principle of no power without accountability was so strong in him that Ismay invoked it to dissuade him from setting up a private office for close advisers like Lindemann and Morton.36 Ismay did not wish to belong to such a body because 'if it were thought that I was trying to exert influence on matters outside my province, I would forfeit all confidence and be useless to him'.37 Unmediated contact with those responsible for a given problem lay at the heart of the 'Winston touch': 'This degree of candour (which was unlike anything I had ever experienced)', wrote a senior official, 'and his readiness to expose the rough workings of his mind added, of course, greatly to the interest of our work. But it did far more than that. It enabled us to serve him far better than we could possibly have done if he had not been willing to let us see far into his thoughts.'38

It is hard to overemphasize how radical Winston was. He always believed that opposition to his ideas sprang from conservatism. 'Being very receptive to new ideas', wrote Lieutenant General Sir Ian Jacob, Military Assistant to the War Cabinet 1939–45, 'he welcomed those who could put them forward, and was naturally inclined to favour those who could speak up boldly, and hold their own in the rough-and-tumble of controversy.'39 He could be very rough indeed, but the purpose was always to test the man as well as his ideas. Brooke found this totally exhausting: his diaries are littered with

332

exclamations when Winston calmly accepted something he had disputed ferociously only a few hours previously. Jacob felt it 'wasted a great deal of time, and created a good deal of misunderstanding and heart-burning, but it made people take great pains to be sure of their ground. If it had not been allied to his immense industry, his driving-power and his personality and prestige, it could have been disastrous.'[40] Not as disastrous, perhaps, as permitting conventional wisdom to go unchallenged.

When the other party understood that Winston's confrontational style was designed to test opinions, not to suppress them, the product was a politico-military synergy that never emerged in Germany, the USA or the Soviet Union. There are many accounts of hard-headed scientists and military men feeling recharged after meeting him. In 1940 the Permanent Under-Secretary of War urged him to meet a general leaving for the USA on an arms-buying mission so that 'he may have the glow of Mount Sinai still on him when he reaches Washington'.[41] All Winston's outbursts were to some extent theatrical—wise men ran for cover when he lapsed into unwonted silence. This happened rarely, and the casualties of his method were not men who stood up to him but those from whom he was unable to strike a spark.[42]

Something else that cannot be stressed too much is how deeply he despised mediocrity, in keeping with an Old Testament outlook deeply offensive to modern sensibilities: 'I know thy works, that thou art neither cold nor hot: I would thou wert cold or hot. So then because thou art lukewarm, and neither cold nor hot, I will spew thee out of my

333

mouth.'[43] He also seems to have found the fabled 'stiff upper lip' tiresome at times, which was unfortunate because British officers prided themselves on their imperturbability above all else. 'Outwardly a commander must inspire confidence in all those serving under him, and equally to his superiors,' wrote Brooke. 'How often have I seen Winston eyeing me carefully, trying to read my innermost thoughts, searching for any doubts that might rest under the surface.'[44] Ismay agreed that 'however black the situation may be, [a staff officer] must never look as if he is rattled or lacking in confidence. In fact he must always give the impression of having time on his hands and a song in his heart.'[45] Some of what the Chiefs of Staff regarded as tiresome wrangling may have been the result of Winston's probing to discover if there was real conviction behind the professional mask.

Most of it, however, was irritation at men who thought more slowly and systematically than he, and at the technique evolved by the chiefs to thwart initiatives they regarded as unsound. This was to agree to his proposals in principle and then bury them deep beneath practical difficulties. The outstanding practitioner was Admiral of the Fleet Sir Dudley Pound, who had been working with him since 1939 and had rapidly decided it was too wearisome to meet him head-on.[46] But it was Air Chief Marshal Sir Charles Portal who triggered what Brooke reckoned among the most violent outbursts of the war at the Chiefs of Staff meeting of 4 December 1941. At issue was Winston's wish, in anticipation of success in a forthcoming offensive in North Africa, to promise Stalin that ten squadrons of RAF fighters and bombers would be detached from the Middle Eastern theatre to assist the Soviet armies. Portal agreed but said the offer was too definite.

> This produced the most awful outburst of temper, we were told that we did nothing but obstruct his intentions, we had no ideas of our own, and whenever he produced ideas we produced nothing but objections, etc. etc! Attlee pacified him once, but he broke out again, then Anthony Eden soothed him temporarily, but to no avail. Finally he looked at his papers for some 5 minutes, then slammed them together, closed the meeting and walked out of the room! It was pathetic and entirely unnecessary. We were only trying to keep him from making definite promises which he might find hard to keep later on. It is all the result of overworking himself and keeping too late hours. Such a pity. God knows where we would be without him, but God knows where we shall go with him![47]

Three days later the Japanese attacked Pearl Harbor and Hitler obligingly declared war on the USA, so this was the last chiefs' meeting at which Winston still thought it possible that Germany would win. Perhaps he erred in concealing too well the doubts under the surface of his apparently indomitable confidence: his military advisers might have served him better if he had bluntly reminded them that for centuries British strategy required a continental ally to carry the brunt of the land fighting. Britain had not done enough to compensate for French deficiencies in 1939–40, and Winston still believed that the Dardanelles operation would have kept Russia in World War I by knocking Turkey out of the war and enabling munitions to be supplied to the tsar's army. He was determined neither error should be repeated but, although Pound unreservedly threw the Royal Navy into getting convoys through to Archangel and Murmansk, Brooke and Portal remained committed to the strategy Winston outlined to the War Cabinet in the midst of the Battle of Britain on 3 September 1940, the first anniversary of the war:

> The Fighters are our salvation, but the Bombers alone provide the means of victory. We must therefore develop the power to carry an ever-increasing volume of explosives to Germany, so as to pulverise the entire industry and scientific structure on which the war effort and the economic life of the enemy depend, while holding him at arm's length from our Island. In no other way at present visible can we hope to overcome the immense military power of Germany.[48]

The chiefs were locked into the view that the only prospect of returning to the continent in order to impose terms on Germany was after blockade and aerial bombardment had created conditions where 'numerically inferior forces can be employed with good chance of success'.[49] They were understandably unwilling to abandon what they believed to be the only way Britain might win the war in order to succour the Soviet Union, whose own appeasement of Germany in 1939–41 had included providing strategic raw materials without which not only the attack in the West but also the assault on the Soviet Union itself could not have taken place. In addition, the chiefs feared that the Russians would collapse and wished to avoid going out on a limb to assist them. Winston had no such qualms, as he made clear in a broadcast on 22 June 1941, the day Germany launched Operation Barbarossa, the invasion of the Soviet Union, with its Finnish, Romanian and Hungarian allies:

> No one has been a more consistent opponent of communism for the last twenty-five years. I will unsay no word I have spoken about it. But all this fades away before the spectacle which is now unfolding. The past, with its crimes, its follies, its tragedies, flashes away. . . . Any man or state who fights on against Nazidom will have our aid . . . It follows therefore that we shall give whatever help we can to Russia and the Russian people.

Winston thought there was a strong case for attacking in Norway to remove the naval and air threat to the convoys to Russia, and to interrupt the flow of Swedish iron ore to Germany, a major strategic objective in its own right. Scandinavia, like the Mediterranean, was an area where naval superiority might tip the balance. The lacklustre 1940 Norwegian campaign had suggested that topography limited German superiority in armour, making it the only place where British infantry might be able to face German on more or less equal terms. Brooke congratulated himself on his long and hard struggle against the project: 'Why he wanted to go back and what he was going to do

337

there, even if he did succeed in capturing Trondheim, we never found out.'[50] In fact it was clear that the operation was intended to keep the Soviet Union in the fight by reducing the German air and maritime threat to convoys steaming round the Norwegian coast, and, in passing, to silence the left's demands for a second front. With the bulk of the Wehrmacht committed to the invasion of the Soviet Union, Winston believed the armed resources of Britain would have enjoyed local preponderance in Norway, something hotly disputed by Brooke and Portal. Ismay thought they were almost certainly right, noting that, although Winston continued to press them for some time, he never over-ruled an outright negative by the chiefs.[51]

Actually, he could not risk it: he could not afford to have an aggrieved ex-chief providing a focal point for the restless, inchoate majority of the dissatisfied that any Prime Minister must deal with, any more than he could ignore the danger that a Halifax or a Cripps might do the same. Assessments of his performance as a 'warlord' commonly fail to appreciate the preferential attention he was obliged to give to the political dimension. He was not a general, an admiral or an air marshal: he was a politician, and his first priority was of necessity the management of his own kind. This is not to suggest that political skills were not needed in his dealings with the chiefs, only that the armed forces are hierarchical and eminently steerable by a Prime Minister. The Commons, however, could be quite the opposite, as Winston knew well from his time as a subversive back-bencher.

On both fronts he was compelled simultaneously to prop up, and to overcome resistance from, the pre-war carapace of authority: a House elected in 1935, and armed forces that had forgotten the lessons of 1914–18. One of his most effective weapons, which he spent hours honing even when apparently more pressing matters awaited his attention, was eloquence. As Ed Murrow put it, he mobilized the English language and sent it into battle. It may be that over-familiarity has dulled our perception of the sheer virtuosity of his most famous peroration, delivered to the Commons on 4 June 1940. His rejection of compromise with Hitler was addressed to domestic capitulationists, and he added both a subtle appeal to the French to continue the struggle from their overseas possessions, and a plea to the Americans to recognize that Britain was now the front line of what would eventually become their fight:

We shall fight in France, we shall fight on the seas and oceans, we shall fight with growing confidence and growing strength in the air, we shall defend our island, whatever the cost may be, we shall fight on the beaches, we shall fight on the landing grounds, we shall fight in the fields and in the streets, we shall fight in the hills [here, under the cover of loud cheers, he muttered to Attlee, seated next to him, 'and we'll fight them with the butt end of broken beer bottles because that's bloody well all we've got']; we shall never surrender. And if, which I do not for a moment believe, this island or a large part of it were subjugated and starving, then our Empire beyond the

339

seas, armed and guarded by the British Fleet, would carry on the struggle, until, in God's good time, the new world, with all its power and might, steps forth to the rescue and the liberation of the old.

Two weeks later on 18 June he told the House, 'The battle of France is over. The battle of Britain is about to begin' and called on it to 'brace ourselves to our duties and so bear ourselves that if the British Empire and its Commonwealth last for a thousand years men will still say: this was their finest hour'.[52] On 14 July, in a broadcast, he spoke directly to Hitler: 'You do your worst, and we will do our best. . . . Here in this strong City of Refuge, which enshrines the title-deeds of human progress and is of deep consequence to Christian civilization . . . we await undismayed the impending assault.'[53] He did not have long to wait.

From bases along all the mainland coasts facing Britain, during 1940's long summer of unforgettably blue skies, Goering launched his Luftwaffe against the RAF to win the air supremacy necessary to cover for a cross-Channel invasion. The British were convinced they faced odds of four to one, although it is now known that the two sides were close to parity in the number of front-line fighter aircraft involved.[54] Winston could not be inactive while the nation's fate was decided high overhead. A frequent visitor to the Uxbridge headquarters of 11 Group, Fighter Command, he sat up in the gantry watching the bulbs on the operations board light up as the squadrons were scrambled. After a fierce battle on 16 August, he first uttered to Ismay the phrase he made famous

340

in the Commons four days later: 'Never in the field of human conflict was so much owed by so many to so few.' He was there on 15 September, during the last great daylight assault on London. Seeing all the bulbs lit up, he exclaimed to the Group Controller, 'Good Lord, man! All your forces are in the air. What do we do now?' The Controller replied, 'Well, sir, we can just hope that the squadrons will refuel as quickly as possible and get up again.' Later, as another wave of German aircraft appeared on the board, Winston asked, 'What other reserves have we?' He had asked the same question of the French on 16 May and received the same reply: there were none. After the crisis was past he descended into the Operations Room to congratulate every member of the staff, as exhausted as if he had fought the battle in person.

On 24 August a flight of German bombers hit central London in error, and Winston ordered a counter-raid two nights later on Berlin, although he had in effect been goading the Germans to attack urban centres since 15 May, when he ordered the first raid of the Strategic Bomber Offensive against the Ruhr.55 The Berlin raid accomplished little in the way of physical destruction but won the battle, because an enraged Hitler changed the priority of the Luftwaffe attacks. Now, instead of attacking the airfields, the bombers were to concentrate on London. The plan was still to destroy Fighter Command in a battle of attrition, but it reprieved the RAF bases, some of which had been abandoned after repeated attacks. The Germans thereby gave up a unilateral advantage, because Bomber Command could not attack the Luftwaffe bases in France by day without suffering appalling

341

losses from German fighters, lacked the means to hit such small targets at night, and was in any case heavily engaged with bombing invasion vessels ominously assembling in the ports across the Channel.

If Winston believed British anti-aircraft and Civil Defence preparations were adequate, he was terribly mistaken. From 7 September London was attacked for 57 consecutive days and/or nights. By mid-November, when attacks were switched to Coventry, Southampton, Birmingham, Liverpool, Bristol and Plymouth, the Germans had dropped over 13,000 tons of high explosive and nearly one million incendiaries on the capital, for a loss of less than 1 per cent of their aircraft, and those mainly to accidents. Most other major industrial cities and ports were heavily attacked before the Blitz ended in May 1941, when German bomber squadrons were redeployed in preparation for the invasion of the Soviet Union. Luftwaffe losses had begun to mount as more searchlights and guns became radar-controlled and a radar-equipped night fighter, the Beaufighter, became operational, but overall only 600 bombers were shot down, a loss rate of 1.5 per cent of all sorties when Bomber Command considered it a good night if it lost less than 4 per cent. The Blitz killed over 43,000 civilians, injured another 139,000, rendered 2.5 million at least temporarily homeless and inflicted severe damage on docks, factories and the railway infrastructure.[56]

The Germans had achieved all of this without using poison gas, the threat that had so transfixed Baldwin and Chamberlain. Since Hitler knew no constraints other than those imposed by an opponent's ability to retaliate, it is fair to assume that whatever else the British obsession with bombers failed to achieve, it was a successful deterrent in this respect. However, the Luftwaffe's ability to bomb by night was an unpleasant surprise, only partially offset by the early discovery of the radio directional beams that made it possible and the rapid development of counter-measures thanks to scientists by-passing the 'correct channels' to put the facts before Winston himself.[57] That they felt compelled to do so was a stern judgement on the Air Staff. Criticism is often levelled at Winston for any errors of appreciation and for riding his favourite hobby-horses, but all too often it fell to him to initiate action. It was certainly not because he consumed all the oxygen in the decision-making process. On the contrary, in the opinion of his officials he was too open to suggestions, the wilder the better, and tended to pursue them almost regardless of feasibility. This was a function of his insatiable curiosity, the incessant 'Why?' that parents of bright children come to dread. But while a parent may fall back on 'Because I say so' as a last resort, it was dangerous to employ any such argument with Winston.[58] When it was one of his own ideas that was being rejected, in the absence of proposals by others his usual interrogation was 'Why not?'

If the Blitz gave Winston the moral *carte blanche* he required to unleash Bomber Command, it simultaneously revealed his doubts about the effectiveness of 'strategic' bombing to be well founded. There was no panic, city life recovered quickly, and although civilian morale temporarily sagged in some particularly hard-hit areas like

Plymouth and Hull this was more a result of a lack of Civil Defence provision and adequate relief efforts than of hostile action. Again, one must ask why it took Winston's personal intervention to jolt the Treasury into setting up a compensation scheme for those whose homes and livelihoods were destroyed. Nobody could accuse the Tory Chancellor, Kingsley Wood, of being unimaginative. As Air Secretary in 1939 he set up the Empire Training Scheme which helped ensure that the supply of aircrew kept up with aircraft availability throughout the war, despite shocking attrition. Along with Keynes, whom he brought into the Treasury in 1941, before his death in 1943 Wood had very largely put in place the structure of economic and social management popularly associated with the post-war Labour government. It was not failure at the ideological or 'big picture' level that characterized the wartime administration, but failure in the little things that matter so much. In this, as in his attention to 'funnies' like specialist tanks, Winston was more representative than the politicians and officials around him of a people capable of outstanding individual or small group initiative, but unwilling or unable to translate it into mass application.[59]

National morale could not have been sustained solely by words or even by the comforting illusion that Bomber Command was repaying the Blitz by targeting German cities. Any opportunity to strike back hard had to be taken and while it was tragic that the first blow should have been against the French navy, attacked in its North African bases, it was a cruel but necessary display of ruthless resolve, a throwing away of the scabbard that met with strong approval in Britain and, perhaps surprisingly, in the USA. The British, it seemed, were not wimps after all. But it was far from being simply a symbolic act. The French had capitulated without giving any guarantee that their navy would not be used as a bargaining chip with the Nazis.[60] The new Vichy regime was Anglophobic, and the tales about Britain abandoning her ally that are still common currency took root at this time. It was actually the other way around: the 52nd Division and four additional squadrons of fighters from the home defence reserve were sent to France *after* Dunkirk, but *perfide Albion* fitted the needs of the moment. At Mers-el-Kebir in Algeria the French had two fully operational battle-cruisers, faster and better armed than their Royal Navy equivalents, and at Dakar, in West Africa, a recently commissioned battleship superior to anything in the British fleet. The two navies together barely outgunned the Italians in the Mediterranean, and the risk that French ships might be thrown into the balance on the Axis side was not to be borne. When the French admirals refused the alternative of seeking internment across the Atlantic, they were fired on in 'an unnatural and painful' episode which still occasionally emerges to sour Anglo-French relations. The battleship *Bretagne* went down with some 800 of her crew, and the battleships *Dunkerque* and *Provence* were damaged: the former was later sunk at her moorings by British aircraft.

Also, in July, even as Brooke was trying to put together a Home Army to face the threat of invasion, he was deprived of four of his remaining armoured regiments, sent around Africa to reinforce General Sir Archibald Wavell, C-in-C Middle East. Winston recalled that he 'purred like six cats' when Wavell advised him, in November, that he intended to attack the Italians who had not only expelled the British from Somalia but also advanced into Egypt from Libya. Winston sent Wavell a stirring telegram of encouragement: 'All acts and decisions of valour and violence against the enemy will, whatever the upshot, receive the resolute support of His Majesty's Government.'61 Ismay confirms that he was 'rapturously' happy. 'At long last we are going to throw off the intolerable shackles of the defensive,' he exclaimed. 'Wars are won by superior will power. Now we will wrest the initiative from the enemy and impose our will on him.'62 After Admiral Sir Andrew Cunningham won local naval supremacy by sinking three battleships in a torpedo bomber attack on the Italian base at Taranto and driving the rest to Genoa, the army advanced to inflict one of the most lop-sided routs of the war, with two British divisions defeating ten Italian and capturing 130,000 prisoners for the loss of only 2000 killed and wounded. Further south, against more determined opposition, Commonwealth forces drove the Italians out of Somalia and Eritrea, clearing the coasts of the Red Sea, and by May 1941 had restored the Abyssinian capital of Addis Ababa to Emperor Haile Selassie.

During the bleakest hours of the Blitz, therefore, the British had something to celebrate, and this helped consolidate Winston's position at home. Bad news was to follow when the advance in North Africa was broken off to send troops to defend Greece, from where the Germans drove them in

April, as they did from Crete the following month. Winston sent Eden and Sir John Dill, Brooke's predecessor as CIGS, to consult Wavell and Cunningham before the decision was taken, and they agreed to the dispersion of effort, explicitly supporting Winston's view that an ally should not be abandoned without a fight.[63] What none of them expected was that their recent gains in North Africa would also be forfeit, and thereby hangs a tangled tale that will keep historians and their readers entertained for many years to come.

As has been seen, Winston used signals intelligence (SIGINT) to direct naval operations during World War I. After the war his implacable enmity towards Bolshevism was nourished by decrypts of Comintern instructions to the faithful to commit acts of subversion and sabotage in Britain.[64] When he became Chancellor in 1924 he begged to be placed on the circulation list for the 'flimsies' (intercepts): 'All the years I have been in office since it began [in 'Room 40' of the Admiralty] I have read every one of these flimsies and I attach more importance to them as a means of forming a true judgement of public policy in these spheres than to any other source of knowledge at the disposal of the State.'[65] His accession in 1940 coincided with the first breakthrough (on 22 May) against the German cipher machine Enigma, and by August the decrypts (first code-named Boniface to suggest an agent source, later known as Ultra) had become Winston's principal source of operational intelligence. 'I do not wish such reports as are received to be sifted and digested by the various Intelligence authorities,' Winston wrote. 'For the present Major [Desmond] Morton will inspect them for me and submit what he considers of major importance. He is to be shown everything and will submit authentic documents to me in their original form.'[66]

It was not until the Official Secrets Act was modified in 1974 that the public learned how important cryptography had been during the war, and not until the 1980s that its full impact became generally known.[67] The revelations cast doubt on all previous interpretations of the war and shed new light on Winston's 'meddling' in operational matters during the Mediterranean campaign of 1940–3. Sadly, there were times during this campaign when the decrypts contributed to Allied defeats because the British did not expect a German general to disobey orders and to misrepresent the strength and battle-readiness of his own forces to his own superiors. Yet that is what soon-to-be Field Marshal Erwin Rommel did during the campaign in order to outmanoeuvre his nominal superior in Italy, only incidentally surprising his enemies in the field whose forces were depleted by the Greek venture.[68]

Thanks to recent speculation about 'dodgy dossiers' devaluing Joint Intelligence Committee (JIC) reports, we are now more aware than ever of the pitfalls of secret intelligence. These are unavoidable and eternal: people tend to lend more credence to information obtained covertly than to what they can glean from overt sources. SIGINT is particularly seductive, but even verbatim records of written or spoken communications require skilled interpretation. The JIC was set up in 1936 to collate information from all sources and to produce balanced assessments, but it was not until Winston became Prime Minister that the relevant Whitehall departments were ordered to channel their information and opinions through the JIC, and not until early 1941 that it actually had the staff to do its job.[69] In time it became competent, but no group of officials could have matched the breadth and diversity of Winston's experience or the sheer range of his contacts. He became his own intelligence analyst and, thanks also to his prodigious memory and a facility for multi-tasking unusual in a man, the maximum advantage was drawn from Ultra, the single greatest British triumph of the war.[70]

I must now draw a line under this far from exhaustive summary of all the ways in which Winston's character made it possible for an unmilitary, unprepared and under-performing nation to avoid seemingly inevitable defeat. There is a passage in his biography of his great ancestor the Duke of Marlborough that defines the standard he set for himself:

Almost any intelligent scribe can draw up a lucid and logical treatise full of laboriously ascertained facts and technical phrases on a particular war situation . . . Nothing but genius, the daemon in man, can answer the riddles of war, and genius, though it may be armed, cannot be acquired, either by reading or by experience. In default of genius nations have to make war as best they can, and since that quality is much rarer than the largest and purest diamonds, most wars are mainly tales of muddle. But when from time to time it flashes upon the scene, order and design with a sense almost of infallibility draw out from hazard and confusion.[71]

This was, as critics never cease to point out, a pre-modern concept of leadership; it was also, however, perfectly adapted to the needs of a pre-modern society, whose moral strength arguably stemmed from the fact that it was neither as 'modern' as Germany nor as 'progressive' as the Soviet Union. Winston was not self-deluding. In 1942, in response to Bevan's sneer that he fed the country on false optimism, he replied: 'I have not made any arrogant, confident, boasting predictions at all. On the contrary, I have stuck hard to my blood, toil, tears and sweat, to which I have added muddle and mismanagement, and that, to some extent, is what you have got out of it.'[72] It is much to his credit that he spurned the temptation of arbitrary power in favour of defending his country through the highly imperfect institutions whose practical failings were, in their way, a reflection of historic distrust of central power and a unique commitment to personal liberty.

It should come as no surprise to find that the only serious challenge to his leadership while the outcome of the war was still in doubt was mounted by men whose passionate advocacy of the Soviet Union concealed, perhaps even from themselves, a secret yearning for the tidiness of totalitarianism, allied to those whose distaste for war extended to Winston for waging it with too much enthusiasm. In January 1942 Bevan gained control of the left-wing journal *Tribune* with the backing of the wealthy businessman Richard Stokes, a Labour MP

350

and extreme pre-war pacifist whose hatred of Winston exceeded even Bevan's own. Another threat was posed by Stafford Cripps, who resigned his ambassadorial post in Moscow and returned to London at this time to make public his view that not enough was being done to help the Russians, to which he attributed the fact that Stalin had treated him with contempt and refused to contemplate a formal alliance. 'Second Front Now' graffiti appeared suddenly all over Britain, and membership of the Communist Party rose from the 12,000 of its 'revolutionary defeatism' stage and the closure of its organ the *Daily Worker* a year earlier to 65,000 in mid-1942.

Cripps refused Winston's offer of the Ministry of Supply but accepted the post of Lord Privy Seal and Leader of the House, where he in effect supported opposition to the government in the debate of 24–25 February on the bombing campaign, maliciously declaring that it had been embarked upon when Britain stood alone, but now that the Russians and Americans were in the war it would be reviewed. It was, by Mr Justice Singleton in April, under terms of reference that precluded any discussion of the issues which Cripps hoped would discredit the government of which he was a member, and just as Bomber Command was at last receiving the equipment necessary to hit Germany hard.[73] In *The Right of the Line* John Terraine quips that 'it is at times difficult . . . to decide whether it is more correct to say that Bomber Command was irrelevant to the war, or the war was irrelevant to Bomber Command'. The same can be said with greater justice of Cripps and his supporters, who sought to halt the only British

351

activity for which Stalin expressed admiration, while simultaneously demanding that more be done to help the Russians.

Only the faithful read *Tribune*, but the 'Second Front Now' campaign was taken up by the *Daily Mirror* and its rival the *Daily Express*, mass circulation newspapers that all politicians took very seriously indeed. Winston's friend the Canadian-born Lord Beaverbrook, proprietor of the *Express*, resigned as Minister of Supply in order to pursue the campaign and may have believed he was strengthening Winston's hand against die-hard Tories and Labour anti-Communists alike. Not so the insidious attacks on the government sponsored by the upper-class socialist Cecil King at the *Mirror*, whose intriguing combination of aristocratic disdain and populism was captured in a January 1942 article on the army by the star columnist William 'Cassandra' Connor: 'At the top you have the military aristocracy of the Guards regiment with a mentality not very foreign to that of Potsdam. In the middle you have a second class snobocracy. And behind it all the cloying inertia of the Civil Service bogged down by regulations from which they cannot extricate themselves.'[74]

On 5 March 1942 Connor and his friend the cartoonist Philip Zec produced a cartoon that laid a blood libel on the government. It showed a sailor clinging to wreckage in stormy seas with the caption: 'The price of petrol has been increased by one penny.' Bevin and Morrison were infuriated by the implication that profiteering was taking place and proposed to the Cabinet that the *Mirror* should be closed down. At Winston's urging they settled for summoning King and giving him the dressing-down of his life. Not long afterwards Connor resigned to join the army, a brave act of contrition that spoke louder than the words of his parting column, in which he protested that he had 'not transgressed' and declared that he was following Winston's advice about 'paths of service open in wartime which are not open in the days of peace, and some of these paths may be paths to honour'. In conclusion he wrote: 'I propose to see whether the rifle is a better weapon than the printed word.'[75]

The long string of defeats that followed Wavell's early victories in North Africa provided grist to the mill of Winston's opponents. While the cream of Commonwealth troops were being evicted from Greece and Crete, Rommel drove the remainder back into Egypt and placed the Libyan port of Tobruk under siege. A prolonged air assault on Malta seemed to presage an invasion which the Royal Navy, severely battered off Crete, would not have been able to prevent. On 24 May the great battle-cruiser *Hood* was destroyed and the new battleship *Prince of Wales* put out of action by the *Bismarck*, a blow to morale not entirely recouped when the Home Fleet caught the crippled German warship three days later. On 21 June, after the failure of two attempts to relieve Tobruk, Winston orchestrated a change of places between Wavell and General Sir Claude Auchinleck, C-in-C India, only to find Wavell's requests for more of everything fully endorsed by his successor. The thunderclap opening of Operation Barbarossa, the German invasion of the Soviet Union, the next day was a mixed blessing. It was the reason why the Axis did not push their advantage in the

Mediterranean, but it meant that much war materiel that might otherwise have come to Britain from the USA was diverted to the Soviet Union, at further great cost to merchant shipping already being lost at an unsustainable rate in the Atlantic. When Auchinleck finally attacked in November 1941 he managed to relieve Tobruk, but at the price of losses that left him exposed to Rommel's counter-attack in January 1942. Reporting this to the Commons, Winston gracefully conceded that 'we have a very daring and skilful opponent against us, and, may I say across the havoc of war, a great general'.

Meanwhile the Japanese sank the *Prince of Wales* and *Repulse* off the coast of Malaya on 10 December: Winston described the news, given him over the telephone by Dudley Pound, as the most direct personal shock he received during the entire war. This was followed by the rout of Empire forces in Malaya, culminating in the surrender of 130,000 men to 55,000 Japanese at Singapore on 15 February 1942, the largest capitulation in British military history.[76] Two days earlier the battle-cruisers *Scharnhorst* and *Gneisenau* called into question the Englishness of the Channel by sailing through it back to Germany. In practice this was a case of prisoners actually escaping into jail, but it was not seen as such by an outraged British public. The nadir, however, came when Rommel attacked again and Tobruk fell on 21 June, with 35,000 men surrendering to a smaller force after perfunctory resistance. When Singapore fell, Mussolini mused: 'I should like to know the effect four British officers, presenting themselves with a white flag of surrender, had had upon those whimsical

Orientals. If it had been us, no one would have attached any importance to it; but they were British.'[77] The panic in Cairo on 1 July 1942, when charred paper filled the air as the authorities burned their files on 'Ash Wednesday', did the same for the mystique of British rule in the Middle East. 'Defeat is one thing', Winston wrote eight years later, 'disgrace is another.'[78]

Singapore, Tobruk and Ash Wednesday were moments from which there could be no recovery, and not only in the eyes of indigenous peoples. Once Winston had to beg for American tanks and guns in order to retrieve the situation in the Middle East, his ability to affect the future course of the war was seriously diminished. His domestic foes also did their best to erode his authority, but he forced the issue by demanding that they proceed to a vote of censure on 1–2 July 1942. Several Conservatives and Winston's old friend Admiral of the Fleet Sir Roger Keyes spoke at cross purposes to propose solutions of dubious constitutionality, and Bevan's spitefulness undermined what might have been a damaging attack from the left. 'The country is beginning to say that [the Prime Minister] fights debates like a war and the war like a debate,' he said, not knowing how truly he spoke. 'If Rommel had been in the British Army he would still have been a sergeant,' he continued, which might have amused the newly promoted field marshal who had joined the Imperial German Army as an officer cadet in 1910. There were plenty of talented French, Czech and Polish generals available, Bevan concluded, any one of whom would be preferable to the best the hated class enemy could produce.

355

Winston savaged his opponents. 'When I was called upon to be Prime Minster, now nearly two years ago', he declared, 'there were not many applicants for the job. Since then perhaps the market has improved.' He raised a laugh at Bevan's expense—it was his favourite tactic in their duels, and always fuelled the Welshman's rage—saying, 'I do not resent criticism, even when, for the sake of emphasis, it parts for the time from reality.' He would permit no change in the structure of war management he had put together. 'I am your servant and you have the right to dismiss me when you please. What you have no right to do is to ask me to bear responsibilities without the power of effective action.'[79] He closed by hinting that it was unpatriotic to undermine him unless he could be replaced to advantage. There was no alternative, any more than there had been two years earlier, and the vote was rejected by 477 votes to 25.

It is unfortunate that the only two MPs who consistently upheld the Commons' right to hold the Prime Minister accountable were Bevan and Stokes, whose personal animosity obscured what were often valid criticisms. Stokes, in particular, asked highly pertinent questions about the inferiority of British weapons, perhaps seeking to goad Winston into making some impolitic remark about the working class. He thought he could not miss with a well-founded lunge about the mechanical unreliability of the new Churchill tank, but Winston turned the joke against him with a masterful sally. 'This tank', he said, 'was ordered off the drawing board and large numbers went into production very quickly. As might be expected, it had many defects and teething troubles and when these became apparent the tank was appropriately rechristened the "Churchill". The defects have now been overcome. I am sure that this tank will prove, in the end, a powerful, massive and serviceable weapon of war.'[80]

With few exceptions, MPs shared the view of Ernest Bevin, who told Winston that the Cabinet knew nothing of war and had 'put him in to win it'. As long as he had their confidence, Bevin said, he should get on with it and not ask them for opinions on matters they knew nothing about.[81] This was also the view of the Dominion Prime Ministers. One gets into the easy habit of saying that Britain stood alone in 1940–1, but it was in fact well accompanied. Americans may be forgiven for referring to the British as 'the English', but even the term 'British' itself was something of a misnomer for what was a truly multinational effort. In North Africa, it was not until the build-up to Alamein that the British Isles component of the 8th Army outnumbered troops from India, Australia, New Zealand, South Africa, Palestine, East and West Africa, as well as national contingents from Poland, France and Greece.[82] Ties of blood and tribal loyalty brought English-speaking volunteers from all over the world to serve what they still regarded as a common cause. The Dominions made significant and unselfish contributions to the war and rocked the Allied boat very little, though their efforts have not received the attention they deserve from British or American military historians.

The Dominion Prime Ministers at the outbreak of war were a robust group of men with much to offer, who declared war in 1939 and accepted that the defence of Britain was the defence of all, despite bad memories, reinforced by even worse myths, about the fate of their troops under British command during World War I. Pro-German feeling was strong in Eire, where de Valera gambled he could squeeze concessions out of the British by remaining neutral. It was stronger still in South Africa, but there Jan Christiaan Smuts led a Cabinet revolt to replace the anti-British Prime Minister Barry Hertzog; thereafter he spent most of the war in London, where he renewed the friendship with Winston begun when Smuts was a member of the Imperial War Cabinet in 1917–18. Having begun his military career as a successful Boer guerrilla leader in 1901–2, Smuts became a British field marshal in 1941 and once again played an active part in the highest British and Allied war councils. He was the only man to sign the founding charters of both the League of Nations and the United Nations. Sadly, in his absence race became the defining issue of South African politics, leading to his defeat in the general election of 1948, the repudiation of the legacy of the Anglo-Boer reconciliation of 1906–10 and the adoption of the institutions of apartheid.[83]

Sir William Mackenzie King, Prime Minister of Canada, led his nation throughout the war and was the friend and confidant of both Winston and FDR. When he retired in 1948 his Liberal Party remained in power for a further nine years through two general elections. In 1940–1 Britain would not have survived as an independent nation had it not been for the agricultural, industrial and financial aid received from Canada. Had the Germans invaded, in all probability the royal family and the government, along with all the other British-based governments in exile, would have transferred to Canada along with the Royal Navy. Canadian assistance included tanks and aircraft produced free of charge under the Canadian Mutual Aid programme; in terms of manpower it produced over a million volunteers for the Allied armed forces, of whom 368,000 served in Europe and 42,000 were killed, from a population base of only 11 million.[84] The Canadian contribution was remarkable: I Canadian Corps fought in Sicily and mainland Italy, II Canadian Corps and later 1st Canadian Army in northern Europe. Canadians were the second largest contingent in Bomber Command, eventually forming their own Group, and from a standing start the Royal Canadian Navy became the fourth largest in the world by sensibly concentrating on smaller convoy escorts and minesweepers, of which 21 were sunk. As usual, only the squeaking wheels get the grease: the quietly competent Canadians and their low-key Prime Minister deserve more credit than they have received, or than I can give them here.[85]

The same can be said of the outstanding contribution made by New Zealand, which mobilized for war more comprehensively than Britain under the leadership of two Labour Prime Ministers, Michael Savage, a ferocious anti-appeaser who died in 1940, and his successor Peter Fraser.[86] Despite having gone to jail to oppose conscription in World War I, Fraser not only introduced it now (along with draconian press censorship) but extended it to a general conscription of labour accompanied by statutory wage regulation and extended working hours. The

New Zealand Division remained under British command for the duration and fought with distinction in Greece, Crete, North Africa, Sicily and Italy. New Zealanders were arguably the most highly regarded national contingent in the integrated crews of Bomber Command, and won a disproportionate number of awards for gallantry. One hundred and forty thousand New Zealanders served overseas from a population base of 1,700,000, and 11,625 were killed, a higher ratio of deaths per million (6684) than in Britain (5123). I doubt if many people outside their islands appreciate what an enormous sacrifice this was for such a small, closely knit society.[87]

Australia went from being the most unconditional supporter of Britain in 1939, when its Prime Minister, Robert Menzies, ruled that the King's declaration of war extended to all his Dominions, to disillusionment under his successor, the Irish-Australian Labour leader John Curtin. Curtin became Prime Minister with the defection of two independent MPs from Menzies' coalition in October 1941. Three volunteer infantry divisions were serving in North Africa and a fourth was lost when Singapore fell in February 1942, followed by Japanese air raids on Darwin in northern Australia from bases in the newly conquered Dutch East Indies. Curtin had already seen the writing on the wall and on 26 December 1941 had broadcast a declaration of independence: 'Without inhibitions of any kind, I make it quite clear that Australia looks to America, free of pangs of any kind as to our traditional links with the United Kingdom.' He demanded the immediate return of the North African divisions to defend the homeland, and two were embarked immediately.[88] The third stayed long enough to play a crucial role at Alamein before also returning home. The Royal Australian Air Force contingent in Bomber Command remained until late 1944, operating four national squadrons in addition to serving as individuals throughout the force. Over a million Australians from a population of 7 million served in the armed forces during the war and 30,000 died, the great majority under British command.[89]

Since 1921 Anzac Day, 25 April, has been a public holiday in Australia and New Zealand.[90] It is the anniversary of the landings at Anzac Cove in Gallipoli in 1915, and as such indissolubly associated with Winston's alleged responsibility for that debacle. Under his overall direction a generation later Australians and New Zealanders suffered defeat and thousands of them became prisoners of war in Greece, Crete, North Africa and Singapore. There are, therefore, few Churchill fan clubs in the southern hemisphere. Yet apart from some mild playing to the Pommy-bashing gallery by Curtin, who was rewarded by a thumping majority in the Australian general election of 1943, the Dominion Prime Ministers did not publicly criticize Winston's war leadership and even in private generally approved of it. Their representatives sat in the War Cabinet, their right to dispose of their own forces was respected even when, as in the withdrawal of the Australians from North Africa, it placed a severe strain on shipping resources urgently needed for other purposes, and at the Dominion Prime Ministers Conference of May 1944 they gave Winston their warm support. Their countrymen may resent how little attention

Winston paid to their efforts in his memoirs, but to a considerable extent Smuts, Mackenzie King, Fraser and even Curtin also took it for granted because it expressed an emotional bond that had shaped their lives. Britain would not have survived without it, which ought to give pause to those whose freedom to sneer at the Empire was thereby preserved.

The paramountcy of character in great events was never more apparent than in 1940–1, when it was condensed in the figure of the dumpy little man in the funny hat with the ever-present cigar and the hand upraised to give the 'V for victory' sign. He was genuinely loved by the people with whom he wept at bomb-sites, by the soldiers who knew that he too had smelt powder, by the airmen knighted by his words, and by a royal family exalted by his example.

He was even admired by the long-suffering staff required to match his impossibly bohemian working hours and demanding standards. When in London he lived at No. 10 Downing Street, sometimes sleeping in the nearby Cabinet War Rooms, usually in quarters on the first floor of what is now the Treasury, and more rarely in the bomb-proofed accommodation below. It is a telling comment on Britain's lack of preparedness for war that the War Rooms had only been conceived of as late as 1936, with an initial funding of just £500. By the war's end they totalled over 150 rooms, with offices, operations rooms and sleeping quarters, where over 600 people worked. Winston went to Chartwell for most weekends, but its proximity to the south coast, coupled with the fact that its gravel drive showed up clearly in the moonlight, encouraged his advisers to persuade him to spend full-moon weekends at Ditchley Park, owned by a Conservative MP and only 4 miles as the crow flies from Blenheim.

Winston usually awoke at about 8.30 a.m., and enjoyed a proper breakfast (cold game was a favourite) before spending the morning reading the most important daily newspapers, and then studying the papers in his despatch box, often in bed. A decent lunch was accompanied by champagne (he had a particular affection for Pol Roger) and after it he retired for a nap. The second phase of the day began when he awoke and began sipping weak whisky and water. It continued through meetings that often went on till 10 p.m. or later, and he retired only after informal conversations that ended well after midnight. Winston scrawled some notes himself, but most documents were dictated to hard-pressed secretaries who then worked through the small hours to get the papers distributed by the next day. If there was an air raid in progress he would often go up on to the roof of what is now the Treasury to watch it, and when the first V-2 rockets began to hit London in 1944 one secretary who rushed out into St James's Park to find out what was happening discovered that Winston had beaten him to it.

He was always on show, whether dressed in morning coat and homburg hat, in one of his uniforms (he was both an honorary air commodore and an honorary colonel), or in a comfortable but unflattering one-piece zip-fronted 'siren suit'. His appearance in newsreels was cheered, his broadcasts reverently heard at home and abroad. 'Do not let us speak of darker days; let us rather speak of sterner days,' he said. 'These are not dark days: these are great days—the greatest days our country has ever lived.'[91] Amid the appalling cascade of bad news that ushered out 1941, he could joke about the moment when he realized France was not only defeated but turning hostile: 'When I warned them that Britain would fight on alone whatever they did, their Generals told their Prime Minister and his divided Cabinet: "In three weeks England will have her neck wrung like a chicken." Some chicken! Some neck!'[92]

And always it was he who drove the machinery of government to wage war better, who devised new mechanisms to cope with outstanding problems, just as when he proclaimed 'The Battle of the Atlantic' on 6 March 1942 to concentrate minds, drew up a campaign directive and formed an all-agency committee to deal with it. He turned his archaic vocabulary to advantage not merely in the Elizabethan resonance of his speeches but even in 'Winston's prayers', from the operative word in his 'Action this Day' memoranda. 'Pray explain', he asked Brooke in the spring of 1942, 'how it is that in the Middle East 750,000 men always turn up for their pay and rations, but when it comes to fighting only 100,000 turn up. Explain to us exactly how the remaining 650,000 are occupied.'[93] How indeed, when Rommel achieved twice as much with half as many. An inability to increase output commensurate with vastly increased input was not a problem confined to British manufacturing.

If I had to choose one document from the thousands he produced during the time when he shouldered the immense burden of resistance to Nazi Germany, it would be the one he wrote on 26

364

May 1942, when Britain's Empire in the East had fallen and it seemed likely that India and the Middle East would follow. In it he described a floating dock to support an invasion across open beaches in France—at a time when the very notion seemed the most towering optimism—and required Combined Operations staff to produce a design and a construction plan. 'Don't argue the matter', he said, 'the difficulties will argue for themselves.'[94] Twenty-five months later the giant 'Mulberry' harbours, obedient to his artifice and will, were towed across the Channel to affirm the return of Allied forces to occupied Europe.

CHAPTER NINE

SUPPORTING ROLE

1942–1944

Grand strategy is the political dimension of war, where means and ends are aligned. It is difficult enough for a single nation, and infinitely more complex for an international coalition where not only aims and interests but relative strengths evolve as a conflict goes on, sometimes as much in response to domestic as to foreign pressures. A government's professional military advisers play a key role in developing military strategy, which drives operations in specific theatres of war, from the broader grand strategy which encompasses all a government's efforts, for instance economic, diplomatic and social as well as the narrowly military. Tensions almost inevitably arise between senior servicemen and the politicians they serve, and within a coalition further fault-lines may develop between nations or interest groups within them. It is generally easier for totalitarian regimes to pursue a single-minded strategy than it is for democratic states to do so with coalition partners, although dictators, spared the often tiresome checks and balances that afflict their democratic opponents, may lose their sense of perspective and when they fall, fall very hard indeed.

In the broadest sense, the story of Anglo-American collaboration during World War II is one of the gradual focusing of American strategic vision

366

in parallel with the growth of the military strength of the USA. The turning-point came in the winter of 1943–4, after which the American view was increasingly dominant in Allied counsels, a process helped by a collective loss of confidence on the part of Winston and his military staff. Winston's exhaustion, mirrored in that of his close collaborators, had much to do with this. While he was bound to lose some authority once the Americans got into their stride, he might have retained more had he not sometimes simply been too ill and too tired to think straight. And it is worth asking whether any other British politician would have had more influence with the USA or Soviet Union in the prevailing circumstances.

If Winston's grand strategic achievement was something less than he had hoped for, it was by no means derisory. He first played a key role in building and sustaining a grand alliance of heterogeneous partners, and then entwined the interests of Britain and the USA so closely that the Empire, despite the American desire to sweep it away in favour of a new world order, survived long enough to permit his successors to mount a dignified retreat. Although the USA emerged as the great winner economically and shrugged off the self-imposed restraints that had previously kept it from being the dominant player on the international stage, this was likely to have occurred whether it had become directly involved in the war or had simply supplied the belligerents.

Initially, FDR's aim was to avoid going to war if American security could be safeguarded by supporting the Chinese, British and Russians. After the Japanese forcefully registered their objection to

367

this policy at Pearl Harbor and then, in one of history's most gratuitous blunders, Hitler declared war on the United States, FDR's main objective was a post-war world benignly presided over by the great powers acting in concert. This was already revealed to be a pipe dream by the time he died on 12 April 1945. It was an outstanding achievement that Winston, FDR and Stalin remained united to the end in their determination to crush Germany so thoroughly that it would not disturb the peace again. All else—including, tragically from a modern perspective, justice for some of the nations conquered by the Germans—was subordinated to that overarching aim.

The seemingly unstoppable success of German arms in 1940–1 induced both Italy and Japan to believe that they were joining the winning side. But conversely, if Britain had not held out at that time, there could have been no Grand Alliance. If Britain had dropped out of the war in the summer of 1940, the Soviet Union would almost certainly have been defeated in 1941 by resources released from the need to guard Germany's flanks. The convoys of supplies the Russians desperately needed to help make good the appalling losses suffered by their armed forces in 1941–2 were also only made possible by Britain's geographical location and its control of the seas and of the Middle East. In addition, the British naval blockade imposed severe constraints on the Germans' operational freedom, helping to bend their 1942 offensive towards the oilfields of the Caucasus and thus creating an exposed flank whose vulnerability the Red Army exploited to the full at Stalingrad. In a speech on 30 September 1942,

Hitler revealed how Britain's peripheral strategy preyed on his mind:

> Had I in front of me a serious opponent I could figure out where the second front would come. But with these military idiots one never knows where they will attack. The maddest enterprise may be launched and—this is the only disagreeable thing—one never knows what next when faced with such lunatics and drunkards. Of course, we must prepare everywhere.[1]

No doubt the drunkard-in-chief chuckled when he read the transcript. In *The Duel*, John Lukacs argues that Winston had the ability to penetrate Hitler's head and thus scramble his judgement. I doubt if he actually spent much time thinking about Hitler as a person: he pursued a peripheral strategy because that was actually all that Britain could do on its own. From the time he became Prime Minister until the USA entered the war Winston was in the classic bind of the weaker side in a long war, almost like George Washington during the Revolutionary War. If he did not actually lose the war then he might eventually win it, while if his opponents did not win it then they must eventually lose it. In the short term, however, the best he could do was, as he put it, to 'KBO'—Keep Buggering On.[2]

The rhetoric of 1940 and the cruel necessity of attacking the French fleet did help convince the Americans that Britain was wholly serious in its purpose and worth supporting, and in the process the USA became so financially committed that it would, in the end, go to war rather than see Britain defeated. The calculation that without Britain it would be impossible to project American power into Europe only became compelling once the USA became a combatant. A common language and some shared cultural values were mainly grease to the gears once national interests were roughly aligned.

Winston had a steep mountain to climb. His first step was to overcome the legacy of what FDR, in private correspondence, referred to as the 'we who are about to die salute thee' attitude of the Chamberlain administration. The new British ambassador, Lord Lothian, had called on the President in 1939 to say that the Americans must take over from the British as 'the guardians of Anglo-Saxon civilization'. FDR commented:

> I got mad clear through and told him that just so long as he or Britishers like him took that attitude of complete despair, the British would not be worth saving anyway. What the British need today is a good stiff grog, inducing not only the desire to save civilization, but the continued belief that they can do it. In such an event, they will have a lot more support from their American cousins.[3]

Winston was 'a good stiff grog' personified, and swiftly spun this perception around. If it is possible to date the change precisely, then the January 1941 visit to Britain by FDR's closest friend and political adviser, Harry Hopkins, is probably the moment when it occurred. Winston handled the visit masterfully, taking Hopkins to review the fleet but

370

also to visit the Communist-dominated and much-bombed Glasgow docks, and by wining and dining him in the company of men and women from all walks of life. Hopkins became convinced that the nation was indeed united behind his host, and was also deeply moved. He ended his visit by telling Winston that the message he would take to FDR was summed up in the Book of Ruth: 'Whither thou goest, I will go; and where thou lodgest, I will lodge; thy people shall be my people, and thy God my God.' Then he added very quietly: 'Even to the end.' Winston's physician was 'surprised to find the PM in tears. He knew what it meant. Even to us the words seemed like a rope thrown to a drowning man.'[4]

The clash of self-images was never easy to reconcile. British and American society had each long believed in its own moral superiority, and the chorus 'God, who made thee mighty, make thee mightier yet', added in 1912 to the evocative and popular 'Land of Hope and Glory', could as easily have been sung in the USA. Although it was to be the last of his major works to be published (in 1956–8), Winston finished *A History of the English-Speaking Peoples* in 1939. He must often have wished it had reached the printers before war broke out, as Anglo-American cultural affinity was a factor in which he placed a fundamental (if often misplaced) faith. In the speech he delivered to a joint session of Congress on 26 December 1941 he mused 'that if my father had been an American and my mother British, instead of the other way around, I might have got here on my own'. He believed that wartime unity would develop into an ever-closer union, and in a speech at Harvard on

371

6 September 1943 expressed the hope that it 'may well some day become the foundation of a common citizenship'. Not while colonialism persisted, was the American reply.5 *Life* magazine, the totem of the American middle class, bluntly declared:

> One thing we are sure we are not fighting for is to hold the British Empire together. We don't like to put the matter so bluntly, but we don't want you to have any illusions. If your strategists are planning a war to hold the British Empire together they will sooner or later find themselves strategizing all alone . . . Our Side [truth, justice and the American way] is plenty big. It always has been big. It is much bigger than the British Raj. It is much bigger than the British Empire. It is bigger than both of us combined.6

Growing contact between British and American troops, and perhaps more especially the latter and British civilians, did not always dispel damaging national stereotypes. When the Americans suffered a reverse at the Kasserine Pass in Tunisia in early 1943 some British quipped, in parody of a best-selling book, 'How green was our Ally', while 'oversexed, overpaid and over here' was a disparaging description of US servicemen in Britain. Many Americans, for their part, found British society at best quaint and at worst feudal. Lieutenant General George S. Patton, who commanded an American army in Europe in 1944–5, had, as his latest biographer observes, 'demonstrated his intense dislike of the British in general and Montgomery in particular' even before he took command of his troops in Normandy.[7] Nations, like individuals, are shaped by their experiences. Few Americans could recognize just how deeply World War I had marked Britain, and even Winston's warmest American supporters had little inkling that, on the very eve of D-Day, the prospect of another Gallipoli still tormented him.

Anglo-American relations were also complicated by a prominent historical chip on the American shoulder. The issue of American ships being stopped and searched on the high seas by the Royal Navy had precipitated Madison's War in 1812, and the memory was revived during World War I to justify a huge battleship-building programme specifically designed to challenge the Royal Navy. FDR was Assistant Secretary of the Navy at the time. In 1937 Winston wrote an article explaining that the only hope for a blockade in any future war was if the USA adopted a policy of cash and carry, because 'ever since the United States built a Navy equal to that of Britain, and even before, it has been impossible for the British Navy to enforce any blockade contrary to the final will of the United States . . . it is now the settled maxim of British policy that without the good will, or at least the acquiescence, of the United States the famous weapon of blockade cannot be used.'[8]

In November 1939 Congress revised the Neutrality Acts of 1935 and 1937, which prohibited the sale of arms to belligerents, to permit cash and carry. Any ship could go to US ports and carry away whatever was first paid for, in practice a measure unilaterally favouring France and Britain who controlled the Atlantic. In September 1939 FDR had initiated contact with Winston at the

Admiralty, although Chamberlain's hostility to what he saw as US interference meant the exchange did not become substantive until Winston became Prime Minister. The fall of France threw US and Soviet calculations into disarray—both had been expecting to benefit from a long-drawn-out stalemate. It reduced Winston's strategic options to one: with the USA victory was possible, without it only survival—and that for a limited time. The most pressing need was to persuade FDR that a war fought on the other side of the Atlantic was preferable to one fought off the US coast. To that end, ten days after becoming Prime Minister Winston sent a blunt warning that, although his government would never surrender, it might not survive a successful invasion and 'if others came in to parley among the ruins, you must not be blind to the fact that the sole remaining bargaining counter with Germany would be the fleet, and if this country was left by the United States to its fate no one would have the right to blame those responsible if they made the best terms they could for the surviving inhabitants'.[9]

Under such circumstances, the residue of the Royal Navy in combination with the French fleet and the Kriegsmarine would have dominated the Atlantic, a prospect no US President could regard with equanimity. However, FDR was facing his second re-election campaign against a background of lingering economic depression and vocal isolationism, and let the State Department handle negotiations. A request for 50 World War I US navy destroyers was met by a demand for the cession of all the British West Indies to cancel remaining World War I debts, payment of which had been suspended in 1932. Failing that, the State Department's next proposal was to demand a public declaration that the Royal Navy would sail to North America if Britain were invaded. Winston rejected both, the first because it was illegal as well as insulting, the second because of the disastrous effect it would have on morale. The final deal, announced on 14 August 1940, was for long leases on naval bases in the British West Indies, Bermuda and Newfoundland to be exchanged for the destroyers.[10] The usefulness of the ships was almost immaterial: what mattered was the precedent. With the election safely over, Winston threw himself on FDR's mercy:

> The moment approaches when we shall no longer be able to pay cash for shipping and other supplies. While we will do our utmost and shrink from no proper sacrifice to make payments across the exchange, I believe that you will agree that it would be wrong in principle and mutually disadvantageous in effect if, at the height of this struggle, Great Britain were to be divested of all saleable assets so that after victory was won with our blood, civilization saved, and time gained for the United States to be armed against all eventualities, we should stand stripped to the bone. Such a course would not be in the moral or economic interests of either of our countries.[11]

Things did not look that way from the other side of the Atlantic, and the pound of flesh was fully taken, not merely in gold, cash and securities but also in

375

patents, licences and rights. The alternative, after all, was to ask the American taxpayer to foot the bill. Ten days after receiving Winston's plea, FDR spoke in a broadcast about supplying arms against a promise to return or repay them after the war (Lend-Lease), saying it was like lending a neighbour a hose to put out a fire that would otherwise spread. In his memoirs Winston called Lend-Lease 'the most unsordid act in the history of any nation'. In fact, like the Marshall Plan of 1947, it was an act of enlightened self-interest, the element of self-interest in no way diminishing the fact that it was infinitely more enlightened than the blunt 'They hired the money, didn't they?' of the previous war. The USA did not create the circumstances in which Britain found itself in 1940, and had the roles been reversed it is hard to see how a British government would have behaved differently towards a beleaguered America. It was a British Prime Minister, Lord Palmerston, who declared, 'We have no eternal allies and we have no perpetual enemies. Our interests are eternal and perpetual and those interests it is our duty to follow.'[12]

Lend-Lease became law on 11 March 1941, with the proviso that British firms could not trade in products made from any material or by any machine obtained under Lend-Lease, or made from material or by a machine freed up by it. Objectively, given its own limited capacity for growth, it was better for Britain that its cash purchases and the surge of US exports into British overseas markets provided the initial impetus for the vast expansion of America's manufacturing base.[13] 'I have today allotted funds for the building of 58 additional shipping ways and 200 additional ships,' FDR wrote in April 1941. 'I have also made arrangements for repairs to merchant ships and for your larger friends [warships].'14 The money would not have produced the same result in Britain. Congress would not have voted to increase taxation unless the domestic benefits were tangible, and Winston helped FDR to sell Lend-Lease as a means of keeping the USA out of the war with a false assurance to the American people in his broadcast of 9 February 1941: 'Give us your faith and your blessing and under Providence all will be well. We shall not fail or falter; we shall not weaken or tire. Neither the sudden shock of battle nor the long drawn trials of vigilance and exertion will wear us down. Give us the tools, and we will finish the job.'

The wonderful rhetoric of these lines concealed a simple truth: even if Britain was given the tools, the country could not finish the job on its own. However, it was tempting for some Americans to believe that Winston meant precisely what he said, and that Lend-Lease was actually a way of keeping America out of the war. How close to the wind FDR was sailing became apparent on 12 August 1941, when Congress voted to extend the draft (conscription, introduced in October 1939) by a margin of only one vote.15 In war the strong grow stronger and the weak can only hope that what is taken from them will be used in the common cause. That hope also animated the governments in exile in London, whose remaining assets served the British cause. Being a junior ally is a cruelly unrewarding role. A major problem for the British during the war, and, indeed, in writing about it

377

since, is that they inexorably became a lesser partner the longer it lasted.

During the war Winston and FDR exchanged more than 1700 letters and telegrams, on average nearly one a day.[16] They also met in person ten times, eight of them at bilateral meetings and the other two with Stalin, spending a total of 120 days in each other's company. History records no comparable association between the leaders of two major nations. Winston was the suppliant, and over one thousand of the messages were his. He also crossed the Atlantic seven times to FDR's three, although the exchange reflected both the fact that the President was head of state and Winston only the king's first minister, and that FDR had been crippled by polio since 1921 and was physically less resilient than his older British colleague. Winston visited Washington four times but FDR refused to visit Britain, consenting to meet twice in Quebec as a mark of limited reciprocity. It was never a relationship between equals, but FDR went far beyond protocol and even personal convenience to honour his guest. By the end his courtesy had frayed along with his health, but he generally treated Winston with the utmost consideration. Yet when the President died on 12 April 1945 Winston did not attend his funeral, which throws a shadow on his protestations of undying friendship.[17]

At the beginning of their relationship, however, there was genuine affinity. Both men were egotistical at the core, and it is highly unlikely that Winston could have successfully feigned a liking he did not feel: FDR was a shrewd judge of character and would have detected it. Instead, the evidence points unequivocally to his feeling a genuine

378

fondness for Winston, and that he found it difficult to deny him. This introduced a Byzantine element into relations between the two governments, with US officials often putting the worst possible construction on all British initiatives in order to offset the perceived bias of their President. It was an article of faith at the US Military and Naval Academies that the British were creatures of infinite cunning, against whom all Americans must be constantly on their guard.[18] Among civilian officials the progressive agenda also played a prominent part, with Winston perceived as a reactionary. An added twist was that the 'best and the brightest' drawn from the elite universities into government service by FDR's New Deal (a package of measures including public works projects, a Social Security Act and a minimum wage) were naïvely credulous about Stalin's Russia. From FDR downwards the US government inclined to regard the Soviet empire in a kindlier light than the British, a sentiment nurtured by Americans recruited by the Soviet secret service who were to be found in the most sensitive policy-making sections of the administration.[19]

British preconceptions were no less tenacious. American soldiers, lumped together as 'Yanks' to the irritation of the mainly southern US army officer corps, were seen as energetic bumpkins in need of guidance. This was not the case in the other two armed services. Even though the profanely Anglophobe Admiral Ernest King was commander of the Atlantic Fleet from February 1941 and of the US Fleet from 30 December that year, the two navies quickly established a mutually respectful working relationship, as they had in

1917–18, while any differences there might be among the senior air force commanders were minor in comparison to their shared belief that the other two armed forces were superfluous. As far as the armies were concerned, it was fortunate for the Allied cause that Pearl Harbor came just after Brooke had replaced General Sir John Dill as CIGS, and that Dill had been made a field marshal prior to being sent to Bombay as governor general. Although Winston did not value Dill, believing that his rationality and intellectual caution made him obstructive, as the senior serving officer Dill accompanied Winston to Washington in December 1941 and remained there as head of the British military mission. Dill's biographer argues that the close comradeship between Dill and George C. Marshall, US army Chief of Staff, was the most special transatlantic relationship to emerge during the war, while FDR even called him 'the most important figure in Anglo-American co-operation'. [20]

Winston's treatment of Dill opens a porthole into the darkest recess of his soul. He mocked and belittled him as 'Dilly-Dally' when he was CIGS, and the Bombay sinecure was a parting insult. Far from appreciating the value of the rapport Dill built up not merely with Marshall but also with Congressional leaders and FDR himself, Winston continued to denigrate him and twice refused him a peerage, doing himself great harm in American eyes. Marshall thought him the best ambassador Britain ever sent to Washington, and when Dill died in Washington on 4 November 1944, successfully petitioned for him to be buried in Arlington National Cemetery, where his grave is marked by one of only two equestrian statues in that American pantheon.²¹ Nor was this all: on 10 January 1945 FDR wrote a letter, very formally addressed to 'My dear Mr Prime Minister', which amounts to a sharp rebuke:

> In connection with the recent posthumous award of an American Distinguished Service Medal to Field Marshal Sir John Dill, I am sending you herewith a copy of a Joint Resolution of Congress enacted on December 20 last, appreciating the services of Field Marshal Sir John Dill. The fact that Congress saw fit to take this action, which is without precedent, and that the Chairman of the Foreign Relations Committee of the Senate, the Honorable Tom Connally, introduced the Resolution, is not only formal recognition of the great service rendered by him in promoting unity of action on the part of our respective countries, but is an evidence of a very wholesome state of mind in the midst of the bickerings that are inevitable at this stage of the war. I think Sir John Dill rendered both our countries a great service and I am delighted to see it written clearly into the record.

Were it not for American tributes one might perhaps discount Brooke's comments about the Winston–Dill relationship, which conclude with the bleak declaration: 'I shall never be able to forgive Winston for his attitude towards Dill.'²² But in the light of FDR's austere letter, Brooke's postscript for 20 October 1941 gains credibility: 'Dill was the essence of straight forwardness, blessed with the highest of principles and an unassailable integrity of character. I do not believe that any of these characteristics appealed to Winston, on the contrary I think he disliked them as they accentuated his own shortcomings in this respect.'[23] It is impossible to deny the spiteful streak in Winston. Desmond Morton, his best intelligence source during the 1930s and the man Winston trusted to review and select Ultra material for him, judged that his 'overwhelming desire to dominate resulted in a feeling of inferiority in regard to anyone who was not in the least afraid of him, nor ever would be, and in whose character he could not detect a flaw'. Morton said the first time he 'ever deeply disliked him and realized the depths of selfish brutality to which he could sink' was when he sacked Wavell as C-in-C Middle East and admitted he had done so to show his power.[24]

The first wartime FDR–Winston meeting (the two had actually met in 1918 at an occasion that Winston subsequently struggled to recall) took place on warships in Placentia Bay (also known as Argentia Harbour), Newfoundland, in August 1941.[25] With the conscription vote looming FDR had little room for manoeuvre and, apart from enabling the two men to take the measure of each other, the main outcome of the meeting was the declaration of principles that came to be known as the Atlantic Charter (see Appendix B). The phrase 'with due respect for their existing obligations' in Clause Four was inserted with reference to Imperial Preference, which the State Department never ceased to attack throughout the war without giving an inch on American protectionism.[26] The whole of Clause Five was inserted at the insistence of the Cabinet in London, convoked by Attlee for an emergency night meeting. The two principals knew that the declaration was a bromide. In February 1945 FDR said: 'The Atlantic Charter is a beautiful idea. When it was drawn up, the situation was that England was about to lose the war. They needed hope, and it gave it to them.'[27] This was disingenuous. He too needed it, for domestic consumption, and, as Winston reminded him a year later with reference to FDR's views on India, among the first consequences of a strict application of the Charter would be the expulsion of the Jewish settlers from Palestine.[28]

Winston wanted some indication that the USA would come into the war soon, but did not get it. On his return he told the newspaper magnate Cecil King that he would prefer to have America in the war and no supplies for six months than double the shipments while it remained neutral—not for any military contribution the Americans could make in the short term but for the impact their entry would have on the struggle for hearts and minds in occupied Europe. He was concerned that the people of Europe might acquiesce in the Nazi new order unless soon convinced they would be liberated. 'In this race for time', he said, 'American participation in the war would be a great psychological point in our favour.'[29] It is possible that FDR regarded the Atlantic Charter as a favour to Britain with this psychological objective in view, but Winston's conversation with King suggests that it may have been more directly a favour to Winston himself, who wanted the Labour Party leaders in his government to have a ringing declaration of intent with which to pacify their left wing.

As soon as practicable following Pearl Harbor, Winston crossed the Atlantic on board the new battleship *Duke of York* (her sister ship *Prince of Wales*, which had carried him to Placentia Bay, was by now at the bottom of the South China Sea), flying the last leg from landfall at Hampton Roads at the mouth of the Potomac River. During the crossing he elaborated his strategic vision in a four-part prospectus. It started with the 'Atlantic Front', in which defeat of the U-boats was the indispensable first step, to culminate in an American occupation of French North Africa which he believed would be unopposed. This would allow free passage through the Mediterranean to the Middle East and the Suez Canal, winning a million tons of merchant shipping by making it no longer necessary for convoys to sail around Africa. This he called 'the ring that is closing' around Germany, from which he took the title of the fifth volume of his memoirs. The second and fourth parts of the prospectus concerned the Pacific, to take second place to the Atlantic because 'the war cannot be ended by driving Japan back to her own bounds and defeating her overseas forces. It can only be ended through the defeat in Europe of the German armies.' The wording was so similar to that of the memorandum the American Chiefs of Staff prepared for FDR after Pearl Harbor that it is fair to assume it reflected the conclusions of the secret Anglo-American joint staff meetings during and after the Placentia Bay summit.[30]

Part Three set out a strategy to close the noose by persuading Turkey to open the Dardanelles for supplies to the Soviet Union via the Black Sea. The plan predicted the internal collapse of Germany, produced by the unfavourable course of the war, economic privation and bombing, and from resistance movements in the occupied countries, to be encouraged by small landings in Norway, Denmark, Holland and Belgium, on the French Channel and Atlantic coasts, as well as in Italy and possibly the Balkans. Meanwhile a 'liberating offensive' of 40 divisions, half of them Commonwealth, was to be prepared for the summer of 1943. The prerequisites were outright air and sea supremacy.[31] The prospectus was accepted with few reservations by the Americans in a long series of staff meetings, which among other things set up the concept of the Combined Chiefs of Staff (CCS) and at subordinate levels followed the British model of discussion in joint services committees where allies worked together and where personal understandings could moderate inter-service as well as inter-allied rivalries. This structure was the single most important British gift to the Allied war effort.[32]

Marshall assigned a comparatively junior general, Dwight D. 'Ike' Eisenhower, as head of the CCS, with orders to prepare a plan for a cross-Channel invasion, inauspiciously scheduled for 1 April 1943, with a contingency plan for a smaller landing in September or October 1942 if it became necessary to save the Soviet Union from collapse.[33] In November 1942 Ike commanded Operation Torch, Allied landings in French Morocco and Algeria that had not been foreseen ten months earlier, for Winston expected British forces to have cleared the Axis from North Africa by then. In July 1943 Ike also headed Operation Husky, the Allied invasion of Sicily, and in September the Allied landings in the south of Italy. The battle of the Atlantic was not won until mid-1943, and it was not until after the long-range Mustang fighter started to escort US bombers in January 1944 that daytime air supremacy over Europe began to be won. The preparatory coastal raids Winston had foreseen did not take place, though there was one ill-starred large landing in Dieppe in August 1942 which did at least teach some useful lessons. At last on D-Day, 6 June 1944, the cross-Channel invasion, Operation Overlord, took place under Eisenhower's overall command; its chances of success were greatly enhanced by changes made to the original plan at the insistence of the ground force commander, General Sir Bernard Montgomery, under whom the 8th Army had defeated Rommel at Alamein in October–November 1942.[34] Although a good deal had changed, not least the timescale, overall the original concept remained much the same.

Winston, the prime author of the strategy, made a well-received speech to Congress on 26 December 1941, after which he suffered the first heart attack of which we have knowledge. However, it was perhaps a sign that Winston's health was causing concern that on this trip he was for the first time accompanied by his physician Sir Charles Wilson, later Lord Moran and later still author of the ethically questionable *Winston Churchill: The Struggle for Survival*. There was no history of cardiac problems in Winston's family, but the effects of cholesterol, alcohol, nicotine, weight and stress could not be denied indefinitely. This episode should condition our understanding of his subsequent behaviour, first because of the possibility that reduced blood flow to the brain dulled his mental acuity, and secondly because it cannot have failed to revive the belief, so influential in his earlier life, that he did not have long to live. This could explain why he threw caution to the wind and used himself up during 1942–3. The famous 'scowling bulldog' photograph taken by Karsh in Ottawa on 31 December 1941 therefore captures a watershed moment in Winston's life.

During 1942 Winston flew back from America, made another return visit to Washington by air in June, and then flew to Cairo to sort out the Middle Eastern command, giving Montgomery the 8th Army (with which he would very soon achieve his famous victory at Alamein), and placing Alexander in overall command. Winston then flew on to Moscow, by way of Tehran, to meet Stalin. The Soviet dictator was well briefed on Winston's habits from reports supplied by his agents in every confidential corner of the British government, and gave his guest a surfeit of his own medicine. Stalin could be insultingly adversarial in meetings that ran long into the night, fuelled with stunning amounts of alcohol—to the quiet amusement of British officials. Winston quickly realized that his host was testing his mettle, while for the first time Stalin encountered someone who was not afraid of him. Laboured consecutive translation neutralized Winston's eloquence, but at the end Stalin waved away the interpreter, saying that he did not need to know what words the Prime Minister had spoken because his spirit spoke for itself.[35] Contrary to all expectations the two formed a good impression of each other.

One may wonder why Stalin did not warm to FDR, given the enormous assistance he directed to the Soviet Union and his undoubtedly heroic triumph over polio. The answer may be that he despised FDR's disloyalty to Winston at Tehran in November–December 1943 and at Yalta in February 1945. Commenting on these attempts by the US President to befriend him at Winston's expense, Stalin said he preferred 'a downright enemy to a pretending friend', and in another left-handed compliment said that while FDR would not take less than a rouble out of your pocket, Winston would snatch the last kopek.[36] Perhaps oddly, for a man as steeped in treachery as Stalin, the proletarian revolutionary valued aristocratic honour. He was visibly moved at the Tehran conference when Winston presented him with a ceremonial sword inscribed 'To the steelhearted citizens of Stalingrad, a gift from King George VI as a token of the homage of the British people', which is still proudly displayed in the Battle of Stalingrad Museum. At Yalta Stalin took Ismay aside to say of Winston, 'There have been few cases in history where the courage of one man has been so important to the future of the world.'[37] Far away in Australia General Douglas MacArthur, the Commander of Allied Forces in the South Pacific, commented to a British SIS officer on his staff:

If disposal of all the Allied decorations were today placed by Providence in my hands, my first act would be to award the Victoria Cross to Winston Churchill. No one of those who wear it deserves it more than he. A flight of ten thousand miles through hostile and foreign skies may be the duty of young pilots, but for a statesman burdened with the world's cares, it is an act of inspiring gallantry and valour.[38]

The sentiment was shared by Marshall and his protégé Eisenhower, and explains why they did not believe that Winston's attempts to delay the invasion of France were born of fear (incubated beneath the dark shadow of Gallipoli and the Somme), well disguised as practical objections. From the very start, plans for the liberation of Europe were bedevilled by complex strategic considerations. Any landing in France in 1942 could, at best, only have established a besieged beach-head whose maintenance would have inhibited a major landing later. If the bulk of US shipping and landing craft had been committed to the European theatre, then conceivably a landing in France might have been made in 1943 with some hope of success. But these resources went preferentially to the Pacific; therefore the arguments that strained Anglo-American relations during meetings in 1943 (at Casablanca in January, Washington in May, Quebec in August and Washington again in September) were enveloped in a cloud of unreality much easier to penetrate now than it was at the time. FDR's signal of 25 November 1942 may be taken as Marshall's fully considered opinion, from which neither he nor FDR budged during 1943:

No one can possibly know whether or not we may have the opportunity to strike across the channel in 1943 and if the opportunity comes we must obviously grasp it. . . . It is my present thought that we should build up as rapidly as present operations permit a growing force in the UK to be used quickly in the event of German collapse or a very large force later if Germany remains intact and assumes a defensive position.[39]

I do not see how FDR and Marshall could have expressed more clearly their belief that an invasion in 1943 depended on the internal German collapse towards which British strategy since 1939 had been directed. If this did not occur, then sterner measures would be called for in 1944. This was, after all, what had been agreed in December 1941, and growing British caution about the invasion was taken by the Americans as proof of backsliding, confirming what they had been taught about British bad faith. The subject has been thoroughly aired by scholars on both sides of the Atlantic, around a dichotomy between 'proponents of British strategy [who] argue that the American approach was wasteful and ignored important political objectives, whereas supporters of US strategy maintain the British approach was incapable of achieving victory, threatened the necessary continuation of their alliance, and was geared to English rather than US political objectives'.[40] This begs an important question about US political objectives in Europe, but on the military plane I do not believe the two views are irreconcilable.

To understand why, it must be remembered that the political dimension of war is domestic as well as international. At the heart of the US war effort was a struggle between competing services, with the dice loaded against Marshall by the difficulty of persuading US public opinion that defeating Germany was more important than punishing Japan as the enemy who had attacked first, as well as by the pronounced bias of FDR, who tended to refer to the navy as 'us' and the army as 'them'. Politically, Marshall could only maintain 'Germany first' against the rival claims of the US navy and of MacArthur in the Pacific by making Europe the major theatre of war as soon as possible. MacArthur, a legendary figure in the US army and also in the eyes of the American people, required particularly careful handling. If the notion of a senior general emerging to mount a political challenge in a wartime election might seem absurd to British readers, it was certainly a possibility that FDR had to consider.

Even amongst those who agreed with the wisdom of dealing with Germany first, it was not easy to be sure how to deal with a German army whose training, organization and leadership enabled it, despite the strategic straitjacket into which it was thrust by Hitler's policies, to excel, time and time again, at the business of fighting battles. The US conscription process sent those judged to be of least social value to the infantry, where they were led by junior officers whose basic training, at least until mid-1944, was inferior to that given to German senior NCOs. The British had already experienced the consequences of throwing a hastily expanded army in the way of the Wehrmacht, and when US troops were badly shaken by their first encounter with the Germans at the Kasserine Pass in Tunisia in February 1943 the pattern was repeated. The failure of Allied armies to overcome German resistance in Italy in 1943–4, despite Allied air and sea supremacy, was not a comfortable portent. Some argued that overwhelming firepower efficiently applied was a necessary substitute for low-level tactical skill. Montgomery was one of the few senior British officers who fully appreciated how the rules of the game had been changed by US resources, which made possible his own preference for that systematic application of machine energy dubbed *Materialschlacht* by the rueful Germans. Montgomery remains scarcely less of a controversial figure than his political master, but amongst his great strengths was the recognition that he was dealing with a citizen army which preferred to let metal, not flesh, bear the brunt of battle.

Senior politicians and military leaders are generally well aware that few things are more likely to damage an alliance than to make disparaging comparisons between one's own and an ally's troops. Winston had paid warm tribute to the great Duke of Marlborough's enormous skill as a coalition manager, with the ability to flatter and cajole, and knew just how difficult it was to raise hard issues about real capabilities. This makes a desperate telegram he sent to FDR on 23 October 1943 all the more revealing. He reported that General von Thoma, captured at the end of the North Africa campaign and placed in a bugged room with other German officers, had said: 'Our only hope is that they come where we can use the army upon them.' Winston confessed this was the real reason for his great concern about Overlord:

the Allied armies were simply not up to it.

> I do not doubt our ability in the conditions laid down [air and sea supremacy] to get ashore and deploy. I am however deeply concerned with the build-up and with the situation that may arise between the 30th and the 60th days. I feel sure the vast movement of American personnel into the United Kingdom and the fighting composition of the units requires to be searchingly examined by the commander who will execute Overlord . . . My dear friend, this is much the greatest thing we have ever attempted, and I am not satisfied that we have yet taken the measures necessary to give it the best chance of success. I feel very much in the dark at present, and unable to think or act in the forward manner which is needed. For these reasons I desire an early conference.[41]

Although World War II wove together a myriad of strategic issues, the strongest thread in the whole skein was the fact that the Red Army ground down the Wehrmacht on the Eastern Front, just as the French and British had ground down the German army on the Western Front a generation before. Its inevitable consequence was that Winston and FDR could do little more than acquiesce to Stalin controlling most of the territory occupied by his forces. As a quid pro quo, Stalin did not retain Austria or add Greece to his collection of satellites—something which was easily within his power. Domestic politics had a powerful impact on Western strategy, from Winston's need of a victory

393

as soon as possible in North Africa, to Marshall's need for the early commitment of the US army against Germany in order to compete for shipping and landing craft with the Pacific theatre. As a result of the prolonged debate over the invasion itself, too little discussion took place about what would happen afterwards, and this helped the Russians to dictate the endgame. The idea that a thrust into the Balkans from Italy or an Allied advance beyond the Elbe might have altered the Cold War boundaries is a fantasy. In his memoirs Winston used it to gloss over his own strategic equivocation because he could not admit it was born of fear that the armies of the English-speaking peoples could not go toe-to-toe with the Germans and win.

Strategy was more clear-cut in the mainland war in the Far East, where American policy was to prop up their client, the Nationalist Chinese leader Chiang Kai-shek, and to bring an early end to British rule in India. FDR's personal emissary to Chiang and also the Chinese leader's Chief of Staff, the aptly nicknamed General 'Vinegar Joe' Stilwell, was a violent Anglophobe who was none the less appointed to command all US forces in the China–Burma–India theatre.[42] It was not until Stilwell was recalled and the Japanese swept the Nationalists from the coasts of China in 1944–5, capturing all the airbases from which the US air force hoped to conduct a strategic bombing campaign against Japan, that the British 14th Army under General Sir William Slim was able to recover operational freedom. Until then it had been, as Winston saw it, 'mis-employed for American convenience' to guard the air-bridge over the

Himalayas 'into their very over-rated China'.43 The remark is more illuminating of Winston's resentment at the supporting role he was forced to play than of the true role of China in Allied strategy. Corrupt and incompetent though the Nationalists were, they tied down more than half the Japanese army and prevented Japan from making the war an anti-colonial and racial struggle of Asians against Caucasians.44

It tends to be overlooked that, although the British population in 1940 was 48 million against Greater Germany's more than 80 million and Italy's 44 million, the Empire encompassed a quarter of the world's population, with over 500 million souls in India alone.45 The Indian army expanded from 189,000 in 1939 to 2,500,000 in 1945, the largest volunteer army in history. It was indispensable in affirming British control in the Middle East in 1941–2, played an important role in the campaigns for North Africa and Italy, and helped salvage imperial authority within the subcontinent during the 'Quit India' uprising of 1942. Winston's principal concern was not to alienate the Muslims, and for the duration of the war British authority in India rested on armed force more nakedly than at any time since the Great Rebellion of 1857.46 It is scarcely surprising that Hindu nationalists have made a hero of Subas Chandra Bose, the leader of the Japanese-sponsored Indian National Army (INA). But the vast majority of Indian army prisoners of war resisted cruel pressure by their German and Japanese captors to join Bose. That they did resist was not by any means out of love for the British, but out of loyalty to a soldierly ideal: this was an army that commanded devotion in its own right.

Winston, professedly the guardian of the British Empire, did not appreciate this. He was singularly unappreciative of Slim, whose success in regrouping and retraining British and Indian forces after their ignominious collapse in 1942, with inadequate resources and little support from Britain, was one of the greatest personal achievements by any Anglo-American commander during the war.[47] One can, however, understand Winston's irritation when FDR, prompted by Chiang, pressed for the immediate declaration of Indian independence, comparing it to the situation in the United States in 1783–9. 'Such a move', he wrote, 'is strictly in line with the world changes of the past half-century and with the democratic processes of all who are fighting Nazism.'[48] Winston replied that he could not 'take responsibility for the defence of India if everything has again to be thrown into the melting pot at this critical juncture'. In *Hinge of Fate*, the fourth volume of his memoirs, he commented bitterly, 'I was thankful that events had already made such an act of madness impossible. The human race cannot make progress without idealism, but idealism at other people's expense and without regard to the consequences of ruin and slaughter which fall upon millions of humble homes cannot be considered as its highest or noblest form.'[49]

The broader aims of US strategy in the Burma–China theatre drew on an almost mystical vision, dating back to the early years of the twentieth century, of how things ought to be rather than of how they really were.[50] Post-war developments were to reveal just how bankrupt this

396

was, but Winston proposed no coherent alternative and never visited the theatre. It is small wonder that Slim's soldiers regarded themselves as 'The Forgotten Army', and that the British component of Slim's army overwhelmingly voted against Winston in 1945. Winston pushed the Chiefs of Staff to the brink of resignation in late 1944, when, to compensate for his inability to affect the course of the war in Europe, he belatedly turned his attention to the Far East and attempted to construct grand strategy out of thin air. Winston did not like being reminded that fundamental strategic decisions could not be altered at his whim. 'I do not want any of your long term projects', Brooke recalled him saying; 'all they do is cripple initiative.'[51] Apart from cosmetic interventions such as producing the charismatic Brigadier General Orde Wingate, author of the Chindit long-range raids behind Japanese lines, like a rather jungly rabbit from a hat at the Quebec conference of August 1943, this theatre was a virtual void in Winston's war leadership, as it was in his world-view in the 1920s and 1930s, for reasons that remain elusive.[52]

It is as well to pause here to examine Winston's views on America and the Americans, because the 'Special Relationship' rests as much on the veneration of his memory in the USA as it does on a community of interests.[53] In 1963 he was the first person to be declared an Honorary Citizen of the USA by Act of Congress (see Appendix C), one of only two so honoured in their lifetime.[54] The reality of Anglo-American relations during the war was captured by the ambiguous thought Brooke confided to his diary in January 1943: 'There is no doubt that we are too closely related to the Americans to make co-operation between us anything but easy.'[55] Winston was miscast as the leader of a nation in decline. His views coincided with the strain of American nationalism expressed by, among others, Admiral King and the flamboyant George Patton, who felt the British no longer possessed the will to dominate and should therefore get out of other people's way. On the other hand Winston's views shocked American progressives like Vice President Henry Wallace, whose diary of the war years makes one grateful that FDR chose Harry Truman as his running mate in 1944.[56] During a lunch at the White House on 22 May 1943, Wallace taxed a well-watered Winston on his notion of Anglo-Saxon superiority:

> [Winston] said why be apologetic about Anglo-Saxon superiority, that we were superior, that we had the common heritage which had been worked out over the centuries in England and had been perfected by our constitution. He himself was half American, he felt that he was called on as a result to serve the function of uniting the two great Anglo-Saxon civilizations in order to confer the benefit of freedom on the rest of the world.

Six weeks before D-Day Patton made a speech to a most improbable audience, the Women's Institute at Knutsford in Cheshire, to the effect that since it was the manifest destiny of the British and Americans to rule the world, they should get to know each other better. Amid much concern about

398

the offence this might give the Russians, Marshall ordered Ike to relieve him of his command. Winston, in contrast, told Ike that 'he could see nothing in it as Patton had simply told the truth'.[57] He liked nothing better than to remind Americans that liberal imperialism was still imperialism. One of the few occasions when he bared his teeth at FDR was prompted by the President's persistent sanctimoniousness in this regard.[58] Sir John Colville, arguably the official closest to Winston during both his premierships, believed 'he was never a party to the Anglo-Saxon folly of supposing that representative government is the only passport to happiness and respectability'.[59] But, barring an occasional lapse such as the one recorded by Wallace, he could usually talk the talk with sufficient conviction. What he did not fully appreciate was that the dominance of the East Coast oligarchy represented by FDR was tenuous. The USA of the 1940s was still 48 rather introspective states lightly overseen by a small Federal government. Washington was a small southern town that came awake for half the year, whereas London was the largest metropolis in the world and had been an imperial capital for centuries. Winston did not make sufficient allowance for the limitations on FDR's power, nor for his need to mobilize public opinion in order to obtain what he wanted from Congress. The descendants of Irish, Italian and German immigrants could be rallied to a specifically American cause, but to do so it was necessary to differentiate that cause as much as possible from the British.

Before the war Winston wrote that 'we produce

few of their clear-cut political types or clear-cut party programmes. In our affairs as in those of Nature there are always frayed edges, borderlands, compromises, anomalies. Few lines are drawn that are not smudged. Across the ocean all is crisp and sharp.'[60] In his memoirs he developed the thought further:

> In the military as in the commercial or production spheres the American mind runs naturally to broad, sweeping, logical conclusions on the largest scale. It is on these that they build their practical thought and action. They feel that once the foundation has been planned on true and comprehensive lines all other stages will follow naturally and almost inevitably. The British mind does not work quite in this way. We do not think that logic and clear-cut principles are necessarily the sole keys to what ought to be done in swiftly changing and indefinable situations. In war particularly we assign a larger importance to opportunism and improvisation, seeking rather to live and conquer in accordance with unfolding events than to aspire to dominate it often by fundamental decisions.[61]

If there is one valid generalization to be made about a people as diverse and a society as decentralized as that of the USA at that time, it is that they waged war in a highly pragmatic manner. Winston may have been referring to something quite different: the sheer size of the USA encouraged a 'think big' mentality alien to the British. The Empire had never involved more than

400

a small proportion of its population in politics, and did not have the cultural effect that the ability to move on in search of pastures new had on the American psyche. Britons who sought these new pastures had emigrated, which in the American view meant that anyone with get up and go had got up and gone, while in the British view those who remained had a more concentrated sense of identity. The two views are not incompatible, but the potential for mutual asperity is manifest.

Despite all this, the two cultures meshed with relatively little serious friction, confounding Hitler's expectation that they would turn on each other. Often the common sense and fellow feeling of those on the ground tolerated a greater degree of wrangling at the top. The sternest test came when Britain experienced something of what it felt like to be an occupied country during the build-up to the invasion of Europe, with all the tensions attendant on the influx of tens of thousands of US and Canadian troops. But the bickering and brawling between servicemen of different nationalities never got out of hand. Part of the reason was that lines of fissure were as often between military specializations as between nationalities, and in bar-room brawls all over the world US and British infantrymen might find themselves fighting shoulder to shoulder against their common enemies: sailors, airmen and their own support personnel.

Wrangling at the top, however, became more pronounced as the war progressed. Winston was determined that post-war Europe should not again be shaped by an American 'big picture' without regard for the detailed consequences, as it had

401

been after World War I. Ralph Ingersoll, an extremely influential American journalist and editor with impeccably progressive credentials, commented: 'They [the British] must have wondered, sometimes, whether history had not committed them to an alliance, at worst with madmen and at best with congenital optimists, the corner stones of whose faith were ignorance and vanity.'[62] A more sinister interpretation, brought into disrepute by the post-war House Un-American Activities Committee and Senator Joe McCarthy, but not for that reason necessarily incorrect, is that US foreign policy in the latter stages of the war was influenced by Soviet agents and sympathizers in the government.[63] Yet Ingersoll's comment provides a more believable reason why FDR signed off State Department drafts to Winston reproving him for, among other things, sending troops to prevent a Communist coup d'état in Athens, limiting Soviet penetration into Persia, seeking to affirm a non-Communist administration in Italy and, the biggest sin of all, failing to make it clear to Stalin 'that we are not establishing any post-war spheres of influence'.[64]

Much of Winston's moral authority rested on his opposition to the policy of setting a good example to dictators by unilaterally foregoing traditional means of dissuasion. Despite this, however, FDR convinced himself that Winston was now the fly in his soup of fellowship with the Soviet tyrant.[65] During private meetings with Stalin at Tehran FDR said that he disagreed with Winston over the need to reconstitute France as a strong nation, because France was not fit to be strong. 'The first necessity', he said, 'is for the French, not only the

Government but the people as well, to become honest citizens.' There was no point in talking about India with Winston, he continued, because he was simply deferring the problem until after the war. FDR said he would like to talk about it with Stalin at some future date, as he thought 'the best solution would be reform from the bottom, somewhat on the Soviet line'.[66] This was music to Stalin's ears, and went far beyond what was necessary if, as FDR's apologists suggest, he was simply trying to establish friendly relations with Stalin at Winston's expense.

Part of the reason for FDR's action lies in the thraldom exercised by Stalin over Western intellectuals, whose past and present culpability Martin Amis explores in his recent *Koba the Dread*. Belief in progress was stronger in the USA than in Britain, and the experience of the Great Depression therefore more shattering. Americans were among the most gullible of Western intellectuals who visited Russia, and the will to see what they wanted to see was strengthened by the heroism of the Soviet people during World War II. Harry Hopkins, much the most influential of FDR's advisers and a man whom no reasonable critic could accuse of being a fellow traveller, believed that since the Soviet Union was the decisive factor in the war 'she must be given every assistance and every effort must be made to obtain her friendship'.[67] In 1944 a party led by Vice President Wallace visited the Kolyma gulag, where 3 million people were killed between 1937 and 1953, and in a *National Geographic* article his aide Professor Owen Lattimore compared it to the Tennessee Valley Authority, the flagship project of

403

FDR's New Deal.[68] The most charitable interpretation of FDR's behaviour towards Winston at Tehran and Yalta is that a policy decision was taken to establish good relations with Stalin at any cost, because without a long-term US commitment to Europe, at that time considered out of the question, the Soviet Union was certain to become the dominant regional power. Underlying this, however, was an intellectual arrogance that prevented many progressives on both sides of the Atlantic from admitting how self-deluding they had been about the Workers' Paradise.

Among the people whose interests were not addressed by FDR's vision of a Europe dominated by Russia were the non-Communist resistance movements in Czechoslovakia, Denmark, Norway, Holland, Belgium, France, Poland and Greece, all of whom looked for support to London. The cold-blooded decision to encourage the resistance, with the certainty that it would lead to savage reprisals and even civil war, was not Winston's. It was the brainchild of Hugh Dalton, one of the public school socialists he so disliked, grudgingly appointed Minister of Economic Warfare in May 1940.[69] Dalton rightly insisted that an agency for irregular ('ungentlemanly', he called it) warfare must be independent of the War Office, a view vigorously pressed by Attlee in the War Cabinet. On 22 July that year the Special Operations Executive (SOE) was brought into being 'to co-ordinate all action by way of subversion and sabotage against the enemy overseas', whose activities 'should not be raised in Parliament'. Dalton was given 'absolute powers of discretion, subject only to the Prime Minister'.

SOE struggled throughout its existence against a rare alliance among the armed forces, the Foreign Office and SIS, and without backing from Winston it could not have become established. Winston's reservations about Dalton, whom he was relieved to move on to the Board of Trade in 1942, were in part personal but also reflected grave misgivings about his ambition to let the genie of revolutionary warfare out of the bottle. Was SOE, as Dalton thought, 'a bloody bone which has been thrown to me in order to appease the Labour Party', or was it simply another example of Keep Buggering On? Either way, Winston was not prepared to arm the Communists, who only sprang to life after Hitler invaded the Soviet Union, unless they were prepared to do serious damage to the Germans in return. He did not want to strengthen resistance groups less concerned with fighting the Germans during the war than with seizing power after it. Ideology was secondary, as was shown when SOE switched its support from the monarchist Draza Mihailovic to the Communist Josep 'Tito' Broz in Yugoslavia in 1943.

The American Office of Strategic Services (OSS) came into the game late, under FDR's appointee the protean 'Wild Bill' Donovan. The strongly Roman Catholic agenda of this World War I hero was more often at variance with official US government policy than with the British, about whom none the less he had the usual Irish-American reservations.[70]

The subject is vast and its ramifications too complex to permit more than a signpost to further reading here.[71] The most tragic area of SOE operations was Poland, at the limit of the RAF's ability to deliver personnel and supplies (only 600 tons, compared with 10,000 tons to France and 18,000 to Yugoslavia), and doomed to fall under Russian control. The Poles were the principal sacrifice Winston was obliged to make on the altar of Allied unity, and his outrageously bullying behaviour towards the Polish government in exile, which did not do him the favour of acquiescing to arrangements reached with Stalin at Tehran and Yalta, betrayed a guilty conscience at work.[72] He was compelled to behave dishonourably towards men who had fought gallantly under British command throughout the war, but as he wrote later, 'terrible and even humbling submissions must at times be made to the general aim'.[73] While the Cold War lasted it was an impossible subject to close, but in 1995 a Polish historian wrote a generous conclusion to a dispassionate review of a situation in which a tidal wave of *realpolitik* remorselessly swamped the frail craft of honour and decency:

> He had no compunction about making full use of Polish manpower, while clearly holding back from making commitments to the Polish government that might have damaging implications [vis-à-vis the Grand Alliance]. . . . Churchill had sympathy for the Polish soldiers. He frequently expressed support for them and at the end of the war made sure that they were neither returned to Poland forcibly, nor left unprovided for in Britain.[74]

Possibly the most thankless supporting role Winston undertook was in favour of France, through the medium of the uniquely awkward General Charles de Gaulle. De Gaulle was not the representative he would have chosen: 'I seek the France that I love', declared Winston, 'and I do not find her in General de Gaulle.'[75] What he did find was someone uncommonly like himself, as he tacitly admitted: 'De Gaulle a great man? Why he's selfish, he's arrogant, he thinks he is the centre of the universe . . . He . . . you're right, he's a great man!'[76] He also saw something of the France he loved in a man capable of uttering the Gallicism: 'I am too weak to make concessions.'[77] For whatever reasons, Winston saved de Gaulle from himself by dint of 'yes, buts' with FDR, who hated the haughty Frenchman.[78] At Casablanca, before de Gaulle bowed to Allied pressure and agreed to cooperate with FDR's candidate for leadership of the Free French, General Henri Giraud, Winston commented: 'His country has given up fighting, he himself is a refugee, and if we turn him down he is finished. Well, just look at him! He might be Stalin with two hundred divisions behind his words!'[79] Winston threatened and cajoled him, usually to no avail, but *au fond* he knew that only de Gaulle could restore to France the greatness that he, unlike FDR, believed to be hers by right. Needless to say, the role of Britain remains a delicate subject. As a French general warned Ismay: 'There will be Frenchmen who will not forgive you for two generations. You made our shame too great by fighting on.'[80]

On his sixty-ninth birthday, during the Tehran conference of 28 November–1 December 1943, Winston saw all too well that the indispensable role Britain under his leadership had played in the

Grand Alliance was coming to an end. 'There I sat', he said, 'with the great Russian bear on one side of me, with paws outstretched, and on the other side the great American buffalo, and between the two sat the poor little English donkey who was the only one who knew the right way home.' Unlike de Gaulle, he was not too weak to make concessions: but nor was he strong enough to refuse them. If any tangible American advantage had followed FDR's humiliation of Winston during the conference, history would judge him to have made a hard but correct decision. But it is still profoundly chastening that a man who considered his nation to be in the vanguard of human civilization sought the friendship of a despot whom he knew to be responsible, among other monstrous crimes, for the murder of some twenty thousand Polish officers and men at Katyn and elsewhere, and made jokes with him about doing the same to the Germans. Winston protested and then strode out. Roy Jenkins glides gently over the episode by observing that Winston handled the situation 'unbuoyantly'.[81] But Winston had just learned that the man in whom he had deposited his hopes for a decent post-war world was an appeaser, and had seen FDR make mock of him while sharing a genocidal jest with a mass murderer. In the circumstances, he can be forgiven for seeming less than buoyant.

Lord Moran wrote that Winston went to bed that night deeply depressed, gloomily predicting another war in which mankind might destroy itself.[82] The 'black dog' persisted, with Winston becoming increasingly listless until he succumbed to pneumonia in Tunis on 11 December. On the

408

night of 14 December Moran thought he was going to die, and on the 15th and 18th his heart fibrillated. And then, as he grew stronger, his workload rose dangerously, until at last on 27 December he was persuaded to take a genuine break at a luxury villa in Marrakech. He stayed there until 14 January, when he flew to Gibraltar and boarded the battleship *King George V* for his return to England. Since leaving for the Casablanca conference on 12 January 1943, he had been out of the country for 172 days. Appearing unexpectedly in the Commons at Question Time on the day of his arrival he was greeted by an outburst of emotion, a standing ovation with MPs cheering themselves hoarse. It was a sublime moment, and it could not have come at a better time for a man more battered in body and spirit than he was ever to admit.

Four days later an operation began that Winston hoped would revitalize the Italian campaign. The amphibious landing at Anzio, which he had championed, was supposed to be followed by a lightning advance inland, unhinging the Gustav Line where the Germans had halted the Allied advance in 1943. But the Germans declined to relinquish their hold on the Gustav Line and resolutely counter-attacked at Anzio, which speedily became a besieged bridgehead, and echoes of Gallipoli resounded.[83] 'I had hoped that we were hurling a wildcat on to the shore', Winston wrote, 'but all we got was a stranded whale.'[84]

The Italian campaign could now only be justified primarily in terms of tying down German troops who would otherwise be available for service elsewhere, most dangerously to counter-attack

Operation Overlord. Michael Howard long ago demolished the idea that the Mediterranean strategy corresponded to a 'British way of warfare', but the question of who was tying down whom in Italy is more difficult to answer.[85] By 6 June 1944, D-Day for Overlord, there were 28 German divisions, including seven panzer or panzergrenadier divisions, facing 25 Allied divisions in Italy. In addition, across the Adriatic Tito's partisans, thanks to strong support from Allied bases in Italy, were tying down more German troops. There were also 18 German divisions garrisoning Denmark and Norway, which should be entered in the credit balance of the peripheral strategy.[86] If the German armoured divisions alone had been able to relocate from Italy to Normandy they could have tipped the balance against Overlord, and limited availability of landing craft meant that Allied divisions withdrawn from Italy could not have been put ashore in Normandy in time to make any difference.[87]

There was, then, a good case for maintaining the pressure in Italy, although many of the soldiers who fought there surmised that their leaders must have been using maps without contours because they had failed to grasp the obstacles that geography placed in an attacker's path. Yet troops were withdrawn from Italy to land in the south of France in mid-August 1944, at the urging of Stalin but also because of American suspicion about British motives, expressed with increasing intemperance from mid-1943.[88] The military logic of this operation, originally codenamed Anvil but rechristened Dragoon to register Winston's feelings about it, was questionable and its results negligible.[89] At Tehran Stalin supported Anvil strongly, saying that Italy and the Balkans were no longer strategically significant.[90] Winston and the British Chiefs of Staff found it hard to adjust to the gloomy fact that their views had become increasingly suspect in the eyes of an ally who was able to monitor their good faith, while those of the ultra-secretive Soviet dictator were no less automatically accepted at face value. This was something far deeper than the issues of ego that disfigure some senior officers' memoirs.[91] Winston's own history of the war created a myth of Anglo-American unity of purpose that successfully diverted the attention of posterity from the dispiriting reality he was obliged to wrestle with in 1944–5. Those who lived through it with him generally followed his lead, but passages here and there testify to an abiding sense of betrayal.[92]

Eisenhower was caught between the rock of Marshall's refusal to contemplate any postponement of Overlord even if the original preconditions of air supremacy and no more than 15 German divisions in northern France were not met, and the hard place of Winston's insistence that these should be fulfilled to the letter. He wisely let Montgomery do most of the talking at a crucial meeting at St Paul's School in west London, the planning headquarters for the operation, on 15 May 1944. King George VI, Winston, the War Cabinet, the South African Prime Minister Smuts, the British Chiefs of Staff and 'Allied generals by the score' were present. Following the formal presentations:

[Winston] made one of his typical fighting

411

speeches, in the course of which he used an expression which struck many of us, particularly the Americans, with peculiar force. He said, 'Gentlemen, I am hardening towards this enterprise', meaning to us that although he had long doubted its feasibility and had previously advocated its further postponement in favour of operations elsewhere, he had finally, at this late date, come to believe with the rest of us that this was the true course of action in order to achieve the victory.[93]

Winston said his words were meant 'in the sense of wishing to strike if humanly possible, even if the limiting conditions we laid down were not exactly fulfilled'.[94] It would have been more in keeping with the majesty of the occasion to express full confidence in the operation, but he seemed unable to break out of the pattern of niggling dissent into which he had by now fallen. The dread of casualties on a World War I scale haunted him. He wanted to witness D-Day from one of the warships offshore, and it took the personal intervention of the King to persuade him to stay home. 'Do you realize that by the time you wake up in the morning twenty thousand men may have been killed?' he said to Clemmie as they went to bed on the evening of 5 June.[95] The reality was much less awful. Barring a near-disaster on Omaha Beach and terrible losses among the airborne divisions, the landings went well and casualties were between 9000 and 10,000, a third of them killed, from approximately 156,000 who landed that day. Sea and air supremacy was nearly absolute. Of nearly 7000 warships involved, one destroyer was torpedoed and sunk and another crippled by a mine, while 11,590 Allied aircraft flew 14,674 sorties for the loss of 127 planes. That was only the beginning, however. In the 35 days between D-Day and the encirclement of the German forces at Falaise, Allied ground and air forces suffered about 1800 casualties per day; Passchendaele, among the bloodiest of World War I offensives, cost an average of 2121 Commonwealth casualties per day. But if D-Day had gone much better than many expected, the battle of Normandy was anything but plain sailing.[96]

The difficulties the Allies encountered in Normandy in the summer of 1944 are blunt evidence that the invasion would certainly have ended in defeat if begun a year earlier. The initial landings were the last time that equal numbers of British Commonwealth and US troops were engaged, and thereafter the imbalance grew. By the end of 1944 US ground forces were double the Commonwealth total, and by the end of the war three times as numerous. The disproportion in transport and logistics was even greater. This background of rapidly declining military stature may explain, although it cannot excuse, why Winston pressed his opposition to the landings in the south of France as far as he did. Even Brooke, who shared his exasperation about Anvil/Dragoon, urged him to say: 'All right, if you insist on being damned fools, sooner than falling out with you, which would be fatal, we shall be damned fools with you.'[97] Instead he argued and complained almost up to the moment when he went to witness the landings in person, and his correspondence with FDR at this time has something of the air of a child seeking reassurance. On 23 June, during a flurry of telegrams which reveal how concerned he was about the unravelling of the relationship, he wrote plaintively: 'I cannot think of any moment when the burden of the war has laid more heavily upon me or when I have felt so unequal to its ever more entangled problems.'[98]

Among these problems were the German V-1 flying bombs that began to fall on London from 13 June. People were tired, beginning to hope the end was in sight and psychologically unprepared for the assault, made worse by the random and impersonal nature of the weapons. Anybody who heard one stopped whatever they were doing to listen, knowing they had only 15 seconds to find shelter after the droning pulse of the jet engine cut out. It was a deeply unnerving experience and affected morale more acutely than the Blitz had done. Winston was hag-ridden by the knowledge that a yet more terrible weapon, the V-2 ballistic rocket, was close to being operational despite the best efforts of Bomber Command in attacking the test and research centre at Peenemunde, and that it might be used to deliver something far worse than high explosive.[99] Impotence piled on impotence, although the new proximity fuses that made London's anti-aircraft artillery effective against the V-1s began to arrive from America. The parabola of Winston's long and lonely crusade against the new barbarism, which had begun with his broadcast warning of 16 November 1934 (see Appendix A), came crashing to earth on 6 July 1944 when rage, frustration and an unbalanced desire to impose his will on circumstances no longer under his control were expressed in an instruction to the Chiefs of Staff to study the merits of drenching German cities with poison gas (see Appendix D).

In a strong rejection dated 26 July the chiefs declared there was no evidence that Germany was about to employ *biological* agents, which suggests that oral discussion of this proposal extended to the possibility that the Germans might be matching the Allies' own top-secret production of weaponized anthrax.[100] Winston did not pursue the matter further, grumbling that 'I cannot make head against the parsons and the warriors at the same time'.[101] This was not the only indication that he had reached the end of his tether. On the same day he wrote the gas proposal he exploded during a meeting of the chiefs, with Attlee, Eden and Oliver Lyttelton, Minister of War Production, present for the War Cabinet. Brooke considered it 'quite the worst we have had with him', a judgement confirmed by others:

He was very tired as a result of his speech in the House concerning the flying bombs, he had tried to recuperate with drink. As a result he was in a maudlin, bad tempered, and drunken mood, ready to take offence at anything, suspicious of everybody, and in a highly vindictive mood against the Americans. In fact so vindictive that his whole outlook on strategy was warped. I began by having a bad row with him. He began to abuse Monty because operations were not going faster, and apparently Eisenhower had said he was over cautious. I flared up and asked him if he could not trust his generals for five minutes instead

415

of abusing them and belittling them. He said he never did such a thing. I then reminded him that during two whole Monday Cabinets in front of a large gathering of Ministers, he had torn Alexander to shreds for his lack of imagination and leadership in continually attacking at Cassino . . . It was not until after midnight that we got onto the subject we had come to discuss, the war in the Far East! Here we came up against all the old arguments that we have had put up by him over and over again. Attlee, Eden and Lyttelton . . . were at last siding with us against him. This infuriated him more than ever and he became ruder and ruder. Fortunately he finished with falling out with Attlee and having a real good row with him concerning the future of India! We withdrew under cover of this smokescreen just on 2 am, having accomplished nothing beyond losing our tempers and valuable sleep!![102]

Men's lives are not as neatly divisible into discrete segments as biographers might wish, but the coincidence of Winston's poison gas minute and his intemperate performance that evening marks a spiritual nadir. Mustard gas lingers and would have filled air raid shelters. In sufficient concentration it inflicts a prolonged and agonizing death, but even in dilute form it permanently damages lungs and eyes. To have contemplated employing it on civilian targets, quite apart from the dreadful consequences that even the most limited of counter-strikes would have had upon crowded London, suggests a temporary mental imbalance. Winston was right to point out that it was no more than a logical extension of area bombing, but that thought takes us back through the evolution of the strategic bombing concept and the unethical expedients to which a defence policy which fails to match commitments with resources can so easily lead.

His behaviour that evening suggests that the galling experience of playing second fiddle in an orchestra brought into existence by his efforts, and of seeing himself gradually written out of the score, had become too much for him. The navy's role was nearly done, the Commonwealth armies were doomed to play roles of decreasing relative importance, and all he had left with which to put a British stamp on unfolding events was Bomber Command and stocks of unused chemical weapons. However, he had surrounded himself with institutional restraints precisely because he knew himself no more immune than any man from the terrible exaltation of absolute power, and for this Winstonian construct we should be profoundly grateful.

'Old age is a shipwreck,' said de Gaulle in reference to his mentor-turned-adversary Pétain. Perhaps it need not be, but the character traits that drive people to achieve eminence often keep them in power too long. It is understandable that politicians in their physical prime should refuse to accept that their moment has passed, but those who persist in remaining at the controls after their bodies have sent them unmistakable signals that they can no longer navigate safely deserve less respect than they are often afforded. Winston was burned out by mid-1944, and while one may admire his rage against the dying of the light, his

417

performance as Prime Minister for the rest of the war and in 1951–5 did his country few favours.

Despite increasing concerns about his health, Winston continued to indulge his need to be there, to see the things and the men, during the last year of the war. On 12 June 1944 he made a day visit to Normandy, and his party had lunch near two hidden German soldiers who, fortunately, were waiting for the opportunity to surrender safely rather than to engage an opportunity target which included Winston, Smuts, Brooke, Marshall, Montgomery, Admiral King and General 'Hap' Arnold, commander of the US Army Air Force. He returned on 22–23 July after a violent storm had destroyed the Mulberry harbour in the American sector and seriously damaged the British one. Between 10 and 29 August he was in Italy and while there pursued a punishing programme which belied his age and health. He sailed to observe the landings he had opposed for so long on the Riviera; had a meeting with the self-appointed Marshal Tito of the Yugoslav Resistance, whom he half-heartedly chided for using the weapons supplied to him against his political rivals; had an audience with Pope Pius XII, in which the main topic of conversation was the Communist threat; and visited the front lines overlooking Florence and at Ancona, where he came under fire.[103] He also made day trips to swim in the famous Blue Grotto at Capri and at other places in the Bay of Naples.

Winston returned to London with a high fever and a recurrence of pneumonia, which was suppressed by one of the early antibiotics before he embarked, within the week, on the fast liner *Queen Mary* for the second Quebec conference with FDR.

Among the first items of business was the draconian Morgenthau Plan for the permanent emasculation of Germany (see Appendix E). This was drafted by Assistant Treasury Secretary Harry Dexter White, one of the genuine Reds under the bed recruited for the Russians by Nathan Gregory Silvermaster.104 It was enthusiastically adopted by his boss, Henry Morgenthau, Secretary of the Treasury since 1932 and the man behind Lend-Lease. Since Winston came to Quebec to seek a 7 billion dollar post-war extension of Lend-Lease, it is not surprising that he agreed to the plan. Before he resigned in late November, FDR's likewise long-serving Secretary of State Cordell Hull led the charge to prevent the plan from becoming US policy, sparing Winston a showdown with the War Cabinet, but its details were widely reported even before Morgenthau published it. By fighting on when defeat was inevitable the Germans incurred the traditional fate of a fortress that compels its besiegers to mount a final bloody assault. Whether this reflected German belief that they were to be obliterated as a nation even if they did surrender (and unconditional surrender was the only sort on offer) awaits dispassionate review.105

In early October Winston flew to Moscow, apparently to defuse any suspicions Stalin might have that the Americans and British had been 'ganging up on him' at Quebec.106 At their first meeting, on the 9th, Winston scribbled his infamous note concerning the percentages of post-war influence by the various great powers in Eastern Europe.107 After Stalin simply ticked the note, it occurred to Winston that it might 'be thought rather cynical if it seemed we had disposed of these issues, so fateful to millions of people, in such an offhand manner'.108 Stalin understood the underlying message. Greece, and to a lesser extent Yugoslavia and Hungary, would be regarded as the trip wires of his intentions. For the rest, the *fait accompli* of Soviet occupation was recognized, and although Poland was not among the countries listed both parties knew Winston had no leverage in negotiations to give the London-based Polish government in exile a post-war role. It is nonsense to equate this with Munich.109 Winston had no power independent of the USA to affect post-war boundaries, and the issue is not what he lost, but what he managed to win with a very weak hand.

On 10 November Winston flew to Paris in order to parade down the Champs Elysées with de Gaulle on Armistice Day, an occasion handled gracelessly by the Frenchman, who did not harbour generosity as his most notable trait. Winston's last overseas expedition of 1944 was to Athens on Boxing Day. He disrupted plans for a family holiday to fly down and impose order on a chaotic situation in which the Communist ELAS guerrilla forces seemed likely to emerge on top: it was also, incidentally, the last time in his life when he came under fire. Despite protests in the press on both sides of the Atlantic, nourished by State Department leaks, he achieved his purpose. The new Secretary of State, Edward Stettinius, had marked his advent by declaring that the government of Italy was a matter to be decided solely by the Italians and that this policy 'would apply to an even more pronounced degree with regard to the governments of the United Nations [the term coined on 1 January 1942 to refer to nations fighting against the Axis powers] in their liberated territories'. Winston bitterly told FDR that it was hardly even-handed to seek to restrict Britain's involvement while at the same time failing to criticize Russian expansionism:

> I do not remember anything that the State Department has ever said about Russia or any other Allied state comparable to this document with which Mr Stettinius has inaugurated his assumption of office. I am sure such things have never been said by the State Department about Russia even when very harsh communications have been received and harsher deeds done.[110]

In Britain, opposition to Winston's Greek policy came mainly from Bevan and fellow left-wingers, but *The Times* and the *Manchester Guardian* both picked up the Stettinius line. On his way to Yalta a month after his foray to Greece, Winston wrote to Clemmie about 'the little band of insulters who have been so forward about Greece', to conclude prophetically:

> Every day come the proofs of how right we were, and I see in today's *Times* . . . that they have learned something from the facts. . . . The bitter misunderstandings which have arisen in the United States, and in degenerate circles at home, are only a foretaste of the furies which will be loosed about every stage of the peace settlement. I am sure in Greece I found one of the best opportunities for wise

421

action that this war has tossed to me from its dark waves.[111]

CHAPTER TEN

FINAL ACT

1945–1965

In January 1945 Winston found himself compelled to use his dwindling capital with the Americans to help Montgomery, who had been entrusted with the command of US as well as British forces to lead the northern pincer—Patton commanded the thrust from the south—of the counter-attack that destroyed the last German offensive of the war, launched on 16 December through the Belgian Ardennes. On 7 January, despite a personal visit from Winston three days earlier to beg him to keep his high opinion of himself better concealed, Monty boasted to the press that he had directed the battle. Even if it had been true, the statement could not have been better designed to disperse American good will. Winston and Brooke forced him to apologize and prevailed on a deeply offended Ike to let him remain, but the price included a counter-exaggeration in the Commons on 18 January, when Winston declared that 'care must be taken not to claim for the British Army an undue share of what is undoubtedly the greatest American battle of the war. I believe the Battle of the Bulge will be regarded as an ever-famous American victory.'

Two days later Winston received a long letter, personally typed by Attlee, in which he was sternly taken to task for his cavalier treatment of recommendations produced by all-party Cabinet committees generally presided over by the deputy Prime Minister. When these were, always belatedly, brought before the War Cabinet, 'it is very exceptional for you to have read them. More and more often you have not even read the note [summary] prepared for your guidance.' More ominously, Attlee warned that he did not find it amusing to have the recommendations Winston disagreed with attributed to 'the malevolent intrigues of socialist Ministers who have beguiled their weak Conservative colleagues'. But the shot across the bows concerned Winston's habit of valuing the opinions of his particular friends Lord Beaverbrook (Lord Privy Seal) and Brendan Bracken (Minister of Information) above those of the Cabinet:

> There is a serious constitutional issue here. In the eyes of the country and under our constitution the eight members of the War Cabinet take responsibility for decisions. I have myself assured members of both Parties who have been disturbed by the influence of the Lord Privy Seal that this was so. But if the present practice continues I shall not be able to do so in the future.[1]

Bracken and Beaverbrook both agreed with Attlee, but Winston's first response was so intemperate that Colville delayed sending it. The revised reply was still insultingly sarcastic: 'I have to thank you for your Private and Personal letter,' it read. 'You may be sure I shall always endeavour to profit by your counsels.'[2] This was arrogant folly quite on a par with Monty's. Attlee had endured many personal slights in the course of loyally and unobtrusively supporting Winston over nearly five years of war, and competently covering for his many absences. A modest act of contrition from Winston was the least he had the right to expect. Nor was Winston on the ball in the one area he jealously reserved for his own exclusive attention. A day after the exchange with Attlee, an exasperated Brooke confided in his diary that he felt he could not 'stand another day working with Winston, it is quite hopeless, he is finished and gone, incapable of grasping any military situation and unable to give a decision'.3

The last meeting of the Big Three—now really the big two-and-a-half—took place at Yalta in the Crimea between 4 and 11 February 1945. Although Winston was well past his best and FDR haggard and slack-jawed from the medication he was taking for extreme hypertension, there is no reason to believe they were misled by Stalin with regard to Poland, any more than Winston had been in Moscow the preceding October. The form of words agreed was diplomatic waffle, political cover for Western domestic consumption.4 The Protocol was a document of appeasement. What distinguishes it from Chamberlain's Munich agreement is that Stalin, unlike Hitler, was effectively appeased. One must not forget that FDR's main objective was to obtain Stalin's agreement to enter the war against Japan and to participate fully in the new United Nations Organization; and that Winston won great power status for France so that neither in occupied Germany nor in the new UN Security Council would Britain be the sole representative of Europe between the Asian and American giants. Stalin obtained territorial security by his occupation of Eastern Europe, and Morgenthau-like provisions for the dismemberment and permanent subjection of Germany. These were not carried out by the Western powers, any more than were free elections in the countries occupied by the Red Army, but Stalin did relinquish the Russian-occupied zone of Austria and refrained from imposing his authority in Yugoslavia, as well as conspicuously refusing to support the Communist ELAS in Greece. It was probably the best that could have been achieved without sacrificing Allied unity.

George Patton believed that a professional soldier should die of 'the last bullet of the last battle of the last war'. He did not quite manage it, although he was fatally injured in a car accident on his last day of active duty.[5] Patton spoke for Winston when he said, 'I only fear the slowing up of the engine inside of me which is pounding, saying—keep going, someone must be on top, why not you?' It is in this light that we should view a poignant episode during Winston's second visit to the Rhine, in the sector won by Lieutenant General W.H. Simpson's 9th US Army, on the right flank of Monty's Army Group. During the first, on 3 March 1945, Winston led Brooke, Monty, Simpson and their respective staffs in a mass urination on the Siegfried Line, asking the photographers present to be discreet. That night he sneaked off by himself to pee into the Rhine, with the Germans holding the other bank, contentedly buttoning himself up with a muttered: 'Most satisfactory.'

But things went beyond boyish pranks during a return visit on 25 March, when he scrambled out along a partly demolished bridge. Brooke recalled:

> General Simpson, on whose front we were . . .
> [said] 'Prime Minister, there are snipers in
> front of you, they are shelling both sides of
> the bridge, and now they have started shelling
> the road behind you. I cannot accept the
> responsibility of your being here, and must
> ask you to come away.' The look on Winston's
> face was just like that of a small boy being
> called away from his sandcastles on the beach
> by his nurse! He put both his arms round one
> of the twisted girders of the bridge, and
> looked over his shoulder at Simpson with
> pouting mouth and angry eyes! Thank heaven
> he came away quietly, it was a sad wrench for
> him.[6]

It is not unreasonable to wonder whether FDR's
death 18 days later did not strike Winston as
robbing him of the timely finale to which he
himself aspired. Nothing he said to those closest to
him at the time or wrote later offers a clue to why
he chose not to pay his last respects in person to
the man with whom his fate had been so closely
bound, and to spurn an invitation to confer with
Harry Truman, FDR's Vice President for only 11
weeks and now his successor, who was anxious to
meet him. Such a flagrant departure from
Winston's normal standards of behaviour, and such
a lapse in his duty as Prime Minister of a nation
that needed US good will more than ever, argues
that some irrational factor was at work. If he
believed the bell announcing the start of his last
round had rung at the time of his first heart attack

in late 1941, now that his opponent was beaten he may have felt that he had spun over his life's culminating point, and was lost without that sense of purpose that had always driven him on. He spent more and more time in bed, shirked his paperwork and had to be carried upstairs in a chair.[7]

Fortunately there was no need for him to put his personal stamp on British foreign policy during the remaining months of his premiership, for it was already indelibly branded with his iron. The foremost British concern from the time FDR declared at Yalta that US forces would be withdrawn from Europe two years after the end of hostilities was to build up French military capability as rapidly as possible and, if possible, to reverse the US decision, something achieved when Attlee's Foreign Secretary, Ernest Bevin, signed the North Atlantic Treaty on 4 April 1949.[8] The errors of the 1920s were not to be repeated and Britain, for the first time in its history, maintained a permanent military presence on the mainland of Europe. On Victory in Europe day, 8 May 1945, Winston broadcast a warning: 'On the continent of Europe, we have yet to make sure the simple and honourable purposes for which we entered the war are not thrust aside or overlooked.' There would be little use in punishing the Nazis, he continued, 'if totalitarian or police Governments were to take the place of the German invaders'. Two days later, in a telegram to Truman pointing out the perils of too rapid withdrawal, he contrasted the openness of Western troop movements with those of the Russians, and employed a phrase he was to make memorable ten months later: 'An iron curtain is drawn down upon their front. We do not know what is going on behind . . . Surely it is vital now to come to an understanding with Russia, or see where we are with her, before we weaken our armies mortally or retire to the zones of occupation. This can only be done by a personal meeting.'[9]

He had missed his chance. There was to be no private conference with the new President before they met at Potsdam, a suburb of ruined Berlin, where Winston, with Attlee in attendance although no longer a member of the government, met Truman and Stalin nine times between 17 and 25 July. There was a break of two days while Winston and Attlee returned to London for the announcement of the general election results, after which the victor Attlee returned with Bevin for four more days of talks and the signature of the Potsdam Declaration on 2 August.[10] Americans and Russians alike were amazed that British policy and the suite of officials at the conference remained unchanged, although after five years of coalition government it would have been more remarkable if there had been any break in continuity. At another level, it was a startling affirmation of democracy at a peculiarly crucial moment, with Attlee becoming the only leader at Potsdam freely elected in his own right.

Moral authority was also added to British reservations about the Soviet Union by Attlee's choice of a Foreign Secretary with impeccably proletarian credentials. Any illusions Bevin might have entertained about Russia had been dispelled when, as Minister of Labour, he had to deal with the British Communists' Moscow-directed attempts to sabotage the war effort in 1940–1.[11] Contrast this with the egregious Harold Laski, chairman of the Labour Party National Executive Committee (NEC) and author of the party's 1945 election manifesto, which affirmed: 'At long last we have made possible full friendship with the Soviet Union.' Attlee disabused Laski of the idea that he would accept direction from the NEC with a laconic note: 'A period of silence from you would now be most welcome.'[12] In total contrast to Winston, Attlee wasted neither words nor time, his economy in both areas being the key ingredient of his 20-year leadership of a party with more than its fair share of bombastic and disorderly personalities.

Continuity was no less evident on the domestic front. There was no serious dispute about the desirability of establishing a Welfare State along lines set out in the Beveridge Report of November 1942.[13] Winston had worked with Beveridge before World War I and the report was an updated plan for the implementation of the Bismarckian scheme both men advocated at that time. He had no objection to accepting the report in principle, but viewed the Labour Party's wish to declare it accepted in its entirety as an unwise commitment in the light of the stringent financial constraints on a post-war government. The broken promises of 1918–22 haunted him, as he explained in a note to the War Cabinet dated 12 January 1943:

A dangerous optimism is growing up about the conditions it will be possible to establish here after the war. . . . While not disheartening our people by dwelling on the dark side of things, Ministers should, in my

430

BRITISH EMBASSY,

CAIRO.

Direction to General Alexander
Commander in Chief in the Middle East

———————

1. Your prime & main duty will be to take
or destroy at the earliest opportunity the German-
Italian Army commanded by Field Marshal
Rommel, together with all its supplies &
establishments in Egypt & Libya.

2. You will discharge or cause to be, discharged
such other duties as pertain to y[ou]r Command
without prejudice to the task described in
paragraph 1. which must be considered paramount
in His Majesty's interests.

W.S.C.

10. Aug. 42

10.8.42

Winston's clear and concise directive to General Sir
Harold Alexander, newly-appointed commander-in-chief
in the Middle East, dated 10 August 1942. On 13 May
1943 Alexander at last reported 'All enemy resistance has
ceased. We are masters of the North African shore.'

Visiting British and Commonwealth troops in the Western Desert in August 1942. General Bernard Montgomery, at Winston's side and wearing an Australian slouch hat, had just been appointed to command the 8th Army. General Sir Alan Brooke, Chief of the Imperial General Staff, is walking a little way behind them.

Winston in his dressing gown with General Eisenhower (left) and General Sir Harold Alexander at Carthage on Christmas Day 1943. Winston, exhausted by work and an unrelenting schedule, had contracted pneumonia. Two days after this photograph was taken he flew to Marrakech to recuperate and plan for the Normandy landings.

Winston addressing a joint session of the US Congress in May 1943. His well-polished speech was a success: a secretary maintained that he had spent nine and a half hours dictating it.

Winston and Monty in Normandy, with Lieutenant General Miles Dempsey in the background and the able Canadian Lieutenant General Guy Simmonds holding the map.

The big three: Winston, FDR and Stalin at the Yalta Conference, February 1945. Winston became increasingly uncomfortable with the worn-out FDR and the triumphant Stalin, and described the place as 'the Riviera of Hades'.

Winston greets cheering crowds from the Ministry of Health balcony overlooking Parliament Street with a 'V' sign following his VE day broadcast on Tuesday 8 May 1945. He told them 'This is your victory!' They replied, 'No, it is yours!'

Winston at his easel, Miami Beach, Florida, in February 1946. He first took up painting in the dark days of 1915 in an effort to keep the 'black dog' of depression at bay, and he was delighted to be elected Royal Academician Extraordinary in 1948.

RIGHT On the campaign trail again. Winston, with Clemmie by his side, gives the 'V' sign from the window of Conservative HQ in South Woodford, 6 October 1951. The general election brought him back to office with a slender majority.

BELOW The slow decline. Winston being entertained by the Greek shipping magnate Aristotle Onassis aboard his yacht *Christina*, on 3 March 1960.

Despite his dismissal of television as a 'tuppenny-ha'penny Punch and Judy show', Winston eventually investigated the political potential of the new medium during his last term as Prime Minister. In 1954 he arranged for a secret screen test at 10 Downing Street. 'I have come here,' he growled, 'to enable me to see what are the conditions under which this thing they call "teevee" is going to make its way in the world. I am sorry, I must admit, to have to descend to this level, but we all have to keep pace with modern improvements, and it is just as well to see where you are in regard to them. There is no point in refusing to move with the age and therefore I have consented to come and have this exhibition, which is for one person and for one person only. And only one person is to judge what is to be done with this. I am that person. [Stretching his arms out wide.] There you are, here you see me! There is no other in this business.' Upon viewing the test he decided that television was not for him and ordered that the film be destroyed. Fortunately, it survived and was unearthed in the late 1980s. Churchill never gave a television interview.

Winston making a speech at Westminster Hall, London, at the unveiling of a portrait by the artist Graham Sutherland presented to him by MPs to mark his eightieth birthday. Clementine hated the painting and had it destroyed after her husband's death.

Churchill's coffin lying in state at Westminster Hall, London, in January 1965. State funerals have been granted to only seven non-royal-family members: Pitt the Elder, Lord Nelson, Pitt the Younger, the Duke of Wellington, Gladstone, Lord Roberts and Churchill.

view, be careful not to raise false hopes, as was done last time by speeches about 'homes for heroes', etc. The broad masses of the people face the hardships of life undaunted, but they are liable to get very angry if they feel they have been gulled or cheated . . . It is because I do not wish to deceive the people by false hopes and airy visions of Utopia and Eldorado that I have refrained so far from making promises about the future. We must all do our best, and we shall do it much better if we are not hampered by a cloud of pledges and promises which arise out of the hopeful and genial side of man's nature and are not brought into relation with the hard facts of life.

Although the Labour Party argued that it fought Tory obstructionism to usher in the new dawn, the 1944 Education Act, named after its sponsor and the first ever Minister of Education, R.A. 'Rab' Butler, which was greeted as a major piece of progressive legislation expressing wartime social solidarity, was based on the recommendations of pre-war reports commissioned by Tory governments. Although Bevin commissioned the Beveridge Report, he did so with Winston's knowledge and consent. The proof that Winston's concern was one not of substance but of timing is that a comprehensive Four Year Plan of social legislation, including a National Health Service Bill, a National Insurance Bill, an Industrial Injury Insurance Bill and a Family Allowance Bill, was announced in the King's Speech of November 1944. In his Address to the Speech Winston expressed no reservations and declared:

> Whatever may be the doubts as to when the election may come . . . there is one thing which is quite certain; all the leading men in both the principal parties—and in the Liberal Party as well—are pledged and committed to this great mass of social legislation, and I cannot conceive that whatever may be the complexion of the new house, they will personally fail to make good their promises and commitments to the people.[14]

The differences boiled down to Labour's determination to nationalize what Lenin in 1922 called 'the commanding heights of the economy'. In Britain these eminences had already been severely eroded, but nobody believed that process to be irreversible in 1945. The younger Winston had expressed a desire to nationalize the transport system, wished he could do the same with the mines at the time of the 1926 General Strike, and as Chancellor often wished he could get his hands around the collective throat of the Bank of England. In general he was no less instinctively statist than many other politicians. What he had always feared, though, was the deadening effect of bureaucracy. The economist Friedrich von Hayek believed his 1944 book *The Road to Serfdom* influenced Winston in 1945.[15] However, both were preceded by Herbert Spencer in his 1884 essay 'The Man Versus the State', and Winston had already set out his own views in an article published in 1937:

The programme of giving the State, that is to say the politicians who have obtained a majority in an election, autocratic control of all means of production, distribution, and exchange, would never commend itself to the individualism of the British race. To have everybody made equal under boards of officials directed by Socialist politicians would be to destroy the whole sparkle and progress of life without in any way raising the average. To join in one fist the authority of the magistrate, of the employer, of the landlord, of the food purveyor, and of the legislator, must be to reduce the wage-earner and his family, equally with more fortunate people, to an absolute subjection.[16]

The addition of one stunningly ill-chosen word pushed the same sentiment, recycled in his election broadcast of 4 June 1945, beyond the limit of acceptable partisanship. That word was 'Gestapo', and it has hung around his neck ever since. He was talking about men who had stood with him against Nazism when his own party was lukewarm. But there was more to it than that: the whole speech was shabby. He said the election had been brought about because the Labour and Liberal parties had put party before country 'and we have been left to carry the nation's burden', and he made a spurious distinction between the Labour colleagues he had worked with for five years and 'this continental conception of human society called Socialism, or in its more violent form Communism'. He was also scathing about the 'Sinclair-Beveridge' Liberals, the two being respectively one of his oldest friends

441

and the author of the social programme to which he himself was committed. But he was just warming up. 'My friends, I must tell you that a Socialist policy is abhorrent to the British ideas of freedom,' he continued. 'Although it is now put forward in the main by people who have a good grounding in the Liberalism and Radicalism of the early part of this century, there can be no doubt that Socialism is inseparably interwoven with Totalitarianism and the abject worship of the State.' Then came the fatal passage:

> No Socialist Government conducting the entire life and industry of the country could afford to allow free, sharp, or violently worded expressions of public discontent. They would have to fall back on some form of Gestapo, no doubt very humanely directed in the first instance. And this would nip opinion in the bud; it would stop criticism as it reared its head, and it would gather all the power to the supreme party and party leaders, rising like stately pinnacles above their vast bureaucracies of Civil [sic] servants, no longer servants and no longer civil.[17]

Labour voters were outraged, but the greatest damage the speech did was probably among working-class Tory voters, who had experienced five years of domestic policy largely run by Labour members of Winston's wartime government, and trusted them. They had won respectability, and it was crass to equate them with Nazi thugs. Thoughtful middle-class voters may also have judged that a Conservative Party that had embraced state control of everything, particularly information, for five years was not in a position to criticize. Lastly, it set up Attlee to make a killing reply, widely judged to have been the making of him as a party and national leader:[18]

> When I listened to the Prime Minister's speech last night in which he gave such a travesty of the policy of the Labour party, I realized at once what was his object. He wanted the electors to understand how great was the difference between Winston Churchill, the great leader in war of a united nation, and Mr Churchill, the party leader of the Conservatives. He feared that those who had accepted his leadership in war might be tempted out of gratitude to follow him further. I thank him for having disillusioned them so thoroughly.

Attlee went on to outline a philosophy that Winston's past prevented him from attacking, as another less personally compromised in the growth of statism might have done. All those fiery speeches in which he had denounced wealth and privilege, and all his eloquent appeals for people to subsume their individual needs in the great national struggle, left him unable to deliver the uppercut when Attlee, in turn, stuck his chin out:

> The Prime Minister made much play last night with the rights of the individual and the dangers of people being ordered about by officials. I entirely agree that people should have the greatest freedom compatible with

the freedom of others. There was a time when employers were free to work little children for sixteen hours a day. I remember when employers were free to employ sweated women workers on finishing trousers at a penny halfpenny a pair. There was a time when people were free to neglect sanitation so that thousands died of preventable diseases. For years every attempt to remedy these crying evils was blocked by the same plea of freedom for the individual. It was in fact freedom for the rich and slavery for the poor. Make no mistake, it has only been through the power of the State, given to it by Parliament, that the general public has been protected against the greed of ruthless profit-makers and property owners. . . . We have to plan the broad lines of our national life so that all may have the duty and the opportunity of rendering service to the nation, everyone in his or her sphere, and that all may help to create and share in an increasing material prosperity free from the fear of want.[19]

The historical detail was false and Attlee, with his long record of work among the voluntary associations, surely knew it. For the rest, he could not have made a more forthright declaration of intent to subordinate the individual to the state. But I do not believe these speeches, although listened to by an audience the BBC can only dream of commanding today, were significant except in the degree to which they posed questions to which the answers could only be negative for the Tories. Did people admire Winston enough to vote for the party that had led them, inadequately prepared, into a life-or-death struggle, or did they want to make a new start under men who had made amends for their pre-war follies in five years of loyal service? Which party was more likely to deal energetically with demobilization and the reintegration of millions into a battered economy with no reserves to fall back on? How could voters ensure that 1945 would not simply recommence the betrayals begun in 1918? Which party offered a vision of a better life and was less likely to betray the expectations of the nation again? Seen in the light of these aspirations it was no contest, and although the result shocked those misled by the crowds that cheered Winston wherever he went, in retrospect the only surprise is that the Labour majority was not even greater. Labour won close to half of the votes cast and an outright majority of 146 in the new Parliament.[20]

Winston recorded waking suddenly just before dawn on 26 July with 'a sharp stab of almost physical pain' and attributed it to a premonition of defeat breaking into his conscious mind. Given his medical history, a small heart infarction is a no less likely explanation. At lunch that day Clemmie suggested it might be a blessing in disguise, to which he replied that if so it was very well disguised. She was certainly correct as to his physical health, but it is more doubtful whether his spirit ever fully recovered. A month later she wrote to their daughter Mary that 'in our misery we seem, instead of clinging to each other, to be always having scenes. I'm sure it's all my fault, but I'm finding life more than I can bear. He is so unhappy and that makes him very difficult. . . . I can't see

445

any future.'[21] In *The Second World War*, writing of an earlier time, Winston quipped that 'the loyalties which centre upon number one are enormous. If he trips he must be sustained. If he makes mistakes they must be covered. If he sleeps he must not be wantonly disturbed. If he is no good he must be pole-axed.' Had he been another man and this any other time the Conservatives would have expected him to resign, and had he not done so they would have deposed him as leader. The fact that he was retained points to a shrewd appreciation among the party professionals that he alone had preserved them from the abyss.

Although they were scarcely mentioned during the campaign, the trade unions lurked like a reef, able to rip the bottom out of any government. The Trades Disputes Act of 1927, whose abolition was one of the Labour Party's foremost objectives, had merely revoked the legally privileged status granted them by the Trades Disputes Act of 1906, strongly supported by Winston at the time. On 2 April 1946, during the debate on the repeal of the 1927 Act, the Attorney General, Sir Hartley Shawcross, spoke the words for which he is best remembered: 'We are the masters at the moment, and not only at the moment but for a very long time to come.' In fact his party remained masters for only a further five years and eight months, thanks in part to granting civil immunity to what were perhaps the most reactionary institutions in British society. Bad labour relations were a chronic condition which could not be conjured away by a wave of the progressive wand.

One might wish that the historic moment when 250 new members took their place in the Commons

446

had been marked by a breath of fresh air, but alas it was business as usual. The American-born Henry Channon, whose nickname 'Chips' reflected the fact that he had shared student lodgings at Oxford with a Mr Fish, was a well-connected Conservative MP who had served as a junior minister during the war. He kept a journal, which eventually ran to 30 volumes and 3 million words, and once wrote: 'What is more dull than a discreet diary?' Its entry for 1 August 1945 is wonderfully descriptive:

I went to Westminster to see the new Parliament assemble, and never have I seen such a dreary lot of people. I took my place on the Opposition side, the Chamber was packed and uncomfortable, and there was an atmosphere of tenseness and even bitterness. Winston staged his entry well, and was given the most rousing cheer of his career, and the Conservatives sang 'For He's a Jolly Good Fellow.' Perhaps this was an error in taste, though the Socialists went one further, and burst into the 'Red Flag' singing it lustily; I thought that Herbert Morrison and one or two others looked uncomfortable.

A little over two weeks later, following the King's Speech, Winston underlined how little separated the two parties in a *tour d'horizon* that included a prophetic summary of the implications of the atom bombs recently used to bring the war with Japan to an end, the morality of which was not at that time seriously questioned: 'The bomb brought peace, but men alone can keep that peace, and henceforward they will keep it under penalties which threaten the survival, not only of civilization but of humanity itself.' It was also during this speech that he made his Pilate-like remark that 'there are few virtues that the Poles do not possess—and there are few mistakes they have ever avoided'. But after a sharp observation that the 'Socialist intelligentsia' might wish to consider why the Trades Union Council felt it necessary to be 'heavily rearmed against State Socialism' he concluded on a conciliatory note:

As to the situation which exists today, it is evident that not only are the two Parties in the House agreed in the main essentials of foreign policy and in our moral outlook on world affairs, but we also have an immense programme, prepared by our joint exertions during the Coalition, which requires to be brought into law and made an inherent part of the life of the people. Here and there there may be differences of emphasis and view, but in the main no Parliament ever assembled with such a mass of agreed legislation as lies before us this afternoon. I have great hopes of this Parliament, and I shall do my utmost to make its work fruitful. It may heal the wounds of war, and turn to good account the new conceptions and powers which we have gathered amid the storm.[22]

We know, now, that these hopes were ill founded and that a further six years of peacetime austerity on top of six years of war continued to sap the vitality of the nation. Although Winston shelled MacDonald's Chancellor Philip Snowden mercilessly in 1929–31, he included him among his *Great Contemporaries* and summed him up in a beautifully crafted sentence (note the use of tenses): 'To him Toryism was a physical annoyance, and militant Socialism is a disease brought on by bad conditions or contagion, like rickets or mange.'23 Aneurin Bevan himself conceded that, if private enterprise could deliver the goods, there would be no argument for socialism and no need for it.24 While it is facile to blame the 'British disease' on the post-war Labour government, the non-Marxist, wealthy Stafford Cripps, Chancellor in 1947–50, relished austerity for its own sake and made it a heart-breaking experience for the general population.25 This had little to do with public ownership of the means of production, everything to do with the intellectual arrogance of a type, rather than a class, of people whose influence had grown steadily since the turn of the century, and which was not confined to the Labour Party.

In the USA the war effort was scarcely 'managed' at all, and estimates of the amount of money wasted range from 30 to 40 billion dollars. 'Waste', however, is a subjective term. Many more people than necessary were conscripted, and there was enormous duplication of effort, but the overall effect was a boom in which gross national product went from 200 billion dollars in 1940 to 300 billion in 1950 and more than 500 billion in 1960. By 1956 a majority of the working population held white-collar jobs and labour militancy waned as large corporations offered their employees benefits comparable to those of the Welfare State in Britain. In the sharpest contrast with contemporary British experience, a populist reaction dealt the

449

prestige of the progressive elite a blow from which it never fully recovered. Thus it was that in the USA the war 'broke the back of the pessimistic expectations that almost everyone had come to hold during the seemingly endless depression. Renewed confidence rather than pent-up demand fuelled America's post-war economic growth.'[26] No such champagne cork popped in Britain: there was too little fizz left in the bottle.

Nor was there in Winston himself, now the figurehead rather than the leader of a party of men 'who adapted themselves to the political reality of Churchill's supremacy, but never truly rose to the level of events, or shared his vision of the role which the British nation could play'.[27] They adapted themselves with greater success to the political reality of their defeat in 1945 and entrusted the task of formulating a new party programme to Butler, a pre-war appeaser third only to Chamberlain and Halifax, who in 1944 sneered at Winston's political beliefs as 'a mixture of old Liberal doctrines of cheap food and free trade, combined with the Tory democracy of his father'.[28] The outcome was the *Industrial Charter*, a policy paper issued in 1947 that accepted nationalization as irreversible, embraced Keynesian demand management and full employment, and proposed a 'workers' charter' for the self-regulation of private enterprise. In a reversal of the situation which prevails today, the Conservatives were able to steal their opponents' clothes without any danger of their own policies being similarly raided. The commitment to 'public ownership of the means of production' in Clause Four of the Labour Party constitution, not revoked

450

until 1995, functioned as a one-way barrier to new ideas and helped make the Labour movement a closed system.

Writing in 1953, Emanuel Shinwell, Minister of Fuel and Power 1945–7 and of War and Defence 1947–51, judged Winston to be 'out of touch with modern social trends' and particularly held against him 'the fatuous declaration that Labour was unfit to govern'.[29] The offending statement dated from the 1920 General Election, and Shinwell might with more wit have recalled that in 1909 Winston declared the Conservative peers to be 'utterly unfit to have any concern with serious affairs' and, later, that the Conservatives were not a party but a conspiracy. Baron Shinwell, as he became, died at the age of 101 in 1984, and was spared the disillusionment of seeing his beloved party judged unfit to govern and out of touch with modern social trends for a further 13 years, until a new generation of politicians sensibly jettisoned that belief in a centrally directed economy by which he had lived. This is not to jeer, simply to stress that one generation's wave of the future is usually the next generation's undertow.

Shinwell was only ten years younger than Winston, and neither of them could have imagined the ever-diminishing role that manufacturing would play in the British economy. Viewed with the hindsight that comes from living in a largely post-industrial society, it is easy to see that both men erred most in what they agreed upon: that a large, interventionist state was necessary in order to moderate, for the greater good, the crude interplay of monopoly capital and monopoly labour. This in turn rested on the myth of a disinterested Civil

451

Service. In 1947 Douglas Jay, Economic Secretary to the Treasury, declared that 'sometimes the gentleman in Whitehall really does know better what is good for the people than the people know themselves'. Today any such comment would be drowned in mocking laughter, but there were no smiles in 1947.

Roy Jenkins wondered why Winston was always hostile to 'upper- middle-class Labour parliamentarians', particularly those educated at Winchester, while he was generally less so to working-class trade union leaders who were far more 'left-wing'.[30] Winston's dislike of public school socialists went back a long way and had little to do with ideology. This was doubly the case with regard to Wykehamists, disproportionately represented in the higher Civil Service, of whom Douglas Jay was representative.[31] A product of Winchester and Oxford, he had pursued careers in academia, journalism and the wartime Civil Service, and only became an MP in 1947. He had not, therefore, served an apprenticeship on the hustings and in Parliament before becoming a minister. Men who slipped comfortably from the Civil Service to active politics were Winston's particular *bêtes noires* because he felt they blurred the line between politicians elected to lead and officials appointed to serve them.

Defeat at the polls permitted Winston to take a long holiday in northern Italy, where he resumed painting, a hobby he took up after his first fall from power in 1915 and continued until shortly before his death. I have concentrated on those aspects of his life that are most revealing of the underlying character, and the last 20 years were by and large replays of familiar themes. His paintings, however, continued to develop. The great majority are landscapes, and it comes as no surprise that he used primary colours for preference and that his preliminary sketches and unfinished paintings have a power and immediacy often lost in the completed works. His body forms are unconvincing, but the very few portraits he attempted are striking. The cold authority in the face of *Lord Darling* (*circa* 1925), the arrogance of beauty in *Miss Cecily Greenwell* (*circa* 1949) and the joyous vivacity in his all-blue study, presumably from a photograph, of *Lady Churchill at the Launching of HMS Indomitable* (*circa* 1954) are, to my untutored eye, his best work.[32] The portraits reveal a human empathy not easily discernible in his writing, and the fact that he could leave them unfinished is an even more startling departure from the Winstonian norm. In *Painting as a Pastime*, a 32-page booklet he published in 1948, the mask also slipped at the end of a bluff, Hemingway-like analogy between painting and battle: 'In painting, the reserves consist in Proportion or Relation. And it is here that the art of the painter marches along the road which is traversed by all the greatest harmonies in thought.' But the black dog was still there, curled up at the foot of his easel. 'Try it if you have not done so—before you die,' he wrote. 'Happy are the painters for they shall not be lonely. Light and colour, peace and hope, will keep them company to the end, or almost to the end, of the day.'

He was even busier with pen than with paintbrush. Between 1948 and 1954 Winston published his six-volume *History of the Second World War*, which brought him not only some

£600,000 at a time when the Prime Minister's salary was about £10,000 a year, but the Nobel Prize for Literature too. He received substantial help from civil servants, led by Cabinet Secretary Sir Edward Bridges, his own research assistant Bill Deakin, and Lieutenant General Sir Henry Pownall. Winston himself affirmed that 'this is not history: this is my case,' and it had no claims to objectivity. The impact of the Eastern Front was understated; Winston's reservations about the Normandy invasion were downplayed; and the long-suffering Alan Brooke found himself treated with Churchillian cavalierishness at its worst. And yet, as David Reynolds recently observed in *In Command of History* the volumes 'offered unique personal impressions of the war and its leaders, voluminous documentary evidence that scholars could not expect to see until the next century, and . . . informed narratives of key battles and diplomacy.' They highlighted 'Britain's contribution to victory at a time when a tide of American memoirs and movies gave the impression that Uncle Sam had won the war single-handed.'

Winston was not an active leader of the opposition, being frequently absent and more concerned with the international situation. When he was present, Attlee thought him a 'mischief-maker', citing an example from 1947 when Winston misrepresented facts over India which had been revealed to him in strict secrecy and:

> put me in perhaps the most embarrassing situation of my whole career, since I could not divulge in detail all the facts of the matter, and therefore could not give the lie to

Winston. I find it very hard to forgive him for this. The extraordinary thing is that I can forgive him. Winston could get away with this. In any other man it would be damnable and utterly unpardonable.[33]

Roy Jenkins, less inclined to view such lapses with charity, cites an occasion in 1951 when Winston sabotaged a speech by Hugh Gaitskell, appointed Chancellor in succession to the ailing Cripps, by rummaging around his seat until Gaitskell was forced to pause. 'I was only looking for a jujube,' Winston explained, and the House was filled with indulgent laughter.[34] By that time, however, he was leading the Tories in a sustained and ultimately successful campaign of harassment against a tired Labour government reduced to a majority of nine in the general election of 1950.[35]

There was good reason for him to concentrate on the international situation, for things were proceeding exactly as he had predicted. In September 1945 he wrote to Clemmie: 'I regard the future as full of darkness and menace ... Very little is known as to what is happening behind the Russian iron curtain, but evidently the Poles and Czecho-Slovakians are being treated as badly as one could have expected.'[36] In early 1946 he spent six weeks enjoying the beaches in Florida and Cuba before seizing with both hands an opportunity granted him by Harry Truman to make perhaps the most portentous speech of his career at Westminster College in Fulton, Missouri. He travelled there and back with Truman on the presidential train, and although both Truman and Attlee may have initially been grateful to him for 'outing' sentiments they could not themselves express, both were compelled to distance themselves from Winston when his speech raised a predictable outcry. The most famous phrases were 'From Stettin in the Baltic to Trieste in the Adriatic, an iron curtain has descended across the Continent', and 'I do not believe that Soviet Russia desires war. What they desire are the fruits of war and the indefinite expansion of their power and doctrines.' But the main thrust of the speech came in the peroration:

If the population of the English-speaking Commonwealths be added to that of the United States, with all that such co-operation implies in the air, on the sea, all over the globe and in science and in industry, and in moral force, there will be no quivering, precarious balance of power to offer its temptation to ambition or adventure. On the contrary, there will be an overwhelming assurance of security. If we adhere faithfully to the Charter of the United Nations and walk forward in sedate and sober strength seeking no one's land or treasure, seeking to lay no arbitrary control upon the thoughts of men; if all the British moral and material forces and convictions are joined with your own in fraternal association, the highroads of the future will be clear, not only for us but for all, not only for now but for a century to come.[37]

This was a vain hope. A major thrust of US foreign policy for much of the twentieth century, as Winston surely knew, was to supplant British

456

international influence. The State Department was possessed by the belief that the USA was free of the taint of colonialism and that it had a liberating mission in the Middle East, Asia and Africa.[38] This attitude dug the chasm between principle and practice into which US foreign policy has fallen repeatedly ever since. Thus the Bell Trade Act, which accompanied the granting of independence to the Philippines in 1946, prohibited the manufacture or sale of any products that might compete with US goods and required the Philippines constitution to grant US citizens and corporations equal access to Philippine markets and natural resources. How this could be construed as differing from colonialism, before or after 1946, is one of the many dialectical curiosities best left for a student of US diplomacy to resolve.

There is no need to venture further into the morass, as it suffices for our purposes to underline the reason behind John Charmley's argument that the 'American illusion' seduced Winston and British Prime Ministers ever since to 'neglect Europe in favour of the special relationship'. Less apparent is whether 'those voices raised in the first half of the 1950s to argue that Britain should take advantage of the unique position she had won in Europe to lead its unification were ignored in favour of Churchill's grander narrative'.[39] At issue is whether or not British influence in the wider world was a force for good. Winston thought it was: the Americans, upon whom the maintenance of that influence increasingly depended after 1941, thought it was not, and that is all that need concern us here.

Charmley's 'American illusion' was simply an

ineluctable fact of life for post-war Britain. Winston's Fulton speech was a harbinger, but the weather changed with Truman's address to Congress on 12 March 1947, announcing that Britain had declared itself unable to sustain its commitments to Greece and Turkey, and that the USA must fill the void. The 'Truman Doctrine', as it came to be known, was that it should be:

> the policy of the United States to support free peoples who are resisting attempted subjugation by armed minorities or by outside pressures. . . . In addition to funds, I ask the Congress to authorize the detail of American civilian and military personnel to Greece and Turkey, at the request of those countries, to assist in the tasks of reconstruction, and for the purpose of supervising the use of such financial and material assistance as may be furnished.

The theme was further developed by George C. Marshall, now Truman's Secretary of State, in his Harvard Commencement address of 5 June 1947:

> Our policy is directed not against any country or doctrine but against hunger, poverty, desperation and chaos. Its purpose should be the revival of a working economy in the world so as to permit the emergence of political and social conditions in which free institutions can exist. Such assistance, I am convinced, must not be on a piecemeal basis as various crises develop. Any assistance that this government may render in the future should provide a

cure rather than a mere palliative. Any government that is willing to assist in the task of recovery will find full cooperation, I am sure, on the part of the United States government. Any government which manoeuvres to block the recovery of other countries cannot expect help from us. Furthermore, governments, political parties, or groups which seek to perpetuate human misery in order to profit therefrom politically or otherwise will encounter the opposition of the United States.

Winston showed himself far more prescient about Europe than many of his successors. After the Fulton speech he toured Europe amassing awards and honorary degrees. The constant theme of his speeches, first mooted as early as November 1945, was the necessity for a United States of Europe. The climax came at the University of Zurich on 19 September 1946. 'I am now going to say something that will astonish you,' he said. 'The first step in the re-creation of the European family must be a partnership between France and Germany. In this way only can France recover the moral leadership of Europe. There can be no revival of Europe without a spiritually great France and a spiritually great Germany.' Few would describe the European Union as 'spiritually great', but it is none the less a creation much as Winston advocated, which, for all its faults, has helped keep the French and Germans from each other's throats and made any resumption of the millennial European civil war unthinkable. Winston's view of Britain's role once again came at the end:

459

The first step is to form a Council of Europe. If at first all the States of Europe are not willing or able to join the Union, we must nevertheless proceed to assemble and combine those who will and those who can . . . In all this urgent work, France and Germany must take the lead together. Great Britain, the British Commonwealth of nations, mighty America, and I trust Soviet Russia—for then indeed all would be well—must be the friends and sponsors of the new Europe and must champion its right to live and shine.[40]

Noting the 'we' in the second sentence, it is clear that Winston saw Britain as a sponsor, not a member, of the European Union. He believed Britain's 'true destiny was the moral leadership of the English-speaking peoples to which she had a historic right endorsed by her championship of freedom'.[41] His vision for the future was of an independent, dynamic Britain, which would be valued both by the USA and by a united Europe as a partner. But this depended on Britain remaining strong. In 1934 he warned that, unless the country was strong, 'you are no kind of European. All you are is a source of embarrassment and weakness to the whole of the rest of the world.'[42]

I will not duplicate the details of Winston's physical decline provided in Moran's account and the gentler chronicle of his last Private Secretary.[43] He was robust enough to lead the Conservatives to victory in the general election of 1951, and wise enough to realize that with the country divided evenly between the two main parties what was needed was a long period of peace to digest the enormous changes that had taken place.[44] That peace was bought at the price of appeasing the trade unions and laying the ground for the great inflation that in due course destroyed the Keynesian consensus and breathed new life into the economic liberalism Winston had abandoned with regret in 1930. When he returned to power in October 1951 the messengers at No. 10 unearthed his fearsome red 'Action This Day' labels and placed them on the Cabinet Room table, but he never used them again.[45] There was, perhaps more than ever, a pressing need to galvanize the bureaucracy, but he no longer had either the desire or the energy to do it. He thought that none of his possible successors for leadership of the party had real fire in their bellies, and he now had none to share. Perhaps, once again, he may even have been the right man for that particular moment. Although he was speaking about American pressure for more rapid progress in creating a European Union, a comment he made to Colville in 1952 applied with even greater force to a Britain that needed to outgrow the consequences of many generations of bad choices. 'It may be better to bear an agonizing period of unsatisfactory time,' he said. 'You may kill yourself in getting strong enough.'[46]

The trade unions were simply too powerful to take on, and their political support was too unconditional to be challenged at this time. The Labour MP George Isaacs did not appear to realize that the following, written in 1953, was profoundly undemocratic:

although the unions have in the past been led into action which, if carried to a logical conclusion, would have taken the supreme economic and political power out of the hands of Parliament, no one who really understood the nature of trade unionism would have expected them to abandon parliamentary democracy as long as it showed itself capable of slow but definite modification into an instrument of social democracy.[47]

In other words, they were prepared to accept parliamentary democracy for as long as it produced the results they wanted. It is not surprising that the Communists never became a national party in Britain, for there was little room left for them outside the broad church of the Labour Party. There were probably as many people intellectually convinced of the rightness of Communism in Britain as there were in France or Italy, but a bedrock of individualism made them unwilling to submit to the discipline of Communist Party membership. The trade unionist Frank Chapple, himself a member of the Communist Party until he turned against it after the Russian invasion of Hungary in 1957, excoriated appeasement of unions in rigged elections, uncounted shows of hands and intimidation. 'In industrial relations', he said, 'if you reward bad behaviour you'll get more of it.'[48]

Internationally, Winston never wavered from the belief, expressed in a minute to Eden in December 1953, that the Russians were 'unreformable creatures of tireless aggression . . .' and in his own eyes, at least, the contest with Russian Communism was what gave his political life the greatest continuity and meaning.[49] Although I believe that Winston was indeed in decline after 1944, even the lion in winter roared resolutely. He had warned of the dangers of Communism for many years, and after 1945 he pressed for *détente* from a position of strength, accompanied by high-level summits, to try to break the stalemate in the Cold War. He believed this was preferable to what became known as mutually assured destruction, and felt that Stalin, and after his death the new Russian leadership, would listen to him. However, the roars drew fewer and fewer answering echoes. Winston endured a number of rejections during his last premiership, notably from Ike, now President Eisenhower, who made it clear that, despite his immense respect for the Winston he had worked with in 1942–5, he did not feel the old man he had to deal with in 1953–5 had anything more to offer. This was true: Winston sought summit meetings more as an affirmation of himself than for any practical good they might achieve. But the most savage act of disrespect came from his beloved House of Commons on his eightieth birthday in November 1954. He was presented with a portrait and an illuminated book signed by the MPs who had subscribed to pay for it: 26 Labour MPs had refused. The portrait, by Graham Sutherland, was intended to be Winston's during his lifetime and then to hang in the Lobby at Westminster. Winston found it redolent of reptilian cruelty, and Clemmie said it preyed on his mind to such an extent that some time later she had it destroyed.

In his acceptance speech Winston took the sting out of the painting by saying it was 'a remarkable example of modern art', pausing for laughter, and that 'it certainly combines force and candour. These are qualities which no active Member of either House can do without or should fear to meet.' He went on to heap more coals with the words: 'I thoroughly understand the position of those who have felt it their duty to abstain. The value of such a tribute is that it should be free and spontaneous.' He then spoke of giving the roar for a lion-hearted people before concluding:

> I am now nearing the end of my journey. I hope I still have some services to render. However that may be and whatever may befall I am sure I shall never forget the emotions of this day or be able to express my gratitude to those colleagues and companions with whom I have lived my life for this superb honour they have done me.[50]

Although not actually his last speech, Winston's address to the Commons on 1 March 1955 in the Defence Debate was intended to be the swansong of a man for whom public life had defined existence. It cannot have escaped him, as he laboured over the text, that he had said it all before. Indeed, he opened by comparing the world situation to that of Europe before the seventeenth-century Thirty Years' War, and the European situation to that of the Mongol invasion in the thirteenth century. The only thing to do was KBO:

> To conclude: mercifully, there is time and hope if we combine patience and courage. All deterrents will improve and gain authority

during the next ten years. By that time, the deterrent may well reach its acme and reap its final reward. The day may dawn when fair play, love for one's fellow-men, respect for justice and freedom, will enable tormented generations to march forth serene and triumphant from the hideous epoch in which we have to dwell. Meanwhile, never flinch, never weary, never despair.[51]

It was part of Winston's inverted vanity to be a great commoner, and although he gladly accepted awards he long declined those which would have changed his form of address. After all, Britain's other great wartime leader had died plain Mr Pitt. When a kind-hearted monarch tried to press the Order of the Garter upon him after his election defeat in 1945, saying that it was his personal award, Winston declined it with the quip that the electorate had given him the Order of the Boot. He eventually accepted the Garter in April 1953, and proudly wore it at the young Queen Elizabeth's coronation in June. The great Duke of Marlborough's father, who had bankrupted himself fighting for King Charles I in the Civil War, had also been Sir Winston Churchill, and the resonance was certainly not lost upon him. Winston gave dinner to the Queen and the Duke of Edinburgh at No. 10 Downing Street on 4 April 1955 and resigned the following day, recommending Anthony Eden as his successor. He was offered the dukedom of London, but turned it down after consultation with his son Randolph, who had no wish to go to the House of Lords. The electors of Woodford duly returned him in the general

465

elections of 1955 and 1959, and he visited his beloved House of Commons for the last time on 27 July 1964. He died on 24 January 1965, 70 years to the day since the death of his father.

CONCLUSION

DEATH SHALL HAVE NO DOMINION

Of recent, sympathetic biographical studies, Andrew Roberts' *Eminent Churchillians* and Geoffrey Best's *Churchill: A Study in Greatness* are suffused with the feeling, so well expressed in Best's closing paragraph, that by the time Winston died Britain had become 'a land in which such a man as he would never again find room to flourish, with a popular culture increasingly inimical to his values and likely therefore not to notice or properly appreciate his achievements'. Winston was deprecated and ridiculed throughout his life by 'right-thinking' people and there is no reason to believe they are any more astute today. Wide diffusion of prosperity and leisure has meant that many more men and women can achieve their full potential, and if they choose not to go into public life that is less a judgement on society at large than on the mediocracy that politics has become.

The paradox of Winston's public life is that while he valued freedom, he loved power more. He was too much of an egoist to care that a bureaucracy powerful enough to contain a man of his volcanic energy would effortlessly stifle his less commanding successors. His was an impossible act to follow, a fact emphasized by the ungrudging admiration of officials he treated like dust beneath his wheels. Thus Sir George Mallaby, Cabinet Office Under-Secretary during the war and later

467

High Commissioner to New Zealand:

> Anybody who served anywhere near him was devoted to him. It is hard to say why. He was not kind or considerate. He bothered nothing about us. He knew the names only of those very close to him and would hardly let anyone else into his presence. He was free with abuse and complaint. He was exacting beyond reason and ruthlessly critical. He continuously exhibited all the characteristics which one usually deplores and abominates in the boss. Not only did he get away with it but nobody really wanted him otherwise. He was unusual, unpredictable, exciting, original, stimulating, provocative, outrageous, uniquely experienced, abundantly talented, humorous, entertaining—almost everything a man could be, a great man.[1]

To all this one must add courage, his most outstanding quality and the one most men value above all others. His was not an unthinking bravery: on the contrary we have his own testimony to the effect that he was playing to the gallery in the Malakand Valley in 1897, and he was almost certainly seeking a Victoria Cross at Diamond Hill in 1900. There may have been an element of death-wish in his performances at Plugstreet in 1916 and on the bridge over the Rhine in 1945, but otherwise he risked his life as a function of getting things done, which included the exercise of moral dominance over men whose chests were quilted with gallantry awards. Even George Patton was in awe of someone who had charged with the 21st

Lancers at Omdurman. Although in old age Winston regretted that none of his many decorations was for valour, men of outstanding courage as diverse as Michael Collins, Lawrence of Arabia and Douglas MacArthur judged him to be one of them.

Moral courage is far rarer than physical bravery. Eisenhower, even as he was keeping Winston at arm's length in 1954, wrote a remarkable assessment of him in a private letter. Bearing in mind that he had the achievements of FDR and his own patron, Marshall, against which to measure Winston's, Ike wrote that greatness in a man was to achieve pre-eminence in some broad field of human thought or endeavour and then to discharge one's duties in such a way as 'to have left a marked and favourable imprint upon the future'. The qualities required were 'vision, integrity, courage, understanding, the power of articulation, and profundity of character'. Winston, he continued, 'came nearer to fulfilling the requirements of greatness than any individual that I have met in my lifetime. I have known finer and greater characters, wiser philosophers, more understanding personalities, but no greater man.'2

If similar praise from British generals is harder to find, it must owe much to the fact that Winston showed little regard for so many of them. But even the hard-pressed Brooke loved him, and the postscript to his diary entry for 27 July 1945, after Winston had lost the election and was gone, lamented his own lack of generosity:

On reading these diaries I have repeatedly felt ashamed of the abuse I had poured on him, especially during the latter years. It must, however, be remembered that my diary was the safety valve and the only outlet for all my pent up feelings. Feelings . . . engendered through friction generated from prolonged contacts of very tired individuals. During the last years Winston had been a very sick man, with repeated attacks of pneumonia, and very frequent attacks of temperature. This physical condition together with his mental fatigue accounted for many of the difficulties in dealing with him, a factor I failed to make adequate allowance for in my diary. I shall always look back on the years I worked with him as some of the most difficult and trying ones of my life. For all that I thank God that I was given an opportunity of working alongside such a man, and of having my eyes opened to the fact that occasionally such supermen exist on this earth.[3]

As I observed at the beginning of this book, when such a superman also devotes his considerable talents to falsifying the historical record the biographer's task is made more than usually fraught by the need to assess not only his deeds but also what he sought to achieve by misrepresenting them. Until 1940 all Winston's writing served the purpose of making himself the man to whom the country would turn in an emergency, and it should be judged in the light of what followed. After World War II it becomes more complex. Did he seek to distance himself from the bombing of Germany because he wished to look good in the eyes of posterity, or because it was inconsistent with the moral legacy he wished to leave? Did he overstate the degree of Anglo-American affinity because he believed it, or because he wished it might be so? Did he, finally, grossly oversimplify the pre-war debate over appeasement in order to exalt himself, or because the situation facing Britain in 1948, when he published the first volume of *The Second World War*, was horrifyingly similar to the dilemma faced by Chamberlain ten years earlier? Intriguingly, it was in his eulogy of his unfortunate predecessor that Winston came closest to defining his philosophy of history:

> It is not given to human beings, happily for them, to foresee or to predict to any large extent the unfolding of events. In one phase men seem to have been right; in another they seem to have been wrong. Then again, when the perspective of time has lengthened, all stands in a different setting. There is a new proportion, there is another scale of values. History with its flickering lamp stumbles along the trail of the past, trying to reconstruct its scenes, to revive its echoes, and kindle with pale gleams the passions of former days.[4]

Yet there were some who thought him more wrong than right. George Bernard Shaw thought Winston had wasted his life with party politics in the Commons. He felt he would have been able to change more as the mayor of a city, and that his real vocation was as a soldier and author.[5] A.J.P. Taylor thought it 'difficult to discern in him any element of creative statesmanship. He responded to events with infinite adaptability and persistent enthusiasm. But he had to be driven from without. Churchill had no vision for the future, only a tenacious defence of the past.'6 Roy Jenkins quotes Jean Monnet, the first general secretary of the League of Nations, proponent of Anglo-French union in 1940 and father of the European Union, to the effect that Winston concentrated on 'being someone' rather than 'doing something'.7 This was to miss the point entirely. Winston had defined himself in 1898, in a letter to Jennie: 'In Politics a man, I take it, gets on not so much by what he does, as by what he is. It is not so much a question of brains as of character and originality.'8

Aneurin Bevan, lashing out not long before he died in 1960, also missed the target: 'Churchill claimed to be the voice of Britain in the Second World War—not the lion, as he put it, but the lion's roar. I do not think he was. He spoke not what thousands of British men and women felt, but what he thought the historic man in the street should feel in circumstances such as these.' On the contrary: Winston's was genuinely inspirational speech, which is why there are pages devoted to him in anthologies of quotations. Bevan, on the other hand, is remembered only for two outbursts of self-damaging partisanship: in 1945, when he declared 'we want the complete political extinction of the Tory Party'; and in 1948, when he stated 'no amount of cajolery, and no attempt at ethical and social seduction, can eradicate from my heart a deep burning hatred of the Tory Party. . . . So far as I am concerned they are lower than vermin.' Bevan defined an orator as one who 'speaks out of a relationship which grows out of his contact with the audience; the dynamic force that drives him is the urge to exert power over his audience, so that they will believe what he believes and act accordingly'. Therefore, he concluded in a bizarre twist of logic, Winston was no orator:

> In peace-time, at any rate, great public figures consistently stand for something or somebody; plead implacably and irresistibly for something they believe in and which a group of men, large or small, want to bring about. Winston was the advocate of no party or cause in particular, did not think much in terms of causes, trusted in men rather than measures, and in any case was not interested in advocacy as such. When the war came, of course, it was quite different. He cast himself in the role of the great advocate who put the case of Britain to the world and the destiny of Britain to the British. His name will stand so long as war is remembered as a symbol of what words can do when there is a strong, brave and devoted nation free and willing to back them up with deeds.[9]

Bevan could not acknowledge that Winston was the ceaseless advocate, throughout his life, of his belief in the British as a great people. Yet of all the MPs who crossed swords with Winston, Bevan was the one who most closely shared his views on the function of debate in a democracy. The following words could have been written of either of them: 'He believed passionately in democracy, and he believed that the vitality of democracy depended upon the serious discussion by an informed electorate of opposed philosophies and a real choice between rival visions of the future.'[10] Both men would have been appalled at the reduction of complex issues to sound-bites and the trivialization of debate that has occurred since their deaths.

Not the least of the rewards gained from researching this book has been to learn that the two men who led the country through the 14 most dangerous and potentially divisive years in its modern history held each other in high regard. The barbed repartee lives on, but Winston's private opinion was that 'Mr Attlee is an honourable and gallant gentleman, and a faithful colleague who served his country well at the time of her greatest need.' He was angry to learn that a quip, attributed to him, was going the rounds: an empty taxi arrived at No. 10 and Mr Attlee got out. 'I should be obliged if you would make it clear whenever an occasion arises that I would never make such a remark about him, and that I strongly disapprove of anyone who does,' he announced.[11] It is comforting to think that if Winston had been the survivor he would have written something almost as fulsome—for more would have been impossible—as Attlee did in 1965:

By any reckoning Winston Churchill was one of the greatest men that history records. . . . He was brave, gifted, inexhaustible and indomitable. 'Talk not of genius baffled, genius is master of man. Genius does what it must. Talent does what it can.' These lines describe him . . . Energy, rather than wisdom, practical judgement or vision, was his supreme qualification . . . However . . . it is not the full story of what he did to win the

474

war. It was the poetry of Churchill, as well, that did the trick. Energy and poetry, in my view, really sums him up. . . . He was, of course, above all, a supremely fortunate mortal. Whether he deserved his great fate or not, whether he won it or had it dropped in his lap, history set him the job that he was the ideal man to do. I cannot think of anybody in this country who has been as favoured in this way so much, and, into the bargain, at the most dramatic moment in his country's history. In this, Winston was superbly lucky. And perhaps the most warming thing about him was that he never ceased to say so.[12]

Winnie and Clem could scarcely have envisaged the mauling of railways, city centres and communities in the name of modernity under their successors, to be replaced by meanly conceived roads and flat-roofed, stained concrete. The Luftwaffe flattened Bristol, but 'town planners' left St Mary Redcliffe, one of the jewels of English ecclesiastical architecture, stranded on a roundabout. They could not have imagined that the educational and welfare provisions they agreed upon would become a brimming trough for some people well able to fend for themselves, and a bureaucratic nightmare robbing others of their self-respect. A passage from the end of what is, in my opinion, one of the best memoirs written by a soldier of World War II speaks of his generation's own sense of betrayal:

The Britain they see in their old age is hardly 'the land fit for heroes' they envisaged—if that land existed in their imaginations, it was probably a place where pre-war values coexisted with decent wages and housing. It was a reasonable, perfectly possible dream, and for a time it existed, more or less. And then it changed, in the name of progress and improvement and enlightenment, which meant the destruction of much that they had fought for and held dear, and the betrayal of familiar things they had loved. Some of them, to superficial minds, will seem terribly trivial, even ludicrously so—things like county names, and shillings and pence, and the King James Version, and yards and feet and inches—yet they matter to a nation.[13]

Collectivists are compelled by their creed to belittle Churchill. Perhaps we should not blame them, because one of his more polite comments on the regime they admired for so long was that 'there is not one single social or economic principle or concept in the philosophy of the Russian Bolshevik which has not been realized, carried into action, and enshrined in immutable laws a million years ago by the White Ant'.[14] Less obvious is why some of a conservative persuasion also attack his memory. But perhaps the explanation is that Winston was a natural liberal forced by circumstances to join the Conservative Party, which only grudgingly accepted him. He was a practical man. His close friend and admirer Professor Lindemann, who, when ennobled, chose the style Lord Cherwell as much to evoke countless stimulating dinners at Chartwell as (less wisely) to claim Oxford's river, thought of him as a scientist who missed his vocation:

476

All the qualities . . . of the scientist are manifested in him. The readiness to face realities, even though they contradict a favourite hypothesis; the recognition that theories are made to fit facts not facts to fit theories; the interest in phenomena and the desire to explore them; and above all the underlying conviction that the world is not just a jumble of events but there must be some higher unity, that facts fit together. He has pre-eminently the synthetic mind which makes every new piece of knowledge fall into place and interlock with previous knowledge; where the ordinary brain is content to add each new experience to the scrap-heap, he insists on fitting it into the structure of the cantilever jutting out from the abyss of ignorance.[15]

'Above all': how often the phrase appears in comments on Winston, and how readily it trips off the fingertips of a biographer. For me the quality that stands out above all is his unconditional love of his country not for what it had been or could be, but for a spirit he believed unique and eternal, and in whose service he found supreme fulfilment.

He was a great complex of a man, compounded of warring ingredients, and full of passion, as well as sentiment. For a little while with him we became dangerous children pursuing visions of glory. In England's desperate need he renewed her youth and fortified her spirit. For him it was never

England right or wrong, but simply, England!16

Since he was Baconian in politics, Elizabethan in heart and Shakespearian in eloquence, let England's greatest poet bid farewell to him:17

His life was gentle; and the elements
So mixed in him, that nature might stand up,
And say to all the world. 'This was a man!'

APPENDIX A

BROADCAST OF 16 NOVEMBER 1934

I have but a short time to deal with this enormous subject and I beg you therefore to weigh my words with the attention and thought which I have given to them.

As we go to and fro in this peaceful country with its decent, orderly people going about their business under free institutions and with so much tolerance and fair play in their laws and customs, it is startling and fearful to realize that we are no longer safe in our island home.

For nearly a thousand years England has not seen the campfires of an invader. The stormy sea and our Royal Navy have been our sure defence. Not only have we preserved our life and freedom through the centuries, but gradually we have come to be the heart and centre of an empire which surrounds the globe.

It is indeed with a pang of stabbing pain that we see all this in mortal danger. A thousand years has served to form a state; an hour may lay it in dust.

What shall we do? Many people think that the best way to escape war is to dwell upon its horrors and to imprint them vividly upon the minds of the younger generation. They flaunt the grisly photograph before their eyes. They fill their ears with tales of carnage. They dilate upon the ineptitude of generals and admirals. They denounce the insensate folly of human strife. Now, all this teaching ought to be very useful in preventing us from attacking or invading any other country, if anyone outside a madhouse wished to do so, but how would it help us if we were attacked or invaded ourselves, that is the question we have to ask.

Would the invaders consent to hear Lord Beaverbrook's exposition, or listen to the impassioned appeals of Mr Lloyd George? Would they agree to meet that famous South African, General Smuts, and have their inferiority complex removed in friendly, reasonable debate? I doubt it. I have borne responsibility for the safety of this country in grievous times. I gravely doubt it.

But even if they did, I am not so sure we should convince them, and persuade them to go back quietly home. They might say, it seems to me, 'You are rich; we are poor. You seem well fed; we are hungry. You have been victorious; we have been defeated. You have valuable colonies; we have none. You have your navy; where is ours? You have had the past; let us have the future.' Above all, I fear they would say, 'You are weak and we are strong.'

After all, my friends, only a few hours away by air there dwell a nation of nearly 70 millions of the most educated, industrious, scientific, disciplined people in the world, who are being taught from childhood to think of war as a glorious exercise and death in battle as the noblest fate for man.

There is a nation which has abandoned all its liberties in order to augment its collective strength. There is a nation, which, with all its strength and virtue, is in the grip of a group of ruthless men, preaching a gospel of intolerance and racial pride, unrestrained by law, by parliament, or by public

480

opinion. In that country all pacifist speeches, all morbid war books are forbidden or suppressed, and their authors rigorously imprisoned. From their new table of commandments they have omitted 'thou shall not kill'.

It is but 20 years since these neighbours of ours fought almost the whole world, and almost defeated them. Now they are rearming with the utmost speed, and ready to their hands is the new lamentable weapon of the air, against which our navy is no defence, and before which women and children, the weak and frail, the pacifist and the jingo, the warrior and the civilian, the front line trenches and the cottage home, all lie in equal and impartial peril.

Nay, worse still, for with the new weapon has come a new method, or rather has come back the most British method of ancient barbarism, namely, the possibility of compelling the submission of nations by terrorizing their civil population; and, worst of all, the more civilized the country is, the larger and more splendid its cities, the more intricate the structure of its civil and economic life, the more is it vulnerable and at the mercy of those who may make it their prey.

Now, these are facts, hard, grim, indisputable facts, and in the face of these facts, I ask again, what are we to do?

There are those who say, 'Let us ignore the continent of Europe. Let us leave it with its hatreds and its armaments, to stew in its own juice, to fight out its own quarrels, and decree its own doom. Let us turn our backs to this melancholy and alarmist view. Let us fix our gaze across the ocean and see our own life in our own dominions and empires.'

There would be very much to this plan if only we could unfasten the British islands from their rock foundations, and could tow them three thousand miles across the Atlantic Ocean, and anchor them safely upon the smiling coasts of Canada; but I have not yet heard of any way in which this could be done.

At present we lie within a few minutes' striking distance of the French, Dutch, and Belgian coasts, and within a few hours of the great aerodromes of Central Europe. We are even within cannon shot of the continent—so close as that. Is it prudent, is it possible, however we might desire it, to turn our backs upon Europe and ignore whatever may happen there? Everyone can judge this question for himself, and everyone ought to make up his mind or her mind, let me say, about it immediately. It lies at the heart of our problems.

For my part, I have concluded, reluctantly I admit, that we cannot get away. Here we are and we must make the best of it, but do not, I beg you, underrate the risks, the grievous risks we have to run. I hope, I pray, and, on the whole, grasping the larger hope, I believe, that no war will fall upon us; but if in the near future the great war of 1914 is resumed again in Europe, no one can tell where and how it would end or whether sooner or later we should not be dragged into it, dragged into it as the United States was dragged in against their will in 1917. Whatever happens, and whatever we did, it would be a time of frightful danger for us, and, when the war was over, or perhaps while it still raged, we should be brought face to face with the victors, whoever they might be. Indeed, with our wealth and vast possessions, we should be the only

482

prize sufficient to reward their exertion and compensate them for their losses.

Then certainly those who had tried to forget Europe would have to turn round very quickly indeed and then it would be too late. Therefore, it seems to me that we cannot detach ourselves from Europe and that for our own safety and self-preservation we are bound to make exertions and run risks for the sake of keeping peace.

There are some who say, indeed it has been the shrill cry of the hour, that we should run the risk of disarming ourselves in order to set an example to others. We have done that already. We have done it for the last five years, but our example has not been followed. On the contrary, it has produced, as I ventured to predict, the opposite results. All the other countries have armed only the more heavily, and the quarrels and intrigues about disarmament have only bred more ill will between the nations.

Everyone would be glad to see the burden of armaments reduced in every country, but history shows on many a page that armaments are not necessarily a cause of war and that the want of them has been no guarantee of peace. If, for instance, all the explosives all over the world could, by a wave of a magic wand be robbed of their power and made harmless, so that not a cannon nor a rifle could fire and not a shell or a bomb detonate, that would be a measure of world disarmament far beyond the brightest dreams of Geneva, but would it insure peace? That is the question. On the contrary, in my belief, war would begin almost the next day when enormous masses of fierce men armed with picks, spades, or with clubs and spears, would pour over the frontiers into the lands they covet.

This truth may be unfashionable, unpalatable, no doubt unpopular, but, if it is the truth, the story of mankind shows that war was universal and unceasing for millions of years before armaments were invented or armies organized. Indeed, the lucid intervals of peace and order only occurred in human history after armaments in the hands of strong governments have come into being, and civilization in every age has been nursed only in cradles guarded by superior weapons and superior discipline.

To remove the causes of war, we must go deeper than armaments. We must remove grievances and injustice. We must raise human thought to a higher plane. We must give a new inspiration to the world. Let moral disarmament come and physical disarmament will soon follow.

That is but one side of this. Is there another? When we look out upon the state of Europe and of the world and of the position of our own country as they are tonight, it seems to me that the next year or two years may contain a fateful turning point in our history. I am afraid that if you look intently at what is moving towards Great Britain, you will see that the only choice open is the old grim choice our forebears had to face, namely, whether we shall submit or whether we shall prepare, whether we shall submit to the will of the stronger nation or whether we shall prepare to defend our rights, our liberties, and indeed, our lives.

If we submit, our submission should be timely. If we prepare, our preparation should not be too late. Submission will entail at the very least, the passing and distribution of the British empire, and the acceptance by our people within and under a Teutonic domination of Europe of whatever future may be in store for small countries like Norway, Sweden, Denmark, Holland, Belgium, and Switzerland.

The difficulty about submission—I state it calmly—the difficulty is that we have already in this island the population of a first-class power, and on our new scale of life as a small state, we could not feed more than perhaps half of those who live here now. Great stresses will arise in deciding which half shall survive. You have perhaps read the story of the raft of Medusa. I will not dwell on that repulsive theme. These are the disadvantages of the submission and of Great Britain definitely releasing her position in the world. Preparation involves statesmanship, expense, and exertion, and neither submission nor preparation are free from suffering and danger.

I should not speak to you, my friends, fellow countrymen, in this way, if I were not prepared to declare to you some of the measures of preparation by which I believe another great war may be averted and our destruction be prevented should war come. First, we must without another day's delay begin to make ourselves at least the strongest air power in the European world. By this means we shall recover to a very large extent the safety which we formerly enjoyed through our navy, and through our being an island. By this means we shall free ourselves from the dangers of being blackmailed against our will, either to surrender our possessions or even hand over such means of defence as we still possess, or of being forced to join in a continental war against our wish or against our feeling of right and justice.

By this means we shall remove from Europe that additional danger to peace which arises when a very wealthy nation and empire is so obviously undefended that it lies an inviting bait or prey to the ambition or appetite of hungry powers.

But that is not all we should do. I look to the League of Nations as being an instrument which, properly sustained and guided, may preserve the threatened peace of the world. I know it is fashionable in some quarters—in many quarters—to mock at the League of Nations, but where is there any other equal hope?

The many countries, great and small, that are afraid of being absorbed or invaded by Germany, should lay their fears and their facts before the League of Nations. If the League of Nations is satisfied that these fears are justified, it should call upon its members to volunteer as special constables for the preservation of peace against a particular danger. Naturally, those would be most ready to volunteer whose homes lay nearest the regions where the outbreak was most likely to occur. It might well be that not only two or three nations but eight or ten would be found willing in their own interests and in the interests of peace to undertake this special obligation. There would then come into being within the League of Nations and under the formal Authority, a special service band of nations who are in danger, and who want to be let alone. It would be a confederation not merely of the peace-loving powers—for everyone will say they are that—but of the peace-interested powers, a league of those who have most to lose by war and are nearest to the danger.

I accept the words which General Smuts used only on Monday last. 'There should be', he said, 'a smaller group within the league, entering into mutual defensive arrangements under the aegis and subject to the control of the league.' Those are words of wisdom and it seems to me that Great Britain should not refuse to bear her share and do her part in this. These volunteer special constables should not only be authorized, but urged by the League of Nations to concert with one another measures of mutual defence against the invasion of any one of them, whether by land, sea, or air; to undertake to maintain forces while the danger lasts.

You have heard the old doctrine of the balance of power. I don't accept it. Anything like a balance of power in Europe will lead to war. Great wars usually come only when both sides think they have good hopes of victory. Peace must be founded upon preponderance. There is safety in numbers. If there were five or six on each side, there might well be a frightful trial of strength, but if there were eight or ten on one side and only one or two upon the other, and if the collective armed forces of one side were three or four times as large as those of the other, then there would be no war.

The practical arrangements which are appropriate to one region of the world may be repeated elsewhere in different combinations for other dangers and in other fields, and it might well be that gradually the whole world would be laced with international insurances against individual aggressors, and confidence and safety would return to mankind.

If the first stage of such a structure could be

487

built up by the League of Nations at the present time—and there may still be time—it would, I believe, enable us to get through the next ten years without a horrible and fatal catastrophe, and in that interval, in that blessed breathing space, we might be able to reconstruct the life of Europe and reunite in justice and good will our sundered and quaking civilization. May God protect us all.

APPENDIX B

THE ATLANTIC CHARTER

Agreed at Placentia Bay, Newfoundland, and dated
14 August 1941

The President of the United States of America and the Prime Minister, Mr Churchill, representing His Majesty's Government in the United Kingdom, being met together, deem it right to make known certain common principles in the national policies of their respective countries on which they base their hopes for a better future for the world.

First, their countries seek no aggrandizement, territorial or other;

Second, they desire to see no territorial changes that do not accord with the freely expressed wishes of the peoples concerned;

Third, they respect the right of all peoples to choose the form of government under which they will live; and they wish to see sovereign rights and self government restored to those who have been forcibly deprived of them;

Fourth, they will endeavor, with due respect for their existing obligations, to further the enjoyment by all States, great or small, victor or vanquished, of access, on equal terms, to the trade and to the raw materials of the world which are needed for their economic prosperity;

Fifth, they desire to bring about the fullest collaboration between all nations in the economic field with the object of securing, for all, improved labor standards, economic advancement and social security;

Sixth, after the final destruction of the Nazi tyranny, they hope to see established a peace which will afford to all nations the means of dwelling in safety within their own boundaries, and which will afford assurance that all the men in all the lands may live out their lives in freedom from fear and want;

Seventh, such a peace should enable all men to traverse the high seas and oceans without hindrance;

Eighth, they believe that all of the nations of the world, for realistic as well as spiritual reasons must come to the abandonment of the use of force. Since no future peace can be maintained if land, sea or air armaments continue to be employed by nations which threaten, or may threaten, aggression outside of their frontiers, they believe, pending the establishment of a wider and permanent system of general security, that the disarmament of such nations is essential. They will likewise aid and encourage all other practicable measures which will lighten for peace-loving peoples the crushing burden of armaments.

APPENDIX C

DECLARATION OF HONORARY CITIZEN OF UNITED STATES OF AMERICA

9 April 1963

BY THE PRESIDENT OF THE UNITED STATES OF AMERICA

A PROCLAMATION

WHEREAS Sir Winston Churchill, a son of America though a subject of Britain, has been throughout his life a firm and steadfast friend of the American people and the American nation; and

WHEREAS he has freely offered his hand and his faith in days of adversity as well as triumph; and

WHEREAS his bravery, charity and valor, both in war and in peace, have been a flame of inspiration in freedom's darkest hour; and

WHEREAS his life has shown that no adversary can overcome, and no feat can deter, free men in the defense of their freedom; and

WHEREAS he has by his art as an historian and his judgment as a statesman made the past the servant of the future;

NOW, THEREFORE, I, JOHN F. KENNEDY, President of the United States of America, under the authority contained in an Act of the 88th Congress, do hereby declare Sir Winston Churchill an honorary citizen of the United States of America.

APPENDIX D

MUSTARD GAS MINUTE OF 6 JULY 1944

GENERAL ISMAY FOR COS COMMITTEE

1. I want you to think very seriously over this question of poison gas. I would not use it unless it could be shown either that (a) it was life or death for us, or (b) that it would shorten the war by a year.

2. It is absurd to consider morality on this topic when everybody used it in the last war without a word of complaint from the moralists or the Church. On the other hand, in the last war bombing of open cities was regarded as forbidden. Now everybody does it as a matter of course. It is simply a question of fashion changing as she does between long and short skirts for women.

3. I want a cold-blooded calculation made as to how it would pay us to use poison gas, by which I mean principally mustard. We will want to gain more ground in Normandy so as not to be cooped up in a small area. We could probably deliver 20 tons to their one and for the sake of the one they would bring their bomber aircraft into the area against our superiority, thus paying a heavy toll.

4. Why have the Germans not used it? Not certainly out of moral scruples or affection for us. They have not used it because it does not pay them. The greatest temptation ever offered to them was the beaches of Normandy. This they could have drenched with gas greatly to the

hindrance of the troops [in 1940 Alan Brooke wrote that if the Germans landed in England 'I . . . had every intention of using sprayed mustard gas on the beaches.' Alanbrooke, *War Diaries*, p. 94.] That they thought about it is certain and that they prepared against our use of gas is also certain. But the only reason they have not used it against us is that they fear the retaliation. What is to their detriment is to our advantage.

5. Although one sees how unpleasant it is to receive poison gas attacks, from which nearly everyone recovers, it is useless to protest that an equal amount of H.E. [high explosive] will not inflict greater casualties and sufferings on troops and civilians. One really must not be bound within silly conventions of the mind whether they be those that ruled in the last war or those in reverse which rule in this.

6. If the bombardment of London became a serious nuisance and great rockets with far-reaching and devastating effect fell on many centres of Government and labour, I should be prepared to do <u>anything</u> that would hit the enemy in a murderous place. I may certainly have to ask you to support me in using poison gas. We could drench the cities of the Ruhr and many other cities in Germany in such a way that most of the population would be requiring constant medical attention. We could stop all work at the flying bomb starting points. I do not see why we should have the disadvantages of being the gentleman while they have all the advantages of being the cad. There are times when this may be so but not now.

7. I quite agree that it may be several weeks or even months before I shall ask you to drench Germany

with poison gas, and if we do it, let us do it one hundred per cent. In the meanwhile, I want the matter studied in cold blood by sensible people and not by that particular set of psalm-singing uniformed defeatists which one runs across now here now there. Pray address yourself to this. It is a big thing and can only be discarded for a big reason. I shall of course have to square Uncle Joe [Stalin] and the President [FDR]; but you need not bring this into your calculations at the present time. Just try to find out what it is like on its merits.

APPENDIX E

THE MORGENTHAU PLAN

Summary from Henry Morgenthau, Jr., Germany is the Problem (New York 1945)

PROGRAM TO PREVENT GERMANY FROM STARTING A WORLD WAR III

1. *Demilitarization of Germany*

It should be the aim of the Allied Forces to accomplish the complete demilitarization of Germany in the shortest possible period of time after surrender. This means completely disarm the German Army and people (including the removal or destruction of all war material), the total destruction of the whole German armament industry, and the removal or destruction of other key industries which are basic to military strength.

2. *New Boundaries of Germany*

(a) Poland should get that part of East Prussia which doesn't go to the USSR and the southern portion of Silesia.

(b) France should get the Saar and the adjacent territories bounded by the Rhine and the Moselle Rivers.

(c) As indicated in 4 below an International Zone should be created containing the Ruhr and the surrounding industrial areas.

3. *Partitioning of New Germany*

The remaining portion of Germany should be divided into two autonomous, independent states, (1) a South German state comprising Bavaria,

Wuerttemberg, Baden and some smaller areas and (2) a North German state comprising a large part of the old state of Prussia, Saxony, Thuringia and several smaller states.

There shall be a custom union between the new South German state and Austria, which will be restored to her pre-1938 political borders.

4. *The Ruhr Area* (the Ruhr, surrounding industrial areas, the Rhineland, the Kiel Canal, and all German territory north of the Kiel Canal)

Here lies the heart of German industrial power. This area should not only be stripped of all presently existing industries but so weakened and controlled that it can not in the foreseeable future become an industrial area. The following steps will accomplish this:

(a) Within a short period, if possible not longer than 6 months after the cessation of hostilities, all industrial plants and equipment not destroyed by military action shall be completely dismantled and transported to Allied Nations as restitution. All equipment shall be removed from the mines and the mines closed.

(b) The area should be made an international zone to be governed by an international security organization to be established by the United Nations. In governing the area the international organization should be guided by policies designed to further the above stated objective.

5. *Restitution and Reparation*

Reparations, in the form of future payments and deliveries, should not be demanded. Restitution and reparation shall be effected by the transfer of existing German resources and territories, e.g.,

(a) by restitution of property looted by the

Germans in territories occupied by them;

(b) by transfer of German territory and German private rights in industrial property situated in such territory to invaded countries and the international organization under the program of partition;

(c) by the removal and distribution among devastated countries of industrial plants and equipment situated within the International Zone and the North and South German states delimited in the section on partition;

(d) by forced German labor outside Germany; and

(e) by confiscation of all German assets of any character whatsoever outside of Germany.

6. *Education and Propaganda*

(a) All schools and universities will be closed until an Allied Commission of Education has formulated an effective reorganization program. It is contemplated that it may require a considerable period of time before any institutions of higher education are reopened. Meanwhile the education of German students in foreign universities will not be prohibited. Elementary schools will be reopened as quickly as appropriate teachers and textbooks are available.

(b) All German radio stations and newspapers, magazines, weeklies, etc. shall be discontinued until adequate controls are established and an appropriate program formulated.

7. *Political Decentralization*

The military administration in Germany in the Initial period should be carried out with a view toward the eventual partitioning of Germany. To facilitate partitioning and to assure its permanence the military authorities should be guided by the following principles:

(a) Dismiss all policy-making officials of the Reich government and deal primarily with local governments.

(b) Encourage the re-establishment of state governments in each of the states (Länder) corresponding to 18 states into which Germany is presently divided and in addition make the Prussian provinces separate states.

(c) Upon the partitioning of Germany, the various state governments should be encouraged to organize a federal government for each of the newly partitioned areas. Such new governments should be in the form of a confederation of states, with emphasis on states' rights and a large degree of local autonomy.

8. *Responsibility of Military for Local German Economy*

The sole purpose of the military in control of the German economy shall be to facilitate military operations and military occupation. The Allied Military Government shall not assume responsibility for such economic problems as price controls, rationing, unemployment, production, reconstruction, distribution, consumption, housing, or transportation, or take any measures designed to maintain or strengthen the German economy, except those which are essential to military operations. The responsibility for sustaining the German economy and people rests with the German people with such facilities as may be available under the circumstances.

9. *Controls over Development of German Economy*

During a period of at least 20 years after surrender adequate controls, including controls over foreign trade and tight restrictions on capital imports, shall be maintained by the United Nations designed to prevent in the newly-established states the establishment or expansion of key industries basic to the German military potential and to control other key industries.

10. *Agrarian Program*

All large estates should be broken up and divided among the peasants and the system of primogeniture and entail should be abolished.

11. *Punishment of War Crimes and Treatment of Special Groups*

A program for the punishment of certain war crimes and for the treatment of Nazi organizations and other special groups is contained in section 11.

12. *Uniforms and Parades*

(a) No German shall be permitted to wear, after an appropriate period of time following the cessation of hostilities, any military uniform or any uniform of any quasi military organizations.

(b) No military parades shall be permitted anywhere in Germany and all military bands shall be disbanded.

13. *Aircraft*

All aircraft (including gliders), whether military or commercial, will be confiscated for later disposition. No German shall be permitted to operate or to help operate any aircraft, including those owned by foreign interests.

14. *United States Responsibility*

Although the United States would have full military and civilian representation on whatever International commission or commissions may be established for the execution of the whole German program, the primary responsibility for the policing of Germany and for civil administration in Germany should be assumed by the military forces of Germany's continental neighbors. Specifically these should include Russian, French, Polish, Czech, Greek, Yugoslav, Norwegian, Dutch and Belgian soldiers.

Under this program United States troops could be withdrawn within a relatively short time.

From President Roosevelt's Foreword to *Germany Is the Problem*:

We bring no charge against the German race, as such, for we cannot believe that God has eternally condemned any race of humanity. For we know in our own land how many good men and women of German ancestry have proved loyal, freedom-loving, peace-loving citizens. . . . The German people are not going to be enslaved—because the United Nations do not traffic in human slavery. But it will be necessary for them to earn their way back into the fellowship of peace-loving and law-abiding nations. And, in their climb up that steep road, we shall certainly see to it that they are not encumbered by having to carry guns. They will be relieved of that burden—we hope, forever.

NOTES AND REFERENCES

INTRODUCTION

1. WSC, *My Early Life* (2002), p. ix.
2. House of Commons, 26 March 1936.
3. Speech to the Royal Society of St George, 24 April 1933.
4. Martin Gilbert, *In Search of Churchill* (1995), p. 6.
5. J.H. Plumb, 'Churchill the Historian', in A.J.P. Taylor (ed.), *Churchill: Four Faces and the Man* (1969), p. 123.
6. Quoted in Frederick Woods, *Artillery of Words* (1992), p. 2.
7. Woods, *Artillery*, p.153.
8. See Clive Ponting, *Churchill* (1994); John Charmley, *Churchill: The End of Glory* (1993) and *Churchill's Grand Alliance: The Anglo-American Special Relationship, 1940–57* (1995).
9. William Shakespeare, *Julius Caesar* Act I Scene 2.
10. Richard Holmes, *Battlefields of the Second World War* (2001), p. 24.
11. House of Commons, 30 July 1934; WSC, *Arms and the Covenant*, p. 160.
12. To his Epping constituents, 23 February 1931.
13. House of Commons, 22 February 1906, about indentured Chinese labourers in South Africa, denying that the terms of their employment constituted slavery.
14. Gilbert, *Search*, p. 86.
15. Washington DC, 26 June 1954.

16. Martin Gilbert, *Churchill: A Life* (2000), p. 862.
17. WSC, *Early Life*, p. 125.
18. *Finest Hour*, Winter 1998–9, p. 51.
19. Violet Bonham Carter, *Winston Churchill as I Knew Him* (1965), p. 135.
20. Lord Beaverbrook, *Men and Power* (1956), p. xiv.
21. Charles de Gaulle, *L'Appel* (1955), opening paragraph.
22. Lord Chandos, *Memoirs of Lord Chandos* (1962), p. 343.
23. This is the main conclusion of Raymond Callahan, *Churchill: Retreat from Empire* (Tunbridge Wells 1984).
24. Some of these were with 'full military honours' as opposed to state funerals; there would have been no significant difference in procession and ceremony.
25. John Lukacs, *Churchill: Visionary, Statesman, Historian* (Yale 2002), p. 174.

CHAPTER ONE: FATHER TO THE MAN 1874–1895

1. Anthony Storr, 'The Man', in A.J.P. Taylor (ed.), *Churchill: Four Faces and the Man* (1969), which must be read bearing in mind that our knowledge of the role of genetics and biochemistry in psychology has advanced enormously since then.
2. On both fronts (women and organized labour), he needed to construct an appealing basket in the bulrushes for his privileged infant self. In

Moses and Monotheism (1939), Sigmund Freud argued that the usual purpose of the exposure myth, first linked to Sargon of Babylon in 2800 BC, was to claim royal parentage for those of lowly birth. For Moses the myth was reversed, to explain how a royal Egyptian was really a birth member of the humble Israelite tribe.

3. Eyewitness account by Patrick Kinna, one of Winston's private secretaries, in Celia Sandys, *Churchill* (2003), p. 111.
4. Extract from 'Crusade in Europe' in Charles Eade (ed.), *Churchill, by His Contemporaries* (1953), pp. 197–8.
5. Simon Jenkins, *England's Thousand Best Houses* (2003), p. 593.
6. Peregrine Churchill and Julian Mitchell, *Jennie, Lady Randolph Churchill: A Portrait with Letters* (1974), pp. 19–20.
7. Churchill and Mitchell, *Jennie*, pp. 43–4.
8. Churchill and Mitchell, *Jennie*, p. 64.
9. Churchill and Mitchell, *Jennie*, p. 98.
10. WSC, *Early Life*, p. 5.
11. WSC, *Early Life*, p. 5.
12. Gilbert, *Life*, p. 4.
13. Gilbert, *Life*, p. 8.
14. The correspondence collected in Celia Sandys, *From Winston with Love and Kisses* (1994), leads irresistibly to this conclusion.
15. WSC, *Early Life*, pp. 9–10.
16. WSC, *Early Life*, p. 17.
17. WSC, *Early Life*, p. 21.
18. William Manchester, *The Last Lion: Alone 1932–1940* (1989), p. 375.
19. WSC, *Early Life*, p. 46.
20. Gilbert, *Life*, p. 38.

21. Gilbert, *Search*, p. 315. I lost my own father the year I went up to Cambridge. I was at my very worst, immature but headstrong, and seldom a day goes by, even now, when I do not regret that he died before he had the chance to take pleasure in some of my modest accomplishments. But I never doubted that he loved me. How much worse must it have been for Winston?

22. WSC, *Early Life*, p. 62: 'She was still at forty young, beautiful and fascinating.'

23. Anthony Montague Brown, *Long Sunset* (1995), p. 122.

24. See *www.winstonchurchill.org/i4a/pages/index.cfm?pageid=105*. Article by John H. Mather, MD.

25. The theatre in question was called the Empire; Winston's pun simultaneously mocked the prudery and the imperialism of the middle-class worthies against whom he led the protest.

26. Gilbert, *Life*, p. 53.

27. In the midst of badgering his mother to pay for polo ponies (letter of 27 April 1895), he wrote: 'I would point out that had not my personal charm induced the Duchess Lily [his uncle's widow] to give me a charger it [the sum he was demanding] would have been £100 or £120 more.' Randolph Churchill, *Winston S. Churchill, Companion to Volume I*, p. 570.

28. R. Churchill, *Companion to Volume I*, pp. 625–38.

29. Oscar Wilde had very recently been imprisoned for 'unnatural practices'.

30. R. Churchill, *Companion to Volume I*, p. 701.

31. Norman Rose, *Churchill: An Unruly Life*

(1994), p. 34.
32. R. Churchill, *Companion to Volume I*, p. 702.

CHAPTER TWO: THE BUBBLE REPUTATION 1895–1901

1. WSC, *Early Life*, p. 59.
2. Possibly the Prince smelled a scandal arising from her affair with young George Cornwallis West, whom she married on 28 July 1900. Yet as late as March that year (R. Churchill, *Companion to Volume I*, p. 1156) Jennie addressed the Prince as '*Très cher Ami et Monseigneur*'.
3. R. Churchill, *Companion to Volume I*, p. 741. Letter of 26 February 1897.
4. R. Churchill, *Companion to Volume I*, p. 746.
5. R. Churchill, *Companion to Volume I*, p. 816.
6. R. Churchill, *Companion to Volume I*, p. 819.
7. R. Churchill, *Companion to Volume I*, pp. 868–9.
8. R. Churchill, *Companion to Volume I*, pp. 870–1. Letter of 30 January 1898.
9. Norman Dixon, *On the Psychology of Military Incompetence* (1976), p. 375.
10. E. T. Williams, 'Churchill', in *Dictionary of National Biography 1961–1970* (1981), p. 205.
11. R. Churchill, *Companion to Volume I*, pp. 863–4. Letter of 26 January 1898.
12. R. Churchill, *Companion to Volume I*, p. 1225.
13. R. Churchill, *Companion to Volume I*, p. 768.
14. R. Churchill, *Companion to Volume I*, pp. 712–13.
15. C.C. O'Brien (ed.), *Burke: Reflections on the*

Revolution in France (1969), p. 23.

16. R. Churchill, *Companion to Volume I*, p. 907.
17. R. Churchill, *Companion to Volume I*, p. 858.
18. R. Churchill, *Companion to Volume I*, p. 724.
19. O'Brien, *Burke*, p. 91.
20. O'Brien, *Burke*, p. 63.
21. WSC, *Early Life*, pp. 59–60.
22. R. Churchill, *Volume 1*, Winston to Jennie, 17 August 1897.
23. Peter Hopkirk, *The Great Game* (2001), pp. 483–98.
24. R. Churchill, *Companion to Volume I*, p. 784. Letter of 5 September 1897.
25. Frederick Woods (ed.), *Winston S. Churchill: War Correspondent 1895–1900* (1992), p. 60. Despatch of 9 November 1897.
26. R. Churchill, *Companion to Volume I*, pp. 792–3. Letter of 19 September 1897.
27. WSC, *Early Life*, p. 143.
28. At that time there were only two gallantry decorations available to officers, the all-ranks Victoria Cross and the officers-only Distinguished Service Order. A Mention, one level below the latter, was awarded for 'gallant and distinguished services' in action or on the staff.
29. R. Churchill, *Companion to Volume I*, p. 839. Letter of 22 December 1897.
30. R. Churchill, *Companion to Volume I*, pp. 833–5.
31. R. Churchill, *Companion to Volume I*, p. 804.
32. R. Churchill, *Companion to Volume I*, p. 807.
33. R. Churchill, *Companion to Volume I*, p.788.
34. R. Churchill, *Companion to Volume I*, p. 810. Letter to his grandmother of 25 October 1897.

35. R. Churchill, *Companion to Volume I*, p. 640.
36. R. Churchill, *Volume I*, pp. 292–3.
37. R. Churchill, *Companion to Volume I*, pp. 979–80.
38. WSC, *Early Life*, p. 170.
39. WSC, *The River War* (1899), II, p. 98.
40. This was not the British army's last cavalry charge: there were several in World War I. The last charge made by a complete regiment of British cavalry took place in Turkey in 1920 during the Chanak crisis, when the 20th Hussars successfully charged a body of Turks. See The Marquess of Anglesey, *History of the British Cavalry*, Vol 8 (1997), pp. 349–52.
41. Woods (ed.), *War Correspondent*, pp. 128–9.
42. WSC, *Early Life*, p. 190.
43. WSC, *Early Life*, pp. 179 and 193.
44. Woods (ed.), *War Correspondent*, p. 145.
45. WSC, *Early Life*, p. 222.
46. *Manchester Courier*, 7 July 1899, quoted in *Volume 1*, p. 449.
47. R. Churchill, *Volume I*, p. 455.
48. Thomas Pakenham, *The Boer War* (1979), p. 32.
49. Celia Sandys, *Chasing Churchill* (2003), p. 52.
50. R. Churchill, *Companion to Volume I*, p. 1067.
51. Although denied a decoration himself, in 1910, when Home Secretary, Winston was instrumental in securing the award of the Albert Medal for the driver and fireman on the train.
52. R. Churchill, *Volume I*, p. 505.
53. Woods (ed.), *War Correspondent*, pp. 224–5.
54. Woods (ed.), *War Correspondent*, p. 318.
55. Woods (ed.), *War Correspondent*, pp. 231–2.

56. Woods (ed.), *War Correspondent*, p. 246.
57. Woods (ed.), *War Correspondent*, p. 264.
58. Woods (ed.), *War Correspondent*, p. 266.
59. Woods (ed.), *War Correspondent*, p. 301.
60. Woods (ed.), *War Correspondent*, p. 322.
61. R. Churchill, *Volume I*, p. 513.
62. Woods (ed.), *War Correspondent*, p. 343.
63. Woods (ed.), *War Correspondent*, pp. 346–7. A fugleman was a trained soldier who once stood in front of his unit to show the correct drill movements and timings.

CHAPTER THREE: THE TATTERED FLAG 1901–1911

1. 'In these somewhat troublesome days when the great Mother Empire stands splendidly isolated in Europe' (George Foster, Canadian House of Commons, 16 January 1896); 'Splendid Isolation' (headline, *The Times*, 22 January 1896).
2. In *The Principles of Political Economy and Taxation* (1817), Ricardo argued that it was mutually beneficial for two countries to trade, even though one of them might be able to produce all the goods it required more cheaply than the other. What mattered was not the cost, but rather the ease (comparative advantage) of production for different goods. Although the most demonstrably true of all economic theories, it remains counter-intuitive and politically hard to defend in the face of populist appeals for protection and subsidy.
3. Andrew Roberts, *Salisbury: Victorian Titan*

(1999), p. 842.
4. R. Churchill, *Companion to Volume II*, p. 346.
5. Until 1918 general elections were held over a period of weeks, freeing early victors like Winston to campaign on behalf of others—and to store up favours for the future. 'Landslides' in first-past-the-post elections are always more apparent than real. The Liberals won 2,565,644 votes, 5.5 per cent more than the Conservatives and Liberal Unionists with 2,278, 076, but this translated into 397 seats over 156. The Labour Party won only 29 seats with 254,202 votes, while the Irish Nationalists were grossly over-represented with 82 seats from 33,231 votes.
6. Robert Rhodes James, *Churchill: A Study in Failure* (1970), p. 41. Roy Jenkins, *Churchill* (2001) is coloured by the same fastidiousness.
7. Salaries for MPs were introduced in the Parliament Act of 1911.
8. Lukacs, *Churchill: Visionary*, p. 164.
9. *The People's Rights* (1910). It was preceded by three pamphlets: *Mr Brodrick's Army* (1903), *For Free Trade* (1906) and *Liberalism and the Social Problem* (1909).
10. In reply to Lord Curzon's statement that 'all civilization has been the work of aristocracies', Winston riposted that 'the upkeep of aristocracies has been the hard work of all civilizations'. Stinging, but hardly rabble-rousing. He was not restrained by *petit bourgeois* 'niceness' when referring to the Tories as a party, but neither were the Tories in their attacks on him.
11. Roberts, *Salisbury*, p. 842.
12. WSC, *Early Life*, p. 35.

13. WSC, *Great Contemporaries* (1990), p. 109.
14. Gilbert, *Life*, p. 227.
15. Martin Gilbert, *Churchill's Political Philosophy* (1981), p. 68.
16. Speech in Glasgow, 11 October 1906.
17. Beatrice Webb, *Our Partnership* (1948), p. 404.
18. Paul Addison, 'Churchill and Social Reform', in Robert Blake and William Roger Louis (eds), *Churchill* (1991), p. 61.
19. WSC, *My African Journey* (1908).
20. For a detailed study of the changes in British imperial policy see Ronald Hyam, *Elgin and Churchill at the Colonial Office 1905–1908* (1968).
21. R. Churchill, *Companion to Volume II*, p. 104. Letter of 23 December 1901.
22. House of Commons, 28 March 1943.
23. R. Churchill, *Volume II*, p. 247.
24. WSC, *The World Crisis and the Aftermath*, Vol. II, pp. 36–8.
25. Bonham Carter, *As I Knew Him*, p. 181.
26. Malcolm Hill, *Churchill: His Radical Decade* (1999) discusses the Land Tax scheme with a passion that illustrates how some issues never go away.
27. WSC, *The People's Rights* (1970), p. 116.
28. WSC, *Rights*, pp. 139–40.
29. Intriguingly, given the prevailing British snobbery about Americans, Teddy Roosevelt lumped Lord Randolph and Winston together as 'cheap characters'.
30. See the essay by G.D.H. Cole at *www.wcml.org.uk/fabianism.html*
31. Speech in Dundee, 5 May 1908.
32. See Chris Cook, 'Liberals, Labour and Local

Elections', in Gillian Peele and Chris Cook (eds), *The Politics of Reappraisal 1918–1939* (1975).

33. Until the 1911 Parliament Act the discretionary term of office was seven years.
34. Including like-minded Independents, the Conservatives and Liberal Unionists won 2,931,008 votes and 273 seats, the Liberals 2,717,748 and 275, Labour 435,770 and 40, the Irish Nationalists 114,185 and 82.
35. The Conservatives and Liberal Unionists won 2,275,400 votes and 272 seats, the Liberals 2,157,256 and 272, Labour 309,963 and 42, the Irish Nationalists 121,649 and 84.
36. Bonham Carter, *As I Knew Him*, p. 186.
37. Letters of 25 and 28 March 1916; Clemmie's thirty-first birthday was on 1 April. Mary Soames (ed.), *Speaking for Themselves* (1998), pp. 195–6.
38. See also Mary Soames, *Family Album* (1982) and *Clementine Churchill* (1979).
39. Jenkins, *Churchill*, p. 178.
40. Gilbert, *Life*, pp. 214–15.
41. See the excellent article at *www.richard.clark32.btinternet.co.uk/hanging1.html*
42. Margot Asquith, cited in William Manchester, *The Last Lion: Visions of Glory* (1983), p. 414.
43. R. Churchill, *Volume II*, p. 417.
44. Apparently for no better reason than his declaration that he would 'not be henpecked on a question of such grave importance'. R. Churchill, *Volume II*, p. 120. His revival of the archaic term rankled.
45. Soames, *Themselves*, p. 64.

46. WSC, *Thoughts and Adventures* (1932), pp. 69–70.
47. Rhodes James, *Failure*, p. 43.
48. Not meant literally, although Winston was indeed a Freemason.
49. Soames, *Themselves*, p. 43.
50. R. Churchill, *Volume II*, p. 365.
51. R. Churchill, *Volume II*, p. 371.
52. WSC, *Great Contemporaries*, p. 187.
53. Speech to the electors of Dundee, 14 May 1908.

CHAPTER FOUR: FIRST LORD 1911–1915 AND 1939–1940

1. WSC, *World Crisis*, Vol. I, p. 47. But see R. Churchill, *Volume II*, pp. 240–2.
2. Bonham Carter, *As I Knew Him*, p. 188.
3. Arthur Marder, *From the Dreadnought to Scapa Flow*, Vol. I (Oxford 1961), p. 6.
4. Technically 'neoteny'—the retention of juvenile characteristics in the adult. Winston had very little body hair, one of the signatures of physical neoteny.
5. The only surviving dreadnought is the USS *Texas*, moored at San Jacinto, near Houston.
6. Vice Admiral Sir Peter Gretton, *Former Naval Person* (1968), p. 319.
7. Edward David (ed.), *Inside Asquith's Cabinet: The Diaries of Charles Hobhouse* (1977), p. 117.
8. Gretton, *Former Naval Person*, pp. 86–9.
9. Marder, *Dreadnought to Scapa Flow*, Vol. I, p. 107.
10. Witness the fierce denunciations in West

Germany of Fritz Fischer, *Germany's Aims in the First World War* (1967), the title in English a bowdlerised translation of *Griff nach der Weltmacht* (The Lunge for World Power). See also the same author's *World Power or Decline: The Controversy over Germany's Aims in the First World War* (New York 1974).

11. Barbara Tuchman, *The Guns of August* (New York 1962), p. 330.
12. Speech in Glasgow, 1 October 1912.
13. R. Churchill, *Volume II*, p. 546.
14. *Glorious* and *Courageous* had eight 15-inch guns (two of the species are outside the Imperial War Museum, London), while *Furious* had two of the only three 18-inch naval guns manufactured in Britain, later mounted in the heavily armoured monitors (shallow-draught warships with heavy guns, designed for shore bombardment) *General Wolfe* and *Lord Clive*. In September 1918 the *General Wolfe* fired on a railway bridge well inland of Ostend, at a range of 36,000 yards (just over 20 miles) the longest shoot ever performed by the Royal Navy.
15. For a full account see Robert Massie, *Dreadnought: Britain, Germany and the Coming of the Great War* (1992).
16. *Lion* was also crippled and a more complete victory lost by signalling failure. No formal investigation was made and therefore no changes in procedure resulted.
17. Tim Slessor, *Ministries of Deception* (2002) shows that this is a constant over time in all government departments, precluding lessons being learned. Whether it is worse in Whitehall than in other national or international

bureaucracies is less easy to say.

18. For a full discussion see Dan van der Vat, *The Ship that Changed the World: The Escape of the* Goeben *to the Dardanelles in 1914* (1985), while the case for something other than gross incompetence is made by Geoffrey Miller, *Superior Force: The Conspiracy behind the Escape of the* Goeben *and the* Breslau (1996).
19. Stephen Roskill, *Churchill and the Admirals* (1977), p. 32.
20. Sir William James, 'Churchill and the Navy' in Eade (ed.), *Contemporaries*. p. 143.
21. WSC, *World Crisis*, Vol I, p. 261.
22. Gretton, *Former Naval Person*, p. 174.
23. The *Blücher* was built in incorrect expectation that Fisher's 'I' class would mount smaller-calibre guns. She was also slower than the *Moltke* class.
24. Gunter Prien in *U-47* used Winston's 'impossible' channel in 1939.
25. WSC, *World Crisis*, Vol. I, p. 398.
26. The Admiralty also had to worry about enemy dreadnoughts in the Mediterranean. Austria-Hungary had four of the 21,500-ton *Viribus Unitis* class and Italy, a pre-war ally of the Central Powers, had five of the 21,700-ton *Conte di Cavour* class, all powerfully armed, sound designs. To oppose these France had in service by 1914 only four slow and suspect 22,000-ton *Courbet* class ships.
27. From *Nonsense Novels* (1911), which many of Winston's critics would have read.
28. Roskill, *Churchill and the Admirals*, p. 36.
29. WSC, *World Crisis*, Vol I, Chapter XV.
30. M. Gilbert, *Volume III*, p. 111.

31. Martin Gilbert, *Winston S. Churchill, Companion to Volume IV*, pp. 886–93. 'Tank' was a cover name coined by Swinton.
32. Gretton, *Former Naval Person*, p. 128. The RAF originated in a merger between the army's Royal Flying Corps (RFC) and the RNAS.
33. M. Gilbert, *Volume III*, p. 429.
34. None the less its agenda-setting effect fully justifies the forensic examination in Robin Prior, *Churchill's 'World Crisis' as History* (1983).
35. WSC, *World Crisis*, Vol. II, p. 9.
36. Confusingly, Volumes III and IV were bound together. There was a later Volume VI, *The Eastern Front*, published in late 1931.
37. Michael Howard, 'Churchill and the First World War', in Blake and Louis (eds), *Churchill*.
38. Gilbert, *Companion to Volume III*, p. 343.
39. Cited in Trumbull Higgins, *Winston Churchill and the Dardanelles* (1963), p. 185.
40. *Sultan Yavuz* (ex-*Goeben*), in December 1914 already damaged by Russian mines beyond satisfactory local repair (the holes were filled with concrete), was further damaged in a battle with Russian pre-dreadnoughts on 10 May 1915, eight days before the Allied assault.
41. Cited in Gretton, *Former Naval Person*, p. 198.
42. Both Fisher and Winston knew that German submarines had arrived off the Dardanelles. On 21 May Winston wrote of them to Asquith: 'My responsibility is terrible. But I know I could sustain it . . .' as one of his many

arguments for clinging to office. (Gretton, p. 223). On 25 May *U-51* sank the old battleship *Triumph* and on the 27th *U-23* sank the more modern *Majestic*, severely curtailing naval bombardment in support of the land operations.

43. Gilbert, *Search*, p. 64.
44. Gilbert, *Companion to Volume III*, p. 932 and *Volume III*, p. 451.
45. Gretton, *Former Naval Person*, p. 199.
46. The German battle fleet, its very existence a strategic blunder of the first order, committed even greater errors. See Robert Massie, *Castles of Steel* (2004).
47. See Edward Spiers, *Haldane: Army Reformer* (Edinburgh 1980).
48. Gilbert, *Search*, p. 92.
49. Gilbert, *Search*, p. 232.
50. John Wheeler-Bennett (ed.), *Action This Day: Working with Churchill* (1968), p. 235.
51. Richard Ollard, 'Churchill and the Navy', in Blake and Louis (eds), *Churchill*, p. 390.
52. See Correlli Barnett, *Engage the Enemy More Closely* (1991) for details of Catherine and much, much more in the same vein.
53. WSC, *Step by Step* (1939), pp. 132–3. Article of 13 May 1937.
54. WSC, *Step by Step*, p. 116. Article of 22 March 1937.
55. WSC, *Step by Step*, p. 320. Article of 12 January 1939.
56. WSC, *Thoughts and Adventures* (1990), p. 89.
57. Gretton, *Former Naval Person*, pp. 264–5.
58. See Captain Vernon Howland's succinct analysis at *www.warship.org/no11994.html*

59. General Lord Ismay, *Memoirs* (1960), p. 110.
60. Piers Mackesy, 'Churchill on Narvik', *RUSI Journal*, Vol. CXV, No. 670. His father, Major General P.J. Mackesy, was the scapegoat for a fiasco made in London.
61. Roskill, *Churchill and the Admirals*, Chapter 8: 'Return to Power and the Norwegian Campaign'.
62. Arthur Marder, *From the Dardanelles to Oran* (Oxford 1974), p. 166, cited in Roskill, *Churchill and the Admirals*, p. 108.

CHAPTER FIVE: THE GREAT BETRAYAL 1914–1929

1. See Simon Ball, *The Guardsmen: Harold Macmillan, Three Friends and the World They Made* (2004).
2. See Gerald Gliddon, *The Aristocracy and the Great War* (2002).
3. Jeffreys retired as a general, and later became Conservative MP for Petersfield. He was given a peerage by Winston in 1952.
4. Soames, *Themselves*, p.119.
5. *Winston S. Churchill*, Vol. III, p. 632.
6. Soames, *Themselves*, p. 148.
7. Soames, *Themselves*, p.164.
8. Soames, *Themselves*, p.176
9. The gross mismatch between a dream of society born of Victorian and Edwardian prosperity and the attempt to implement it in greatly reduced circumstances is dissected in Correlli Barnett, *The Audit of War: The Illusion and Reality of Britain as a Great Nation* (1986).

10. WSC, *Contemporaries*, p. 83.
11. Walter Runciman, the shipping magnate, was another leading Liberal who made an obscene amount of money during the war. As President of the Board of Trade under Asquith, along with Lloyd George he negotiated a non-strike agreement with trade union representatives covering only firms concerned with war production—which included shipping.
12. The phrase became famous when repeated by the Liberal John Maynard Keynes in *The Economic Consequences of the Peace* (1920).
13. WSC, *Early Life*, p. 328.
14. *Illustrated Sunday Herald*, 23 November 1919.
15. House of Commons, 16 February 1922.
16. WSC, *World Crisis*, Vol. V, pp. 335–6.
17. WSC, *World Crisis*, Vol. I, p. 183.
18. WSC, *Early Life*, p. 328.
19. He was a dead shot with any firearm. In 1944, aged 70, he challenged some Guards officers and Generals Bradley and Eisenhower to a competition with M-1 carbines. He scored nine out of ten bullseyes and an inner; nobody else scored even one.
20. *www.historylearningsite.co.uk/black_and_tans.html*
21. *Schrecklichkeit*, a signature of the German occupation of South West Africa and Belgium.
22. Debate of 8 July 1920.
23. Jenkins, *Churchill*, p. 350.
24. In the general election of 14 December 1918 the electorate had almost trebled since 1910 and, although voter turnout was down (from 81 per cent to 57 per cent), more than double the number of pre-war votes were cast. Coalition

Conservatives won 3,393,167 and 332 seats; Lloyd George Liberals 1,318,844 and 127; minor Coalition members 206,749 and 14; Labour 2,171,230 and 57, Asquith Liberals 1,355,398 and 36; anti-Coalition Conservative and Unionists 640,985 and 50; and minor parties won 14 seats. Irish Nationalists (who did not take their seats) won 80.

25. In the 15 November 1922 general election voter participation rose to 73 per cent: the Conservatives won 5,411,326 votes and 347 seats; Labour 4,076,655 and 142; Asquith Liberals 2,601,486 and 62; Lloyd George (National) Liberals 1,355,366 and 53; ten other parties 303,457 votes and 11 seats.

26. Morel was MacDonald's Chief Adviser at the Foreign Office during the first Labour government in 1923–4.

27. Soames, *Clementine*, p. 386.

28. Their lives were closely interwoven, with Amery always off the pace. He was First Lord of the Admiralty in 1922 and Colonial Secretary 1924–9. It is ironic that, since he was a persistent critic, his 'In God's name, go' speech cleared the way for Winston in 1940. Amery was Secretary of State for India during the war, but the hanging of his son John for high treason in 1945 darkened the last ten years of his life.

29. Jenkins, *Churchill*, pp. 372–3.

30. Voter participation in the general election of 6 December 1923 was 71 per cent: the Conservatives won 5,286,159 votes and 258 seats; Labour 4,267,831 and 191; the reunited Liberals 4,129,922 and 158; ten other parties

225,105 and 8.
31. WSC, *Thoughts and Adventures* (1932), p. 154.
32. Arthur Maundy Gregory, the individual most closely identified with Lloyd George's sale of honours, probably murdered Victor Grayson, the man who publicly described and threatened to name him in 1920. Winston is unlikely to have been unaware of what was going on.
33. David Cannadine, 'Churchill and the Pitfalls of Family Piety', in Blake and Louis (eds), *Churchill*.
34. WSC, *Thoughts and Adventures* (1932), pp. 38–9.
35. Addison, 'Churchill and Social Reform', in Blake and Louis (eds) *Churchill*, p. 66. The proposal is associated with the Labour intellectual Hugh Dalton; he made it four years later.
36. Gilbert, *Life*, p. 438.
37. A common and often self-fulfilling presentiment among the substance-dependent.
38. Soames, *Clementine*, pp. 278–9.
39. In the general election of 29 October 1924 voter turnout was 77 per cent: the Conservatives won 7,418,983 votes and 412 seats; Labour 5,281,626 and 151; Liberals 2,818,717 and 40; Constitutionalists 185,075 and 7; nine other parties won 151,814 and 5.
40. In the general election of 30 May 1929 voter turnout was 76.3 per cent: the Conservatives won 8,252,527 votes and 260 seats; Labour 8,048,968 and 287; Liberals 5,104,638 and 59; nine other parties won 279,646 and 9.
41. So did Adam Smith, Jeremy Bentham, David Ricardo, John Stuart Mill, Karl Marx and

Friedrich Engels, to name but a few.

42. WSC, *Early Life*, p. 3.
43. See Max Beloff, 'The Role of the Higher Civil Service 1919–39' and bibliography in Gillian Peele and Chris Cook (eds), *The Politics of Reappraisal* (1975). For a broader sweep see Peter Hennessy, *Cabinet* (Oxford 1986), *The Great and the Good* (1986) and *Whitehall* (1989).
44. The power of the Civil Service is a huge subject, strangely absent from most political histories. See Andrew Boyle, *Montagu Norman* (1967); Eunan O'Halpin, *Head of the Civil Service: A Study of Sir Warren Fisher* (1989); D.E. Moggridge, *British Monetary Policy 1924–31* (Cambridge 1972); and Robert Boyce, *British Capitalism at the Crossroads 1919–1932* (Cambridge 1987) for the problems Winston confronted.
45. Jenkins, *Churchill*, Chapter 21: 'Gold and Strikes'.
46. Gilbert, *Companion to Volume V*, pp. 437–8.
47. Much the same can be said about the demonization of Winston's role in the General Strike. It was a challenge to the sovereignty of Parliament and, as in the strikes of 1911 or against the Northern Irish Protestants in 1914, he was ready to use troops to defeat it.
48. Tony Blair's keynote speech to the Labour Party conference, 28 September 1999.
49. Paul Kennedy, *The Rise and Fall of the Great Powers* (1989), pp. 197–201.
50. Rhodes James, *Failure*, pp. 155–8.
51. Gilbert, *Companion to Volume V*, p. 1623.
52. Richard Holmes, *Battlefields*, p. 41.

53. Soames, *Themselves*, p. 172.
54. Walmer Castle is the official residence of the Lord Warden of the Cinque Ports, a title held by Winston from 1946 until his death. In 1915–16 it was being used by the Asquith family as a forward base for closer communications with France.
55. Soames, *Themselves*, p. 175. Letter of 13 February 1916.

CHAPTER SIX: CLIMACTERIC 1929–1935

1. Victor Germains, *The Tragedy of Winston Churchill* (1931).
2. One might also reflect on the fact that 'If' was written in praise of Dr Leander Jameson, who led the ignominious raid into Boer territory in 1895 that set the stage for the war in which Winston rose to national prominence.
3. Although he also believed it healthy for the individual service ministers to compete for their share of defence spending.
4. Gilbert, *Companion to Volume V*, p. 356.
5. See Phillips O'Brien, 'Churchill and the US Navy, 1919–29', in R.A.C. Parker (ed.), *Winston Churchill: Studies in Statesmanship* (1995).
6. See Dixon, *Military Incompetence*.
7. Roskill, *Former Naval Person*, pp. 254–5.
8. See Robert O'Neill, 'Churchill, Japan, and British Security in the Pacific 1904–1942', in Blake and Louis, *Churchill*.
9. See Beloff, 'The Role of the Higher Civil Service', in Peele and Cook (eds), *The Politics of Reappraisal*, pp. 224–7.

10. See 'Consistency in Politics', in WSC, *Thoughts and Adventures*, pp. 23–30.
11. Soames, *Themselves*, p. 111.
12. WSC, *World Crisis*, Vol. II, p. 500.
13. WSC, *World Crisis*, Vol. III, p. 339.
14. Gilbert, *Volume IV*, p. 123.
15. WSC, *World Crisis*, Vol. IV, pp. 454–5.
16. WSC, *Thoughts and Adventures*, p.174.
17. WSC, *Thoughts and Adventures*, pp.176–81.
18. For a perceptive account of the former see 'Conservation: The National Trust and the National Heritage', in David Cannadine, *In Churchill's Shadow* (2003), pp. 224–43. Lytton Strachey's biographies of Cardinal Manning, Florence Nightingale, Dr Arnold and General Gordon in *Eminent Victorians* (1918) are representative of the latter.
19. WSC, *Thoughts and Adventures*, pp. 24 and 32.
20. In 1914–18 the USA went from being the largest debtor to the largest creditor in the world financial system. It lacked the institutions, the skills and above all the psychological preparation to handle the pivotal role it now played in world affairs.
21. See Philip Williamson, *National Crisis and National Government* (Cambridge 1992).
22. In the elections of 27 October 1931 the Conservatives won 11,377,022 votes (55 per cent) and 470 seats (76 per cent). The Liberals were split into three factions, the two supporting the National Government polling 2,108,276 votes and 67 seats. National Labour won 316,741 and 13, the National Party 100,193 and 4, for a total of 13,902,232 votes (67 per cent) and 554 seats (90 per cent). Labour won

6,339,306 (30.6 per cent) and 52 (8.5 per cent), the Lloyd George Liberals 103,528 and 4. Fourteen other small parties won 302,060 and 5.

23. WSC, *Thoughts and Adventures*, pp. 169–70.
24. Royal Albert Hall, 18 March 1931.
25. Gilbert, *Volume V*, pp. 595–6.
26. Gilbert, *Volume V*, p. 603.
27. That is, in the conditions prevailing in 1935. Neither his arguments nor his motives at the beginning of his campaign bear close examination.
28. Gillian Peele, 'The Revolt over India', in Peele and Cook (eds), *The Politics of Reappraisal*, pp. 124–5.
29. Gilbert, *Companion to Volume V*, p. 1245.
30. Gilbert, *Volume V*, p. 617.
31. Rhodes James, *Failure*, p. 235.
32. House of Commons, 28 January 1931.
33. During the 1931 election the normally mild Baldwin spoke of the press barons with killing contempt: 'Power without responsibility, the prerogative of the harlot through the ages.'
34. Bob Boothby and Desmond Morton, without whom Winston could not have sustained his 1930s campaign, discovered this once their usefulness was exhausted.
35. Donald Cameron Watt, 'Chamberlain's Ambassadors', in Michael Dockrill and Brian McKercher (eds), *Diplomacy and World Power: Studies in British Foreign Policy, 1880–1950* (Cambridge 1996), p. 169.
36. Andrew Roberts, *Eminent Churchillians* (1994), p. 6.
37. Rhodes James, *Failure*, p. 226.

38. The previous Comintern line had been insurrectionary. Having contributed greatly to the destabilization of the Weimar Republic, the German Communists created the preconditions for the rise of National Socialism and their own ruin.
39. This conceit, inseparable from 'Manifest Destiny', was first expressed by John Winthrop, the first governor of the Massachusetts Bay Colony, who wrote: 'We shall find that the God of Israel is among us . . . when he shall make us a praise and glory, that men of succeeding generations shall say, "The Lord make it like that of New England". For we must consider that we shall be as a City upon a Hill, the eyes of all people are upon us.'
40. Rhodes James, *Failure*, p. 233.
41. The RAF College at Cranwell was originally a Royal Navy establishment.
42. See Hubert Allen, *The Legacy of Lord Trenchard* (1972).
43. Gilbert, *Volume IV*, p. 72.
44. Geoff Simons, *Iraq: From Sumer to Saddam* (1994), pp. 179–81.
45. On 16–17 March 1988 the Saddam Hussein regime used air-dropped lethal chemical agents against the Kurdish inhabitants of Halabja. Comment is superfluous.
46. WSC, *Arms and the Covenant*, p. 34.
47. House of Commons, 23 November 1932.
48. WSC, *Arms and the Covenant*, p. 48.
49. Rhodes James, *Failure*, p. 227.
50. Holmes, *Battlefields*, pp. 21–2.
51. WSC, *Arms and the Covenant*, p. 225.
52. WSC, *Arms and the Covenant*, p. 47.

53. See Richard Holmes, *Tommy: The British Soldier on the Western Front* (2004).
54. Manchester, *Alone*, p. 46; Jenkins, *Churchill*, p. 473.
55. WSC, *Arms and the Covenant*, p. 158.
56. In the general election of 14 November 1935 the National ticket won 11,183,908 votes and 429 seats, of which the Conservatives gained 10,025,083 and 387, National Liberals 784,608 and 33, National Labour 321,028 and 8, and Nationals 53,189 and 1. Labour won 7,984,988 and 154, the opposition Liberals 1,414,010 and 21. Independents and others won 11 seats.
57. Manchester, *Alone*, pp. 192–4.
58. WSC, *Arms and the Covenant*, pp. 384–5.
59. Rhodes James, *Failure*, pp. 265–6.
60. WSC, *Arms and the Covenant*, pp. 385–6.

CHAPTER SEVEN: IN THE WINGS 1936–1940

1. The Do-17 and the He-111 could be fitted with long-range fuel tanks, with a corresponding reduction in bomb-load.
2. Donald Cameron Watt, 'Churchill and Appeasement', in Blake and Louis (eds), *Churchill*, p. 204.
3. See *www.radarworld.org* for a concise account.
4. Dowding's unpardonable offence in Winston's eyes was that he advised Chamberlain to buy time at any cost for the integration of the new fighters and Chain Home radar in a practical system of 'passive' air defence.
5. The same 'not invented here' pettiness very nearly prevented the production of De

Havilland's superb multi-role Mosquito and to its grudging deployment in all the many roles where it greatly outperformed aircraft built to Air Ministry specifications.

6. The Stirling's short, fat wings made it markedly lower-flying than the Halifax and Lancaster and hence more vulnerable to flak. It was also the preferred target for German night fighters, although the Stirling could out-turn them on the rare occasions that they were spotted in time.

7. The specification originally also required the aircraft to 'glide-bomb' at an angle of 30 degrees and drop torpedoes. Handley Page were unable to install its pioneering leading-edge flaps because the requirement for barrage balloon cable cutters on the wings persisted even after the glide-bombing role had been tacitly abandoned. The Lancaster's cavernous bomb bay was the more fortunate legacy of the likewise abandoned torpedo-dropping requirement.

8. Before World War I he had established a world-class reputation in quantum physics, and after it he founded the Clarendon Laboratory in Oxford; he was Winston's principal scientific adviser during World War II and afterwards instrumental in setting up the United Kingdom Atomic Energy Authority. Winston made him Baron Cherwell in 1941 and a viscount in his resignation honours, the year before Lindemann died, in 1956.

9. For the full story of this extraordinary man see the recent biography by the highly qualified Adrian Fort, *Prof: The Life and Times of*

Frederick Lindemann (2003).
10. Barnett, *Audit of War*, Chapters 7–9.
11. WSC, *Step by Step*, p. 236. Article of 28 April 1938.
12. WSC, *Step by Step*, pp. 279–80. Article of 1 September 1938.
13. WSC, *Step by Step*, p. 318. Article of 12 January 1938.
14. Francis Hinsley, *Power and the Pursuit of Peace* (1963), Chapter 15.
15. WSC, *Step by Step*, p. 343. Article of 24 March 1939.
16. WSC, *Step by Step*, p. 143. Article of 25 June 1937.
17. WSC, *Thoughts and Adventures*, p. 192.
18. Paolo Pombeni, 'Churchill and Italy, 1922–40', in Parker (ed.), *Studies in Statesmanship*, p. 73.
19. *News of the World*, 10 October 1937.
20. Pombeni, 'Churchill and Italy', p. 81.
21. WSC, *Thoughts and Adventures*, p. 165.
22. WSC, *Thoughts and Adventures*, p. 173.
23. On 16 February 1936 the Popular Front won 47.1 per cent of the popular vote, the National Front 45.6 per cent, centrist parties the rest.
24. WSC, *Arms and the Covenant*, pp. 409–10. Speech of 14 April 1937.
25. Reminiscent of the acid comment by Prince Talleyrand about Napoleon's judicial murder of the Duc d'Enghien: 'It is worse than a crime; it is a mistake.'
26. WSC, *Great Contemporaries*, p. 165.
27. WSC, *Great Contemporaries*, pp. 170–1.
28. WSC, *Step by Step*, p. 100. Article of 22 January 1937.
29. Schacht was president of the Reichsbank again

in 1933–9, Minister of Economic Affairs and Plenipotentiary for the War Economy 1935–7, and Minister without Portfolio until 1943.

30. John Weitz, *Hitler's Banker* (1998) is good on personality, less so on the context.

31. WSC, *Step by Step*, p. 170. Article 'Friendship with Germany' of 17 September 1937.

32. Cameron Watt, 'Chamberlain's Ambassadors', in Dockrill and McKercher (eds), *Diplomacy and World Power*, p. 169.

33. Hobbes also urged societies 'to be sociable with them that will be sociable, and formidable to them that will not'. This was Winston's point of view exactly.

34. Gilbert, *Volume V*, p. 662.

35. A game not without its perils, then as now. Ralph Wigram, the link between Winston and Sir Robert Vansittart, Permanent Under Secretary at the Foreign Office, may have committed suicide in 1936, and Group Captain Lachlan MacLean, who performed the same valuable service for Air Chief Marshal Sir Edgar Ludlow-Hewitt of Bomber Command, was forced to resign in 1937.

36. WSC, *Step by Step*, pp. 143–4. Article of 25 June 1937.

37. WSC, *Step by Step*, pp. 232–3. Article of 14 April 1938.

38. WSC, *Step by Step*, pp. 60–1. Article of 4 September 1936.

39. 'Zionism versus Bolshevism', *Illustrated Sunday Herald*, 8 February 1920.

40. Of which, one hopes, Christopher Andrew and Vasili Mitrokhin, *The Mitrokhin Archive* (2000) will be definitively the last.

41. Martin Allen, *Hidden Agenda* (2000) is built on one of the very few documentary traces not destroyed or buried under the hundred-year rule. See also Roberts, *Eminent Churchillians*, p. 5.
42. Manchester, *Alone*, p. 232. Boothby said it was the only occasion he ever saw Winston drunk.
43. Jenkins, *Churchill*, pp. 505–18, gives a wonderfully concise synthesis of Winston in 1937.
44. House of Commons, 25 May 1938.
45. Charles A. Lindbergh, *The Wartime Journals of Charles A. Lindbergh* (New York 1970), p. 22.
46. WSC, *Step by Step*, p. 275. Article of 18 August 1938.
47. WSC, *Step by Step*, p. 284.
48. Chamberlain was inviting comparison with Disraeli's return from the Congress of Berlin in 1878, where he earned the respect of the German Chancellor, Bismarck. Manchester, *Alone*, pp. 356–8.
49. First woman (Conservative) MP 1919–45, she was at the hub of the strongly pro-appeasement 'Cliveden Set', taken seriously chiefly by its members.
50. House of Commons, 5 October 1938.
51. WSC, *Step by Step*, p. 303. Article of 17 November 1938.
52. House of Commons, 28 June 1939.
53. Jenkins, *Churchill*, p. 543.
54. Manchester, *Alone*, p. 394.
55. Gilbert, *Companion to Volume V*, p. 1545.
56. Paul Addison, *Churchill on the Home Front 1900–1955* (1992), p. 336.
57. Michael Dockrill, 'The Foreign Office and

France during the Phoney War', in Dockrill and McKercher (eds), *Diplomacy and World Power*, p. 178.

CHAPTER EIGHT: CENTRE STAGE 1940–1942

1. John Lukacs, *The Duel: Hitler vs Churchill 10 May–31 May 1940* (1990) and *Five Days in London: May 1940* (1999) are a good starting point.
2. Unemployment was down to a hard core of 200,000 a year later.
3. Ismay, *Memoirs*, p. 105.
4. John Colville, *The Churchillians* (1981).
5. Roberts, 'The Tories versus Churchill during the Finest Hour', in *Eminent Churchillians*, p. 210.
6. Lord Bridges in Wheeler-Bennett (ed.), *Action This Day*, p. 219.
7. Addison, *Home Front*, p. 333.
8. Geoffrey Best, *Churchill: A Study in Greatness* (2001), p. 331.
9. William Crozier (ed. A.J.P. Taylor), *Off the Record: Political Interviews 1933–1943* (1973), p. 323.
10. Addison, *Home Front*, p. 355.
11. John Colville in Wheeler-Bennett (ed.), *Action This Day*, p. 53.
12. John Colville in Wheeler-Bennett (ed.), *Action This Day*, p. 58.
13. He could not resist mocking the earnest nutritionists, of whom Lindemann was one: 'Almost all the food faddists I have ever known, nut-eaters and the like, have died young after a

long period of senile decay. . . . The way to lose the war is to try to force the British public into a diet of milk, oatmeal, potatoes, etc., washed down on gala occasions with a little lime juice.'

14. The mechanism involved in this transfer of power is analyzed from different aspects in 'Political Science and War', 'War and Economic Growth' and 'War Finance' in Richard Holmes (ed.), *The Oxford Companion to Military History* (Oxford 2001).

15. Lord Attlee, 'The Churchill I Knew', in Eade (ed.) *Contemporaries*, p. 35.

16. A 'sheep in sheep's clothing' and a 'modest man with a great deal to be modest about' were among the many slings and arrows.

17. Ismay, *Memoirs*, p. 146.

18. A member of the Imperial Defence Committee since 1926, he retired in 1946 to serve as Chief of Staff to Mountbatten, then Viceroy of India. In 1951 he was made Secretary of State for Commonwealth Relations and in 1952–7 held the post of first Secretary General of NATO.

19. Field Marshal Lord Alanbrooke (eds Alex Danchev and Daniel Todman), *War Diaries 1939–1945* (2001).

20. In addition to those of the contributors to Wheeler-Bennett (ed.), *Action This Day*, there are more intimate accounts by his bodyguard Walter Thompson in *I Was Churchill's Shadow* (1951) and his personal assistant C.R. Thompson in Gerald Pawle, *The War and Colonel Warden* (1963).

21. David Reynolds, 'Churchill and the British "Decision" To Fight On in 1940', in Richard Langhorne (ed.), *Diplomacy and Intelligence*

during the Second World War (1985), p. 154.
22. Ismay, *Memoirs*, p. 147.
23. Ismay, *Memoirs*, p. 155.
24. 'Churchill in Epigram', in Observer, *Churchill by his Contemporaries*, p. 100.
25. Said of Confederate General 'Stonewall' Jackson, who rebuked a subordinate for lamenting the need to kill brave men. 'Shoot them all', said Jackson, 'I do not wish them to be brave.'
26. Alanbrooke, *Diaries*, pp. 188–9.
27. Dupuy, Trevor A., *A Genius for War: The German Army and General Staff, 1807–1945* (Englewood Cliffs, New Jersey, 1977), pp. 253–4.
28. See Martin van Creveld, *Fighting Power* (1983) for a comparison of German and US methods.
29. WSC, *The Second World War*, Vol. II, p. 16.
30. See Ismay, *Memoirs*, Chapter XIII 'Mr Churchill's Machinery of War Direction'.
31. This theme is developed in greater detail in my *Battlefields of the Second World War*.
32. Giving rise to his edit on a document in which the author had made an heroic effort to avoid ending with a preposition: 'This is the sort of thing up with which I will not put.'
33. WSC, *The Second World War*, Vol. II, p. 262.
34. 'There but for the grace of God goes God himself,' Winston muttered after one post-war encounter. He admired the Jehovah-like arrogance that everyone else found insufferable.
35. John Colville in Wheeler-Bennett (ed.), *Action This Day*, p. 78.
36. Winston's view of technocrats was that they

'should be on tap but never on top'.

37. Ismay, *Memoirs*, pp. 167–8.
38. Lord Bridges in Wheeler-Bennett (ed.), *Action This Day*, p. 223.
39. Sir Ian Jacob in Wheeler-Bennett (ed.), *Action This Day*, p. 173.
40. Sir Ian Jacob in Wheeler-Bennett (ed.), *Action This Day*, p. 186.
41. Gilbert, *Volume VI*, p. 697.
42. Lord Bridges in Wheeler-Bennett (ed.), *Action This Day*, pp. 235–6.
43. Revelation 3:15.
44. Alanbrooke, *Diaries*, p. 174.
45. Ismay, *Memoirs*, p. 132.
46. Note the ambiguous title chosen by Robin Brodhurst, *Churchill's Anchor: Admiral of the Fleet Sir Dudley Pound* (2000).
47. Alanbrooke, *Diaries*, p. 207.
48. David Reynolds, 'Churchill the Appeaser?', in Dockrill and McKercher (eds), *Diplomacy and World Power*, p. 215.
49. Reynolds, 'Churchill the Appeaser?', p. 213.
50. Alanbrooke, *Diaries*, p. 187.
51. Ismay, *Memoirs*, pp. 164–5.
52. A clear reference to Hitler's 'Thousand Year Reich'.
53. Gilbert, *Volume VI*, p. 1273.
54. See: *www.battleofbritain.net/contents-index.html*
55. Appeasement continued after the war began: Chamberlain had forbidden Bomber Command to attack any target where there was a probability of civilian casualties.
56. See Richard Holmes, *War Walks 2* (1997), Chapter 6 and bibliography.
57. See R.V. Jones, *Most Secret War* (1978).

58. Or, indeed, any other of Aristotle's logical fallacies. Winston employed them freely to advance his own views, but was intolerant of them when used against him.
59. Jose Harris, 'Great Britain: The People's War', in David Reynolds, Warren F. Kimball and A.O. Chubarian, *Allies at War* (1994) is a balanced and acute analysis of the phenomenon.
60. The surrender terms stated that the French fleet would be *contrôlé* by German or Italian representatives. It means 'supervised', but languages have never been a British strong suit.
61. Ismay, *Memoirs*, p. 209.
62. Ismay, *Memoirs*, p. 195.
63. In June 1940, when Ismay suggested delaying the despatch of the 52nd Division to Brittany in what they knew was a lost cause, Winston replied, 'Certainly not. It would look very bad in history if we were to do any such thing.'
64. Christopher Andrew, *Secret Service: The Making of the British Intelligence Community* (1986), Chapters 9 and 10.
65. Andrew, *Secret Service*, p. 449.
66. Francis Hinsley, 'Churchill and Special Intelligence' in Blake and Louis (eds), *Churchill*, p. 410.
67. Peter Calvocoressi, *Top Secret Ultra* (1980), was the first reliable guide. F.H. Hinsley, Anthony Simkins and Michael Howard, *British Intelligence in the Second World War*, 5 Vols (1979–90) is likely to remain the definitive study. Stephen Budiansky, *Battle of Wits* (2000) contains new material and calls some cherished recent certainties into question.

68. He was also well informed of his opponents' strength and intentions through Allied breaches of basic communications security. See Hans-Otto Behrendt, *Rommel's Intelligence in the Desert Campaign, 1940–1943* (1985).
69. Christopher Andrew, 'Churchill and Intelligence', in *Intelligence and National Security* Vol. 3.3 (1988), p. 191.
70. It was not until the cash-starved cryptanalysts appealed to him directly in October 1941 that their requests received 'extreme priority'. Andrew, 'Churchill and Intelligence', p. 189.
71. WSC, *Marlborough*, Vol. I (1947), pp. 568–70.
72. Eade (ed.), *Churchill, by his Contemporaries*, p. 435.
73. See 'Bomber' in Holmes, *Battlefields*.
74. Brian Gardner, *Churchill in His Time* (1968), p. 146.
75. 'Cassandra', *Daily Mirror*, 27 March 1942.
76. See Louis Allen, *Singapore* 1941–1942 (1977) and the poignant *Battleship* (1977) by Martin Middlebrook and Patrick Mahoney.
77. Gardner, *Churchill in His Time*, p. 160.
78. *The Second World War*, Vol. IV, p. 344.
79. *Winston S. Churchill*, Vol. VII, p. 139.
80. Eade (ed.), *Contemporaries*, pp. 434–5.
81. Alex Danchev, 'Great Britain: The Indirect Strategy', in Reynolds, Kimball and Chubarian (eds), *Allies at War*, p. 6.
82. The RCAF contingent of the Desert Air Force was also significant, but their ground forces did not join the 8th Army until the invasion of Sicily.
83. See Bernard Friedman, *Smuts: A Reappraisal* (1976). In 1926 Smuts published *Holism and*

Evolution ('holism' was a term he coined), in which he argued that evolution was a sequence of ever-closer integrations, of which the Empire was a prime example.

84. Conscription was introduced in 1944, but no conscript served overseas.

85. See J.L. Granatstein, *Canada's War: The Politics of the Mackenzie King Government* (Toronto 1975) and John English and J.O. Stubbs, *Mackenzie King: Widening the Debate* (Toronto 1978).

86. When Savage came to London for the coronation of King George VI he scandalized the 'respectable tendency' by his outspoken denunciation of Chamberlain's policy.

87. See James Thorn, *Peter Fraser, New Zealand's Wartime Prime Minister* (1952) and Ian McGibbon, *New Zealand and the Second World War* (2004).

88. A move complicated by the fact that one of them was besieged at Tobruk.

89. See Clem Lloyd and Richard Hall (eds), *Backroom Briefings: John Curtin's War* (Canberra 1997) and David Day, *Menzies and Churchill at War* (North Ryde 1986), *The Great Betrayal: Britain, Australia and the Onset of the Pacific War 1939–42* (1988) and *Reluctant Nation: Australia and the Allied Defeat of Japan 1942–45* (1992).

90. For a recent revisionist account see Eric Montgomery Andrews, *The Anzac Illusion: Anglo-Australian Relations during World War I* (1994).

91. Speech at Harrow School, 29 October 1941.

92. Canadian Parliament, 30 December 1941.

'Neck' was Canadian slang for insolent audacity.

93. Ronald Lewin, *Churchill as Warlord* (1973), p. 133.

94. Sir John Martin in Wheeler-Bennett (ed.), *Action This Day*, p. 149. He had first proposed something similar in 1917, for a landing on the German island of Borkum. Ismay, *Memoirs*, p. 346.

CHAPTER NINE: SUPPORTING ROLE 1942–1944

1. Adolf Hitler, 'Churchill the Hated Enemy', in Eade (ed.), *Contemporaries*, p. 214. The disastrous Dieppe raid had taken place on 19 August 1942.

2. Gilbert, *Volume VI*, p. 1273.

3. Cannadine, *Shadow* (2003), pp. 196–7.

4. Lord Moran, *Winston Churchill: Struggle for Survival 1940–1965* (1966), p. 6.

5. See Roger Louis, *Imperialism at Bay* (1978).

6. *Life*, 12 October 1942.

7. Carlo D'Este, *Decision in Normandy* (1994), p. 307.

8. WSC, *Step by Step*, p. 136. Article of 31 May 1937.

9. Reynolds, 'Decision to Fight', p. 165.

10. For the service record of the 'four stackers' see: *www.navsource.org/Naval*

11. Francis Loewenheim, Harold Langley and Manfred Jonas (eds), *Roosevelt and Churchill: Their Secret Wartime Correspondence* (1975), p. 125. Telegram of 7 December 1940.

12. He also said, 'England is one of the greatest powers in the world, no event or series of events bearing on the balance of power, or on probabilities of peace or war can be matters of indifference to her, and her right to have and to express opinions on matters thus bearing on her interests is unquestionable.'
13. Richard Overy, 'Great Britain: Cyclops', in Reynolds, Kimball and Chubarian (eds), *Allies at War*, p. 123.
14. Loewenheim, *Roosevelt and Churchill*, p. 136.
15. See *www.ihr.org/jhr/v03/v03p-15_Martin.html* for another view of these events.
16. See Warren Kimball (ed.), *Churchill and Roosevelt: The Complete Correspondence*, 3 vols (1984).
17. This slight was reciprocated when President Johnson did not join heads of state from all over the world at Winston's funeral in 1965.
18. See John Gooch, 'Hidden in the Rock: American Military Perceptions of Great Britain, 1919–1940', in Lawrence Freedman, Paul Hayes and Robert O'Neill (eds), *War, Strategy, and International Politics* (Oxford 1992).
19. Andrew and Mitrokhin, *Archive*, p. 144. These included Alger Hiss and Laurence Duggan at the State Department, and Harry Dexter White at the Treasury.
20. Alex Danchev, *Very Special Relationship: Field-Marshal Sir John Dill and the Anglo-American Alliance 1941–44* (1986).
21. The other marks the grave of Major General Philip Kearny, killed in the Civil War.
22. Alanbrooke, *Diaries*, p. 617.

23. Alanbrooke, *Diaries*, p. 192.
24. Reginald Thompson, *The Yankee Marlborough* (1963), p. 315.
25. See Theodore A. Wilson, *The First Summit* (rev. ed. Kansas 1991).
26. See the exchange of telegrams of February 1942 about US attempts to link Lend-Lease to the abolition of Imperial Preference (the system of tariffs imposed on non-Empire goods). Loewenheim, Langley and Jonas (eds), *Roosevelt and Churchill*, pp. 174–8.
27. Loewenheim, Langley and Jonas (eds), *Roosevelt and Churchill*, p. 71 fn.
28. Loewenheim, Langley and Jonas (eds), *Roosevelt and Churchill*, p. 234.
29. Reynolds, 'Decision to Fight', p. 161.
30. Jenkins, *Churchill*, p. 670.
31. See the summary in Danchev, 'Great Britain: the Indirect Strategy', in Reynolds, Kimball and Chubarian (eds), *Allies at War*, pp. 14–16.
32. Danchev, 'Indirect Strategy', p. 9.
33. Loewenheim, Langley and Jonas (eds), *Roosevelt and Churchill*, p. 195.
34. Ismay, *Memoirs*, p. 344.
35. Loewenheim, Langley and Jonas (eds), *Roosevelt and Churchill*, p. 238.
36. David Reynolds, 'Legacies: Allies, Enemies and Posterity', in Reynolds, Kimball and Chubarian (eds), *Allies at War*, p. 421.
37. Ismay, *Memoirs*, p. 157.
38. Gilbert, *Volume VII*, p. 217.
39. Loewenheim, Langley and Jonas (eds), *Roosevelt and Churchill*, p. 286.
40. Mark Stoler, 'The United States: The Global Strategy', in Reynolds, Kimball and Chubarian

(eds), *Allies at War*, p. 73.
41. Loewenheim, Langley and Jonas (eds), *Roosevelt and Churchill*, p. 388.
42. Theodore White (ed.), *The Stilwell Papers* (1949) is a useful reminder that deeply impolitic diaries and memoirs are not the exclusive preserve of British generals.
43. Soames, *Themselves*, p. 501.
44. Stoler, 'The Global Strategy', p. 67.
45. In 1940 the population of China was approximately 520 million, that of the Soviet Union 195 million, USA 132 million, Japan 71 million, France 36 million and Poland 27 million.
46. WSC, *The Second World War*, Vol. IV, pp. 185–7. Also, since the dismemberment of the Ottoman Empire Britain had become the largest Muslim power in the world, as well as ruling over most Hindus. The subject awaits comprehensive treatment in English, but Mushirul Hassan (ed.), *Communal and Pan-Islamic Trends in Colonial India* (1981) and A. Moin Zaidi (ed.), *Congress, Nehru and the Second World War* (1985) are useful introductions.
47. Slim's *Unofficial History* (1959) and *Defeat into Victory* (rev. ed. 1961) are considered, at least by me, amongst the most honest memoirs ever written by a British general.
48. Loewenheim, Langley and Jonas (eds), *Roosevelt and Churchill*, p. 192.
49. Loewenheim, Langley and Jonas (eds), *Roosevelt and Churchill*, pp. 202–4.
50. Barbara Tuchman, *Sand against the Wind: Stilwell and the American Experience in China*

1911–1945 (1971) puts Stilwell's mission in the broader context.

51. Alanbrooke, *Diaries*, p. 376.
52. See Robert O'Neill, 'Churchill, Japan and British Security in the Pacific 1904–1942', in Blake and Louis (eds), *Churchill*, for some answers. Winston's fascination with Wingate was shared by FDR and the CCS. The Chindit leader was killed in an air crash in March 1944 and his remains, intermingled with those of his mainly American companions, are buried at Arlington.
53. See Robert Pilpel, *Churchill in America: An Affectionate Portrait* (1977), and Kay Halle (ed.), *Winston Churchill on America and Britain* (1970).
54. The other was Mother Teresa in 1996. Posthumous awards were made in 1981 to Raoul Wallenberg, the Swedish diplomat and Holocaust hero murdered by the Russians; in 1984 to William and Hannah Penn, the founders of Pennsylvania; and in 2002 to the Marquis de Lafayette for his service during the American Revolution of 1775–83.
55. Alanbrooke, *Diaries*, p. 360.
56. John Blum (ed.), *The Price of Vision: The Diary of Henry A. Wallace 1942–1946* (1973).
57. See diary extract at: *www.loc.gov/exhibits/churchill/wc-trans215.html*.
58. Loewenheim, Langley and Jonas (eds), *Roosevelt and Churchill*, p. 499.
59. John Colville in Wheeler-Bennett (ed.), *Action This Day*, p. 74.
60. WSC, *Thoughts and Adventures*, p. 33.
61. WSC, *The Second World War*, Vol. III, p. 673.

62. Cited in Thompson, *The Yankee Marlborough*, p. 349.
63. John Earl Haynes, *Red Scare or Red Menace* (1996) is a post-hysterical account.
64. Loewenheim, Langley and Jonas (eds), *Roosevelt and Churchill*, p. 532.
65. See FDR's 'Stalin likes me better' signal of 18 March 1942.
66. Loewenheim, Langley and Jonas (eds), *Roosevelt and Churchill*, p. 396.
67. Andrew and Mitrokhin, *Archive*, p. 147.
68. Lattimore was neither a Soviet agent nor even a Communist, which makes his Kolyma article all the more incomprehensible. His heavily edited FBI file is at *foia.fbi.gov/owenlatt.html*
69. See Ben Pimlott, *Hugh Dalton* (1985).
70. See Anthony Cave Brown, *The Last Hero: Wild Bill Donovan* (1982).
71. See M.R.D. Foot, *SOE in France* (1966), *Resistance* (1976), *SOE: An Outline History* (1984) and *SOE in the Low Countries* (2001), also David Stafford, *Britain and European Resistance* (1980) and Ken Robertson (ed.), *War Resistance and Intelligence* (1999). For a different perspective see Henri Michel, *The Shadow War: Resistance in Europe 1939–1945* (1972).
72. See Józef Garlinski, *Poland, SOE and the Allies* (1969), and Jan Nowak, *Courier from Warsaw* (1982).
73. WSC, *The Second World War*, Vol. VI, p. 124.
74. Anita Prazmowska, 'Churchill and Poland', in Parker (ed.), *Studies*, p. 123.
75. François Kersaudy, 'Churchill and de Gaulle', in Parker (ed.), *Studies*, p.129.

76. Kersaudy, 'Churchill and de Gaulle', p. 132.
77. Kersaudy, 'Churchill and de Gaulle', p. 128.
78. See Charles Williams, *The Last Great Frenchman* (1993), and Simon Berthon's book of the excellent BBC series *Allies at War* (2001).
79. Moran, *Struggle for Survival*, p. 81.
80. Ismay, *Memoirs*, p. 381.
81. Jenkins, *Churchill*, pp. 723–4.
82. Moran, *Struggle for Survival*, pp. 136–41.
83. Ismay, *Memoirs*, p. 322.
84. WSC, *The Second World War*, Vol. V, p. 432.
85. Michael Howard, *Mediterranean Strategy in the Second World War* (1968).
86. Brian Bond, 'Alanbrooke and Britain's Mediterranean Strategy, 1942–1944', in Freedman, Hayes and O'Neill (eds), *War, Strategy, and International Politics*, p. 190.
87. Bond, 'Alanbrooke', p. 191.
88. Alanbrooke, *Diaries*, pp. 405–6.
89. The Germans had denuded the area of first-class troops, there was little serious fighting and most of the 100,000 prisoners taken were only too happy to surrender. It had no influence on the battle of Normandy and Patton's lightning advance in fact reached Dijon before the troops advancing up the Rhône valley joined him on 12 September.
90. Ismay, *Memoirs*, p. 399.
91. See Alex Danchev, 'Being Friends: The Combined Chiefs of Staff and the Making of Allied Strategy in the Second World War', in Freedman, Hayes and O'Neill (eds), *War, Strategy, and International Politics*.
92. See, in particular, the memoirs of Anthony Eden *Full Circle* (London 1960) and *Facing the*

Dictators (London 1962).
93. Dwight Eisenhower, 'Churchill as an Ally in War', in Eade (ed.), *Contemporaries*, p. 203.
94. WSC, *The Second World War*, Vol. V, p. 543.
95. Gilbert, *Volume VII*, pp. 793–4.
96. Shelford Bidwell and Dominick Graham, *Fire Power* (1982), p. 291.
97. Alanbrooke, *Diaries*, p. 565.
98. Loewenheim, Langley and Jonas (eds), *Roosevelt and Churchill*, p. 541.
99. See Mark Walker, *German National Socialism and the Quest for Nuclear Power* (1988) and Thomas Powers, *Heisenberg's War: The Secret History of the German Bomb* (1993).
100. See *www.vectorsite.net/twgas.html*
101. Gilbert, *Volume VII*, p. 865.
102. Alanbrooke, *Diaries*, pp. 566–7.
103. WSC, *The Second World War*, Vol. VI, p. 107.
104. Andrew and Mitrokhin, *Archive*, pp. 137–48.
105. For David Irving's view on the matter, see his introduction to a folio of related documents published in Germany at *www.fpp.co.uk/bookchapters/Morgenthau.html*.
106. Colville unpublished diary entry cited in Jenkins, *Churchill*, p. 757.
107. Romania: Russia 90 per cent, 'the others' 10 per cent; Greece: 'Great Britain (in accord with the USA)' 90 per cent, Russia 10 per cent; Yugoslavia and Hungary 50–50; Bulgaria: Russia 75 per cent, 'the others' 25 per cent.
108. WSC, *The Second World War*, Vol. VII, p. 198.
109. See Charmley, *End of Glory*.
110. Loewenheim, Langley and Jonas (eds), *Roosevelt and Churchill*, pp. 619–21.

111. Soames, *Themselves*, p. 512.

CHAPTER TEN: FINAL ACT 1945–1965

1. Kenneth Harris, *Attlee* (1982), p. 243.
2. Gilbert, *Volume VII*, p. 1156.
3. Alanbrooke, *Diaries*, p. 649.
4. For the text of the Yalta Protocol see
    www.yale.edu/lawweb/avalon/wwii/yalta.html
5. His car was hit by a truck on 9 December 1945
    and he died 12 days later.
6. Alanbrooke, *Diaries*, p. 667–8.
7. WSC, *The Second World War*, Vol. VI, pp.
    512–13.
8. Jenkins, *Churchill*, p. 780.
9. The term was first used by Josef Goebbels, the
    Nazi Propaganda Minister, in an article
    commenting on Yalta published in *Das Reich*,
    25 February 1945: 'If the German people lay
    down their weapons, the Soviets, according to
    the agreement between Roosevelt, Churchill
    and Stalin, would occupy all of East and
    Southeast Europe along with the greater part
    of the Reich. An iron curtain would fall over
    this enormous territory controlled by the Soviet
    Union, behind which nations would be
    slaughtered.'
10. Text at:
    *www.yale.edu/lawweb/avalon/decade/decade17.h
    tml*
11. Bevin's massive official biography has recently
    been republished in more accessible form: see
    Alan Bullock (ed. Brian Brivati), *Ernest Bevin*
    (2002).

12. Harris, *Attlee*, p. 252.
13. For a summary see: *www.fordham.edu/halsall/mod/1942beveridge.html*
14. House of Commons, 29 November 1944.
15. Interview in Addison, *Home Front*, p. 383. They met in 1948 and Winston told Hayek that, although he was right in principle, 'it would never have happened in England'.
16. WSC, *Step by Step*, p. 148. Article of 9 July 1937.
17. David Cannadine (ed.), *Blood, Toil, Tears and Sweat* (1989), pp. 270–7.
18. Jenkins, *Churchill*, p. 793.
19. Election broadcast of 5 June 1945.
20. In the 5–19 July 1945 general election 72.8 per cent of an electorate of 33,240,391 voted. Labour won 11,557,821 votes (48 per cent of votes cast) and 393 seats and the Conservatives 8,716,211 and 197. Liberals won 2,177,938 (9 per cent) and 12 seats. A handful of seats went to a dozen small parties.
21. Soames, *Clementine*, p. 391.
22. Cannadine, *Blood, Toil, Tears*, pp. 279–94.
23. WSC, *Great Contemporaries*, p. 186.
24. House of Commons, 23 June 1944. John Campbell, *Nye Bevan and the Mirage of British Socialism* (1987), p. 130.
25. He published the pamphlet *Towards a Christian Democracy* at the time of his readmission to the Labour Party in 1945. See Peter Clarke, *The Cripps Version* (2002).
26. Theodore Wilson, 'The United States: Leviathan' in Reynolds, Kimball and Chubarian (eds), *Allies at War*, p. 196.

27. Roberts, *Eminent Churchillians*, p. 4.
28. Addison, *Home Front*, p. 358.
29. 'Churchill as a Political Opponent', in Eade (ed.), *Contemporaries*.
30. Roy Jenkins, 'Churchill: The Government of 1951–1955', in Blake and Louis (eds), *Churchill*, p. 500.
31. Cripps was a Wykehamist, as were Hugh Gaitskell and Richard Crossman.
32. David Coombs, *Churchill: His Paintings* (1967), pp. 105, 223 and 75.
33. Attlee, 'The Churchill I Knew', in The Observer, *Churchill by His Contemporaries*, p. 29.
34. Jenkins, *Churchill*, p. 837.
35. In the 23 February 1950 general election 83.9 per cent of an electorate of 34,271,754 voted. Labour won 13,266,176 votes (46.1 per cent of votes cast) and 315 seats. Conservatives won 12,492,404 (43.4 per cent) and 298. Liberals won 2,621,487 (9.1 per cent) and 9. Others won 391,057 and 3.
36. Soames, *Themselves*, p. 541.
37. Cannadine, *Blood, Toil, Tears*, pp. 296–308.
38. See Donald Cameron Watt, *Succeeding John Bull: America in Britain's Place 1900–1975* (1984).
39. John Charmley, 'Churchill and the American Alliance', *Transactions of the Royal Historical Society*, 6th Series, Vol. XI (2001).
40. Cannadine, *Blood, Toil, Tears*, pp. 310–14.
41. John Colville in Wheeler-Bennett (ed.), *Action This Day*, p. 97.
42. House of Commons, 30 July 1934; WSC, *Arms and the Covenant*, p. 160.

43. Montague Brown, *Long Sunset*.
44. In the 25 October 1951 general election 82.6 per cent of an electorate of 34,919,331 voted. Labour won 13,948,883 votes (48.8 per cent of votes cast) and 295 seats. Conservatives won 13,718,199 (48 per cent) and 321. The Liberals fell to 730,546 and 6. Others won 198,966 and 3.
45. John Colville, *The Fringes of Power: Downing Street Diaries 1939–1955* (1985), p. 634.
46. Colville, *Fringes*, p. 660.
47. George Isaacs, 'Churchill and the Trade Unions', in Eade (ed.), *Contemporaries*, p. 388.
48. Roberts, *Eminent Churchillians*, p. 284.
49. David Carlton, 'Churchill and the Two "Evil Empires"', *Transactions of the Royal Historical Society*, 6th Series, Vol. XI (Cambridge 2001).
50. Cannadine, *Blood, Toil, Tears*, pp. 335–7.
51. Cannadine, *Blood, Toil, Tears*, pp. 339–51.

CONCLUSION: DEATH SHALL HAVE NO DOMINION

1. Basil Liddell Hart, *History of the Second World War* (1970) p. 199.
2. Stephen Ambrose, 'Eisenhower and the Second World War' in Blake and Louis (eds), *Churchill*, p. 406.
3. Alanbrooke, *Diaries*, p. 712.
4. WSC, *The Unrelenting Struggle* (1942), pp. 1–2. House of Commons, 12 November 1940.
5. Gardner, Brian, *Churchill in His Time*, p. 313.
6. A.J.P. Taylor (ed.), *Churchill: Four Faces and the Man* (1969), p. 51.

7. Jenkins, 'Churchill: The Government of 1951–55,' in Blake and Louis (eds), *Churchill*, p. 493. It is actually an adaptation of an aphorism by Dwight Morrow, the US financier and diplomat: 'The world is divided into people who do things and people who get the credit. Try, if you can, to belong to the first class. There's far less competition.'

8. R. Churchill, *Companion to Volume I*, p. 863. Letter of 26 January 1898.

9. Aneurin Bevan, 'History's Impresario', in Observer, *Contemporaries* (1965), p. 63.

10. Campbell, *Nye Bevan*, p. 376.

11. Harris, *Attlee*, p. 244.

12. Attlee, 'The Churchill I Knew', in Observer, *Contemporaries*, p. 35.

13. George MacDonald Fraser, *Quartered Safe Out Here* (2000), p. 264.

14. WSC, *Thoughts and Adventures*, p. 185.

15. R.V. Jones, 'Churchill and Science', in Blake and Louis (eds), *Churchill*, p. 432.

16. Thompson, *The Yankee Marlborough* (1963), p. 354.

17. Shakespeare, *Julius Caesar* Act V Scene V. 'Gentle' in this context means well-bred or noble.

FURTHER READING

Published in London unless otherwise specified

Addison, Paul, *Churchill on the Home Front 1900–1955* (1992)

Alanbrooke, Field Marshal Lord (ed. Alex Danchev and Daniel Todman), *War Diaries 1939–1945* (2001)

Allen, Hubert, *The Legacy of Lord Trenchard* (1972)

Allen, Martin, *Hidden Agenda* (2000)

Andrew, Christopher, *Secret Service: The Making of the British Intelligence Community* (1986)

Andrew, Christopher, 'Churchill and Intelligence', in *Intelligence and National Security*, Vol 3.3 (1988)

Andrew, Christopher and Vasili Mitrokhin, *The Mitrokhin Archive: The KGB in Europe and the West* (2000)

Anglesey, Marquess of, *History of the British Cavalry*, Vol. 8 (1997)

Ball, Simon, *The Guardsmen: Harold Macmillan, Three Friends and the World They Made* (2004)

Barnett, Correlli, *The Audit of War: The Illusion and Reality of Britain as a Great Nation* (1986)

Barnett, Correlli, *Engage the Enemy More Closely* (1991)

Barnett, Correlli, *Lost Victory* (1995)

Beaverbrook, Lord, *Men and Power* (1956)

Behrendt, Hans-Otto, *Rommel's Intelligence in the Desert Campaign, 1940–1943* (1985)

Berthon, Simon, *Allies in War* (2001)

Berlin, Isaiah, *Mr Churchill in 1940* (n.d., published in magazines 1949)

Best, Geoffrey, *Churchill: A Study in Greatness* (2001)

Bidwell, Shelford and Dominick Graham, *Fire-Power* (1982)

Blake, Robert and W. Roger Louis (eds.), *Churchill* (Oxford 1993):
- Paul Addison, 'Churchill and Social Reform'
- Stephen Ambrose, 'Eisenhower and the Second World War'
- Donald Cameron Watt, 'Churchill and Appeasement'
- David Cannadine, 'Churchill and the Pitfalls of Family Piety'
- Peter Clarke, 'Churchill's Economic Ideas'
- Gordon Craig, 'Churchill and Germany'
- Sarvepali Gopal, 'Churchill and India'
- John Grigg, 'Churchill and Lloyd George'
- Francis Hinsley, 'Churchill and Special Intelligence'
- Michael Howard, 'Churchill and the First World War'
- Roy Jenkins, 'Churchill: The government of 1951–55'
- Douglas Johnson, 'Churchill and France'
- R.V. Jones, 'Churchill and Science'
- Richard Ollard, 'Churchill and the Navy'
- Robert O'Neill, 'Churchill, Japan and British Security in the Pacific 1904–1942'

Blum, John (ed.), *The Price of Vision: The Diary of Henry A. Wallace 1942–1946* (1973)

Bond, Brian, *British Military Policy Between the Two World Wars* (Oxford 1980)

Bonham Carter, Violet, *Winston Churchill as I*

Knew Him (1965)

Boog, Horst (ed.), *The Conduct of the Air War in the Second World War* (Oxford 1992)

Boyce, Robert, *British Capitalism at the Crossroads 1919–1932* (Cambridge 1987)

Boyle, Andrew, *Montagu Norman* (1967)

Brodhurst, Robin, *Churchill's Anchor: Admiral of the Fleet Sir Dudley Pound* (Barnsley 2000)

Browning, Christopher, *Ordinary Men: Reserve Police Battalion 101 and the Final Solution in Poland* (2001)

Budiansky, Stephen, *Battle of Wits* (2000)

Bullock, Alan (ed. Brian Brivati), *Ernest Bevin* (2002)

Callahan, Raymond, *Churchill: Retreat from Empire* (Tunbridge Wells 1984)

Calvocoressi, Peter, *Top Secret Ultra* (1980)

Cameron Watt, Donald, *Succeeding John Bull: America in Britain's Place 1900–1975* (Cambridge 1984)

Campbell, John, *Nye Bevan and the Mirage of British Socialism* (1987)

Cannadine, David (ed.) *Blood, Toil, Tears and Sweat* (1989)

Cannadine, David, *The Decline and Fall of the British Aristocracy* (1992)

Cannadine, David, *In Churchill's Shadow* (2003)

Cave Brown, Anthony, *The Last Hero: Wild Bill Donovan* (1982)

Chandos, Lord, *Memoirs of Lord Chandos* (1962)

Charmley, John, *Churchill: The End of Glory* (1993)

Charmley, John, *Churchill's Grand Alliance: The Anglo-American Special Relationship, 1940–57* (1995)

Churchill, Peregrine and Julian Mitchell, *Jennie,*

Lady Randolph Churchill: A Portrait with Letters (1974)

Churchill, Randolph, *Winston S. Churchill*, 2 vols (1966–7) (see also Gilbert, Martin):
- Vol. I, *Youth, 1874–1900* + 2-part *Companion Volume* (1966)
- Vol. II, *Young Statesman, 1900–1914* + 3-part *Companion Volume* (1967)

Churchill, Winston, *The River War*, 2 vols (1899)

Churchill, Winston, *Lord Randolph Churchill*, 2 vols (1906)

Churchill, Winston, *My African Journey* (1908)

Churchill, Winston, *The World Crisis and the Aftermath*, 5 vols (1923–31)

Churchill, Winston, *Marlborough: His Life and Times*, 4 vols (1933–8)

Churchill, Winston, *Arms and the Covenant* (1938)

Churchill, Winston, *Step by Step* (1939)

Churchill, Winston, *The Unrelenting Struggle* (1942)

Churchill, Winston, *Painting as a Pastime* (1948)

Churchill, Winston, *The Second World War*, 6 vols (1948–53)

Churchill, Winston, *A History of the English-Speaking Peoples*, 4 vols (1956–8)

Churchill, Winston, *The People's Rights* (1910/1970)

Churchill, Winston, *The Story of the Malakand Field Force* (1898/1989)

Churchill, Winston, *Great Contemporaries* (1937/1990)

Churchill, Winston, *Thoughts and Adventures* (1932/1990)

Churchill, Winston, *My Early Life* (1930/2002)

Churchill, Winston, *The Boer War* [combining *London to Ladysmith via Pretoria* and *Ian Hamilton's March*] (1900/2002)

Clarke, Peter, *The Cripps Version* (2002)
Colville, John, *The Churchillians* (1981)
Colville, John, *The Fringes of Power: Downing Street Diaries 1939–1955* (1985)
Coombs, David, *Churchill: His Paintings* (1967)
Crozier, William (ed. A.J.P. Taylor), *Off the Record: Political Interviews 1933–1943* (1973)
Danchev, Alex, *Very Special Relationship: Field-Marshal Sir John Dill and the Anglo-American Alliance 1941–44* (1986)
David, Edward (ed.) *Inside Asquith's Cabinet: The Diaries of Charles Hobhouse* (1977)
Day, David, *Menzies and Churchill at War* (North Ryde 1986)
Day, David, *The Great Betrayal: Britain, Australia and the Onset of the Pacific War 1939–42* (1988)
Day, David, *Reluctant Nation: Australia and the Allied Defeat of Japan 1942–45* (1992)
Dean, Sir Maurice, *The Royal Air Force and Two World Wars* (1979)
De Gaulle, Charles, *L'Appel* (1995)
D'Este, Carlo, *Decision in Normandy* (1994)
Dixon, Norman, *On the Psychology of Military Incompetence* (1983)
Dockrill, Michael and Brian McKercher (eds), *Diplomacy and World Power: Studies in British Foreign Policy, 1890–1950* (Cambridge 1996):
• Donald Cameron Watt, 'Chamberlain's Ambassadors'
• Michael Dockrill, 'The Foreign Office and France during the Phoney War'
• Brian McKercher, 'Old Diplomacy and New'
• David Reynolds, 'Churchill the Appeaser?'
• Geoffrey Warner, 'From Ally to Enemy'
Dupuy, Trevor, *A Genius for War* (New York 1977)

Eade, Charles (ed.), *Churchill, by His Contemporaries* (1953):
- Dwight Eisenhower, 'Churchill as an Ally in War'
- Adolf Hitler, 'Churchill the Hated Enemy'
- George Isaacs, 'Churchill and the Trade Unions'
- Sir William James, 'Churchill and the Navy'
- Emanuel Shinwell, 'Churchill as Political Opponent'
- Paul Reynaud, 'Churchill and France'

Eden, Anthony Sir, *Full Circle* (1960)

Eden, Anthony Sir, *Facing the Dictators* (1962)

English, John and J.O. Stubbs, *Mackenzie King: Widening the Debate* (Toronto 1978)

Finest Hour, the society journal of the Chuchill Centre, Washington DC

Fischer, Fritz, *Germany's Aims in the First World War* (1967)

Fischer, Fritz, *World Power or Decline: The Controversy over Germany's Aims in the First World War* (New York 1974)

Foot, M.R.D., *SOE in France* (1966)

Foot, M.R.D., *Resistance* (1976)

Foot, M.R.D., *SOE: An Outline History* (1984)

Foot, M.R.D., *SOE in the Low Countries* (2001)

Fort, Adrian, *Prof: The Life and Times of Frederick Lindemann* (2003)

Fraser, David, *Alanbrooke* (1982)

Freedman, Lawrence, Paul Hayes and Robert O'Neill (eds), *War, Strategy, and International Politics* (Oxford 1992):
- Brian Bond, 'Alanbrooke and Britain's Mediterranean Strategy, 1942–1944'
- Alex Danchev, 'Being Friends: The Combined Chiefs of Staff and the Making of Allied Strategy in the Second World War'

- Michael Carver, 'Britain and the Alliance'
- John Gooch, 'Hidden in the Rock: American Military Perceptions of Great Britain, 1919–1940'

Friedman, Bernard, *Smuts: A Reappraisal* (1976)

Freud, Sigmund, *Moses and Monothesim* (1939)

Gardner, Brian, *Churchill in His Time* (1968)

Garlinski, Józef, *Poland, SOE and the Allies* (1969)

Germains, Victor, *The Tragedy of Winston Churchill* (1931)

Gilbert, Martin, *Winston S. Churchill*, 6 vols (1971–88); (see also Churchill, Randolph):
- Vol. III, *Challenge of War, 1914–1916* + 2-part *Companion Volume* (1971)
- Vol. IV, *Stricken World*, 1917–1922 + 3-part *Companion Volume* (1975)
- Vol. V, *Prophet of Truth*, 1922–1939 + 3-part *Companion Volume* (1976)
- Vol. VI, *Finest Hour*, 1939–1941 + *War Papers* (1983)
- Vol. VII, *Road to Victory, 1941–1945* + *War Papers* (1986)
- Vol. VIII, *Never Despair, 1945–1965* (1988)

Gilbert, Martin, *Churchill's Political Philosophy* (Oxford 1981)

Gilbert, Martin, *In Search of Churchill* (1995)

Gilbert, Martin, *Churchill: A Life* (2000)

Gliddon, Gerald, *The Aristocracy and the Great War* (Norwich 2002)

Granatstein, J.L., *Canada's War: The Politics of the Mackenzie King Government* (Toronto 1975)

Gretton, Peter, *Former Naval Person* (1968)

Halle, Kay (ed.), *Winston Churchill on America and Britain* (New York 1970)

Harris, Kenneth, *Attlee* (1982)

Hassan, Mushirul (ed.), *Communal and Pan-Islamic Trends in Colonial India* (New Delhi 1981)
Haynes, John Earl, *Red Scare or Red Menace* (1996)
Hennessy, Peter, *Cabinet* (Oxford 1986)
Hennessy, Peter, *The Great and the Good* (1986)
Hennessy, Peter, *Whitehall* (1989)
Higgins, Trumbull, *Winston Churchill and the Dardanelles* (1963)
Hill, Malcolm, *Churchill: His Radical Decade* (1999)
Hinsley, Francis, *Power and the Pursuit of Peace* (Cambridge 1963)
Hinsley, F. H., Anthony Simkins and Michael Howard, *British Intelligence in the Second World War*, 5 vols (1979–90)
Holmes, Richard, *Firing Line* (1985)
Holmes, Richard, *War Walks* (1996)
Holmes, Richard, *War Walks 2* (1997)
Holmes, Richard, *The Western Front* (1999)
Holmes Richard (ed.), *The Oxford Companion to Military History* (Oxford 2001)
Holmes, Richard, *Battlefields of the Second World War* (2001)
Holmes, Richard, *Tommy: The British Soldier on the Western Front* (2004)
Hopkirk, Peter, *The Great Game* (2001)
Howard, Michael, *The Mediterranean Strategy in the Second World War* (1993)
Hyam, Ronald, *Elgin and Churchill at the Colonial Office 1905–1908* (1968)
Ismay, General Lord, *Memoirs* (1960)
Jablonsky, David, *Churchill, the Great Game and Total War* (1991)
Jenkins, Roy, *Churchill* (2002)

Jenkins, Simon, *England's Thousand Best Houses*
  (2003)
Jones, R.V., *Most Secret War* (1978)
Kennedy, Paul, *The Rise and Fall of the Great
  Powers* (1989)
Keynes, John Maynard, *The Economic
  Consequences of the Peace* (New York 1920)
Keynes, John Maynard, *The Economic
  Consequences of Mr. Churchill* (1925)
Kimball, Warren (ed.), *Churchill and Roosevelt: The
  Complete Correspondence*, 3 vols (1984)
Kimball, Warren, *Forged in War: Churchill,
  Roosevelt and the Second World War* (1997)
Langhorne, Richard (ed.), *Diplomacy and
  Intelligence during the Second World War*
  (Cambridge 1985):
• Donald Boadle, 'Vansittart's Administration of
  the Foreign Office in the 1930s'
• A.E. Campbell, 'Franklin Roosevelt and
  Unconditional Surrender'
• Sheila Lawlor, 'Britain and the Russian Entry
  into the War'
• Bradford Lee, 'Strategy, Arms and the Collapse
  of France 1930–40'
• David Reynolds, 'Churchill and the British
  "Decision" to Fight On in 1940'
Lewis, Ronald, *Churchill as Warlord* (1973)
Liddle Hart, Basil, *History of the Second World War*
  (1970)
Lindbergh, Charles A., *The Wartime Journals of
  Charles A. Lindbergh* (New York 1970)
Lloyd, Clem and Richard Hall (eds), *Backroom
  Briefings: John Curtin's War* (Canberra 1997)
Louis, Roger, *Imperialism at Bay* (1978)
Loewenheim, Francis, Harold Langley and

Manfred Jonas (eds), *Roosevelt and Churchill: Their Secret Wartime Correspondence* (1975)

Lukacs, John, *The Duel: Hitler vs. Churchill 10 May–31 May 1940* (1990)

Lukacs, John, *Five Days in London: May 1940* (Yale 1999)

Lukacs, John, *Churchill: Visionary, Statesman, Historian* (Yale 2002)

MacDonald Fraser, George, *Quartered Safe Out Here* (2000)

McGibbon, Ian, *New Zealand and the Second World War* (2004)

Manchester, William, *The Last Lion: Visions of Glory 1874–1932* (1983)

Manchester, William, *The Last Lion: Alone 1932–1940* (New York 1988)

Marder, Arthur, *From the Dreadnought to Scapa Flow* (Oxford 1961)

Marder, Arthur, *From the Dardanelles to Oran* (Oxford 1974)

Massie, Robert, *Dreadnought: Britain, Germany and the Coming of the Great War* (1992)

Massie, Robert, *Castles of Steel* (2004)

Messenger, Charles, *'Bomber' Harris and the Strategic Bombing Offensive* (1984)

Michel, Henri, *The Shadow War: Resistance in Europe 1939–1945* (1972)

Miller, Geoffrey, *Superior Force: The Conspiracy behind the Escape of the* Goeben *and the* Breslau (1996)

Moggeridge, D.E., *British Monetary Policy 1924–31* (Cambridge 1972)

Montague Brown, Anthony, *Long Sunset* (1995)

Montgomery Andrews, Eric, *The Anzac Illusion: Anglo-Australian Relations during World War I*

(1994)
Moran, Lord, *Anatomy of Courage* (1945)
Moran, Lord, *Winston Churchill: Struggle for Survival 1940–1965* (1966)
Nowak, Jan, *Courier from Warsaw* (1982)
O'Brien, C.C. (ed.), *Burke: Reflections on the Revolution in France* (1969)
The Observer (newspaper), *Churchill by His Contemporaries* (1965):
• Lord Atlee, 'The Churchill I Knew'
• Aneurin Bevan, 'History's Impresario'
O'Halpin, Eunan, *Head of the Civil Service: A Study of Sir Warren Fisher* (1989)
Overy, Richard, *Why the Allies Won* (1995)
Overy, Richard, *The Dictators: Hitler's Germany and Stalin's Russia* (2004)
Pakenham, Thomas, *The Boer War* (1979)
Parker, R.A.C., *Struggle for Survival: The History of the Second World War* (Oxford 1989)
Parker, R.A.C. (ed.), *Winston Churchill: Studies in Statesmanship* (1995):
• François Kersaudy, 'Churchill and de Gaulle'
• Warren Kimball, 'Churchill, Roosevelt and Post-war Europe'
• Wolfgang Krieger, 'Churchill and the Defence of the West, 1951–55'
• Brian McKercher, 'Churchill, the European Balance of Power and the USA'
• Phillips O'Brien, 'Churchill and the US Navy, 1919–29'
• Ritchie Ovendale, 'Churchill and the Middle East, 1945–55'
• Paolo Pombeni, 'Churchill and Italy, 1922–40'
• Anita Prazmowska, 'Churchill and Poland'
Parker, R.A.C., *Churchill and Appeasement* (2000)

Pawle, Gerald, *The War and Colonel Warden* (1963)
Peele, Gillian and Chris Cook (eds), *The Politics of Reappraisal 1918–1939* (1975):
• Max Beloff, 'The Whitehall Factor' and 'The Role of the Higher Civil Service 1919–39'
• John Campbell, 'The Renewal of Liberalism: Liberalism without Liberals'
• Cook, Chris, 'Liberals, Labour and Local Elections'
• David Harkness, 'England's Irish Question'
• Gillian Peele, 'The Revolt over India'
• John Stubbs, 'The Impact of the Great War on the Conservative Party'
Pilpel, Robert, *Churchill in America: An Affectionate Portrait* (1977)
Pimlott, Ben, *Hugh Dalton* (1985)
Ponting, Clive, *Churchill* (1994)
Powers, Thomas, *Heisenberg's War: The Secret History of the German Bomb* (1993)
Prior, Robin, *Churchill's 'World Crisis' as History* (1983)
Reynolds, David, *In Command of History* (2004)
Reynolds, David, Warren Kimball and A.O. Chubarian (eds), *Allies at War* (1994):
• Alex Danchev, 'Great Britain: The Indirect Strategy'
• Jose Harris, 'Great Britain: The People's War'
• Richard Overy, 'Great Britain: Cyclops'
• David Reynolds, 'Great Britain: Imperial Diplomacy'
• David Reynolds, 'Legacies: Allies, Enemies and Posterity'
• Mark Stoler, 'The United States: The Global Strategy'
• Theodore Wilson, 'The United States:

Leviathan'

Rhodes James, Robert (ed.), *Chips: The Diaries of Sir Henry Channon* (1967)
Rhodes James, Robert, *Churchill: A Study in Failure* (1970)
Roberts, Andrew, *Eminent Churchillians* (1994)
Roberts, Andrew, *Salisbury: Victorian Titan* (1999)
Robertson, Ken (ed.), *War Resistance and Intelligence* (1999)
Rose, Norman, *Churchill: An Unruly Life* (1994)
Roskill, Stephen, *Churchill and the Admirals* (1977)
Sandys, Celia, *From Winston with Love and Kisses* (1994)
Sandys, Celia, *Chasing Churchill* (2003)
Sandys, Celia, *Churchill* (2003)
Simons, Geoff, *Iraq: From Sumer to Saddam* (1994)
Slessor, Tim, *Ministries of Deception* (2002)
Slim, Viscount, *Unofficial History* (1959)
Slim, Viscount, *Defeat into Victory* (rev. ed. 1961)
Soames, Mary, *Clementine Churchill* (1979)
Soames, Mary, *Family Album* (1982)
Soames, Mary, *Speaking for Themselves* (1998)
Spiers, Edward, *Haldane: Army Reformer* (Edinburgh 1980)
Stafford, David, *Britain and European Resistance* (1980)
Strachey, Lytton, *Eminent Victorians* (1918)
Taylor, A.J.P. (ed.), *Churchill: Four Faces and the Man* (1969):
• Basil Liddell Hart, 'Churchill the Military Strategist'
• J.H. Plumb, 'Churchill the Historian'
• Robert Rhodes James, 'Churchill the Politician'
• Anthony Storr, 'The Man'
• A.J.P. Taylor, 'Churchill the Statesman'

Terraine, John, *The Right of the Line* (1985)
Thompson, Reginald, *The Yankee Marlborough* (1963)
Thompson, Reginald, *Churchill and Morton* (1976)
Thompson, Walter, *I Was Churchill's Shadow* (1951)
Thorn, James, *Peter Fraser, New Zealand's Wartime Prime Minister* (1952)
Transactions of the Royal Historical Society, 6th Series, Vol. XI (2001):
• Paul Addison, 'The Three Careers of Winston Churchill'
• Stuart Ball, 'Churchill and the Conservative Party'
• David Carlton, 'Churchill and the Two "Evil Empires"'
• John Charmley, 'Churchill and the American Alliance'
• David Reynolds, 'Churchill's Writing of History'
Tuchman, Barbara, *The Guns of August* (New York 1962)
Tuchman, Barbara, *Sand against the Wind: Stilwell and the American Experience in China 1911–1945* (1971)
Van Creveld, Martin, *Fighting Power* (1983)
Van der Vat, Dan, *The Ship that Changed the World: The Escape of the* Goeben *to the Dardanelles in 1914* (1985)
Walker, Mark, *German National Socialism and the Quest for Nuclear Power* (1988)
Webb, Beatrice, *Our Partnership* (1948)
Wheeler-Bennett, John (ed.), *Action This Day: Working with Churchill* (1968):
• Lord Normanbrook (Cabinet Secretariat 1941–46, Secretary to the Cabinet 1947–62)

- John Colville (Assistant Private Secretary [PS] 1940–1, 1943–5, Parliamentary Private Secretary [PPS] 1951–5)
- Sir John Martin (PS 1940–1, PPS 1941–5)
- Lt Gen. Sir Ian Jacob (Military Assistant to the War Cabinet 1939–45)
- Lord Bridges (Secretary to the Cabinet 1938–46)
- Sir Leslie Rowan (PS 1941–5, PPS 1945)

White, Theodore (ed.), *The Stilwell Papers* (1949)

Williams, Charles, *The Last Great Frenchman* (1993)

Williamson, Philip, *National Crisis and National Government* (Cambridge 1992)

Wilson, Theodore A., *The First Submit* (rev. ed. Kansas 1991)

Woods, Frederick, *Artillery of Words* (1992)

Woods, Frederick (ed.), *Winston S. Churchill: War Correspondent 1895–1900* (1992)

Zaidi, A. Moin (ed.), *Congress, Nehru and the Second World War* (New Delhi 1985)

USEFUL WEBSITES

www.winstonchurchill.org
—Churchill Centre, Washington DC (includes articles from the society journal *Finest Hour*)
www.churchill-society-london.org.uk
—Churchill Society, London
www.yale.edu/lawweb/avalon/wwii/wwii.html
—important documents
www.fpp.co.uk/index.html
—website featuring the revisionist works of David Irving
www.nizkor.org/hweb/people/i/irving-david
—condemnation of the above
www.battleships-cruisers.co.uk
—general history, all navies
www.pinetreeweb.com/perspectives.html
—comprehensive history of the Boer War
www.election.demon.co.uk/geresults.html
—general election results
uboat.net/index.html
—operational details of the U-boat war
www.vectorsite.net/twgas.html
—overview of chemical and bacteriological weapons
www.raf.mod.uk/bombercommand/aircraft/index.html
www.battleofbritain.net
www.radarworld.org

PICTURE CREDITS